WORKING WITH
NATURE
AGAINST POVERTY

Indonesia Project
The Australian National University

WORKING WITH
NATURE
AGAINST POVERTY

Development, Resources and the
Environment in **Eastern Indonesia**

Edited by
**Budy P. Resosudarmo
and Frank Jotzo**

ᒪᔆᓄᔆ
INSTITUTE OF SOUTHEAST ASIAN STUDIES
Singapore

First published in Singapore in 2009 by
ISEAS Publishing
Institute of Southeast Asian Studies
30 Heng Mui Keng Terrace, Pasir Panjang
Singapore 119614

E-mail: publish@iseas.edu.sg
Website: http://bookshop.iseas.edu.sg

ISEAS Library Cataloguing-in-Publication Data

Working with nature against poverty : development, resources and the
     environment in eastern Indonesia / edited by Budy P. Resosudarmo and
     Frank Jotzo.
　　1.　Economic development—Environmental aspects—Indonesia.
　　2.　Environmental policy—Indonesia.
　　3.　Sustainable development—Indonesia.
　　4.　Poverty—Indonesia.
　　I.　Resosudarmo, Budy P.
　　II.　Jotzo, Frank.
HC450 E5R43　　　　　　　　　　　　2009

ISBN 978-981-230-959-4 (soft cover)
ISBN 978-981-230-960-0 (PDF)

Cover photo: Shark-fishing hooks on a small boat from the port of Dobo, November 2004. Reproduced with kind permission of Professor James Fox.

Typeset by Beth Thomson, Japan Online, Canberra
Indexed by Angela Grant, Sydney
Printed in Singapore by Utopia Press Pte Ltd

FOREWORD

The development challenge is joined by humanity in many different environments. Small and isolated communities face many special challenges. This book describes and analyses those challenges in an important and interesting context: three eastern provinces of the Republic of Indonesia.

Small and/or isolated economies face unusually large costs in participating in trade and specialization. They find it difficult to catch the attention of owners of capital in all its forms. They are at a disadvantage in the supply of public goods of all kinds that are necessary for development—from governance, to transport, to communications infrastructure—because costs fall with scale.

These and other disadvantages of small size and isolation are well represented in the stories presented in this book about development and the environment in Papua, Maluku and East Nusa Tenggara. Budy P. Resosudarmo and Frank Jotzo present a set of chapters that brings out in rich detail the nature of the development challenge in these provinces, the response to it and the lessons from experience so far.

These are relatively poor regions within Indonesia, in income, health, education and other ways. Poverty has so far been impervious to development efforts.

In these three eastern Indonesian provinces, limitations on scale are even more acute below the level of the province. In each of them, internal integration is blocked by ocean, swamp or mountain, so that the effective economic size of communities for purposes of development is smaller again.

These characteristics of scale and location are as old as human society in these regions. This means that populations have not expanded as close to the limits of resource availability as in places that are better located for trade, specialization and economic growth. As a result, natural resource endowments tend to be large relative to population. The three provinces are all rich in natural resources relative to population, with Papua being exceptional on a global as well as a national scale. This offers both a source of potential and a source of challenge for development. An abundance of natural resources can be a blessing or a curse for development. As the authors of individual chapters in this book observe, whether a high per capita endowment of natural resources is a blessing or a curse depends above all on the quality of governance.

These are environments in which the nature of the development challenge requires large inputs from government, but in which resources of good governance are scarce. Governance resources are scarce because of the absence of a history of large-scale organization of society, government and business. The requirements of government are especially important in resource-rich environments because there is the special challenge of reconciling economic growth with sustainability, and because the utilization of opportunities for development requires effective government to collect revenues from the resource-based industries and apply them to the provision of public goods and services. These are challenging governance issues anywhere. They are especially challenging in poor and underdeveloped communities with weak governance systems.

The editors of this book have brought together rich material on development in an unusual and interesting setting. I have learned a great deal from the book, and commend it to others who are interested in the challenges of development and its interaction with the environment.

Ross Garnaut
Vice-Chancellor's Fellow and Professorial Fellow in Economics,
University of Melbourne and
Distinguished Professor, Australian National University
Canberra, December 2008

CONTENTS

FIGURES AND MAPS

FIGURES

MAPS

TABLES

CONTRIBUTORS

Dedi S. Adhuri, Scientist, Policy, Economics and Social Science, WorldFish Center, Penang, Malaysia

Hidayat Alhamid, Scientist, Forestry Research and Development Agency, Ministry of Forestry, Manokwari, Indonesia

Chris Ballard, Fellow, Division of Pacific and Asian History, Research School of Pacific and Asian Studies, College of Asia and the Pacific, The Australian National University, Canberra, Australia

Glenn Banks, Associate Professor, School of People, Environment and Planning, College of Humanities and Social Sciences, Massey University, Palmerston North, New Zealand

Colin Barlow, Visiting Fellow, Department of Political and Social Change, Research School of Pacific and Asian Studies, College of Asia and the Pacific, The Australian National University, Canberra, Australia

David Campbell, Senior Economist, Desert Knowledge Cooperative Research Centre: Livelihoods in Land & Centre for Remote Health, Alice Springs, Australia

Michelle Carnegie, Post-doctoral Fellow, Department of Human Geography, Research School of Pacific and Asian Studies, College of Asia and the Pacific, The Australian National University, Canberra, Australia

Astia Dendi, Senior Advisor, GTZ Good Local Governance, Mataram, Indonesia

Rili Djohani, Country Director, The Nature Conservancy in Indonesia, Jakarta, Indonesia

Ian M. Dutton, Deputy Regional Director, Asia–Pacific Region, The Nature Conservancy, Alaska, United States

Karla M. Dutton, Alaska Program Director, Defenders of Wildlife, Alaska, United States

James J. Fox, Professor, Resource Management in Asia–Pacific Program, Research School of Pacific and Asian Studies, College of Asia and the Pacific, The Australian National University, Canberra, Australia

Ria Gondowarsito, Member, Nusatenggara Association, Canberra, Australia

Suriadi Gunawan, Senior Researcher, National Institute of Health Research and Development, Ministry of Health, Jakarta, Indonesia

Heinz-Josef Heile, Former Program Director, GTZ PROMIS-Nusa Tenggara, Mataram, Indonesia

Bambang Heru, Director, Directorate of Animal Husbandry, Fishery and Forestry Statistics, Statistics Indonesia (BPS), Jakarta, Indonesia

Frank Jotzo, Research Fellow, Resource Management in Asia–Pacific Program, Research School of Pacific and Asian Studies, College of Asia and the Pacific, The Australian National University, Canberra, Australia

Peter Kanowski, Professor, Fenner School of Environment and Society, College of Medicine, Biology and Environment, The Australian National University, Canberra, Australia

Stephanus Makambombu, Former Senior Advisor, GTZ PROMIS-Nusa Tenggara, Waingapu, Indonesia

Chris Manning, Associate Professor, Arndt-Corden Division of Economics, Research School of Pacific and Asian Studies, College of Asia and the Pacific, The Australian National University, Canberra, Australia

Lydia Napitupulu, Lecturer, Faculty of Economics, University of Indonesia, Depok, Indonesia

Ditya A. Nurdianto, PhD Candidate, Arndt-Corden Division of Economics, Research School of Pacific and Asian Studies, College of Asia and the Pacific, The Australian National University, Canberra, Australia

Budy P. Resosudarmo, Fellow, Arndt-Corden Division of Economics, Research School of Pacific and Asian Studies, College of Asia and the Pacific, The Australian National University, Canberra, Australia

Ida Aju Pradnja Resosudarmo, Post-doctoral Scholar, Fenner School of Environment and Society, College of Medicine, Biology and Environment, and Crawford School of Economics and Government, College of Asia and the Pacific, The Australian National University, Canberra, Australia

Agus P. Sari, Country Director, Ecosecurities Indonesia, Jakarta, Indonesia

Setijati D. Sastrapradja, Senior Scientist, Indonesian Institute of Sciences, Jakarta, Indonesia

Endang R. Sedyaningsih, Senior Researcher, National Institute of Health Research and Development, Ministry of Health, Jakarta, Indonesia

Elina Situmorang, Lecturer, Faculty of Economics, Papua State University, Manokwari, Indonesia

Tom Therik, Lecturer, Artha Wacana Christian University, Kupang, Indonesia

Craig Thorburn, Senior Lecturer, School of Geography and Environmental Science, Faculty of Arts, Monash University, Melbourne, Australia

Velix Wanggai, Staff Member, National Agency for Development Planning (Bappenas), Jakarta, Indonesia

ACKNOWLEDGMENTS

This book had its origins in an international workshop on the theme 'Development and Environment in Eastern Indonesia: Papua, Maluku and East Nusa Tenggara'. The workshop was held at the Australian National University (ANU) in Canberra on 8 April 2006.

The Australian Agency for International Development (AusAID) was the principal financial sponsor of the workshop and this book, through a grant to the Indonesia Project at the ANU. We thank the agency for its support. We also thank the Indonesia Project, the National Institute of Economics and Business at the ANU, the Decentralization Support Facility Eastern Indonesia (SOfEI) and the German aid agency GTZ for financial assistance to offset the costs of travel. Another source of generous support was the Research School of Pacific and Asian Studies (RSPAS) at the ANU. Its Director, Robin Jeffrey, was a major source of encouragement. Within RSPAS, the Arndt-Corden Division of Economics, led by Hal Hill and Peter Warr, and the Resource Management in Asia–Pacific Program, led by Colin Filer, provided moral and material help. We thank them for their contributions.

We are grateful to Karen Guest and Trish van der Hoek of the Indonesia Project, as well as Lydia Napitupulu, for helping to organize the workshop and make it a success. We would also like to thank Yogi Vidyattama for his invaluable assistance. Our colleagues at the Indonesia Project, Chris Manning, Hal Hill and Ross McLeod, provided consistent support for the workshop and the book. We benefited greatly from their helpful suggestions.

Our appreciation goes to all those who reviewed the papers after the workshop: Mukhtar Adam, Jamal Bake, Chris Ballard, Chakriya Bowman, Harold Crouch, Jim Douglas, Kate Duggan, Hal Hill, Terence Hull, Suna Jayadiningrat, Teddy Kristedi, Kuntala Lahiri-Dutt, Christian von Luebke, Minggus Male, Chris Manning, John McCarthy, Peter McCawley, Rod McGibbon, Neil McCulloch, Andrew McWilliam, Agus Heri

Purnomo, Purwanto, Ida Aju Pradnja Resosudarmo, Hendra Yusran Siry, Melinda Spink and Craig Thorburn. We also thank Laode Ida, Vice-Chair of the Indonesian Regional House of Representatives, for giving an excellent opening speech at the workshop.

We thank Cartographic Services, Research School of Pacific and Asian Studies, College of Asia and the Pacific, ANU, for granting us permission to reproduce six maps showing different parts of Indonesia in this book.

We would like to express our particular thanks to Beth Thomson for the outstanding job she has done in copy editing and typesetting this book. Our thanks also go to Triena Ong and her staff at the Institute for Southeast Asian Studies for their support in seeing the book through to print.

Finally, we would like to commend all the speakers at the workshop and the authors who contributed to this book. We are grateful to them for their hard work and for their patience during the preparation of this book.

Budy P. Resosudarmo and Frank Jotzo
Canberra, January 2009

We dedicate this book to our familes:

Daju Omang, Dhika, Yana and Sesa
and especially my mother
Satimah Sudjiran Resosudarmo
28 December 1925 – 29 October 2008
Budy P. Resosudarmo

Sally, Benjamin and Alana
Frank Jotzo

GLOSSARY

abangan	nominal (Muslims)
adat	tradition, customs, customary laws
AMDAL	*analisis mengenai dampak lingkungan* (environmental impact analysis)
APIA	*alokasi penangkap ikan asing* (foreign fishing vessel allocation)
AusAID	Australian Agency for International Development
Bapedal	Badan Pengendalian Dampak Lingkungan (Environmental Impact Management Agency)
Bappeda	Badan Perencanaan Pembangunan Daerah (Regional Development Planning Agency)
Bappenas	Badan Perencanaan Pembangunan Nasional (National Development Planning Agency)
BBM	Buginese, Butonese and Makassarese
BKKBN	Badan Koordinasi Keluarga Berencana Nasional (National Family Planning Coordination Agency)
BMZ	Bundesministerium fuer Wirtschaftliche Zusammenarbeit (German Ministry for Economic Cooperation)
bodi susun	a slightly larger version of a *bodi* with a better cabin
bodi	a small vessel fitted with an engine and used for illegal shark fishing
BPN	Badan Pertanahan Nasional (National Land Agency)
BPS	Badan Pusat Statistik (Statistics Indonesia), Indonesia's central statistics agency
Brimob	Brigade Mobil (Mobile Brigade), crack police forces
bupati	district head
CARDI	Consortium for Assistance and Recovery toward Development in Indonesia
CDK	Cabang Dinas Kehutanan (Provincial Forestry Service)

CEO	chief executive officer
CSIRO	Commonwealth Scientific and Research Organization (Australia)
DAK	Dana Alokasi Khusus (Specific Purpose Fund)
DAU	Dana Alokasi Umum (General Purpose Fund)
desa	village
Dewan Adat Papua	Papuan Tribal Council
dinas	office or agency
Dinas Perindustrian	Industry Office
Dinas Pertanian	Agriculture Office
DPR	Dewan Perwakilan Rakyat (People's Representative Council, also known as the 'House of Representatives' and as 'parliament')
DPRD	Dewan Perwakilan Rakyat Daerah (regional assembly)
DPRP	Dewan Perwakilan Rakyat Papua (Papuan People's Representative Council), the provincial parliament
dusun	hamlet (there are usually 4-5 hamlets in each village)
EIA	environmental impact assessment
FKM	Forum Kedaulatan Maluku (Christian Maluku Sovereignty Forum)
FPI	Front Pembela Islam (Muslim Defenders Front)
GDP	gross domestic product
GMIT	Gereja Majilis Injili Timor (Calvinist Church of Timor)
Golkar	orig. Golongan Karya (the state political party under the New Order, and one of the major post-New Order parties)
GTZ	Deutsche Gesellschaft für Technische Zusammenarbeit, German Society for Technical Cooperation
hak asal-usul	customary or original rights
halal	food prepared in a manner suitable for Muslims to eat
HDI	human development index
HPH	*hak pengusahaan hutan* (large-scale timber harvesting concession)
HTI	*hutan tanaman industri* (industrial forest plantation concession)
ICMC	International Catholic Migration Commission
IDP	internally displaced person
IDT	Inpres Desa Tertinggal (Neglected Villages Program, a special presidential program for poor villages)
ILO	International Labour Organization
IMC	International Medical Corps

Inpres	Instruksi Presiden (Presidential Instruction), a program of special grants from the central government
IPB	Institut Pertanian Bogor (Bogor Agricultural Institute)
IPK	*izin pengusahaan kayu* (small to medium-scale timber harvesting permit)
ISAI	Institut Studi Arus Informasi (Institute for the Study of the Free Flow of Information)
ITCQ	individual transferable catch quota
kabupaten	district
kain timur	traditional textiles
kampong/kampung	village
kapubaten	district
kecamatan	subdistrict
kelompok	cooperative, group
kepala kampong/kampung	village head
KfW	Kreditanstalt für Wiederaufbau (German government-owned development bank)
KNIL	Koninklijk Nederlands Indisch Leger (Royal Dutch Indies Army)
Kopassus	Komando Pasukan Khusus (Special Forces Command)
Kostrad	Komando Strategi Angkatan Darat (Army Strategic Reserve Command)
kota	city, municipality
KPAP	Komisi Penanggulangan AIDS Provinsi Papua (Papua Province AIDS Commission)
KPH	Kesatuan Pemangkuan Hutan (Local Forestry Service)
KPK	Komisi Pemberantasan Korupsi (Commission for the Eradication of Corruption)
KPM	Koalisi Pengungsi Maluku (Maluku IDP Coalition)
KSK	*koordinator statistik kecamatan* (subdistrict statistical coordinator)
kW	kilowatt
ladang	clearing for special cultivation
Lakpesdam NU	Lembaga Kajian dan Pengembangan Sumber Daya Manusia Nahdlatul Ulama (Nahdlahtul Ulama Institute for Human Resource Studies and Development)
lambo perahu	sailing boat of a kind used by Butonese and Bajau; it is described by Australian authorities as a 'type 2' boat
Laskar Jihad	Holy War Warriors
LEMASA	Lembaga Adat Masyarakat Suku Amungme (Amungme Traditional Council)

LIPI	Lembaga Ilmu Pengetahuan Indonesia (Indonesian Institute of Sciences)
Litbang Pertanian	Agriculture Institute
LKMD	Lembaga Ketahanan Masyarakat Desa (Village Community Resilience Council)
LMD	Lembaga Musyawarah Desa (Village Consultative Council)
LNG	liquefied natural gas
LPMAK	Lembaga Pembangunan Masyarakat Amungme dan Kamoro (Amungme and Kamoro Community Development Institution)
Mam	lowlanders (Papua) [specific to Papua]
Mbrei	non-Papuans (Papua) [specific to Papua]
Min	highlanders (Papua) [specific to Papua]
MOU	memorandum of understanding
MOU Box	the area off the northwest continental shelf of Australia to which 'traditional' Indonesian fishermen would be given access
MPR	Majelis Permusyawarahan Rakyat (People's Consultative Assembly), the national house of representatives
MRP	Majelis Rakyat Papua (Papuan People's Assembly), the Papuan house of representatives
mtd	metric tonnes per day
MUI	Majelis Ulama Indonesia (Council of Indonesian Ulama)
musyawarah	participative conference, discussion, or meeting
MW	megawatt
negeri	village (Maluku)
negeri adat	a traditional village
negeri administratif	an administrative ('new') village (Maluku)
nekey	tribal elder (Papua) [specific to Papua]
New Order	the government led by President Soeharto, 1965–98
NGO	non-government organization
NIT	Negara Indonesia Timur (Federation of East Indonesian States)
NTB	Nusa Tenggara Barat (West Nusa Tenggara)
NTT	Nusa Tenggara Timur (East Nusa Tenggara)
OCHA	Office for the Coordination of Humanitarian Affairs
OPIC	(US) Overseas Private Investment Corporation
OPM	Organisasi Papua Merdeka (Free Papua Movement)
padi	wet rice field
PAN	Partai Amanat Nasional (National Mandate Party)

Pancasila	the five guiding principles of the Indonesian state (belief in God, humanitarianism, nationalism, democracy and social justice)
PDAM	Perusahaan Daerah Air Minum (Municipal Drinking Water Enterprise)
PDI-P	Partai Demokrasi Indonesia-Perjuangan (Indonesian Democratic Party of Struggle)
PemProv Papua	Pemerintah Provinsi Papua (Papua Provincial Government)
perahu	traditional sailing boat
perda/Perda	*peraturan daerah* (local/regional regulation)
perdasi/Perdasi	*peraturan daerah provinsi* (provincial regulation)
perdasus/Perdasus	*peraturan daerah khusus* (special regional regulation)
PHKA	(Direktorat Jenderal) Perlindungan Hutan dan Konservasi Alam ((Directorate General of) Forest Protection and Nature Conservation)
PKM/ACE	Program Kebangkitan Masyarakat/Association for Community Empowerment (Community Recovery Program)
PKS	Partai Keadilan Sejahtera (Prosperity and Justice Party)
PLN	Perusahaan Listrik Negara (the state electricity company)
posyandus	integrated community health care post
PP	Peraturan Pemerintah (Government Decree or Regulation)
PPK	Proyek Pembangunan Kecamatan (Subdistrict Development Project)
PPP	Partai Persatuan Pembangunan (United Development Party)
preman	standover man, thug
PROMIS	Program Penanggulangan Kemiskinan dan Dukungan Pemerintahan Daerah (Poverty Alleviation and Support for Local Governance Program)
Proyek Pesisir	Indonesia Coastal Resources Management Project
puskesmas	community health centre
reformasi	the post-Soeharto period of political and social reform
Repelita	Rencana Pembangunan Lima Tahun (Five Year Development Plan)
RMS	Republik Maluku Selatan (Republic of South Maluku)
SDO	Subsidi Daerah Otonom (Autonomous Regional Subsidy), central government grants to finance regional government expenditure before the 2001 decentralization

SEAMEO Biotrop	Southeast Asian Regional Centre for Tropical Biology (Bogor)
SIKPI	*surat ijin kapal pengangkutan ikan* (licence for vessel transporting fish)
SIUP	*surat ijin usaha perikanan* (fishery business licence)
SPI	*surat penangkapan ikan* (fishing licence)
STD	sexually transmitted disease
suanggi	sorcerer (Papua) [specific to Papua]
Susenas	Survei Sosial Ekonomi Nasional (National Socio-Economic Survey)
tenun ikat	woven cloth
TNI	Tentara Nasional Indonesia (Indonesian National Army)
ummat	Islamic community
UN	United Nations
UNAIDS	Joint United Nations Programme on HIV/AIDS
UNDP	United Nations Development Programme
UNESCO	United Nations Educational, Scientific and Cultural Organization
UNFPA	United Nations Population Fund
UNHCR	United Nations High Commissioner for Refugees
UNICEF	United Nations Children' Fund
UNIPA	Universitas Negeri Papua (State University of Papua)
USAID	United States Agency for International Development
VOC	Vereenigde Oost-Indische Compagnie (Dutch East Indies Company)
WALHI	Wahana Lingkungan Hidup Indonesia (Friends of the Earth Indonesia)
walikota	mayor
WHO	World Health Organization
WVI	Wahana Visi Indonesia (World Vision Indonesia)
YPMD	Wahana Lingkungan Hidup Indonesia (Rural Community Development Foundation)

Currencies

A$	Australian dollar
Rp	Indonesian rupiah
US$	US dollar

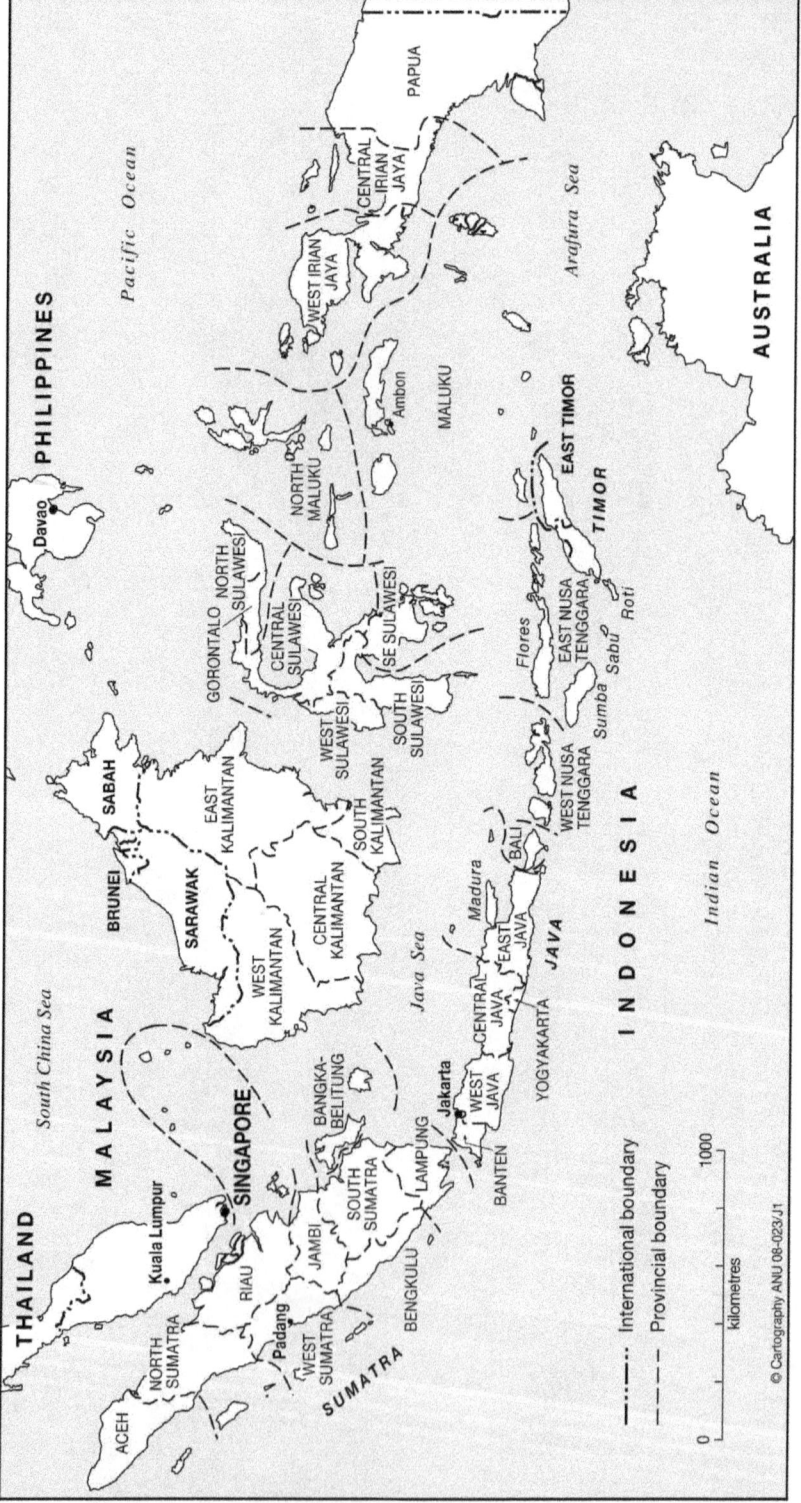

Map 1.1   The Republic of Indonesia

1 DEVELOPMENT, RESOURCES AND ENVIRONMENT IN EASTERN INDONESIA

Budy P. Resosudarmo and Frank Jotzo

Eastern Indonesia has for a long time epitomized the problems of development in Indonesia, with the region having lower incomes, higher poverty and worse social indicators than most other regions in Indonesia. The challenge is to achieve economic development. But much economic development relies on more intensive use of resources, which places great pressure on the environment. In some parts of the region this could undermine the future sustainability of the economy. In others it threatens unique environmental systems that are of significance not just for Indonesia but for the world.

This book brings together contributions from leading experts on eastern Indonesia. It provides comprehensive information on current economic, social, political and environmental developments in the region. The goal is to provide a framework for balancing environmental and social concerns against the need to promote economic development, particularly in areas where poverty is prevalent. Understanding the interactions, trade-offs and synergies between development and environment is a prerequisite for better policies to benefit both the people of eastern Indonesia and the environment.

The existing literature on eastern Indonesia—especially research on the nexus between resources, environment and development—is sparse. Earlier publications of note include Barlow and Hardjono (1995) and Pannell and von Benda-Beckmann (1998). The present book has its origins in a symposium held at the Australian National University in 2006, which brought together some of the leading researchers on eastern Indonesia.

1 BACKGROUND

Indonesia is the world's largest archipelagic state and one of the most spatially diverse nations on earth in terms of resource endowments, population settlements, locations of economic activity, ecology and ethnicity (Tomascik et al. 1997; Hill, Resosudarmo and Vidyattama 2008). Stretching across 8 million square kilometres of land and sea between the Indian and Pacific oceans, it links the continents of Asia and Australia (Map 1.1). Indonesia's 17,000 islands have a land area of close to 2 million square kilometres. Many parts of the country have abundant natural resources, such as fossil fuels and minerals, as well as rich forests and diverse marine habitats.

In 2005 Indonesia had a population of approximately 220 million, expanding at an annual rate of 1.5 per cent. Of its roughly 350 ethnic groups, the three largest are Javanese (45 per cent), Sundanese (14 per cent) and Malay (7.5 per cent). The vast majority of the population is Muslim (88 per cent), with smaller numbers of Protestants (5 per cent), Catholics (3 per cent) and Hindus (2 per cent).

Ever since Indonesia gained independence in 1945, policy makers and academics have grappled with the problem of development imbalances between regions. Infrastructure such as roads, universities and hospitals has always been more readily available in Java than in the outer islands. In the early 2000s, per capita income in the richest province, East Kalimantan, was around 16 times that in the poorest, Maluku. Poverty ranged from 3 per cent of the population in Jakarta to 42 per cent in Papua (Hill, Resosudarmo and Vidyattama 2008). The discrepancies between rich and poor regions have aroused, and exacerbated, resentment between ethnic groups.

The Indonesian government typically refers to eastern Indonesia as comprising Kalimantan, Sulawesi, East and West Nusa Tenggara, Maluku and Papua. The literature commonly focuses on four of these provinces: West Nusa Tenggara, East Nusa Tenggara, Maluku and Papua. This book concentrates on just three—East Nusa Tenggara, Maluku and Papua— because West Nusa Tenggara is now well connected to Bali. These three provinces are generally considered to be the least developed in Indonesia and the most challenging in which to conduct development activities. They have a combined population of 8.8 million people, a total area of close to 2 million square kilometres and a land mass of 600,000 square kilometres. Each of the provinces we look at has distinct environmental assets, and faces distinct challenges.

2   DEVELOPMENT IN EASTERN INDONESIA

Comparisons with Other Parts of Indonesia

For any Indonesian region, the natural point of comparison is Java, the most populous island and the one generally considered to be the most advanced. Java still has backward rural areas, but most parts of the province have access to the electricity grid as well as reasonable road access to nearby urban areas where goods and services, including health and higher education, are available.

Average per capita income in eastern Indonesia was approximately half that in Java in 2004, rising to three-quarters if Jakarta is removed from the indicators for Java because of its special characteristics (Table 1.1). If per capita income in eastern Indonesia continued to grow at the average rates observed since the mid-1970s, namely 3–4 per cent per year, then it would take 10–20 years for eastern Indonesia to achieve the current level of per capita income observed in Java without Jakarta. However, the long-term growth rate of per capita income in eastern Indonesia is well below that in Java and the Indonesian average, implying that even as eastern Indonesia attains the levels of development currently prevailing in Java, the gap in income will in fact widen over time.

Trends in the poverty data also evoke scepticism about whether eastern Indonesia could achieve Java's present standard of living in just a decade or two. The proportion of poor people in eastern Indonesia was almost 30 per cent in 2004 (Table 1.1), compared with just 22 per cent in Java in the early 1990s (Resosudarmo and Vidyattama 2007).[1] Poverty rates have been declining, with the proportion of poor people in eastern Indonesia falling by 11.4 per cent between 1996 and 2004. This is a greater relative reduction than achieved almost anywhere else in Indonesia, but even so poverty remains very high in eastern Indonesia.

Social indicators other than poverty suggest that eastern Indonesia is lagging even further behind Java without Jakarta (Table 1.1). In 2004, eastern Indonesia recorded levels of infant mortality, life expectancy and education about the same as those for Java without Jakarta in the late 1980s (Miranti 2007). Life expectancy in Papua is a particularly depressing story. Whereas average life expectancy in Indonesia increased by 20.5 years between 1971 and 2002, in Papua it rose by only 8.5 years — the worst result of any province in the country. This reflects poorly on the pace of improvement in health services in Papua. Maluku started out with rela-

---

1   Here we use the Indonesian government's definition of poor people — essentially those whose total income (measured by their expenditure) falls below a provincial poverty line (see Appendix A2.1, Chapter 2).

Table 1.1   *Indonesia: Provincial Economic and Social Indicators*

Region	Population (million people)	GDP per Capita (Rp million)	Growth in GDP per Capita (% p.a.)		
	2004	2004	1976–90	1991–2004	1976–2004
Eastern Indonesia	8.6	5.8	2.8	3.0	2.9
East Nusa Tenggara	4.1	3.1	4.9	4.0	4.5
Maluku	2.1	3.0	5.4	0.1	2.8
Papua	2.5	12.6	0.3	2.9	1.5
Java	121.5	10.2	6.5	2.7	4.6
Java without Jakarta	112.8	7.8	6.3	2.6	4.5
Bali	3.3	8.5	8.7	3.4	6.1
West Nusa Tenggara	4.3	5.5	5.0	5.9	5.4
Sumatra	45.5	10.8	1.0	2.2	1.6
Kalimantan	12.3	17.3	5.1	3.0	4.1
Sulawesi	15.8	5.9	5.2	4.0	4.6
Indonesia	**211.4**	**10.1**	**4.8**	**2.7**	**3.8**

tively high levels of education in 1971 and has recorded slightly higher than average rates of improvement. East Nusa Tenggara, on the other hand, has been lagging behind other regions in educational achievement: from roughly average performance in 1971, it has been growing below the national average ever since.

There are two defining differences between eastern Indonesia and Java, both with major consequences for development. First, eastern Indonesia has a far lower population density. As a result, it cannot hope to achieve the scale effects that were so beneficial for development in Java. Second, geographical conditions are far more challenging in eastern Indonesia. Governments have struggled to provide transport across the scattered small islands of Maluku and East Nusa Tenggara, or to extend communications into the rugged and remote interior of Papua. Inevitably, the costs of transport and communications are far higher in eastern Indonesia than in Java (Hill 1989). Rather than adopting the Java development model, therefore, eastern Indonesia needs its own development path — one that takes local conditions, local economic and social structures and local patterns of resource use and interaction with the environment into account.

Table 1.1 (continued)

Region	Poverty (%) 2004	Infant Mortality (deaths per 1,000 live births) 2000	Life Expectancy (years) 2002	Average Schooling (years in school) 2002
Eastern Indonesia	29.9	59.2	65	6.4
East Nusa Tenggara	27.7	57.0	64	5.8
Maluku	23.9	66.2	66	8.0
Papua	38.4	57.0	65	6.0
Java	15.9	48.6	67	7.1
Java without Jakarta	16.8	50.4	66	6.8
Bali	6.8	36.0	70	7.6
West Nusa Tenggara	25.3	89.0	59	5.8
Sumatra	17.4	48.0	67	7.8
Kalimantan	10.9	55.3	66	7.2
Sulawesi	16.7	53.9	68	7.3
Indonesia	**16.6**	**47.0**	**66**	**7.1**

Source: BPS (various years).

The development gap between eastern Indonesia and Sumatra or Bali is at least as great as that between eastern Indonesia and Java (Table 1.1). Although, like Java, Sumatra has some very poor areas, overall it is more developed than eastern Indonesia. Kalimantan, the richest of Indonesia's regions, is also well ahead of eastern Indonesia on most economic and social development indicators, even if its wealthiest province, East Kalimantan, is excluded from the data. But despite the wide gap between them, eastern Indonesia has more in common with Kalimantan than with Java. Kalimantan is a resource-based economy with many remote areas and a few urban areas in which wealth is concentrated. If per capita indicators for eastern Indonesia keep growing at their historic pace, then in one or two decades the economy of eastern Indonesia, particularly Papua, could resemble that of Kalimantan today. That is, natural resource exploitation and industry would dominate the economy and wealth would be concentrated in just a small number of cities.

In terms of income and many social indicators, eastern Indonesia has most in common with Sulawesi and West Nusa Tenggara (Table 1.1), although Sulawesi has performed far better with respect to poverty.

Importantly, comparison at the regional level again masks strong differences within regions. Parts of Sulawesi and West Nusa Tenggara, namely Manado, Makassar and Mataram, are well connected to Java and Bali, and these areas are relatively advanced. But other, less favoured areas have much lower levels of development, similar to those in many parts of eastern Indonesia.

Comparisons within Eastern Indonesia

There are marked differences in development status between the three eastern Indonesian provinces discussed in this book. Economically, Papua is far more advanced than the other two provinces. It is a much richer place in terms of natural resources, principally coal, copper, natural gas and forests (Marshall and Beehler 2007). Exploitation of copper and gold began in the 1970s, initiating development in several parts of the province. Another source of development was the central government, keen to reduce the influence of the Papuan independence movement by delivering visible progress. However, the remoteness of much of Papua meant that central government programs were concentrated in cities such as Jayapura, Biak, Sorong, Manokwari and Merauke. In absolute terms, Papua enjoyed relatively high growth in gross domestic product (GDP) of 3.0 per cent per annum between 1976 and 2004. But in per capita terms growth was relatively slow, at just 1.5 per cent per annum, because of Papua's high rates of population growth, driven by migration.

This highly uneven pattern of development has succeeded in increasing average incomes, but has generally not been effective in improving social conditions or lifting people out of poverty. Tellingly, the proportion of poor people in Papua is higher than that in either Maluku or East Nusa Tenggara, despite Papua's far higher levels of per capita GDP. Between 1996 and 2004, the proportion of poor people fell by 11.2 per cent in East Nusa Tenggara and 20.6 per cent in Maluku, but by just 3.9 per cent in Papua. Papua has the highest poverty rate in the country, and will continue to do so at these rates of change.

Maluku and East Nusa Tenggara are broadly similar on many economic and social indicators. In 1999, before social and political conflict ruined its economy, Maluku was slightly better off than East Nusa Tenggara economically (Hill, Resosudarmo and Vidyattama 2008). It has always had relatively high levels of education by Indonesian standards but has performed poorly on health.

Conflict has been a major obstacle to development in eastern Indonesia. Both Maluku and Papua have witnessed episodes of violence that have been deeply disruptive to social stability and economic development. On a lesser scale, parts of East Nusa Tenggara have also been exposed to the flow-on effects of the conflict in East Timor. Although other parts of Indonesia have experienced conflict over the last decade or two, it has not been as persistent or as damaging as it has in eastern Indonesia.

Overall it is difficult to judge which of the three provinces is the least developed. Papua is the best endowed but poverty is more severe there. Each of the three faces distinct challenges.

International Comparisons

Indonesia is not alone in having backward regions. An example in the immediate neighbourhood is Mindanao in the Philippines, which has consistently lagged behind other regions, in part because of its long history of conflict (Balisacan and Hill 2007). Examples further afield include the northern parts of Thailand, the western regions of China and many parts of India. There is certainly nothing unique about eastern Indonesia's development status *vis-à-vis* the rest of Indonesia.

Aggregate economic and social indicators for eastern Indonesia, the poorer countries of northern Southeast Asia (such as Laos) and many states in the Pacific are similar. Some of the underlying structural impediments to development are the same, such as low population densities, long distances, lack of infrastructure and poorly developed markets.

In all of these cases, the question is whether and how development can be accelerated. Crucial in this regard is the extent to which a country's development status is a function of policies and institutions that can be improved, and the extent to which it is inevitable because of structural factors such as poor soil, an adverse climate or difficult geographical conditions. Lessons learned from successes and failures in other Asia–Pacific countries are important for eastern Indonesia.

3   RESOURCE ENDOWMENTS AND ENVIRONMENTAL ASSETS

Although Papua stands out as one of Indonesia's richest regions in terms of natural resources, Maluku and East Nusa Tenggara are not without assets of their own. Mining is significant in the northern part of Maluku. Although levels of activity have dropped off since conflict broke out in 1999, Newcrest continues to mine coal on the island of Halmahera and BHP Billiton is still extracting nickel on Gag island. Forestry also contributes to the economy, with logging operations spread out across the province. East Nusa Tenggara is not well endowed with either forests or minerals, but like the other two provinces it has access to the marine resources of the Arafura Sea, one of the richest fishing grounds in the country.

With all three provinces having access to at least some natural resources, one might speculate that natural resource extraction could act as the engine of growth for the region. Doubts have been expressed, however, about the effectiveness of natural resource extraction as an engine of economic growth. History shows that rich endowments of natural resources can be either a 'curse' or a 'blessing' for a region. Sachs and Warner (2001: 828) found that:

> there is virtually no overlap between the set of countries with large natural resource endowments—and the set of countries that have high levels of GDP ... [Moreover] extremely resource-abundant countries such as the Oil States in the Gulf, or Nigeria, or Mexico and Venezuela, have not experienced rapid economic growth ... [Hence] resource intensity tends to correlate with slow economic growth.

In many developing countries, natural resource extraction is a source of conflict—among resource-extracting firms, between firms and local communities, between firms and authorities, among the various levels of government, between local communities and local authorities, and within local communities (Azis and Salim 2005).

Nevertheless, many resource-abundant Southeast Asian economies have experienced periods of sustained economic growth, indicating that they may be different in some way from the group of countries examined by Sachs and Warner (Coxhead 2005). In Indonesia, two of the four best endowed provinces, East Kalimantan and Riau, have become increasingly prosperous without any major disruption to the peace. But two others, Aceh and Papua, have experienced serious conflict (at least until the early 2000s). Lack of equity in the distribution of mining revenues is a longstanding source of conflict between the central government and the Acehnese and Papuan elites, and between mining companies and locals. It is one of the main grievances fuelling separatist movements. Conflict over mining has also occurred in Maluku and many other parts of Indonesia. However, even in Aceh and Papua socio-economic conditions have improved, and on the whole it appears that rich endowments of natural resources are more an advantage than a curse for most Indonesian regions (Hill, Resosudarmo and Vidyattama 2008).

Eastern Indonesia has an exceedingly rich natural environment, with diverse and unique land and marine ecosystems (Marshall and Beehler 2007; Tomascik et al. 1997). But the region's biological riches are under threat from forest conversion, overharvesting, mining and other activities, as elsewhere in Southeast Asia and in tropical developing countries more generally (Sodhi et al. 2004). Environmental degradation is happening in Indonesia at an alarming rate (Resosudarmo 2005).

The strong negative externalities from resource extraction range from landslides at the local level to climate change at the global level. Deforestation, forest degradation and water pollution from mine tailings are some of the causes. It is no easy task to marry environmental and development objectives, especially where environmental conservation competes directly with economic activity and people's need to earn a livelihood. For conservation to be effective, governments may need to compensate those who face losses when high-conservation areas are closed to overexploitation, and devise programs that give local farmers and fishers the tools to find other ways of sustaining a livelihood. This is particularly difficult for governments that have very limited finances, and may require resource transfers from developed countries that have an interest in preserving environmental values.

4 LOOKING AHEAD

What can be done to close the development gap between eastern Indonesia and the rest of the country? Better connections to the global economy would certainly help, as international studies and the experience of several fast-growing Indonesian regions, particularly Jakarta, Bali and Batam, attest (Hill 2007; Hill, Resosudarmo and Vidyattama 2008). At present there are no direct flights between eastern Indonesia and Java, let alone between eastern Indonesia and the rest of the world. It typically takes a full day to fly between Java (the heart of the Indonesian economy) and any of the eastern Indonesian capitals. Ferries tend to run infrequently, although East Nusa Tenggara has benefited from the development of a road and ferry network connecting Lombok in West Nusa Tenggara with Bali and, by extension, Java.

Industrial activity is known to stimulate regional growth (Fujita, Krugman and Venables 2000; Hill 2007) but cannot occur without a good internal transport and communications network. The literature indicates that this is important to lower the costs of production, and so help create industrial clustering and increasing returns to scale. Given eastern Indonesia's low population density, it would be hard to create the kind of industrial clustering seen in Jakarta, Bali or Balikpapan. It is nevertheless important to improve transport and communications within eastern Indonesia, to encourage industrial development.

Good institutions and governance are also universally important for regional development (Shleifer and Vishny 1993; Knack and Keefer 1995; Easterly, Ritzan and Woolcock 2006). In the case of eastern Indonesia, the two aspects of governance that can be expected to have the most immediate impact on growth are to improve the quality of public sector human capital and to eliminate corruption. The quality of local government staff in eastern Indonesia is generally poor. As a consequence, many local governments are incapable of formulating high-quality development programs for their areas. The situation is not as bad in East Nusa Tenggara and Maluku as it is in many other provinces, but the same cannot be said of Papua, where significant improvements in the quality of personnel are urgently needed. Eliminating corruption is also of great importance, because it diverts large sums of money that might otherwise be used for development to the elite. Again, this is particularly important in the case of Papua.

Private sector engagement is another universally important aspect of development; in fact, private sector business activity can be seen as a fundamental prerequisite for economic prosperity in any region. To achieve sustained economic development, private sector activity in eastern Indonesia needs to expand significantly. Better infrastructure (including better connectivity) and better governance would help to remove some of the obstacles to private sector growth, but may not be sufficient to attract business on a large scale. Direct policies to promote business, such as subsidies or tax concessions (as in the case of Batam), may work if other preconditions are met, but raise the question of whether they are a good use of public funds. It should also be remembered that large-scale industrial activity can undermine environmental systems and compromise local livelihoods, as comes into sharp view with, for example, some mining projects.

Natural resources clearly play a major role in regional development. However, the utilization of such resources must take into account issues of equity and sustainability, and the possibility of negative externalities. Resources need to be extracted in a sustainable way to ensure that present and future generations are able to reap the benefits of local resources. Prudent management of resources and the environment pays for itself by preserving economic opportunities for the future.

In rural eastern Indonesia, where extractable resources are scarce and sizeable manufacturing or service activities unlikely to spring up, economic and social development will most likely have to come from improvements in productivity and better management of agriculture, fisheries and forestry. Hence, better watershed and environmental management, the provision of technical assistance to farmers and fishers and the creation of strong institutions to underpin agriculture, fisheries and forestry will be of paramount importance. The Indonesian experience shows the importance of having programs directly targeted at alleviating poverty (Resosudarmo and Vidyattama 2007). In this context, traditional development strategies such as programs to provide better education and health facilities, to direct credit to the poor and to expand irrigation networks clearly have a role to play.

The list of what can and should be done is long, and the right strategy is very specific to the local context. For development to be sustainable, the eastern Indonesian provinces need clear frameworks to promote economic development, accelerate poverty alleviation and preserve environmental conditions. A more holistic understanding of developmental and environmental issues in eastern Indonesia is a prerequisite. This book aims to go some way in that direction.

5   OVERVIEW OF THE BOOK

This book consists of 14 chapters organized into three parts. Part I describes economic, social and political conditions in each of the three provinces, with a particular focus on poverty alleviation and development strategies.

Chapter 2, by Budy P. Resosudarmo, Lydia Napitupulu, Chris Manning and Velix Wanggai, describes political developments in Papua since the collapse of Soeharto's New Order administration. Perhaps the most momentous of these was the passage of the Special Autonomy Law (Law No. 21/2001), which gave the province greater financial resources and more say over its own development path. While diminishing the calls for an independent Papua, the law has encountered problems that the authors detail. The chapter then turns to another defining feature of the province: its high rates of demographic change, mainly due to in-migration. As well as affecting population growth rates, this has changed the ethnic, religious, migrant versus indigenous and urban versus rural composition of the province. Next, the chapter reviews social and economic indicators for Papua, including its ranking on the human development index (HDI) and its performance with respect to trade and GDP. It concludes with an in-depth look at poverty trends across Papua.

In Chapter 3, Budy P. Resosudarmo, Lydia Napitupulu and Chris Manning turn their attention to the fiscal impact on Papua of the central government's decentralization and special autonomy policies. The authors explore both the opportunities the new policies have created to implement more effective economic development policies in Papua, and the challenges to doing so. On the plus side, they note the huge increase in provincial and local government budgets, and the commensurate increase in local responsibilities and control. On the minus side, they point to the destructive effects of the increase in the number of new districts and the challenges posed by corruption, poor infrastructure and lack of private investment.

Chapters 2 and 3 both make extensive use of statistical data. Chapter 2 therefore provides an appendix on the quality and reliability of Indonesian statistics in general, and of the Papuan poverty and GDP statistics in particular. Appendix A2.1 is written by Bambang Heru, a staff member of the Indonesian statistical agency, BPS.

In Chapter 4, Budy P. Resosudarmo outlines administrative, demographic, social and economic conditions in Maluku, against the background of the conflict of 1999–2003. Like other provinces, Maluku has seen a plethora of new districts established since 1999, with the usual problems of disruption to local government finances and development programs. Population statistics reflect the effects of the conflict, with the population actually declining between 1999 and 2000. Social indicators are mixed: the province slid backward on the HDI but continues to score above the national average; educational outcomes are relatively good; and health indicators have worsened. Economically, Maluku is struggling. Poverty has also worsened since 1999, if not to the extent one might expect. The chapter highlights the need for prudent fiscal policy, to get Maluku back on its feet.

The final chapter in this section, by Colin Barlow and Ria Gondowarsito, focuses on rural development in East Nusa Tenggara. The chapter first provides a comprehensive review of economic, social, political, geographical and agricultural conditions in East Nusa Tenggara. It then discusses poverty, and how it might be alleviated. The authors highlight practical measures to achieve rural development, such as better infrastructure and improved production and marketing techniques. They also offer a brief assessment of several initiatives already on the ground, the success of which is closely related to their ability to engage the local community.

Part II of the book explores the tension between natural resource exploitation and environmental protection. Chapter 6 by Ian M. Dutton, Rili Djohani, Setijati D. Sastrapradja and Karla M. Dutton argues the need to balance biodiversity conservation and development in eastern Indonesia. The biological diversity of eastern Indonesia is of global importance from both an evolutionary biology and socio-political perspective. The region's resources are increasingly coming under pressure, however, as global demand for all types of natural resources increases, as comparable resources in western and central Indonesia are depleted and as the regional population expands. On a more hopeful note, the chapter offers four case studies of innovative approaches currently being used in Central Sulawesi, North Sulawesi, Komodo island and West Papua to conserve biological diversity and secure sustainable livelihoods for the local community.

Chapter 7 by Chris Ballard and Glenn Banks discusses the evolving corporate strategies of Freeport, owner of the hugely profitable Grasberg mining complex in Papua, as it adapts to the post-Soeharto political environment. The authors first review the company's long history of involvement in mining in Papua, which extends back to the 1960s. They then discuss the company's mining, political and environmental strategies, its troubled relations with local landowners and its close relationship with the Indonesian military. The authors conclude that Freeport will continue to conduct 'business as usual' in Papua for many years to come, based on the ability it has demonstrated to withstand dramatic transformations at the global, national and provincial levels.

In Chapter 8, Budy P. Resosudarmo, Lydia Napitupulu and David Campbell investigate the subject of illegal fishing in the Arafura Sea. The authors describe the national legal regime for fishing in Indonesian territorial waters, the nature of illegal fishing and the jurisdictional inconsistencies created by the new decentralization laws. They argue that the most dangerous and destructive perpetrators of illegal fishing are large-scale operators with international networks and close connections to the Indonesian elite. Not only do their activities deplete fish stocks, but they drain national finances, deprive local fishermen of their livelihoods and place social and economic pressures on local communities. The chapter concludes by reviewing the progress that is being made to combat illegal fishing and by offering some policy options to prevent and mitigate the effects of illegal fishing.

Chapter 9 by James J. Fox, Dedi S. Adhuri, Tom Therik and Michelle Carnegie turns to the subject of illegal fishing by Indonesian fishermen in Australian territorial waters. The chapter discusses the driving forces behind the fishermen's activities and describes their networks of operation. It stresses the importance of generating alternative livelihoods for those engaged in illegal fishing as part of an overall policy to eliminate illegal fishing in Australia's northern waters.

In Chapter 10, Hidayat Alhamid, Peter Kanowski and Chris Ballard discuss the issue of forest tenure in Papua. Drawing on the case of the Rendani Protection Forest adjacent to the town of Manokwari in the Bird's Head peninsula region, they investigate indigenous forest management practices and indigenous forest utilization regimes. They review the history of conflict over forest access and use in Rendani, as a microcosm of the conflict over resource use in Papua more generally.

Chapter 11 is about climate change. Frank Jotzo, Ida Aju Pradnja Resosudarmo, Ditya A. Nurdianto and Agus P. Sari summarize the anticipated effects of climate change in Indonesia and options to reduce greenhouse gas emissions. Research is evolving on this topic and data are especially patchy for eastern Indonesia. However, enough information is available for the authors to draw some options for climate change mitigation and adaptation policies to support the development of eastern Indonesia.

Part III focuses on issues related to conflict, local development and health. Chapter 12 by Craig Thorburn provides an in-depth look at the situation in Maluku since conflict broke out in 1999. The author discusses the historical, economic and cultural roots of the conflict and describes how and why it spread. Although the conflict officially ended with the signing of the Malino Peace Accord in 2002, its reverberations continue. Thorburn singles out two issues in particular for discussion: the plight of internally displaced persons and the role of local government reform in effecting a lasting recovery.

In Chapter 13, Astia Dendi, Heinz-Josef Heile and Stephanus Makambombu assess the performance of one of the programs set up to alleviate poverty in East Nusa Tenggara, in order to extract lessons for other livelihood development programs. The Poverty Alleviation and Support for Local Governance Program (PROMIS) takes a two-pronged approach to livelihood development: it aims to assist rural populations to expand their economic activities, and it aims to strengthen local institutions. The authors find that this integrated approach to poverty alleviation is one of the strongest aspects of the program. They conclude that the success of the program hinges on its ability to align its goals with those of the community and harness individual, community and local government participation.

The final chapter of the book, by Endang R. Sedyaningsih and Suriadi Gunawan, discusses health conditions in Papua in relation to the goals of Healthy Indonesia 2010, a Ministry of Health initiative. The chapter describes the historical and more recent development of health services in Papua. It details the nature and extent of communicable diseases such as malaria, tuberculosis and HIV/AIDS, and reviews the nutritional status of Papuans. The chapter concludes by discussing the action needed to close the gap between the current health status of Papuans and the targets set for the province by Healthy Indonesia 2010.

6   MAIN FINDINGS

This book covers a broad range of issues to do with development, resources and the environment in eastern Indonesia. In its pages, many researchers bring specialist knowledge and different points of view to bear on the challenges facing the region. Here we attempt to distil the 10 main messages that we, as editors, have drawn from their work. We know that not everyone will agree with our emphases and interpretations, but we nevertheless hope to capture the essence of the main issues.

First, there is strong evidence that development in eastern Indonesia has lagged behind that in Java, Sumatra, Bali and Kalimantan. Of course, it is not the only backward region in the country; Sulawesi without Manado and Makassar and West Nusa Tenggara without Lombok are equally poor. It is also important to note that over the last three decades, development in eastern Indonesia has not been without progress. Eastern Indonesia has grown at about the same rate as other regions, particularly in terms of economic indicators, but less so in terms of social indicators. It has also done better than many South Pacific countries with similar geographical conditions. Nevertheless, how to alleviate poverty remains a key policy challenge for the region.

Second, adverse initial conditions and difficult geography are the two main factors behind the current lack of development in eastern Indonesia. In the face of these difficulties, government and non-government organizations alike have struggled to find an approach to rural poverty alleviation that works. It appears that an integrated approach consisting of credit provision, technical support, knowledge transfer and active community involvement might work. What is not known is whether such a program can be implemented effectively on a large scale.

Third, as is apparent in Papua and Maluku, conflict is an important obstacle to socio-economic development. To ensure that local arguments do not escalate into destructive social and political conflict, local governments need to establish transparent mechanisms to resolve such disputes. The current democratization and decentralization process is contributing to the prevention of conflict, but more remains to be done.

Fourth, the status of public health in eastern Indonesia is of great concern. Rates of malaria, tuberculosis and HIV/AIDS are significantly higher in eastern Indonesia than in other parts of Indonesia. Difficult geographical conditions, lack of funding and poor human capital are the main hurdles to delivering better health services across eastern Indonesia. The most difficult policy challenge facing local government is how to deliver better health services in rural and remote areas. At the very least, the situation requires closer cooperation and alignment of goals between government, the private sector and civil society.

Fifth, the decentralization policy implemented in 2001 presents opportunities for more rapid development in eastern Indonesia. Regional governments now have larger budgets and more power to formulate their own development policies. In the case of Papua, the special autonomy policy has given Papuans more control over the province's resources, softening demands for independence. However, throughout eastern Indonesia, there is the question of whether the additional funds from decentralization are being spent judiciously on strategic infrastructure, public services and improving the business and investment climate. If revenues are spent in a suboptimal way — most notably, if they are spent on creating new districts or squandered through corruption — eastern Indonesia risks losing the present momentum to build a strong base for future improvements in welfare.

Sixth, natural resource extraction is playing a vital role in advancing economic growth in eastern Indonesia, particularly Papua. In general, local people have benefited from the multiplier impacts of resource extraction, particularly in the form of schools, markets, roads, health centres and, to some extent, increased incomes. Nevertheless, the spread of these benefits has been unable to solve the problems of poverty and health, particularly among indigenous people in rural areas. Finding better ways to distribute the benefits from natural resource extraction, and to avoid resource-related conflict, will require a strong commitment from all involved: the central government, local governments and the local communities themselves.

Seventh, it is time to take a fresh approach to the issue of land and natural resource tenure. Ignoring traditional rights over land and natural resources simply creates conflict, especially between extractors supported by the central government on one side and local communities on the other side. The solution lies in creating a regime in which the validity of both traditional and government laws on land tenure and natural resource ownership are acknowledged. Large companies need to work more closely with local communities and governments so that their operations are actively 'welcomed' by the locals. To win their trust, they need to act with greater transparency and accountability than they have in the past, share their profits with the host community, maintain the environment and support local economic activities. At the same time, local governments need to prepare for the future by giving their communities the resources to sustain alternative means of livelihood. In particular, this means putting more resources into education and improving the technical skills of the population.

Eighth, urgent action is needed to address the problem of illegal extraction of natural resources. Contrary to popular perception, most of this is carried out, not by small operators struggling to earn a living, but by large-scale networks linked with international markets. Tackling this problem must begin at the top, by disrupting the connections between 'bosses' and influential central and local government officers. Other measures would include clearer legislation, stronger enforcement of laws and regulations, and improvements in monitoring capability. Once again it is essential to stress the importance of education and skills in giving local people a way of earning a living without resorting to illegal and destructive fishing practices.

Ninth, it is apparent that development is placing great strains on the sustainability of ecosystems in eastern Indonesia. Key threats to the environment include overexploitation or overharvesting of forests and seas, destructive harvesting (such as blast fishing or the inappropriate use of fire) and habitat conversion (of forests to agriculture and plantations, for example). The extent of the problem in each area is greatly influenced by the nature of government and community control and management, the preparedness to enforce laws, the degree of corruption and the prices paid for resources and the economic incentives to exploit them. Pure environmental concerns are difficult to accommodate in a situation in which people lack the basic necessities of life. One of the challenges of biodiversity conservation, therefore, is to make it more relevant to the lives and livelihoods of local communities. Some conservation projects designed as 'learning experiments' do hold out hope of balancing conservation and development interests. Upscaling these projects to cover larger territories will be the main challenge.

Finally, Indonesia can expect to face major adverse impacts from climate change in the form of devastated ecosystems. In many areas this can be expected to negate any progress made by development efforts. A combination of sea-level rise and changing hydrological cycle will affect already stretched supplies of water and food. Adapting to climate change will happen automatically in many cases, but in other cases will require intervention. In any event, it will require additional economic resources.

It is true that the challenges of developing eastern Indonesia are enormous. With serious and consistent efforts by the government, the private sector, civil society and local communities, it should be possible to overcome many of these challenges. Without such efforts, eastern Indonesia could become permanently dependent on aid and remittances — something that the people of the region certainly do not want.

REFERENCES

Azis, I.J. and E. Salim (2005), 'Development Performance and Future Scenarios in the Context of Sustainable Utilisation of Natural Resources', in B.P. Resosudarmo (ed.), *The Politics and Economics of Indonesia's Natural Resources*, Institute of Southeast Asian Studies, Singapore, pp. 125–44.

Balisacan, A.M. and H. Hill (eds) (2007), *The Dynamics of Regional Development: The Philippines in East Asia*, Edward Elgar, Cheltenham.

Barlow, C. and J. Hardjono (1995), *Indonesia Assessment 1995: Development in Eastern Indonesia*, Institute of Southeast Asian Studies, Singapore.

BPS (Badan Pusat Statistik) (various years), *Statistik Indonesia* [Statistics of Indonesia], Jakarta.

Coxhead, I. (2005), 'International Trade and the Natural Resource "Curse" in Southeast Asia: Does China's Growth Threaten Regional Development?', in B.P. Resosudarmo (ed.), *The Politics and Economics of Indonesia's Natural Resources*, Institute of Southeast Asian Studies, Singapore, pp. 71–91.

Easterly, W., J. Ritzan and M. Woolcock (2006), 'Social Cohesion, Institutions, and Growth', Working Paper No. 94, Center for Global Development, Washington DC.

Fujita, M., P. Krugman and A. Venables (2000), *The Spatial Economy: Cities, Regions and International Trade*, MIT Press, Cambridge MA.

Hill, H. (ed.) (1989), *Unity and Diversity: Regional Economic Development in Indonesia since 1970*, Oxford University Press, Singapore.

Hill, H. (2007), 'Regional Development: Analytical and Policy Issues', in A.M. Balisacan and H. Hill (eds), *The Dynamics of Regional Development: The Philippines in East Asia*, Edward Elgar, Cheltenham, pp. 68–92.

Hill, H., B.P. Resosudarmo and Y. Vidyattama (2008), 'Indonesia's Changing Economic Geography', *Bulletin of Indonesian Economic Studies*, 44(3): 407–35.

Knack, S. and P. Keefer (1995), 'Institutions and Economic Performance: Cross-country Testing Using Alternative Institutional Measures', *Economics and Politics*, 7(3): 207–27.

Marshall, A.J. and B.M. Beehler (2007), *The Ecology of Papua: Part II*, Periplus, Singapore.

Miranti, R. (2007), 'Determinants of Regional Poverty in Indonesia 1984–2002', PhD thesis, Australian National University, Canberra.

Pannell, S. and F. von Benda-Beckmann (1998), *Old World Places, New World Problems*, Centre for Resource and Environmental Studies, Australian National University, Canberra.

Resosudarmo, B.P. (2005), 'Introduction', in B.P. Resosudarmo (ed.), *The Politics and Economics of Indonesia's Natural Resources*, Institute of Southeast Asian Studies, Singapore, pp. 1–12.

Resosudarmo, B.P. and Y. Vidyattama (2007), 'East Asian Experience: Indonesia', in A.M. Balisacan and H. Hill (eds), *The Dynamics of Regional Development: The Philippines in East Asia*, Edward Elgar, Cheltenham, pp. 123–53.

Sachs, J. and A. Warner (2001), 'The Curse of Natural Resources', *European Economic Review*, 45: 827–38.

Shleifer, A. and R. Vishny (1993), 'Corruption', *Quarterly Journal of Economics*, 108(3): 599–617.

Sodhi, N.S., L.P. Koh, B.W. Brook and P.K.L. Ng (2004), 'Southeast Asian Biodiversity: An Impending Disaster', *Trends in Ecology and Evolution*, 19(12): 654–60.

Tomascik, T., A.J. Mah, A. Nontji and M.K. Moosa (1997), *The Ecology of the Indonesian Seas: Part I and Part II*, Periplus, Singapore.

PART I

Economic Development
and Poverty Alleviation

2   PAPUA I: CHALLENGES OF ECONOMIC DEVELOPMENT IN AN ERA OF POLITICAL AND ECONOMIC CHANGE

Budy P. Resosudarmo, Lydia Napitupulu, Chris Manning and Velix Wanggai

---

Economic development has been uneven in Papua,[1] and poverty in the region remains high by Indonesian (though not necessarily South Pacific) standards. Part of the problem has been neglect of the poor — too little or the wrong kind of government support from Jakarta and Jayapura. A major factor in this is the extraordinarily high cost of delivering goods and services to large numbers of isolated communities, in the absence of a developed road or river network (the latter in contrast to Kalimantan) providing access to the interior and the highlands (Garnaut and Manning 1974; Manning and Rumbiak 1991). Intermittent political and military conflict and tight security controls have also contributed to the problem (McGibbon 2006), but with the exception of some border regions and a few pockets in the highlands, this has not been the main factor contributing to underdevelopment.

This chapter outlines the important political, social and economic developments that have occurred in Papua since the collapse of Soeharto's New Order administration. It sets the stage for the discussion of development policies that follows in Chapter 3.

---

1   Called West Irian when formally annexed by Indonesia in 1969, the province was renamed Irian Jaya in 1973 and Papua in 2001. Although it is currently divided into two provinces, Papua and West Papua, in this chapter we define Papua to include both provinces. The administrative divisions are shown in Map 2.1.

Map 2.1 The Administrative Divisions of Papua, 2007

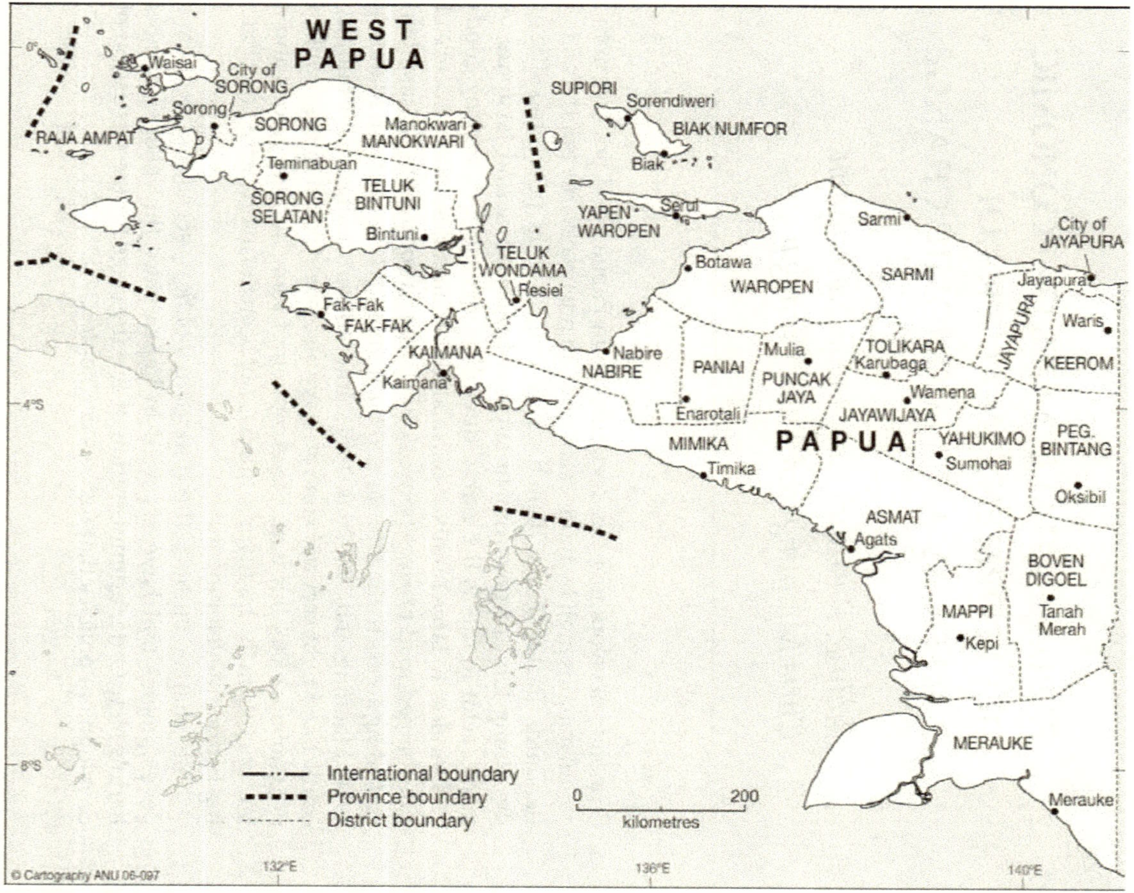

1 THE POLITICS OF SPECIAL AUTONOMY FOR PAPUA

Since Papua's annexation by Indonesia in 1969, many among the Papuan elite have indicated a preference for the formation of an independent Papuan state. There has been a longstanding, low-level (though sometimes quite violent) struggle for independence both at home and abroad, including sporadic guerrilla activity in Papua, mostly led by a loose political organization called the Free Papua Movement (OPM) (McGibbon 2006; Timmer 2007). Tensions between Jakarta and Papua were not helped by the fact that most of the revenues generated by the region's natural resources, especially those from the hugely profitable Freeport mine in Mimika district, went straight to Jakarta and delivered only limited development to indigenous Papuans. We argue in this chapter that the concerns of Papuans are well justified: the central government has been unable to support a level of social and economic development in Papua commensurate with the value of the rents generated from natural resource exploitation in the province.

The most critical political time in the relationship between Jakarta and Papua occurred in the years between 1998 and 2001. The resignation of President Soeharto in mid-1998 and East Timor's successful demand for a referendum on independence intensified separatist hopes in Papua. When Abdurrahman Wahid became president at the end of 1999, he introduced a more accommodative and culturally sensitive approach to the question of ethnic conflict and separatist demands in Papua (Sumule 2003; McGibbon 2004, 2006). The president sought to maintain good relations with the Papuan elite and endorsed the development of a draft bill on special autonomy for the province. After a long series of debates, in late 2001 the national parliament finally enacted Law No. 21/2001 on Special Autonomy for Papua.

The Special Autonomy Law instilled hope among Papuans that the province would gain greater control over the revenues from natural resource extraction in the province and a far greater say in the direction of economic and political development. But while the provincial government has indeed been the recipient of increased revenues, the central government's approach to implementing the new law has disappointed various groups in Papua, especially the Jayapura elite. In particular, the central government was criticized for its tardiness in establishing the political institutions required by Law No. 21/2001, its deliberate weakening of those institutions and its decision to split Papua into two provinces. This situation renewed resentment against the central government, leading to further conflict between Jakarta and Jayapura. In August 2005, the Papuan Tribal Council (Dewan Adat Papua) and other Papuan groups decided to reject the largely unimplemented Special Autonomy Law.

This is indicative of the high level of disappointment among Papuans with the political arrangements for implementation of the law.

Three issues in particular contributed to the souring of relations between Jakarta and Jayapura. The first concerned the establishment and role of the Papuan People's Assembly (MRP). The Special Autonomy Law required the establishment of an upper house of parliament consisting of equal numbers of customary, religious and female representatives, as the highest institution in Papua (see Box 2.1). However, the formation of the MRP was delayed during the Megawati presidency (2001–04) because of differences between the central government and Papuans about its specific responsibilities. In particular, the minister for home affairs, Hari Sabarno, wanted to ensure that the MRP did not have excessive powers to curtail the authority of the province's executive and legislative arms of government (*Republika*, 10 September 2003).

When Susilo Bambang Yudhoyono became president in 2004, one of his first acts was to endorse a draft bill establishing the MRP. In December 2004, he put the bill into effect as a 'Christmas gift' to the Papuan people. Under this regulation (PP No. 54/2004), the MRP is mandated to protect the basic rights of Papuans by considering, providing advice on and approving gubernatorial and national (MPR) candidates and international agreements. In common with the lower-level provincial parliament, the DPRP, the MRP has the right to prepare and enact special regional regulations (*perdasus*).[2]

On 31 October 2005, 42 Papuans were inducted as members of the first MRP. They immediately faced the immense challenge of making the MRP functional. To establish the institution's credibility, and their own as legislators, they first needed to demonstrate that they had the ability to produce relevant advice on matters within their jurisdiction. They also needed to establish good working relations with the central, provincial and district governments, as well as with the Papuan and the West Papuan DPRP.

The second source of conflict between Jakarta and Jayapura concerned the transfer of authority for the management of the region's natural resources. From the start, the central and provincial governments disagreed on the extent of the transfer. For example, based on Law No. 41/1999 on Forestry, the forestry minister, M.S Kaban, argued that his ministry should retain the right to issue forest concessions. However, the governor of Papua, the late J.P Solossa, insisted that the Special Autonomy Law gave the provincial government authority over all matters related to forestry, including the issuing of concessions. This matter

---

2 The MRP sits in Jayapura. At present there are two provincial parliaments, one in Papua and one in West Papua.

BOX 2.1   KEY FEATURES OF
THE SPECIAL AUTONOMY LAW

After a long and high-profile process of drafting and consultation, Law No. 21/2001 on Special Autonomy for Papua was enacted in November 2001 (Sumule 2003). The five key features of the law are as follows.

First, the Special Autonomy Law gives the provincial government authority over decision making in all sectors except international affairs, defence, monetary and fiscal policy, religion and the Supreme Court. Papua may conduct international trade and investment and take part in international exchanges of culture and technology. Moreover, all treaties affecting Papua are subject to the approval of the Papuan provincial government.

Second, the law states that the provincial parliament is to consist of two chambers: an indigenous upper house (MRP) consisting of equal numbers of customary, religious and female representatives, and a lower house (DPRP) consisting of elected political-party representatives. The responsibilities of the MRP include approving gubernatorial candidates, approving Papua's candidates to the national People's Consultative Assembly (MPR) and drafting special regional regulations (*perdasus*), the highest level of regional regulation in Papua. The DPRP may enact both special regional regulations and provincial regulations (*perdasi*) and is responsible for approving the provincial budget. The provincial governor is responsible in the first instance to the DPRP.

Third, apart from the usual Indonesian symbols of state, the law allows Papua to have its own flag, symbol and anthem, and permits the formation of local political parties.

Fourth, the law gives Papua a higher share of the revenues originating in Papua (see also Chapter 3, this volume). At least 30 per cent of the proceeds from oil and gas mining must be spent on education, and 15 per cent on health.

Fifth, the law requires the provincial government to protect the existence of customary laws and traditions, including the rights of traditional communities over customary land and the natural resources (and other economic activities) on that land. The law provides for the establishment of both traditional and human rights-based court systems.

remains unresolved, and is a good example of what the Papuan elite sees as the central government's strategy to retain responsibilities that should be transferred to the province.

The third issue concerned the administrative division of Papua. In 1999, the central government passed Law No. 45/1999 dividing Papua into three provinces: Papua, West Irian Jaya and Central Irian Jaya. The official establishment of the three new provinces in February 2003 (under Presidential Instruction No. 1/2003) evoked a storm of protest from Papuans. Jakarta managed to establish West Irian Jaya but was forced to abandon its plans for the third province of Central Irian Jaya. After a judicial review, in November 2004 the Constitutional Court declared Law No. 45/1999 unconstitutional and therefore invalid, but recognized the *de facto* establishment of West Irian Jaya. But while the new province had been established *de facto*, *de jure* matters remained unresolved. The Special Autonomy Law of 2001 made no mention of Law No. 45/1999 but stated that any division of Papua into provinces had to be approved by the MRP and DPRP. Based on the views expressed by the people of West Irian Jaya over a two-week consultation period, in February 2006 the newly established MRP decided to oppose the establishment of the province (*Kompas*, 18 February 2006).

Nevertheless, the central government continued to push ahead with its plans, conducting gubernatorial elections in March 2006 and—in a concession to Papuans—renaming West Irian Jaya 'West Papua' in April 2007. Abraham O. Atururi was elected governor in the west (perhaps surprisingly, with overwhelming support), while Barnabas Suebo, a former governor of Papua under Soeharto and a popular local leader, was elected governor in the east. The dispute continues and in a legal sense is yet another unresolved issue in relation to special autonomy. Nevertheless, it seems highly unlikely that politically there can be any return to a single Papuan province, given the fissures that have developed between the elites in the eastern and western parts of the region (McGibbon 2006).

It is important to note that debate about the division of Papua is not new, but goes back several decades (ICG 2003). In the early 1980s, the then governor of Irian Jaya, Busiri Suryowinoto, proposed splitting Papua into three provinces (*Suara Pembaruan*, 25 March 1994). The discourse on this issue has continued since that time, even though it has not always been reported widely in the media. In the mid-2000s, Solossa suggested splitting Papua into five provinces: South Papua, East Papua, North Coast, Sorong and Central Highlands (Solossa 2006). No doubt the issue of the administrative division of the province will continue into the future as political and economic interests shift. A matter that will need to be given close attention is the impact of potentially greater fragmentation on the political and administrative capacity of local governments, as discussed in the next chapter of this book.

While the three issues identified above are of concern to elite Papuans, the grassroots concerns of ordinary Papuans are more closely related to the recognition and fulfilment of their basic needs and associated rights, and acknowledgment of their distinct identity, history and culture (Yappika 2001). Local government officials and NGOs highlight the generally lower standard of living of Papuans compared with other Indonesians, the periodic cases of famine in isolated regions, the lack of benefits flowing to the province from both legal and illegal natural resource extraction, and the continuing political dominance of the military (Rathgeber 2005).

The political situation in Papua is likely to remain challenging for some time to come, as is perhaps to be expected given the size and diversity of the region. It is important to remember, however, that there is general agreement that special autonomy provides the best way forward for resolving the various challenges facing Papua. Accordingly, there is a need for political commitment on the part of all parties to implement the Special Autonomy Law. It provides a political umbrella to help ensure that Papua remains part of the unitary state of Indonesia (notwithstanding the prospect of several more provinces being formed in the future). More importantly, it provides huge opportunities to improve the welfare of Papuans. The law gives local governments significantly increased budgets and far greater freedom to engineer their own development programs. As we argue in this and the next chapter, after several decades of domination by Jakarta, future resolution of the 'Papua problem' now lies firmly in the hands of Papuans themselves, who have the means to significantly improve the living standards of the people.

2   DEMOGRAPHIC AND SOCIAL CHANGE

For better or for worse, Papua today is certainly not the Papua of the late 1960s when the region was annexed by Indonesia. Large-scale migration and successive waves of development have changed the face of Papua. This section highlights the demographic and other changes that have occurred over the past two decades in particular.

Demographic Change

Papua has long had a diverse population characterized by competition between local ethnic groups seeking to improve their standard of living. With the high rates of in-migration since the 1970s, the population has increased significantly and become even more diverse. Although competition between local ethnic groups still exists, many indigenous Papuans view migrants as a more significant threat to their ability to improve their standard of living (Manning and Rumbiak 1991; McGibbon 2004). However, the increased diversity of the population can also be viewed as an opportunity to improve the knowledge base of the society and provide the indigenous population with more opportunities to build a better society.

Figure 2.1   Papua: Estimated Population Growth Rates, 1980–2005 (% p.a.)

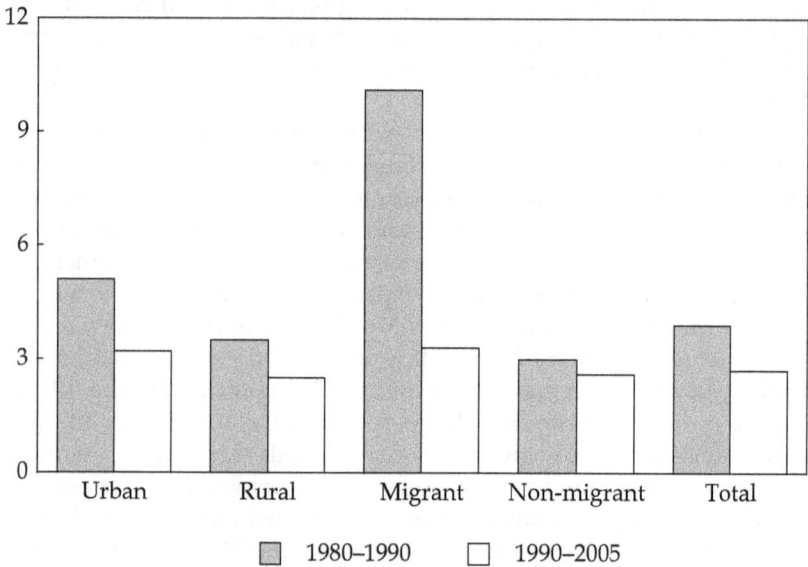

Source: BPS (1981, 1991, 2001, 2006b).

Population census data collected by the central statistics agency, BPS, show that the Papuan population increased rapidly during the 1980s (Figure 2.1).[3] Based on the censuses conducted in 1980, 1990 and 2000, it appears that the population grew at an average annual rate of 3.5 per cent in 1980–90 and 3.1 per cent in 1990–2000, faster than the national rates of 2.0 per cent and 1.4 per cent respectively.[4] However, population growth rates have been slowing since 1990, largely due to lower rates of in-migration in the 15 years to 2005. According to the 2005 intercensal survey, Papua had a population of approximately 2.5 million in 2005, compared with less than 1 million when Indonesia formally took control of the province in 1969. The data imply an average annual growth rate of 2.6 per cent between 2000 and 2005 (BPS 2006a).

Population growth rates are highest in the major urban centres, especially Sorong, Jayapura and Timika. Owing to rapid urbanization, the proportion of people living in urban areas has also increased. As

---

3   The population census was restricted to urban areas in 1971, so it is not possible to make reliable estimates of population growth during the ensuing decade.

4   Note that the population figures for 2000 are problematic owing to the substantial undercoverage of the 2000 census, mainly as a result of political unrest. See Appendix A2.1 for a discussion of some of the data problems.

Table 2.1 shows, approximately 26 per cent of the population was living in urban areas in 2005, a far higher proportion than 25 years earlier
(McGibbon 2004; BPS-Papua 2004). One important reason for the high
urban growth rates has been the large number of migrants moving to
Papua. The majority settled in urban areas, and constituted about 38 per
cent of the total urban population in 2005. In the rapidly growing cities
along the north coast (Jayapura, Biak, Manokwari and Sorong), the proportion of migrants born outside the province is even higher — around 50
per cent of the total population. In 2000 most lifetime migrants were from
Java (47 per cent), followed by South Sulawesi (23 per cent), other parts
of Sulawesi (11 per cent) and Maluku (10 per cent). Migrants from South
Sulawesi (most of them short-term or 'spontaneous' migrants working
in the informal sector) congregated disproportionately in urban areas,
although even here Javanese still dominated in 2000.

The central government's transmigration program brought large numbers of people to Papua in the 1980s. Whereas non-indigenous Papuans
accounted for only 9 per cent of the total population in 1980, this share
had nearly doubled to 16 per cent by 1990. As Figure 2.2 indicates, the
biggest increase (in relative terms) took place in rural areas. However,
in contrast to the popular perception, by 1990 the share of migrants had
begun to stabilize, and increased only slightly to 17 per cent over the
ensuing 15 years.

While migrants tend to live in the cities, indigenous Papuans continue
to live in rural areas, mainly in the central highlands and along the south
coast. In 2000, over 86 per cent of indigenous Papuans living in rural
areas were engaged in agriculture. The largest of Papua's 312 indigenous
tribes were the Biak-Numfor/Mafoorsch/Noefor group inhabiting the
coastal regions of the Biak and Numfor islands, and the Lani and Dani/
Ndani groups occupying the fertile valleys of the interior. Each of these
three tribal groupings had a population of around 150,000, twice the
population of the next largest ethnic group. The 10 largest ethnic groups
combined accounted for 53 per cent of the total indigenous population
in 2000. The remaining 47 per cent comprised around 300 ethnic groups,
two-thirds of them with a population of less than 1,000 and 100 with a
population of less than 100 (BPS 2001; McGibbon 2004).

The large influx of migrants to Papua has also changed the province's religious composition. In the 2005 intercensal survey, 76 per cent of
Papuans identified themselves as Christian (59.1 per cent Protestant and
16.4 per cent Catholic), 24 per cent as Muslim and less than 1 per cent
as 'other' (Table 2.1).[5] In contrast, in 1971 around 90 per cent of the total

---

5 In the 2000 census, a far higher proportion of the population (24 per cent)
   identified themselves as Catholic, and a slightly lower proportion as Protestant or Muslim.

Table 2.1   Papua: Demographic and Social Characteristics of the Population, 2005

	Urban	Rural	Total
Total population	637,000	1,803,000	2,440,000
Share (%)	26.1	73.9	100.0
Migration			
Lifetime migrants/total population (%)	38.2	10.4	17.6
Distribution of migrants by birthplace[a]			
Java	33.1	68.5	47.0
South Sulawesi	28.7	10.2	23.2
Other Sulawesi	12.9	3.5	11.2
Maluku	14.6	5.3	10.1
Other	10.7	12.5	8.4
Total	**100.0**	**100.0**	**100.0**
Religion			
Protestant	44.0	64.4	59.1
Muslim	45.2	16.9	24.3
Catholic	10.5	18.5	16.4
Other	0.3	0.2	0.2
Total	**100.0**	**100.0**	**100.0**
Population aged 7–24 currently attending school[b]			
Ages 7–12	95	70	75
Ages 13–15	93	62	70
Ages 16–18	68	31	39
Ages 19–24	16	7	9
Educational attainment among population aged 19+			
No schooling	2.5	39.0	29.1
Less than primary	3.6	11.9	9.6
Primary	14.1	22.6	20.3
Junior secondary	20.3	14.3	15.9
Senior secondary[c]	49.3	11.3	21.6
Tertiary	10.2	0.9	3.5
Total	**100.0**	**100.0**	**100.0**

a   The figures refer to 2000; no urban/rural breakdown of migrants by birthplace is given in the officially published data for 2005.

b   The figures given here are gross enrolment rates, so cannot be compared directly with the figures cited in the text on net enrolments (see footnote 7).

c   Includes Diplomas 1 and 2 (one and two years' training after high school respectively).

Source: BPS (2001, 2006b).

Figure 2.2   Papua: Lifetime Migrants as a Share of the Urban/Rural Population, 1980–2005 (%)

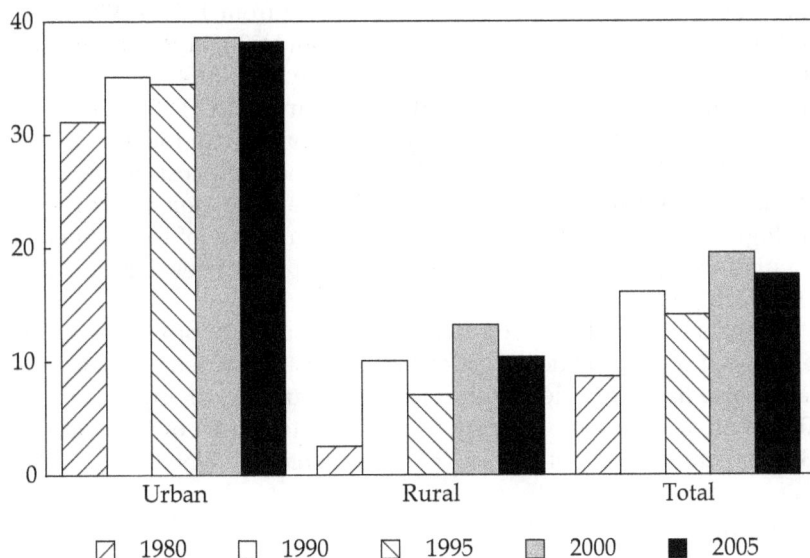

Source: BPS (1981, 1991, 2001, 2006b).

(urban) population was Christian. The large increase in the Muslim population is attributable to the rapidly growing migrant population, 66 per cent of whom were recorded as Muslim in 2000. As one would expect, the proportion of Muslims is highest in urban areas — close to 50 per cent in several large cities (Jayapura, Biak and Sorong) in 2000. However, among indigenous Papuans religious composition has not changed much: in 2000 around 96 per cent said they were Christian. The small proportion of indigenous Papuans who are Muslim (4 per cent) have long lived in the Bird's Head region (some for more than a century) and nearby regions such as Kokas, Kaimana, Sorong, Raja Ampat and Fak-Fak.

Clearly the structure of the Papuan population has become far more diverse, although whether this has benefited indigenous Papuans is a matter of contention (Manning and Rumbiak 1991; McGibbon 2004). We pursue some of the issues associated with demographic change later in this chapter.

Social Change

Human Development Index

In general, social indicators on Papua show an improvement over the last two decades, although many would argue that the speed of the improvement has not been fast enough. Papua's score on the human development index (HDI) — a single measure of life expectancy, literacy, educational attainment and income — increased from 49.9 in 1990 to 60.1 in 2002. It then rose to 64.8 in West Papua and 62.1 in Papua in 2005.[6] For Indonesia as a whole, the HDI score rose from 63.4 in 1990 to 65.8 in 2002, then to 69.6 in 2005 (BPS, Bappenas and UNDP 2001, 2004; BPS 2006c). The poor performance of Papua compared with the rest of Indonesia reflects in part the extreme difficulty and high cost of delivering educational and health services to small, relatively isolated groups in the highland regions in particular, where the majority of the indigenous population lives. This is probably the most important development challenge facing Papua.

Papua's HDI ranking dropped from 25th out of 27 provinces in 1990 to 29th out of 30 provinces (just ahead of West Nusa Tenggara) in 2002. Papua also had the widest within-province variation of any province in 2002, with an HDI score ranging from 47 in the district of Jayawijaya to 73 in the municipality of Sorong (BPS, Bappenas and UNDP 2001, 2004).

Education

In the last three decades, large numbers of new schools have been established in Papua. In 2003, the region had around 2,400 primary schools, 380 junior secondary schools and 140 senior secondary schools, as well as 10 universities or tertiary-equivalent institutions. The literacy rate among adults (those aged 15 or over) stood at 74 per cent in 2002, up slightly from 71 per cent in 1999 (PemProv Papua, Bappenas and UNDP 2005). The net enrolment ratio in primary education (number of children attending primary school to total number of children aged 7–12 years) rose from 55 per cent in 1984 to 70 per cent in 1991 and 81 per cent in 2000. While still below the national figures, of 88 per cent in 1984, 89 per cent in 1991 and 93 per cent in 2000, this indicates significant progress. The net enrolment ratio at junior secondary level (number of children attending junior secondary school to total number of children aged 13–15 years) should be a matter of concern: it remained stuck at around 40 per cent while the ratio for Indonesia as a whole increased from 41.1 per cent in 1984 to 60.3 per cent in 2000 (BPS, various years).

Within Papua, there are significant variations in net enrolment ratios across regions, with urban areas typically recording higher ratios. The

---

6 Note that the formula used to calculate the HDI changed during this period; the formula used in 1990 also took account of the infant mortality rate. However, even after correcting for this difference, the relative scores remain much the same.

municipalities of Sorong and Jayapura recorded the highest net enrolment rates, and several highland areas the lowest. The district of Jayawijaya in the central highlands had the lowest net enrolment ratios for all age groups in 2000 (BPS, various years). The gap between urban and rural areas is especially evident at the senior secondary level: over two-thirds of the total student population aged 16–18 was attending school in urban areas in 2005, but only one-third in rural areas (Table 2.1).[7]

Educational attainment among workers has also been improving. The average number of years of schooling of people in the workforce rose from around four in the early 1980s to six in 2003 (compared with nine at the national level) (BPS, various years). Once again, educational attainment among adults was far higher in urban than in rural areas (Table 2.1). Clearly human capital has been progressing in Papua. However, the province still has a long way to go to catch up with the rest of Indonesia.

Employment

The Papuan workforce is estimated to have increased at an average rate of 4.3 per cent per annum between 1990 and 2003. The total workforce (those aged 15 or above) rose from 679,000 in 1990 to 1.2 million in 2003 (of whom roughly 90,000 were unemployed or looking for work). Compared with several decades ago, the sectoral composition of the workforce has probably not changed much. The agricultural sector still dominated in 2003, employing about 75 per cent of the workforce. This was followed by community, social and personal services (9 per cent) and trade, hotels and restaurants (5 per cent). The mining industry, the largest sector in the Papuan economy, directly employed only 6,584 people—less than 1 per cent of the workforce—although its indirect impact on jobs in services and other sectors was far greater than this figure suggests, especially in the Timika region (BPS-Papua 2004).

The government sector grew from about 25,000 employees in 1978 to 53,000 in 1988, 74,000 in 1998 and 78,000 in 2001. That is, it expanded rapidly in the 1980s, then grew relatively slowly in the 1990s. Following decentralization and the granting of special autonomy, it seems likely that the rate of growth has begun to rise sharply once again. Average annual growth in the civil service was 5.1 per cent in 1978–2001, higher than the national rate of 3.4 per cent.

---

7 Note that Table 2.1 only gives an indication of this, since many of the students aged 16–18 may have been enrolled in junior secondary or even primary school—not senior secondary school as one would expect.

Health

Papua had around 200 community health centres (*puskesmas*) and 25 hospitals in 2002, a substantial rise from 140 *puskesmas* and 19 hospitals in 1980. Nevertheless, progress in improving the health status of the population has been slow. Illnesses such as diarrhoea, cholera, dysentery, tuberculosis and malaria are rife. In 2003, for example, an estimated 540,000 people — almost a quarter of the population — were afflicted with clinical malaria, and there were hundreds of thousands of cases of diarrhoea and cholera.[8]

Famine occurs regularly in some pockets of Papua, especially in isolated regions in the highlands. In the remote and mountainous Yakuhimo region, for instance, it was only after the media began to report deaths due to starvation that assistance was finally mobilized (*Kompas*, 9 December 2005). Even then, the effort to help the highlanders was delayed by several days due to bad weather and poor transport infrastructure. As this example demonstrates, poor communications hinders efforts to avert food shortages in remote areas, and hampers rapid response measures when communities are affected by a crisis.

Variations across regions can also be gleaned from the health data. The infant mortality rate for the whole of Papua, for example, was 50 deaths per 1,000 live births in 2003 (compared with a national average of 43.5 deaths per 1,000 live births). The rate for Merauke, however, was 74 deaths per 1,000 live births, the highest rate in Papua (PemProv Papua, Bappenas and UNDP 2005).

3   ECONOMIC DEVELOPMENT

Economic Growth

Papua's gross domestic product (GDP) grew at a faster rate than the national average until, and throughout, the financial crisis of 1997–98 (Figure 2.3). However, the differences are much smaller if mining is excluded from provincial GDP. Given that most mining revenues were commandeered by the central government until the Special Autonomy Law was passed in 2001, provincial GDP without mining is most likely a better measure of Papuan GDP during the pre- and immediate post-crisis periods. On a per capita basis, the GDP growth rates for both Papua and Indonesia are lower than those for total GDP. However, the gap between

---

8 See Chapter 14 for a more detailed discussion of the health situation in Papua.

Figure 2.3   Papua and Indonesia: Growth in GDP, 1972–98 (% p.a.)

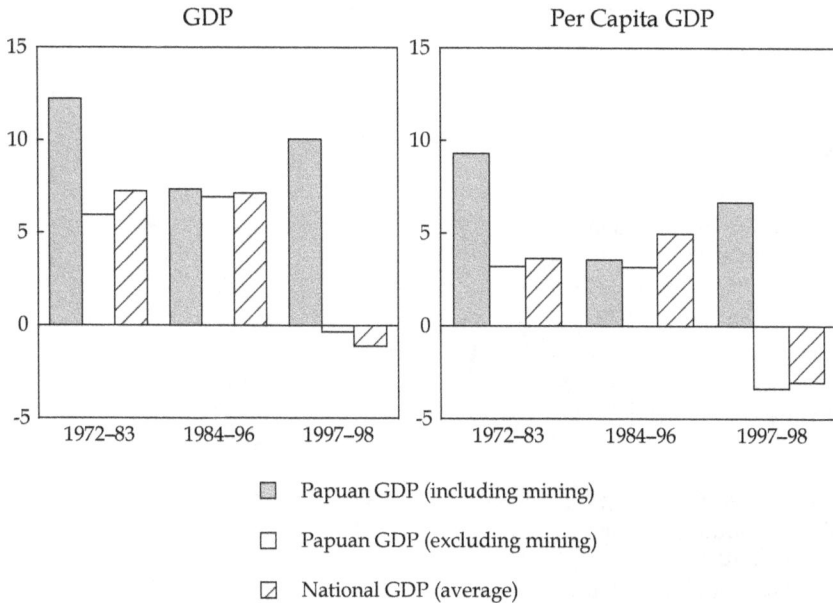

▣	Papuan GDP (including mining)
☐	Papuan GDP (excluding mining)
▨	National GDP (average)

Source: BPS (various years).

per capita GDP and total GDP is larger for Papua than for Indonesia as a whole, reflecting Papua's high population growth rates.

Average annual growth in provincial GDP ran at about 3 per cent per annum in 2000–05, below the national figure of 5 per cent (Table 2.2). Capital investment grew steadily until 2003, only to decline significantly in 2004–05. Although the political and social turmoil of the early 2000s has subsided somewhat (Chauvel and Bhakti 2004; McGibbon 2006), it has certainly contributed to this pattern of investment.

Exports declined steeply in real terms, from Rp 6.4 trillion in 1999 to Rp 2.1 trillion in 2003 (in 1993 rupiah). This was mainly due to a slump in gold and copper prices and a slowdown in production at the dominant mine at Timika. In 2005 exports staged a sharp recovery, reaching Rp 6.7 trillion (in 1993 rupiah) or Rp 29 trillion (in current prices), largely as a result of the skyrocketing international prices for copper and gold, which have been Papua's most important exports for three decades.

Overall, one can conclude that the Papuan economy has been growing fairly rapidly since the 1970s. If mining is included in provincial GDP, the Papuan economy has grown significantly faster than the national average; if it is excluded, the economy has grown at about, or a bit below, the national average.

Table 2.2   Papua: GDP by Expenditure, 1999 and 2005[a]

Expenditure Composition	1999	2005	Average Annual Growth Rate, 2000–05
Papua			
Household consumption (%)	44.9	32.0	1.5
Non-profit organization consumption (%)	0.3	0.9	16.4
Government consumption (%)	7.3	6.2	–0.4
Capital investment (%)	19.4	17.3	–3.4
Exports (%)	85.6	66.6	0.7
Imports (%)	61.8	43.1	–1.6
Change in stock (%)	4.3	20.1	22.1
Total	**100.0**	**100.0**	
GDP including mining (Rp billion)	18,249	43,615	2.9
GDP excluding mining (Rp billion)	6,709	12,366	1.7
GDP per capita including mining (Rp million)	8.4	23.3	5.4
GDP per capita excluding mining (Rp million)	3.1	6.6	4.2
Indonesia			
GDP (Rp billion)	992,322	2,729,708	4.5
GDP per capita (Rp million)	4.7	12.5	3.2

a   Expenditure composition is in current prices; growth rates are in constant 1993 prices. Total expenditure = household consumption + non-profit organization consumption + government consumption + capital investment + exports + change in stock – imports.
Source: BPS (various years).

It is also instructive to compare Papua's economic growth rates with those of several developing countries situated, like Papua, along the equator. Table 2.3 shows that in terms of average annual GDP per capita, Papua performed better than many other developing countries in Africa, Latin America and the Pacific between 1994 and 2004.

Table 2.4 compares Papua and its closest neighbour, Papua New Guinea, with respect to a number of socio-economic indicators. The two regions share a similar demographic, cultural and geographical profile but Papua performs better on several indicators. Papua is ahead on per capita GDP, infant mortality, school enrolment, life expectancy and literacy. However, Papua has a far higher maternal mortality rate (as does

Table 2.3   Papua and Selected Developing Countries: Average Annual Growth in per Capita GDP, 1994–2004 (% p.a.)

Country	Growth Rate	Country	Growth Rate
Papua	3.6	Cameroon	1.7
Papua New Guinea	–1.4	Gabon	0.0
Fiji	1.6	Kenya	0.3
Micronesia	–0.6	Tanzania	2.3
Solomon Islands	–2.6	Brazil	1.2
Vanuatu	–0.8	Columbia	0.7
Tonga	2.1	Ecuador	1.1
Democratic Republic of the Congo	–3.4	Peru	2.6
Republic of the Congo	–0.9	Venezuela	–1.0

Source: World Bank (2007).

Indonesia more generally), and a lower score on the human poverty index (HPI). As we argue below, Papua's low score on the poverty index is a critical indicator of continuing underdevelopment in the province.

Trade

Despite increasing only slightly in real terms (see Table 2.2), in nominal terms exports from Papua showed a significant increase, from US$1.4 billion in 1999 to US$2.3 billion in 2005. Imports remained relatively steady at US$0.6 billion in 1999 and US$0.7 billion in 2005. Raw materials accounted for 98 per cent of the total value of exports in 2005. Next in value were exports of animal and vegetable oils and fats (mainly palm oil) (0.9 per cent) and exports of foodstuffs and live animals (0.4 per cent) (BPS-Papua 2004, 2008).

The main export commodities in 2005 (and subsequent years) were copper and gold (US$1.35 billion), plywood (US$44.9 million), shrimp (US$24.2 million) and fish (US$17.6 million). Almost all of the copper and gold was exported from Amamapare port in Timika. The main export destinations were Australia, Singapore and the United States.[9]

---

9   It is important to note that there are many problems with the data on exports from Papua (and other Indonesian provinces). They include: (1) a high level of interisland trade, with commodities from Papua being shipped to Surabaya, Makassar or even Manado, and then exported; (2) very weak data collection; and (3) a high level of illegal exports, especially of timber and fish.

Table 2.4   Papua and Papua New Guinea: Comparison of Selected Socio-economic Indicators[a]

Indicator	Papua	Papua New Guinea
GDP (US$ billion)	2.6	2.8
GDP excluding mining (US$ billion)	1.3	
GDP per capita (US$)	1,046	523
GDP per capita excluding mining (US$)	530	
Population (thousand)	2,470	5,378
Labour force (thousand)	1,170	2,665
Fertility rate (births per woman)	4.3	4.1[b]
Infant mortality rate (deaths per 1,000 live births)	51	70
Maternal mortality rate (deaths per 100,000 live births)	1,116	300
School enrolment rate (% of children aged 7–12 years enrolled in primary school)	87	69
Life expectancy at birth (years)	65	54
Human development index (HDI)	60	54
Human poverty index (HPI)	31	37[c]
Adult literacy rate (literacy among population aged 15+)	74	65
Births attended by skilled/medical personnel (%)	52	53[d]
Physicians (per 100,000 people)	17	6[e]
Gender-related development index[f]	54	54[g]

a   Data are for 2002 unless indicated otherwise.
b   Average for 2000–05.
c   Data are for 2004.
d   Average for 1995–2002.
e   Average for 1990–2003.
f   The gender-related development index (GDI) measures the human development achievements of women. If there is no gender-based inequality, the GDI will be identical to the HDI.
g   Data are for 2004.
Source: World Bank (various years); UNDP (2004, 2005); BPS-Papua (2004).

The main imports in 2005 were mining products and machinery (including heavy transport vehicles). Most imported goods passed through Amamapare port, presumably on their way to PT Freeport Indonesia's mine in Mimika district.

Clearly Papua's trade is dominated by non-renewable natural resources, supported by potentially renewable resources (forestry and fisheries), which have been exploited more rapidly in recent years. A major challenge facing Papua is how to promote greater diversification of trade towards more sustainable agricultural activities, such as estate crops.

The Structure of the Economy

From the preceding analysis of economic growth and trade in Papua, it is apparent that mining has been the most important sector in the regional economy for a long time. It has contributed more than 50 per cent of Papuan GDP since the mid-1970s (Manning and Rumbiak 1991). Within the mining sector, PT Freeport Indonesia is easily the dominant player,[10] although going forward the large BP gas operation at Tangguh can be expected to counterbalance the impact of Freeport to some extent.[11]

Although mining still contributed around 72 per cent of provincial GDP in 2005, growth in mining revenues slowed to just 3.6 per cent per annum in 2000–05 (Table 2.5). This might suggest that the contribution of mining will decline in the future. However, once construction of the Tangguh liquefied natural gas project is completed, the contribution of mining to provincial GDP is expected to increase significantly once again (Anggraeni 2007).

Besides mining, there are at least three other important economic sectors (excluding the government sector) in the Papuan economy. The first is agriculture, particularly food crops, forestry and fisheries (see Table 2.5) (Manning and Rumbiak 1991; Anggraeni 2007). Agriculture made up 10.4 per cent of provincial GDP in 2005 but grew at an average rate of only 0.1 per cent per annum in 2000–05. The second important sector is trade, hotels and restaurants, which contributed 4.0 per cent of provincial GDP in 2005. Within this sector, trade contributed most to provincial

---

10 See Chapter 7 for a more detailed discussion of the Freeport mine and its social, economic and political effects.

11 With the division of Papua into two provinces, Freeport is currently the main source of revenue for the province of Papua, while Tangguh can be expected to play a similar role in underpinning development expenditure in West Papua. Given that there are likely to be only two major mining projects in the entire region in the foreseeable future, any further division would greatly complicate the allocation of resource rents across Papua.

GDP. However, the subsector with the highest growth rate was hotels, which grew at 13.2 per cent per annum in 2000–05. The third important sector is transport and communications, which contributed 3.4 per cent of provincial GDP in 2005. The sector grew at an average annual rate of 5.3 per cent in 2000–05, slightly below the national level. Within the sector, sea transport, air transport and communications performed particularly well. The role of private enterprise in developing communications and air transport has become increasingly significant. Since private enterprise will only expand if businesspeople see good prospects to make a profit, this is certainly an encouraging development.

At current rates of growth, the transport and communications sector could support the development of agriculture in Papua. However, we suspect that, so far, most of the growth in communications has been between the rapidly expanding urban areas of Jayapura, Timika, Sorong and Manokwari, and between them and the rest of Indonesia. Nevertheless, in the medium term, improved communication networks may create opportunities for Papua to shift from heavy dependence on the mining sector to greater reliance on the agricultural sector. With good international demand for palm oil anticipated in the medium term, production of this commodity could be expanded. However, the negative effects of deforestation on the local environment should be a major consideration in the selection of new areas for this and any other plantation crop.

Manufacturing and banking make up a tiny proportion of the regional economy and experienced negative growth in 2000–05 (Table 2.5). Poor infrastructure and lack of human capital are the most likely reasons for the poor performance of manufacturing. In addition, the costs of manufacturing are typically very high in Papua, as they are in many other outer island regions of Indonesia. Both within Indonesia and in the world economy, Papua's comparative advantage will continue to lie in agriculture and natural resource-based industries for a long time to come. A more significant role for manufacturing is unlikely given the far lower cost of labour and better infrastructure in Java. But provided that there are substantial improvements in infrastructure and communications, over the longer term manufacturing can be expected to cluster around activities related to agriculture—for example, food processing.

4   POVERTY: THE KEY DEVELOPMENT ISSUE

What effect has economic growth had on personal consumption expenditure (PCE)[12] and poverty in Papua, bearing in mind the province's low

---

12 That is, per capita household consumption expenditure.

Table 2.5 Papua: Composition of GDP by Sector, 1999 and 2005 (%)[a]

Sector	1999	2005	Average Annual Growth, 2000–05
Agriculture	**16.4**	**10.4**	**0.1**
Food crops	6.3	4.7	3.3
Estate crops	0.8	0.5	–1.1
Livestock	1.0	0.6	3.1
Forestry	4.9	1.9	–8.4
Fisheries	3.5	2.8	1.6
Mining	**63.2**	**71.6**	**3.6**
Oil & gas	3.2	0.0	–100.0
Mining	59.8	71.4	4.3
Quarrying	0.3	0.3	2.1
Manufacturing	**4.1**	**1.6**	**–5.7**
Electricity & water	**0.2**	**0.2**	**–5.7**
Electricity	0.2	0.1	–6.5
Clean water	0.1	0.0	–3.8
Construction	**2.7**	**3.5**	**4.9**
Trade, hotels & restaurants	**4.2**	**4.0**	**4.9**
Trade	3.8	3.6	9.4
Hotels	0.1	0.2	13.2
Restaurants	0.3	0.2	2.1
Transport & communications	**2.5**	**3.4**	**5.3**
Land transport	0.8	0.7	–3.3
Sea transport	0.3	0.4	4.2
River transport	0.1	0.1	–13.2
Air transport	0.3	0.6	17.1
Transport support services	0.1	0.1	1.5
Communications	0.8	1.6	11.9
Financial, rental & corporate services	**1.0**	**0.8**	**–0.3**
Banking	0.3	0.3	8.1
Non-bank financial institutions	0.1	0.1	–3.3
Rental services	0.4	0.3	–3.8
Corporate services	0.1	0.1	–4.1
Other services	**5.7**	**4.3**	**3.6**
Government services	5.4	3.9	3.0
Social services	0.1	0.2	6.7
Entertainment & recreation	0.1	0.1	12.8
Personal services	0.1	0.1	9.9
Total	**100.0**	**100.0**	

a Sectoral compositions are calculated based on current prices; growth rates are in constant 1993 prices.

Source: BPS (various years).

Figure 2.4   Papua and Indonesia: Nominal and Real Personal Consumption
Expenditure (PCE), 1987–99 (Rp thousand)

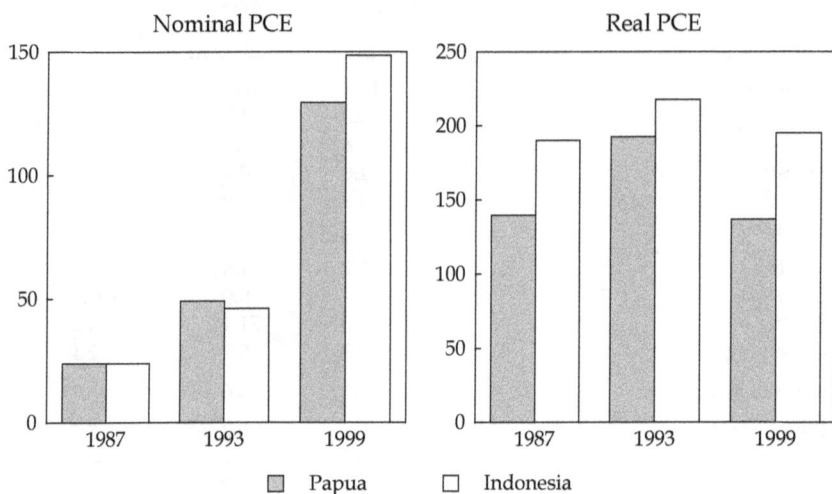

Nominal PCE   Real PCE

[Papua   Indonesia]

Source: BPS, National Socio-Economic Survey (Susenas) data.

(but growing) average per capita income (without mining) and the dominant impact of the Freeport mine on overall economic growth rates? The
provincial and national trends in PCE, in both nominal and real terms,
are shown in Figure 2.4. In nominal terms, provincial and national PCE
were much the same until the early 1990s. A gap then opened up, and
by 1999 Papua's nominal PCE had fallen around 13 per cent below the
national level.[13] In real terms, PCE in Papua has been well below the
national average, particularly in isolated urban centres where the cost
of living is very high.[14] Thus it appears that, in general, the higher GDP
growth associated with the mining sector in the 1970s and early 1980s
has not enabled Papuans to enjoy a higher level of PCE than the average Indonesian household. Mining revenues during that period clearly
did not trickle down sufficiently to the average Papuan (Manning and
Rumbiak 1991).

At the national level, the upward trend in PCE was accompanied by
a fall in poverty, or the percentage of the population living below the

---

13 Unfortunately, at the time of writing data for Papua were only available
through to the late 1990s.
14 The significantly higher cost of living in Papua is indicated, for example, by
its score on the construction price index. According to this index, Papua has
the highest construction costs in Indonesia (PemProv Papua, Bappenas and
UNDP 2005).

Figure 2.5   *Papua and Indonesia: Poor People as a Share of the Total Population, 1996–2004 (%)*

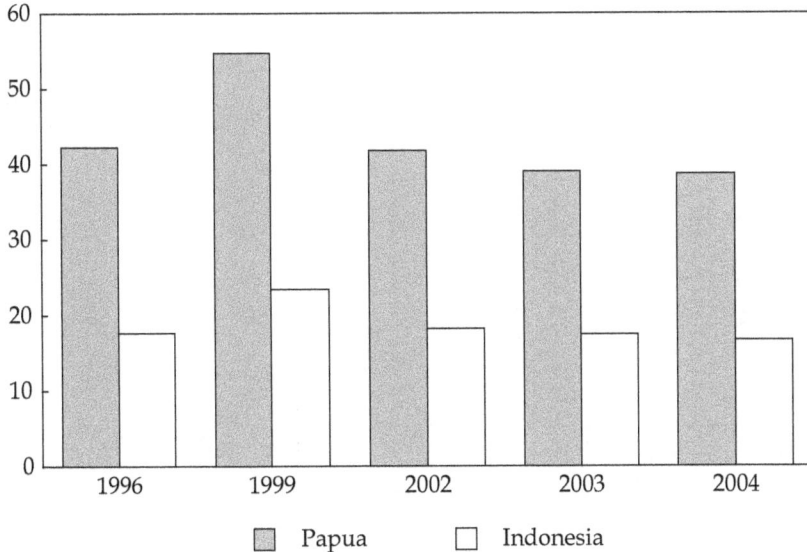

Source: BPS (various years).

poverty line (as defined by BPS). Poverty declined from 54 per cent in 1976 to 18 per cent in 1996, then rose during the crisis before resuming its downward trend (BPS, various years). Given the many data collection problems in Papua, we cannot be perfectly sure of the extent of poverty reduction in the province during this period (see Appendix A2.1). But most indicators seem to show a significant reduction, even if at a slower pace than for the nation as a whole.

Nevertheless, the overall poverty rate remains substantially higher in Papua than at the national level (Figure 2.5). The incidence of poverty rose from 42 per cent in 1996 to a peak of 55 per cent in 1999, before falling back to just under 40 per cent in 2004. Throughout the 1990s and early 2000s, the proportion of poor people in Papua was around twice the national average. However, the official data suggest that Papua's Gini ratio (measuring the degree of income inequality) has improved in recent years, from about 0.39 in 1996 to 0.32 in 2003 (BPS, various years).

BPS has developed a broader measure of poverty—the human poverty index, or HPI—by combining four indicators: the probability of a person not living to age 40; the adult literacy rate; the proportion of people without access to safe water; and the proportion of children who are malnourished (BPS, Bappenas and UNDP 2004). In 2002, Papua's score on this index ranged from 14 (in the municipality of Jayapura) to 51 (in

*Figure 2.6   Papua: Poor People as a Share of the Urban/Rural Population,
1996–2004 (%)*

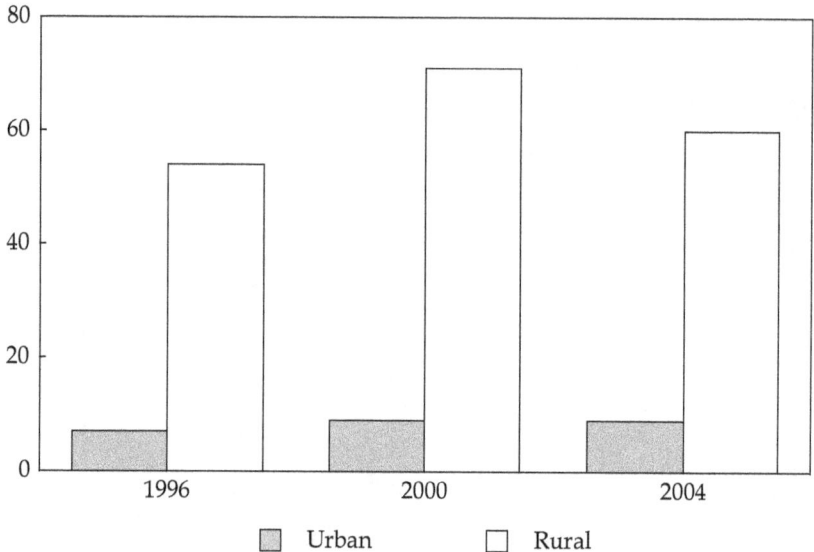

Source: BPS (various years).

the district of Jayawijaya), with an overall provincial score of 30.9 (down
slightly from 31.3 in 1999). Papua ranked 28th among Indonesia's 30
provinces on the HPI, ahead of West Kalimantan and Gorontalo. As one
of the richest provinces in terms of its natural resources and associated
economic indicators, Papua's high levels of poverty undoubtedly constitute the major development challenge facing the province—especially
when one considers that several other natural resource-rich provinces,
such as East Kalimantan and Riau, rank well ahead of it on the HPI.

Figure 2.6 gives a breakdown of poverty in Papua by urban/rural
area. The proportion of poor people living in rural areas is far higher
than the proportion living in urban areas, giving Papua the highest ratio
of rural to urban poor in Indonesia. Indeed, Papua has one of the highest
ratios in the developing world, reflecting a situation closer to that in some
African countries than in most countries in the Asia–Pacific region.

Table 2.6 shows the proportion of poor people by district in 2004. It
can be seen that the five districts with the highest proportion of poor
people (45–50 per cent) included the relatively isolated regions of Paniai,
Puncak Jaya and Manokwari. In contrast, the five districts with the lowest proportion of poor people (20–30 per cent)—the city of Jayapura,
the district of Jayapura, the nearby districts of Keerom and Sarmi, and
Merauke—were located in or close to urban centres.

Table 2.6   Papua: Total Population and Share of Poor People by District, 2004

District/ Municipality	Total Population (thousand)	Poor People (%)
Biak Numfor & Supiori	112	44.87
Jayapura district	92	28.39
Keerom	38	26.16
Sarmi	31	27.88
Jayawijaya	209	46.21
Pegunungan Bintang	88	47.85
Tolikara	44	45.15
Yahukimo	135	45.74
Merauke	156	28.15
Asmat	61	31.37
Boven Digoel	31	28.76
Mappi	65	29.97
Mimika	126	30.75
Nabire	160	43.01
Paniai	111	49.09
Puncak Jaya	110	50.67
Yapen Waropen	71	42.62
Waropen	21	44.48
Jayapura municipality	199	22.98
Fak-Fak	59	37.43
Kaimana	37	35.17
Manokwari	151	49.55
Teluk Bintuni	47	53.70
Teluk Wondama	20	54.94
Sorong district	65	33.15
Raja Ampat	29	31.73
South Sorong	48	28.95
Sorong municipality	183	36.08

Source: BPS (2005).

Table 2.7 gives a picture of the educational and occupational backgrounds of the poor in 2004. It shows that very few poor people had a high school diploma or tertiary degree, and most worked in the agricultural sector – in many areas, the proportion working in agriculture was 80 per cent or more. In both cases, however, the largest cities of Jayapura and Sorong were exceptions; both have a heavy concentration of migrant labour.

Table 2.7 Papua: Poor People by Educational Attainment and Employment Status, 2004 (%)[a]

District/Municipality	Educational Attainment				Employment Status			
	Less than Primary	Primary or Secondary	Post-secondary	Total	Not Working	Agriculture	Non-agriculture	Total
Biak Numfor & Supiori	48.85	46.70	4.45	100	12.67	78.21	9.12	100
Jayapura district	47.89	47.18	4.93	100	27.12	67.80	5.08	100
Jayawijaya	85.71	11.43	2.86	100	1.69	96.61	1.70	100
Merauke	76.80	23.20	0.00	100	4.95	94.06	0.99	100
Mimika	66.38	32.76	0.86	100	8.70	89.13	2.17	100
Nabire	51.02	48.98	0.00	100	8.33	75.00	16.67	100
Paniai	83.33	14.81	1.86	100	20.00	78.18	1.82	100
Puncak Jaya	61.22	32.65	6.13	100	3.13	96.87	0.00	100
Yapen Waropen	68.40	29.32	2.28	100	1.03	98.97	0.00	100
Jayapura municipality	18.92	33.78	47.30	100	20.69	0.00	79.31	100
Fak-Fak	75.28	24.72	0.00	100	14.71	82.35	2.94	100
Manokwari	75.69	23.76	0.55	100	9.47	89.47	1.06	100
Sorong district	57.69	37.50	4.81	100	9.30	86.05	4.65	100
Sorong municipality	25.86	43.10	31.04	100	44.44	14.81	40.75	100

a   Keerom and Sarmi are included in Jayapura district; Pegunungan Bintang, Tolikara and Yahukimo are included in Jayawijaya; Asmat, Boven Digoel and Mappi are included in Merauke; Waropen is included in Yapen Waropen; Kaimana is included in Fak-Fak; Teluk Bintuni and Teluk Wondama are included in Manokwari; and Raja Ampat and South Sorong are included in Sorong district.

Source: BPS (2005).

The demographic section of this chapter indicated that most indigenous Papuans live in rural areas where they constitute the majority of the population. Most are engaged in agriculture. The statistics presented in this section indicate that the majority of poor people live in rural areas, have low educational attainment and work in the agricultural sector. Although not easy to document from the available statistics, it seems clear that the vast majority of poor people in Papua are indigenous Papuans.

Deeper research is certainly needed to understand the main factors contributing to poverty in Papua. However, so far it seems clear that mining revenues and successive government budgets have mainly benefited urban areas, creating enclaves of rapid development in the towns and cities while rural areas lag behind. It also seems clear that people living in heavily populated but isolated highland regions like Jayawijaya and Paniai are especially vulnerable to poverty. Poor communications and low agricultural productivity appear to be the major constraints to raising incomes in these regions. This suggests that improving the incomes of farmers, facilitating greater participation in the non-farm economy in rural areas and connecting rural economies to urban economies are likely to be important strategies for poverty alleviation in Papua.

5 CONCLUSION

In this chapter, we have documented both the advances made in Papua over the past several decades and some of the enduring problems faced by its peoples. We have drawn attention in particular to the stark contrast between the largely rural indigenous population and the newcomers born in other parts of Indonesia, many of whom came to Papua as the economy prospered in the 1980s and 1990s.

Despite intermittent political instability, economic and social development has taken place in Papua over the last three decades, albeit slowly and unevenly. Growth has been on a par with the national average. In fact, in terms of growth in provincial GDP (including mining), Papua has consistently exceeded the national average. On indicators such as non-mining GDP and personal consumption expenditure, however, the region has performed less well. On most social indicators, Papua is among the worst in the country. It ranked 29th out of 30 provinces on the HDI in 2002. In 2004, just under 40 per cent of Papuans were living below the poverty line, compared with a national average of 17 per cent. Most were indigenous Papuans living in rural areas and working in the agricultural sector.

Our research indicates that government programs utilizing the large revenues from mining and other sources have mostly induced enclave development in a few urban areas, such as Jayapura, Sorong and Timika. The benefits of this income have not trickled down sufficiently to rural areas. Papua's lower level of development when it joined Indonesia in 1969 as well as its topography and rough terrain have been the main barriers to development. Topography remains a major constraint today: much of the highlands and other remote areas are still difficult to reach. A more concerted effort is therefore needed to improve the levels of development in rural areas in particular.

There are reasons to be optimistic that Papua will do better in the future. First, the implementation of special autonomy is contributing to the resolution of the intermittent political conflict between Jakarta and Jayapura. Second, since Indonesia adopted a decentralized system of government in 2001, the regional government has received larger transfers of funds from the centre. As a consequence, Papua now has far greater flexibility to design its own development programs. This is important, because locals are likely to have a better understanding of what is required in an environment with such dramatic regional variations in topography, ecology, settlement patterns and communication networks.

The next chapter of this book documents government policies and expenditure patterns in Papua, and explores some of the challenges posed by decentralization.

APPENDIX A2.1   INDONESIAN STATISTICS AND THE CHALLENGES OF COLLECTING DATA IN PAPUA[15]

This appendix first describes the role of BPS and how the data for several basic economic development indicators are collected. Next, it discusses the problems and challenges facing the central statistics agency, BPS, in collecting data in Papua. Finally, it looks at how the economic development indicators are calculated.

The Role of BPS

The head office of BPS is located in Jakarta. In 2006, it had 33 provincial and roughly 350 district/municipality (*kabupaten/kota*) branches throughout Indonesia. In each branch there is at least one coordinator responsible for activities at the subdistrict (*kecamatan*) level. All branch activities are supervised by head office. The chair of BPS is accountable to the president.

BPS collects primary data through various censuses and surveys, as well as obtaining secondary data from other government agencies and several private institutions. Three types of census are conducted every 10 years: a population census (in years ending with a zero), an agricultural census (in years ending with the number 3) and an economic census (in years ending with the number 6).

The best known BPS survey is the National Socio-Economic Survey (Susenas). It is used as the main data source for calculating many important social and economic indicators, including poverty. Other surveys include an integrated survey on household business activities, a survey aimed at estimating the cost structure of agricultural activities, a survey of large and medium-sized businesses, and an intercensal survey conducted every 10 years between two population censuses (in years ending with the number 5).

The main difficulty facing BPS in undertaking data collection is inadequate facilities and resources, particularly off-Java. In collecting secondary (administrative) data, there is also the problem of getting other agencies to submit a consistent set of data. Although BPS constantly strives to improve the reliability and accuracy of its data, it is important for users to understand how BPS collects and uses data, in order that they can use the data appropriately.

---

15 This appendix was prepared by Bambang Heru, a staff member of BPS. This note was written in a personal rather than professional capacity.

How Data Are Collected: The Case of the Susenas

To better understand how BPS collects data, the process of collecting Susenas data is described here. For the whole of Indonesia, there are around 18,000 Susenas census blocks, of which 500 (about 2.7 per cent) are in Papua. Each census block consists of roughly 16 households chosen at random. Hence the total Susenas sample consists of about 250,000–280,000 households, the same as for the intercensal survey.

All respondents fill out a 'core' questionnaire consisting of a household roster listing the age, sex, marital status and educational attainment of all household members, as well as a section on basic welfare indicators. It is supplemented by 'modules' to collect additional information on health care and nutrition, household income and expenditure, labour force experience and so on. The modules cover a much smaller sample of about 65,000 households chosen randomly from the larger sample. They are rotated to ensure that, over time, all areas of interest will be covered.

The Susenas modules (especially the expenditure module on which poverty figures are based) are intended to be used to estimate indicators at the provincial level, *not* the district/municipality level. If a district/municipality government wants BPS to estimate economic indicators at the local level, BPS may have to ask it to provide additional funding so that the total number of samples can be increased.

To undertake the survey, BPS district/municipality offices recruit individual enumerators (typically subdistrict officials) to interview household respondents. These enumerators are trained by regional instructors (*instruktur daerah*), who in turn are trained by national instructors (*instruktur nasional*). The minimum qualification for a national instructor is a bachelor's degree or equivalent qualification. They are trained by principal instructors (*instruktur utama*) who are involved in the development of the concepts, definitions and questions used in the survey. In undertaking the interviews, subdistrict enumerators are guided and coordinated by a subdistrict statistical coordinator (*koordinator statistik kecamatan*, or KSK).

BPS applies strict validation at every stage of data collection and processing to minimize misinterpretation of data at the provincial and district/municipality levels. Because the Susenas is intended to measure national and provincial-level performance, the problems posed by remote areas (as in Papua) do not matter much, as these comprise only a small proportion of the total sample.

Data Collection in Papua

The response rate and the quality of data collected in Papua are typically below those of other regions, for several reasons. First, the region's difficult terrain, poor transport and communications infrastructure and dispersed population make it difficult for enumerators to reach respondents. Many district capitals and subdistricts can only be reached by air, with no regular flight schedule. For example, Elikobel, the capital of Yahukimo district, can only be reached by small airplane from Merauke, 400 kilometres away. The main towns in Yahukimo's seven subdistricts are even more difficult to reach. Because of the cost of collecting data in Papua, the government cannot afford to be as active in collecting data there as it is, for example, in Java. Hence, the data from Papua are biased towards relatively large urban areas.

Second, there are not enough statistical coordinating staff in Papua. The most important person in collecting census or survey data for BPS is the KSK. Typically each subdistrict has at least one KSK. But in the early 2000s Papua had only 131 coordinators serving a total of 296 subdistricts (Table A2.1). That is, many subdistricts had no coordinator. Such subdistricts usually (but not always) remain unrepresented in surveys and tend not to be included in the census. Table A2.1 also shows the ratio between the number of coordinators and the number of subdistricts. The quality of data from districts with a low ratio can be expected to be poorer than that from districts with a high ratio. It can be seen that 16 of Papua's 29 districts had a ratio of less than 0.5, whereas only six—the districts of Teluk Wondama, Sorong, Supiori and Biak Numfor, and the cities of Sorong and Jayapura—had a ratio of 0.8 or higher.

Third, not only is there a shortage of KSK staff in Papua, but they are likely to be less skilled than those in Java. Better-qualified staff typically do not want to be assigned to Papua. This situation also contributes to the poor statistical record in Papua.

Fourth, since decentralization many new districts—and therefore many more government agencies—have been formed in Papua. This has made it more difficult for BPS both to maintain its contacts at the existing agencies (since many of their staff have been transferred to new agencies) and to establish contacts at the new agencies (which can take time).

Fifth, even when enumerators do reach respondents, they often have difficulty obtaining accurate answers because respondents have trouble understanding the survey questions.

Finally, the high level of illegal or unrecorded economic activity in Papua further complicates the compilation of accurate statistical information. For example, illegal logging is known to be rampant in Papua but information on illegal logging activities is almost nonexistent. Although common in many places, barter also goes unrecorded in the official statistics.

BPS is attempting to overcome these challenges in several ways. First, since the mid-1980s it has strengthened its programs at the Jakarta

Table A2.1   *Papua: Number of Subdistrict Statistical Coordinators (KSK)*
by District/Municipality, 2004

District/ Municipality	Number of KSK	Number of Subdistricts	Number of KSK per Subdistrict
West Papua	**46**	**101**	**0.46**
1 Manokwari	7	29	0.24
2 Teluk Wondama	7	7	1.00
3 Teluk Bintuni	2	11	0.18
4 Sorong district	12	12	1.00
5 Sorong municipality	4	5	0.80
6 South Sorong	5	14	0.36
7 Raja Ampat	3	10	0.30
8 Fak Fak	4	9	0.44
9 Kaimana	2	4	0.50
Papua	**85**	**195**	**0.44**
1 Merauke	8	11	0.73
2 Asmat	2	7	0.29
3 Boven Digoel	4	6	0.67
4 Mappi	4	6	0.67
5 Jayawijaya	5	15	0.33
6 Tolikara	2	10	0.20
7 Pegunungan Bintang	2	7	0.29
8 Yahukimo	3	7	0.43
9 Mimika	3	12	0.25
10 Jayapura district	7	18	0.39
11 Paniai	5	21	0.24
12 Nabire	6	12	0.50
13 Waropen	1	9	0.11
14 Puncak Jaya	6	15	0.40
15 Yapen Waropen	5	7	0.71
16 Jayapura municipality	4	4	1.00
17 Sarmi	4	11	0.36
18 Keerom	3	5	0.60
19 Supiori	2	2	1.00
20 Biak Numfor	9	10	0.90
Total	**131**	**296**	**0.44**

Source: BPS-Papua, unpublished data.

Academy of Statistics, most of whose graduates join BPS. This is expected to raise standards at all BPS branch offices, including those in Papua. Second, head office now supplies all data-processing hardware and software used by BPS branches, and trains staff to use the equipment appropriately. To minimize mistakes and ensure standardized results, most calculations for general regional indicators are now carried out using ready-to-use software. Third, BPS tries to maintain good relations with the various Papuan agencies supplying secondary data to it. If they are able to collect data properly, this is preferable to BPS collecting the data itself.

Given the nature of the problems associated with collecting data in Papua, one can predict that the data for coastal areas will be more accurate than those for highland areas. In particular, data for the city of Sorong, the city of Jayapura and the districts of Sorong, Biak Numfor and Supiori are likely to be more accurate and reliable than those for other regions — including Teluk Wondama, which has one KSK per subdistrict but is relatively isolated.

Data collection is inherently difficult in Papua. The main challenges for researchers are to be sensitive to possible data deficiencies; to use good judgment and common sense in interpreting data; and to indicate the possible margins of error when interpreting key figures on population distribution, economic activity and welfare.

How Indicators Are Calculated: Poverty and Regional GDP

In general, BPS implements the methodologies commonly used throughout the world, while adapting some formulas to meet specific local conditions. This section describes, first, how BPS calculates the number and proportion of poor people, and second, how it calculates regional GDP.

BPS first published data on the number and proportion of poor people in Indonesia in 1984, using data from the consumption module of the Susenas. Since then, BPS has published this information annually, distinguishing between urban and rural areas. In 1990, BPS published information on poverty at the provincial level, although data for nine provinces (Jambi, Bengkulu, East Timor, Central Kalimantan, East Kalimantan, Central Sulawesi, Southeast Sulawesi, Maluku and Irian Jaya) had to be combined because of the small sample size in those provinces. BPS has made poverty data for every province available since 1993, and for the district/municipality level since 2002. Nowadays this information is needed to calculate general block grant (DAU) transfers from the central government to the provincial and district/municipality levels of government.

In absolute terms, people are defined as poor if they are unable to fulfil their minimum basic consumption needs. Transforming this into financial terms gives us a poverty line. Poor people, then, are those whose total income (commonly measured by their expenditure) is below the poverty line. BPS defines the components of basic needs as food (equivalent to 2,100 calories) and non-food items. The minimum expenditure required to fulfil these basic needs can be seen in Table A2.2.

Note that for each region, poverty lines are recalculated each year to take inflation and regional price differences into account. Table A2.3 shows the provincial poverty lines for 2004. Knowing the poverty line for each province allows us to estimate the number and proportion of poor people in each.

Regional GDP is a summation of the net output of goods and services produced in a certain area over a specified period of time (that is, one year). Also known as value added, net output is obtained by subtracting the cost of intermediate inputs from gross output (the value of production). Thus, regional GDP is the sum of value added from all economic activities.

Regional GDP has been constructed and published annually for all provinces and districts/municipalities since 1980. It is important to note that the numbers for national, provincial and district/municipality GDP are constructed independently; hence, there is a statistical discrepancy between national GDP and the sum of all provincial GDP, and between provincial GDP and the sum of all district/municipality GDP in that province.

BPS constructs national GDP and provincial GDP based on both the production and expenditure approaches. At the district/municipality level, however, only the production approach is used due to the limited availability of data. To construct the numbers, BPS collects data on all economic activities from BPS censuses and surveys, and obtains administrative data from government agencies and the private sector. Typically two types of information are needed for each sector: price and quantity.

The main problems in constructing regional GDP are as follows. First, data supplied by other institutions may not be in the form required by BPS. Second, BPS has limited control over the quality of the data supplied by other agencies. Third, securing data from other institutions is often difficult, since there is no dedicated computing facility linking them to BPS, or, indeed, linking the various BPS branches. A related problem is that other institutions may use software that is not compatible with that used by BPS. Finding ways to improve communications and share information with other institutions, particularly in the regions, is therefore the main focus of BPS's activities to improve the quality of the data used to calculate regional GDP.

*Table A2.2   Indonesia: Expenditure Required to Fulfil Basic Needs at the
National Level, 2002 (Rp per capita per month, in current prices)*

Basic Needs	Urban		Rural	
	Rp	Calories	Rp	Calories
Average expenditure on basic food	**59,366**	**1,335**	**51,754**	**1,488**
1 Rice & rice-related products	27,076	958	27,478	1,067
2 Corn & wheat	304	13	868	57
3 Tubers & tuber-related products	560	26	767	47
4 Fish	2,850	10	1,860	8
5 Meat, dairy & poultry products	6,342	42	2,983	20
6 Vegetables	4,674	15	4,315	21
7 Nuts & soybeans	3,939	57	2,461	39
8 Fruit & fruit products	2,759	108	2,640	126
9 Other	10,862	106	8,381	104
Required expenditure on basic food[a]	**93,356**		**73,020**	
Average expenditure on non-food items	**37,148**		**23,482**	
1 Housing	19,795		12,942	
2 Clothing	7,711		5,449	
3 Education	1,374		791	
4 Health related	4,122		2,537	
5 Other	4,146		1,763	
Total basic needs (national poverty line)	**130,504**		**96,502**	
Average expenditure of Indonesians on food & non-food items	322,009		163,720	

a   That is, the expenditure on basic food required to achieve a minimum calorie consumption of 2,100 calories per day.

Source: Calculated from raw data from the 2002 Susenas.

Table A2.3   Indonesia: Provincial Poverty Lines, 2004 (Rp per capita per month, in current prices)

Province	Urban	Rural
Aceh	141,926	124,857
North Sumatra	142,966	114,214
West Sumatra	181,506	128,610
Riau	198,075	164,921
Jambi	160,203	117,428
South Sumatra	154,768	108,457
Bengkulu	148,156	102,335
Lampung	146,566	108,611
Bangka Belitung	162,288	143,114
Jakarta	197,306	n.a.
West Java	152,144	122,475
Central Java	140,391	116,998
Yogyakarta	148,247	114,671
East Java	138,792	119,405
Banten	150,384	115,988
Bali	158,639	136,166
West Nusa Tenggara	144,001	99,686
East Nusa Tenggara	142,351	94,886
West Kalimantan	160,491	103,400
Central Kalimantan	148,964	128,382
South Kalimantan	148,413	111,821
East Kalimantan	163,976	170,296
North Sulawesi	148,343	132,207
Central Sulawesi	154,043	116,373
South Sulawesi	136,222	107,309
Southeast Sulawesi	140,925	108,260
Gorontalo	126,612	94,889
Maluku	152,194	123,769
North Maluku	174,000	107,142
Papua	160,866	130,649
Indonesia	**143,455**	**108,725**

Source: BPS (2005).

REFERENCES

Anggraeni, D. (2007), 'Pattern of Commercial and Industrial Resource Use in Papua', in Andrew J. Marshall and Bruce M. Beehler (eds), *The Ecology of Papua: Part Two*, Periplus, Singapore, pp. 1,149–66.

BPS (Badan Pusat Statistik) (various years), *Statistik Indonesia* [Statistics of Indonesia], Jakarta.

BPS (Badan Pusat Statistik) (1981), *Penduduk Indonesia: Hasil Sensus Penduduk Tahun 1980* [Population of Indonesia: Results of the 1980 Population Census], Jakarta.

BPS (Badan Pusat Statistik) (1991), *Penduduk Indonesia: Hasil Sensus Penduduk Tahun 1990* [Population of Indonesia: Results of the 1990 Population Census], Jakarta.

BPS (Badan Pusat Statistik) (2001), *Penduduk Indonesia: Hasil Sensus Penduduk Tahun 2000* [Population of Indonesia: Results of the 2000 Population Census], Jakarta.

BPS (Badan Pusat Statistik) (2005), *Data dan Informasi Kemiskinan Tahun 2004* [Data and Information on Poverty, 2004], Jakarta.

BPS (Badan Pusat Statistik) (2006a), *Statistik Indonesia* [Statistics of Indonesia], Jakarta.

BPS (Badan Pusat Statistik) (2006b), *Penduduk Papua: Hasil Survei Penduduk Antar Sensus Tahun 2005* [Population of Indonesia: Results of the 2005 Intercensal Survey], Jakarta.

BPS (Badan Pusat Statistik) (2006c), *Indonesia: Indeks Pembangunan Manusia 2005* [Indonesia: Human Development Index 2005], Jakarta.

BPS, Bappenas and UNDP (Badan Pusat Statistik, Badan Perencanaan Pembangunan Nasional and United Nations Development Programme) (2001), *Indonesia Human Development Report 2001. Towards a New Consensus: Democracy and Human Development in Indonesia*, Jakarta.

BPS, Bappenas and UNDP (Badan Pusat Statistik, Badan Perencanaan Pembangunan Nasional and United Nations Development Programme) (2004), *Indonesia Human Development Report 2004. The Economics of Democracy: Financing Human Development in Indonesia*, Jakarta.

BPS-Papua (Badan Pusat Statistik Provinsi Papua) (2004), *Papua dalam Angka 2003* [Papua in Statistics 2003], Jayapura.

BPS-Papua (Badan Pusat Statistik Provinsi Papua) (2008), *Papua dalam Angka 2007* [Papua in Statistics 2007], Jayapura.

Chauvel, R. and I.N. Bhakti (2004), 'The Papua Conflict: Jakarta's Perception and Policies', Policy Studies No. 5, East-West Center, Washington DC.

Garnaut, R. and C. Manning (1974), *Irian Jaya: The Transformation of a Melanesian Economy*, Australian National University Press, Canberra.

ICG (International Crisis Group) (2003), 'Dividing Papua, How Not To Do It', Asia Briefing No. 24, Jakarta/Brussels.

Manning, C. and M. Rumbiak (1991), 'Irian Jaya: Economic Change, Migrants, and Indigenous Welfare', in Hal Hill (ed.), *Unity in Diversity: Regional Economic Development in Indonesia since 1970*, Oxford University Press, Singapore, pp. 77–106.

McGibbon, R. (2004), 'Secessionist Challenges in Aceh and Papua: Is Special Autonomy the Solution?', Policy Studies No. 13, East-West Center, Washington DC.

McGibbon, R. (2006), *Pitfalls of Papua*, Lowy Institute for International Policy, Sydney.

PemProv Papua, Bappenas and UNDP (Pemerintah Provinsi Papua, Badan Perencanaan Pembangunan Nasional and United Nations Development Programme) (2005), *Sintese Kapasitas Pembangunan Papua* [Synthesis of Papua's Development Capacity], Jayapura.

Rathgeber, T. (ed.) (2005), *Economic, Social and Cultural Rights in West-Papua: A Study on Social Reality and Political Perspectives*, Foedus-Verlag, Wuppertal.

Solossa, J.P. (2006), *Otonomi Khusus Papua, Mengangkat Martabat Rakyat Papua di dalam NKRI* [Special Autonomy for Papua: Raising the Status of Papuans within the Unitary Republic of Indonesia], Sinar Harapan, Jakarta.

Sumule, A. (ed.) (2003), *Mencari Jalan Tengah Otonomi Khusus Provinsi Papua* [Finding the Middle Ground on Special Autonomy for Papua], PT Gramedia Pustaka Utama, Jakarta.

Timmer, J. (2007), 'A Brief Social and Political History of Papua, 1962–2005', in A.J. Marshall and B.M. Beehler (eds), *The Ecology of Papua: Part Two*, Periplus, Singapore, pp. 1,098–124.

UNDP (United Nations Development Programme) (2004), *Human Development Report 2004. Monitoring Human Development: Enlarging People's Choices*, New York NY.

UNDP (United Nations Development Programme) (2005), *Human Development Report 2005. International Cooperation at a Crossroads: Aid, Trade and Security in an Unequal World*, New York NY.

World Bank (various years), *World Development Indicators*, Washington DC.

World Bank (2007), *World Development Indicators*, Washington DC.

Yappika (2001), *Suara dari Papua: Identifikasi Kebutuhan Masyarakat Papua Asli* [Voices from Papua: Identifying the Needs of the Native Papuan People], Jakarta.

3 PAPUA II: CHALLENGES FOR PUBLIC ADMINISTRATION AND ECONOMIC POLICY UNDER SPECIAL AUTONOMY

Budy P. Resosudarmo, Chris Manning and Lydia Napitupulu

With the implementation of decentralization in 2001 and special autonomy in 2002, Papua was given a historic opportunity to dramatically improve the living standards of the mass of the rural population. There are two factors in Papua's favour at present. First, the flow of funds to the province is substantially higher than ever before in Papuan history, including during the last years of the Dutch occupation and the period of United Nations administration in the 1960s. Second, decentralization has been more extensive in Papua than in any other province in Indonesia (or almost anywhere else in the developing world). This has brought regional governments much closer to the people than they were in the past, giving them greater freedom to implement their own programs.

The short-term challenges and costs are substantial, however. Most importantly, an astonishingly large number of new government structures needs to be put in place following the significant increase in the number of districts. Moreover, the extraordinary increase in the public budget has created opportunities for widespread corruption, especially given the weak, and sometimes nonexistent, governance structures needed to guide public administration and economic management. Another major challenge is that of dealing with transition: from a centralized regime to a decentralized one; and from local governments starved of funds and dictated to from outside, to governments with large surpluses, supported by the local population, with the potential to develop and implement local initiatives. The process of establishing and strengthening Papua's political and government institutions may take a decade or more, and should be a central goal of government efforts. In this respect Papuans have much to learn from some of the successful, and especially the less successful, development experiments in other developing regions in the Pacific, where the economic challenges related to demography and geography are very similar.

1   THE FISCAL IMPACT OF DECENTRALIZATION AND SPECIAL AUTONOMY

Before Indonesia's decentralization policy was implemented in 2001, most of the government revenues from mining and other natural resource extraction activities (in the form of royalties, taxes and so on) accrued to the central government. Like other provinces, Papua was heavily dependent on transfers from the central government (PemProv Papua, SOfEI and World Bank 2005), which typically made up 60–85 per cent of total budget revenue. These funds were intended to cover specific budgetary items, mainly civil servant salaries and administration. During the 1970s and early 1980s the proportion of routine expenditure in the provincial budget declined (from around 70 per cent in the 1970s to 55 per cent in the early 1980s) as the share allocated to development increased.[1] The Papuan government became more active in developing infrastructure in the 1980s, supplementing the efforts of the central government. Towards the end of the 1990s, however, the share of budgetary expenditure allocated to development fell, indicating a decline in the priority given to development activities.

Table 3.1 shows the regional budget for Papua in 1999/2000 (the year before the decentralization policy took effect), 2001 (the year in which decentralization was implemented) and 2002 (the year in which special autonomy was implemented), covering allocations at the provincial, district and municipality levels of government. It can be seen that almost all income came from the central government in all three years. In 1999/2000, the Autonomous Regional Subsidy (SDO) made up the largest part of these central government transfers, followed by grants made under the Presidential Instruction (Inpres) program. The purpose of SDO transfers was to cover civil servant salaries, while the purpose of Inpres grants was to fund development activities. Inpres grants were of

---

1   Routine expenditure typically covers civil servant salaries, government administration and maintenance, and other routine bureaucratic expenses. Development expenditure covers the development of human and physical infrastructure.

Table 3.1   Papua: Total Provincial, District and Municipality Budget, 1999/2000, 2001 and 2002 (Rp billion)

	1999/2000	2001	2002
TOTAL INCOME	**1,207**	**3,521**	**4,764**
Transfer from previous year	**46**	**87**	**235**
Own revenue	**51**	**115**	**165**
Regional tax	26	53	76
Levies & other income	25	62	89
Transfer from the centre	**1,111**	**3,297**	**4,172**
Tax revenue sharing	132	337	321
Non-tax revenue sharing	205	361	199
SDO/DAU[a]	415	2,430	2,111
Inpres/DAK[a]	358	169	1,541
Other		**22**	**192**
TOTAL EXPENDITURE	**1,168**	**3,262**	**4,625**
Routine expenditure	**750**	**2,027**	**2,373**
Development expenditure	**418**	**1,235**	**2,252**
Industry	2	6	5
Agriculture	23	75	138
Irrigation	11	26	60
Trade	19	74	91
Mining	87	9	19
Telecommunications	2	12	9
Transport	20	296	483
Regional development	21	66	125
Environment	35	35	39
Education	20	145	276
Health	23	102	198
Housing	7	91	66
Science	31	13	38
Judicative apparatus	2	4	8
Government apparatus	33	231	250
Security	21	19	399
Other	59	30	48

a   Figures for 1999/2000 are Autonomous Regional Subsidy (SDO) or Presidential Instruction (Inpres) grants; figures for 2001 and 2002 are General Purpose Fund (DAU) or Specific Purpose Fund (DAK) grants.

Source: Department of Finance, <http://www.sikd.djapk.go.id/>.

two types: block grants and specific purpose grants. In theory at least, block grants, together with the income from revenue sharing and the revenue raised by the provincial government itself, could be spent on Papuan government priorities. The purpose of specific purpose grants was to fund development and other activities considered a high priority by Jakarta, such as transport, regional development, environment, health and education. The nature of the investments in those sectors was determined by the central government.

In 1999/2000, most budgetary expenditure was allocated to routine items and only 36 per cent to development. Surprisingly, a significant share of the development budget went to the mining sector, most likely for infrastructure development in the Timika region. Total funding for education, science and health comprised only 18 per cent of development expenditure, or 6 per cent of total expenditure.

On 1 January 2001, Indonesia began to implement the far-reaching decentralization measures set out in Law No. 22/1999 and Law No. 25/1999 (since replaced by Law No. 32/2004 and Law No. 33/2004 respectively). These laws delegated much greater authority to Indonesia's 400-odd districts and municipalities in the areas of education, agriculture, industry, trade and investment, and infrastructure (Alm, Aten and Bahl 2001), leaving security, foreign relations, and monetary and fiscal policy with the central government (Government Regulation (PP) No. 25/2000). Together with their much greater powers and responsibilities, quite suddenly district and municipality heads (*bupati* and *walikota*) acquired large numbers of civil servants who had previously been employed by the provincial and district offices of central government agencies. Because of these huge changes, many analysts have used the term 'big bang' to describe Indonesia's decentralization process.

Under the new decentralization policy, the SDO and Inpres mechanisms were eliminated and two new mechanisms for central government transfers introduced: the General Purpose Fund (DAU) and the Specific Purpose Fund (DAK). Regional governments were given the authority to decide how DAU transfers would be spent. DAK transfers were earmarked for specific purposes in line with central government priorities — mainly reforestation in 2001. The rules for revenue sharing between the central government and regional governments were also changed in favour of the latter (Table 3.2).

The nominal value of the Papuan budget almost tripled between 1999/2000 and 2001 (Table 3.1). The main source of income was DAU transfers from the central government. It is interesting to observe that development still comprised only 38 per cent of total expenditure (compared with 36 per cent in the previous year), although in absolute terms the amount increased several-fold. Like many other local governments,

Table 3.2   *Papua: Revenue-sharing Arrangements before and after Decentralization (Law No. 25/1999) and Special Autonomy (Law No. 21/2001)*

Item	Before Decentralization (to December 2000)	After Decentralization (from January 2001)	After Special Autonomy (from 2002)
Taxes	*Property tax*[a] centre: 100% (later allocated to regions) *Fee for transfer of property title*[b] centre: 100% (later allocated to regions)	*Property tax*[a] centre: 10%; local: 90% *Fee for transfer of property title*[b] centre: 20%; local: 80%	*Property tax*[a] centre: 10%; local: 90% *Fee for transfer of property title*[b] centre: 20%; local: 80% *Personal income tax* centre: 80%; local: 20%
Royalties & proceeds from natural resource extraction	*Forest concession licence fee* centre: 30%; local: 70% *Fisheries* unclear *Mining exploitation & exploration fee*[d] centre: 20%; province: 16%; district: 64% *Oil & gas revenues net of tax* not shared	*Forest concession licence fee*[c] centre: 20%; province: 16%; producing district: 64% *Fisheries* centre: 20%; split among all districts: 80% *Mining exploitation & exploration contribution*[d] centre: 20%; province: 16%; producing district: 32%; split among districts in producing province: 32% *Oil & gas revenue net of tax* centre: 85% (oil), 70% (gas); province: 3% (oil), 6% (gas); producing district: 6% (oil), 12% (gas); other districts in producing province: 6% (oil) 12% (gas)	*Forestry, fisheries & mining* centre: 20%; local: 80% *Oil & gas* centre: 30%; local: 70% (for 25 years until 2026, thereafter 50%)
DAU & DAK	Not applicable	National formula	National formula + special infrastructure fund + special autonomy fund[e] (the latter equal to 2% of total national DAU for 20 years until 2021)

a   Pajak Bumi dan Bangunan.
b   Bea Perolehan Hak atas Tanah dan Bangunan.
c   Iuran Hak Pengusahaan Hutan.
d   Iuran Eksplorasi dan Iuran Eksploitasi.
e   Dana Otsus.
Source: Alisjahbana (2005); Law No. 25/1999; Law No. 21/2001.

Papua's district governments were unable to significantly increase the share of development expenditure in 2001 for several reasons. First, they had to absorb large numbers of civil servants from central government line agencies (especially in education and health). Second, there was a tendency for districts to enlarge their administrative structures so that they could accommodate more local residents in the local bureaucracy. Third, despite having the authority to develop their own development programs, local governments had not yet acquired the requisite capacity, knowledge or experience to do so.

Law No. 21/2001 on Special Autonomy for Papua came into operation in early 2002. It entitled Papua to most of the proceeds from its natural resources and other economic activities, as summarized in Table 3.2. Total regional income consequently increased from Rp 3.5 trillion in 2001 to Rp 4.8 trillion in 2002 — a rise of 35 per cent (Table 3.1). The budget in 2002 was equivalent to about US$217 per capita, a much higher amount per person than in any other province in Indonesia (PemProv Papua, SOfEI and World Bank 2005). The highest increase was in DAK grants, under provisions in the Special Autonomy Law establishing a special autonomy fund (Dana Otsus) focused on education and health, as well as an ad hoc infrastructure fund directed at reducing the longstanding disparities between Papua and other provinces. DAK grants rose from just Rp 169 billion in 2001 to Rp 1.5 trillion in 2002.

The division of revenue between the various levels of government is governed by Regional Regulation (Perda) No. 2/2004 of the province of Papua. It stipulates that revenue related to the Special Autonomy Law is to be divided between the provincial and district/municipality governments in a ratio of 40 to 60,[2] but it does not provide clear guidance on how the 60 per cent is to be distributed among districts and municipalities. This is an important issue, since inequality of per capita revenue among districts/municipalities is considered to be high in Papua. For example, Sorong district's per capita revenue was almost five times that of Biak Numfor in 2003 (PemProv Papua, SOfEI and World Bank 2005).

Regional governments in Papua (and elsewhere in Indonesia) have a relatively high degree of freedom to draw up their own budgets. The Special Autonomy Law states only that at least 30 per cent of revenue from oil and gas is to be allocated to education and 15 per cent to health. The National Education Law (Law No. 20/2003) requires all regional governments to direct at least 20 per cent of their expenditure towards education. However, there is no law or regulation stipulating the proportion of development expenditure in total regional government expenditure.

---

2 Before the enactment of this regulation, 60 per cent of such monies went to the provinces and 40 per cent to the districts and municipalities.

As noted, the funds available to the provincial government increased sharply in 2002, resulting in an increase in the development budget from Rp 1.2 trillion in 2001 to Rp 2.3 trillion in 2002. With the exception of government administration, the largest items in the 'development' budget were transport (Rp 483 billion) and security (Rp 399 billion) — the latter up from Rp 19 billion in 2001 — followed by education (Rp 276 billion) and health (Rp 198 billion). The Papuan government almost doubled its funding for health and education in 2002 to meet its obligations under the Special Autonomy Law. Nevertheless, its expenditure on education was still only 6 per cent of total expenditure, far less than that required by the National Education Law. In fact, so far no regional government has been able to meet the national target (PemProv Papua, SOfEI and World Bank 2005).

Regional income has continued to increase since 2002, although not as dramatically as it did between 2001 and 2002. Observing this situation, one could conclude that lack of funds is not the main constraint to development in Papua, at least in the near to medium term. Rather, it is the ability of Papuans themselves to use that money wisely and generate appropriate development policies.

2 THE CHALLENGES

Papua must overcome many challenges if governments at all levels are to formulate and implement the policies needed to significantly improve the living standards of the majority of the population. Four of these challenges will be discussed in this section: the increase in the number of districts, corruption, public infrastructure and the investment climate.

The Growing Number of Districts

Although the division of Papua into two provinces has attracted much public debate (see Chapter 2), more problematic for local development is the continual formation of new districts. The number of districts has grown rapidly since 1999, creating political uncertainty and disrupting many local development programs.[3]

Historically, the establishment of new districts in Papua is not a new phenomenon. In 1969 the central government passed Law No. 12/1969, which established nine districts (Biak Numfor, Fak-Fak, Jayapura, Jayawijaya, Manokwari, Merauke, Paniai, Sorong and Yapen Worapen) under

---

3 See Map 2.1 (Chapter 2) for a guide to the administrative divisions of Papua in 2007, and Table 2.6 for details of the population of each of Papua's districts in 2004.

the provincial government of Irian Jaya. The administrative municipality of Jayapura was established in 1979 (PP No. 26/1979) and became a full municipality in 1993 (Law No. 6/1993).[4] In 1996, several further changes were made: (1) Paniai district was divided into three regions (the district of Nabire and the administrative districts of Paniai and Puncak Jaya) (PP No. 52/1996); (2) the administrative district of Mimika was hived off from Fak-Fak district (PP No. 54/1996); and (3) a new administrative municipality of Sorong was created (PP No. 31/1996). Hence, at the time of the fall of Soeharto, Papua had nine districts (Biak Numfor, Fak-Fak, Jayapura, Jayawijaya, Manokwari, Merauke, Nabire, Sorong and Yapen Waropen); three administrative districts (Paniai, Mimika and Puncak Jaya); one municipality (the city of Jayapura); and one administrative municipality (the city of Sorong).

The speed at which new districts were being established increased from 1999. In addition to splitting Papua into three provinces, Law No. 45/1999 upgraded Paniai, Mimika and Puncak Jaya to full districts and Sorong to a full municipality. In 2002, an astounding 14 new districts were established under Law No. 26/2002, resulting in an almost doubling of the total number of districts.[5] In 2003, Biak Numfor was divided into two districts: Biak Numfor and Supiori (Law No. 35/2003). This brought the total number of districts to 27 (plus two municipalities), three times that in 1969.[6] On 15 March 2007, Mamberamo Raya district was established, covering areas that were originally part of Sarmi and Waropen (Law No. 19/2007). On 6 December 2007, Jakarta approved the establishment of another six new districts.[7] Given the vast area of Papua, it seems likely that further new districts will be established in the future.

---

4   The difference between an administrative district or municipality and a (normal) district or municipality is that an administrative district/municipality does not have a regional parliament.

5   The new districts were: Sarmi and Keerom (formerly part of Jayapura district); South Sorong and Raja Ampat (formerly part of Sorong); Pegunungan Bintang, Yahukimo and Tolikara (formerly part of Jayawijaya); Waropen (formerly part of Yapen Waropen); Kaimana (formerly part of Fak-Fak); Boven Digoel, Mappi and Asmat (formerly part of Merauke); and Teluk Bintuni and Teluk Wondama (formerly part of Manokwari).

6   These districts/municipalities were: Fak-Fak, Kaimana, Manokwari, Raja Ampat, Sorong, South Sorong, Teluk Bintuni and Teluk Wondama, and the municipality of Sorong, in West Irian Jaya; and the districts of Asmat, Biak Numfor, Boven Digoel, Jayapura, Jayawijaya, Keerom, Mappi, Merauke, Mimika, Nabire, Paniai, Pegunungan Bintang, Puncak Jaya, Sarmi, Supiori, Tolikara, Waropen, Yahukimo and Yapen Worapen, and the municipality of Jayapura, in Papua.

7   These districts were: Lanny Jaya, Yalimo, Nduga and Central Mamberamo (originally part of Jayawijaya district), Dogiyai (originally part of Nabire) and Puncak (originally part of Puncak Jaya) (*Kompas*, 6 December 2007).

There are a number of problems associated with the formation of new districts at such a rapid pace. First, the administrative costs of establishing a new district are significant; they include the costs of transferring and recruiting staff, constructing new offices and establishing new political and governmental institutions. Local businesses are also put to the trouble and expense of changing the status of their permits and licences when they are summarily transferred from one jurisdiction to another.

Second, it could take a decade or more to establish strong new political and governmental institutions that function properly and deliver development to the local community. In the meantime, government programs are likely to be disrupted as new administrations seek to re-align them in line with the policies of the new district head.

Finally, before and after the establishment of a new district, local politics is typically in turmoil, throwing plans for the district into disarray and quite often leading to physical conflict among local groups, especially different ethnic and language groups. The prospect of being able to gain government approval for the division of an existing district creates political instability and uncertainty. For example, members of local elites who have failed to gain traction through local elections may view the option of establishing a new district as an alternative means of increasing their political influence.

All of these issues are likely to disrupt the progress of local development in Papua.

Corruption

It has been argued that one immediate effect of Indonesia's decentralization policy was to spread corruption. Under the centralized political system of the Soeharto era, corruption was a centralized 'one-stop shop'. But with the decentralization of governmental power and authority, corruption has become much more diffuse. The more fragmented bribe collection system that now prevails involves government officials, military and police, and legislative members at the national and regional levels (Resosudarmo 2005; Resosudarmo and Kuncoro 2006). Corruption has become rampant in the regions.

For a number of reasons, it seems possible that the opportunities (and temptations) for corruption are likely to be greater in Papua than in other parts of Indonesia. First, the amount of funds being disbursed throughout the region is huge. In 2003, total regional government expenditure reached Rp 5.4 trillion, equivalent to about Rp 2 million per capita or Rp 8 million per family (BPS-Papua 2004). Second, control by higher-level governmental institutions and judicial bodies is weak, especially in Papua where many of these institutions are newly formed. Given that a high proportion of the population has little education and lives in relatively isolated rural areas, the control exerted by the public through political and social institutions is also weak. Third, much of the revenue comes from natural resource rents and is highly concentrated in just a few regions. The temptation for local officials to misuse the easy wind-falls from the resource sector is therefore strong. In this respect Papua is just as exposed to the 'curse' of natural resource abundance as many other resource-rich regions and countries. In the resource-rich districts in particular, some local government leaders have become very powerful, often being referred to as 'kings' (*raja*). Moreover, they have the capacity not only to determine spending priorities but also to levy various taxes and charges.

There is mounting evidence that corruption has become such a sig-nificant problem in Papua that it may hamper future development. Large sums of money have allegedly disappeared into the private purses of high-ranking local government officials. In 2005, one high-profile case of alleged corruption involved the district head of Jayawijaya district. He was suspected of creating several fictitious projects in 2002–03 to cover his illicit activities, including the 'acquisition' of two Fokker F27s and one Antonov airplane and the 'purchase' of steel and other construction materials. It was alleged that the loss of public revenue from his activities amounted to as much as Rp 56 billion. On 10 November 2005, the presi-dent gave permission for the attorney general's office to investigate this case (*Kompas*, 11 November 2005).

In another case, a high-ranking official in Mimika district was sus-pected of misusing as much as Rp 14 billion of the district budget in 2001. In his defence, the official argued that he did not use the funds for personal purposes, but rather to entertain central government officials who were visiting the region (*Kompas*, 30 April 2004). There have also been reports of the involvement of several government officials in illegal trading activities. For example, four military officials and the head of the forestry service in Manokwari, as well as four police officials in Papua, were accused in 2005 of being involved in illegal logging activities (*Kompas Cybermedia*, 30 March 2005; *Kompas*, 24 March 2005). Another case involved a Pertamina official in Sorong who was suspected of selling fuel acquired at Indonesia's heavily subsidized prices to foreign ships (*Suara Karya*, 3 March 2006). Allegations of corruption have even stalked mem-bers of the local legislature. In 2005, for example, 35 members of the Mer-auke district parliament were reported to have misappropriated as much as Rp 5 billion of parliamentary funds (*Kompas*, 19 February 2005).

The central government has taken several initiatives to combat cor-ruption. In 2002 it set up the Commission for the Eradication of Cor-ruption (KPK) to improve the effectiveness and efficiency of efforts to eradicate criminal acts of corruption (Law No. 30/2002). In collaboration with other authorized institutions, the commission has succeeded in identifying numerous cases of alleged corruption by regional government officials and members of parliament, and in bringing them before the courts. It has also turned its attention to Papua, where progress has been visible but slow. On 29 August 2006, the district head of Jayawijaya district was sentenced to one year in prison and fined Rp 400 million by the Wamena court in Jayawijaya after being found guilty of three counts of corruption. He is currently appealing to a higher court (*Kompas*, 30 August 2006). At the end of 2007, the district head of Nabire was also under investigation for corruption (*Detikcom*, 21 September 2007).

Efforts are also being made to clean up the judicial system. For example, in September 2007 seven public prosecutors in Papua were dismissed from their positions for mishandling an illegal fishing case (*Tempo Interaktif*, 4 September 2007).

It will take time to curb Papua's high levels of corruption. However, as more corruption cases are brought before the courts and tighter monitoring of the judicial system is conducted, the number of successful prosecutions should increase, acting as a disincentive to the misappropriation of public funds. Corruption must be brought under control if governments and other agencies are to have confidence in the integrity of their development programs.

Public Infrastructure

When Papua became part of Indonesia in 1969, its infrastructure was very poor. Although progress was made in the 1970s, Papua remained extremely deficient in infrastructure. In 1980, for example, the province had a mere 627 kilometres of paved roads, or about 1.6 kilometres for every 1,000 square kilometres of territory. The average for the whole of Indonesia in the same year was 27.8 kilometres per 1,000 square kilometres. The situation improved during the 1980s and early 1990s, so that by 1994, Papua had about 3,700 kilometres of paved roads, or 9 kilometres per 1,000 square kilometres. This equated to a growth rate of 17.6 per cent per annum, much faster than the national average of 9.2 per cent and behind only Central Kalimantan (25.7 per cent) and South Sulawesi (18.8 per cent). But between 1994 and 2004, the pace of growth slowed to just 1.1 per cent per annum, almost the slowest rate in the country. In 2002 Papua still had only 9.8 kilometres of roads per 1,000 square kilometres of territory (BPS, various years).[8]

---

8 Papua was not the worst, however; Central Kalimantan, which also relies heavily on river transport, had only 1.4 kilometres of paved roads per 1,000 square kilometres of territory in 2002.

Better road transport is a precondition for the expansion of economic activity and trade in many highland areas, on the larger islands and along some parts of the north coast. But of course, other modes of transport are also important in Papua. River transport is the preferred (and, indeed, only practical) mode of transport for the movement of goods and people over large parts of the lowlands in southern Papua. The density of air transport has increased in recent years, although this is of limited significance for most of the population because of the cost of air travel.

Electrification has also lagged behind the rest of Indonesia. In 2003, the installed capacity of the national electricity company (PLN) in Papua was around 145MW, which translates to around 15.8kW per billion rupiah of gross domestic product (GDP) per annum in 1993 prices (or 0.06kW per capita). This compares with the national level of 21,204MW, or 48kW per billion rupiah of GDP in 1993 prices (BPS-Papua 2004; BPS, various years).

It is important to bear in mind the reasons for Papua's poor infrastructure, especially the very poor initial conditions in the 1960s, the region's hostile terrain and low population density, and the high cost of building infrastructure by national and international standards. Although there were periods in which infrastructure performed better than the national average in Papua, the rate of growth has not been nearly fast enough to allow the province to catch up with the rest of Indonesia. The large amounts of revenue now flowing to the provincial and district governments should make significant improvements possible.

The Investment Climate

There has been little in the way of new private capital investment in Papua in recent years. This is apparent from data on private investment flows during the six years from 1999 to 2005 (Figure 3.1). Large investments tend to be concentrated in mining. Thus, foreign investment jumped in 2001, when BP invested around US$5 billion in a large liquefied natural gas project in Tangguh. However, the implementation of that project has been relatively slow, and in February 2006 it was only 30 per cent complete. Registered domestic investment has consistently been small over the entire period.

Investment outside mining (much of it probably not reflected in the data shown in Figure 3.1) has typically been in forest-based activities (Cannon 2007). In 2003 Papua had around 10 million hectares under forest concessions—just under one-third of the province's total forest cover, estimated at 32 million hectares in 2004 (Ministry of Forestry 2004). This was a very large area by national standards, accounting for approximately 30 per cent of the total area under forest concessions in Indonesia, and equal to the total area of forest concessions in the Indonesian part of

Figure 3.1   Papua: Approved Domestic and Foreign Direct Investment
             (US$ billion)

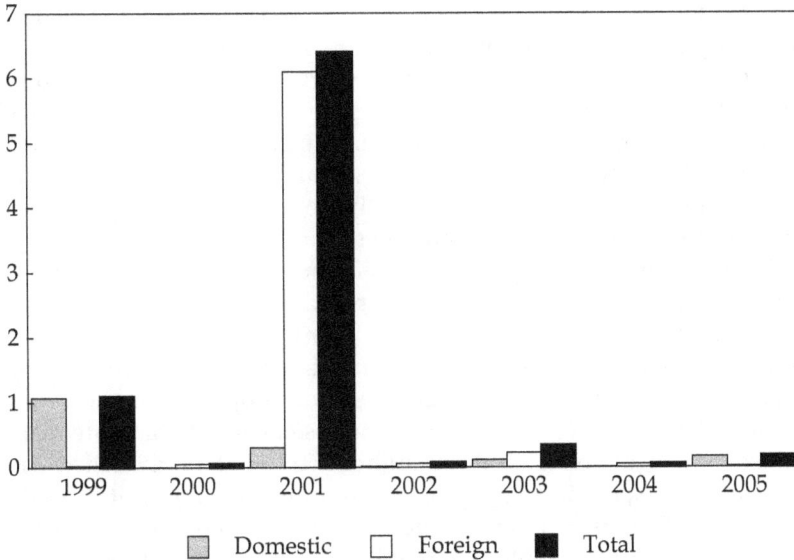

Source: BPS (various years).

Kalimantan (Ministry of Forestry 2004). As touched on above, appropriating the benefits from forest exploitation for local and regional populations has been a major challenge in Papua, given problems of supervision of private sector logging and the involvement of powerful political and military figures in forestry operations.

Investment in estate crops has been lower in Papua than in the other large islands, and than in some parts of Papua New Guinea. In 2001, the total area of smallholder plantations stood at around 109,000 hectares, mainly producing coconuts (around 42,000 hectares), while the total area of large plantations, including nucleus estate arrangements, was 56,000 hectares, mainly producing palm oil (50,000 hectares) (BPS-Papua 2004). The government set a goal of increasing the area under estate crops to 170,000–200,000 hectares by 2006. But even if this target is achieved, Papua will still account for only 1 per cent of the total area devoted to estate crops in Indonesia, despite having a land mass that accounts for around 20 per cent of the national total (*Kompas*, 27 February 2006).

3   CONCLUSION

In this chapter, we have documented both the opportunities and the challenges for Papua. Decentralization and special autonomy present opportunities for more rapid development in Papua. The special autonomy policy provides a way out of the political dispute between the Papuan elite and the Indonesian government over Papuan independence. It has given Papuans greater control over their own resources and their own development path. Under both the decentralization and special autonomy policies, greatly increased revenues are available to establish development programs. Provincial income in the 2005 budget, for example, was almost four times that before special autonomy was implemented. In addition, regional governments (both provincial and local) now have much more say in how these funds are spent.

If the new revenue is spent judiciously, on strategic infrastructure, on public services and on improving the business and investment climate to support the development of sectors other than mining, Papua should be able to lay a strong foundation for future economic and social development. The agricultural sector and rural development should receive special attention, since development in these areas has the potential to induce more equitable growth throughout Papua. If, on the other hand, the revenue is spent in a suboptimal way—most notably, if it is used to create new districts or is squandered through corruption—Papua risks losing the present momentum to build a strong base for future improvements in welfare.

The wise allocation of present revenue and the creation of effective and efficient administrative institutions, rather than too much emphasis on looking for additional funds, should be a central part of government efforts in Papua. If the present opportunity for advancement is lost, the social and economic gap between Papua and the rest of Indonesia is only likely to widen in the medium to longer term.

REFERENCES

Alm, J., R.H. Aten and R. Bahl (2001), 'Can Indonesia Decentralize Successfully? Plans, Problems and Prospects', *Bulletin of Indonesian Economic Studies*, 37(1): 83–102.

Alisjahbana, A. (2005), 'Does Indonesia Have the Balance Right in Natural Resource Revenue Sharing?', in Budy P. Resosudarmo (ed.), *The Politics and Economics of Indonesia's Natural Resources*, Institute of Southeast Asian Studies, Singapore, pp. 109–24.

BPS (Badan Pusat Statistik) (various years), *Statistik Indonesia* [Statistics of Indonesia], Jakarta.

BPS-Papua (Badan Pusat Statistik Provinsi Papua) (2004), *Papua dalam Angka 2003* [Papua in Figures 2003], Jayapura.

Cannon, J.B. (2007), 'Natural Resource Economics of Papua', in Andrew J. Marshall and Bruce M. Beehler (eds), *The Ecology of Papua: Part Two*, Periplus, Singapore, pp. 1,167–91.

Ministry of Forestry (2004), *Forestry Statistics of Indonesia*, Jakarta.

PemProv Papua, SOfEI and World Bank (Pemerintah Provinsi Papua, Support Office for Eastern Indonesia and World Bank) (2005), *Papua Public Expenditure Analysis: Regional Finance and Service Delivery in Indonesia's Most Remote Region*, Jayapura.

Resosudarmo, B.P. (2005), 'Introduction', in B.P. Resosudarmo (ed.), *The Politics and Economics of Indonesia's Natural Resources*, Institute of Southeast Asian Studies, Singapore, pp. 1–12.

Resosudarmo, B.P. and A. Kuncoro (2006), 'The Political Economy of Indonesian Economic Reform: 1983–2000', *Oxford Development Studies*, 34(3): 341–55.

4   A NOTE ON SOCIO-ECONOMIC DEVELOPMENT IN MALUKU

Budy P. Resosudarmo

History tells us that the Maluku (or Moluccan) islands were famous for their spice products, and so were named the Spice Islands. As the dominance of these islands in the spice trade came to an end, the local economy began to decline. Data from the early 1980s show that Maluku was one of the poorest and most poverty-stricken regions in Indonesia. The violence that broke out in 1999 set the province back even further: thousands of people died, tens of thousands became refugees, and houses and other infrastructure were destroyed. The conflict continued more or less uninterrupted until 2003, although by most accounts 2001 was a slightly more peaceful year than 2000. In the northern part of Maluku, the violence had pretty much tapered off by 2001.[1]

The province of Maluku was formally established in 1957 by Emergency Law No. 22/1957 (replaced in 1958 by Law No. 20/1958). Maluku is made up of over 1,000 islands (Map 4.1) The provincial capital is Ambon, located on the island of Ambon. The three largest islands are Halmahera, Seram and Buru. The province covers a territory of approximately 850,000 square kilometres, making it one of the largest provinces in Indonesia. However, more than 90 per cent of it is ocean, and the total land area is only 75,000–85,000 square kilometres.[2] The distance from the northernmost to the southernmost part of Maluku is nearly 1,000 kilo-

---

1 See van Klinken (2001), Brown, Wilson and Hadi (2003), Duncan (2005a) and Pariela (2007), as well as Chapter 12 by Thorburn, for a detailed discussion of the conflict and its consequences.

2 These figures are for Maluku before it was divided into two provinces in 1999.

Map 4.1   Maluku

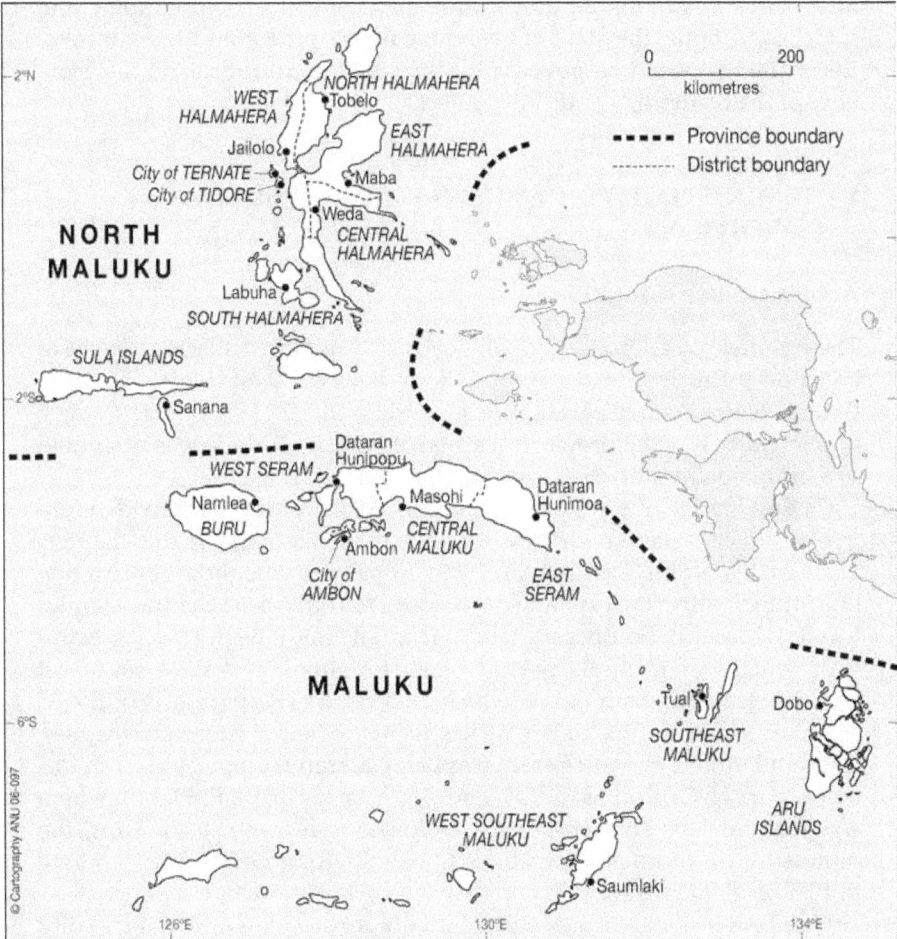

metres, equal to the distance from Jakarta to Medan. These geographical conditions pose a serious challenge to attempts to develop the region (Meyer and Hardjodimedjo 1989; Monk, de Fretes and Reksodiharjo-Lilley 1997; Brown, Wilson and Hadi 2003).

Maluku is urgently in need of well-considered development policies underpinned by a thorough understanding of current socio-economic trends. Although reliable data are hard to obtain, this chapter will attempt to describe Maluku's administrative arrangements, demographic and social conditions, the state of economic development and the nature of the challenge posed by poverty. It also analyses the effects on the economy of the recurring conflict of 1999–2003.

1   ADMINISTRATIVE, DEMOGRAPHIC AND SOCIAL CONDITIONS

Administrative Conditions

The province of Maluku originally consisted of four districts (*kabupaten*) and one municipality (*kota*).[3] The four districts were North Maluku, Central Halmahera, Central Maluku and Southeast Maluku. The single municipality was the provincial capital of Ambon. Ternate was upgraded to a municipality in 1999 (Law No. 11/1999).

Following the outbreak of violence in 1999, Maluku was divided into two provinces: Maluku (or 'new Maluku' as we will call it in this chapter) and North Maluku (Law No. 46/1999). Initially new Maluku consisted of one municipality (the capital, Ambon) and four districts: Central Maluku (capital: Masohi); Southeast Maluku (capital: Tual); Buru (capital: Namlea), which was formerly part of Central Maluku; and West Southeast Maluku (capital: Saumlaki), which was formerly part of Southeast Maluku. In 2003, three new districts were created: East Seram (capital: Dataran Hunimoa), West Seram (capital: Dataran Hunipopu) — both formerly part of Central Maluku — and Aru Islands (capital: Dobo), which was formerly part of Southeast Maluku (Law No. 40/2003). Thus, the number of districts/municipalities in new Maluku has grown from five in 1999 to eight currently.

The province of North Maluku initially consisted of one municipality (Ternate) and two districts: North Maluku (capital: Ternate) and Central Halmahera (capital: Tidore). The capital of the province is Sofifi on the

---

3   Provincial governments are the highest level of regional government in Indonesia. Districts (*kabupaten*) and municipalities (*kota*) comprise the second highest level. Below them are the subdistricts (*kecamatan*) and villages (*kelurahan* or *desa*).

island of Halmahera. While infrastructure is being built in Sofifi, Ternate is functioning as the provincial capital. In 2003, one new municipality (Tidore) and four new districts were formed in this province (Law No. 1/2003). The new districts were North Halmahera (capital: Tobelo), South Halmahera (capital: Labuha), Sula Islands (capital: Sanana) — all originally part of North Maluku district — and East Halmahera (capital: Maba), which was hived off from Central Halmahera district (new capital: Weda). At the same time the name of North Maluku district was changed to West Halmahera (new capital: Jailolo). Thus, the number of districts/municipalities in North Maluku has grown from three to eight in the decade since the province was formed.

As in Papua and many other regions, the establishment of new districts in Maluku was seen as a 'solution' to resolve conflicts among local elites, as well as being triggered by an expectation that the newly created districts would benefit from higher central government transfers. The costs, however, have been significant, in terms of both the funding needed to establish new district administrations and the disruption to existing development programs (ICG 2007).

Demographic Conditions

The population of Maluku doubled from slightly over 1 million in 1971 to approximately 2.1 million in 2005. About 27 per cent of the population lives in urban areas, and almost half of the total urban population resides in the city of Ambon. About 1.2 million people live in the province of new Maluku and the rest in North Maluku (BPS 2006b).

Figure 4.1 shows average annual population growth in Maluku for four periods between 1971 and 2005. The population grew at about 3 per cent per annum — 1 per cent above the national average — until 1998, but fell sharply in 1999–2001 as people fled the province to escape the violence and political and social instability caused by the conflict (BPS 2006b). The extent of the decline dragged population growth for the entire decade into negative territory.

The proportion of migrants in the total population was approximately 9 per cent in 1980, increasing slightly to 10 per cent in 1990 (BPS 1981, 1991). This indicates the importance of migration in the overall population growth rate. However, the proportion of migrants had declined to 6 per cent by 2005, from around 187,000 migrants in 1990 to 137,000 in 2005. The conflict wracking the province undoubtedly contributed to this decline: most of those who left Maluku were migrants, many of them returning to nearby parts of Sulawesi from whence they had originally come (Duncan 2005b).

In 1990, 85 per cent of migrants in Maluku came from five provinces: Southeast Sulawesi (28 per cent), East Java (23 per cent), Central Java (15

Figure 4.1   Maluku: Average Annual Population Growth, 1971–2005 (%)

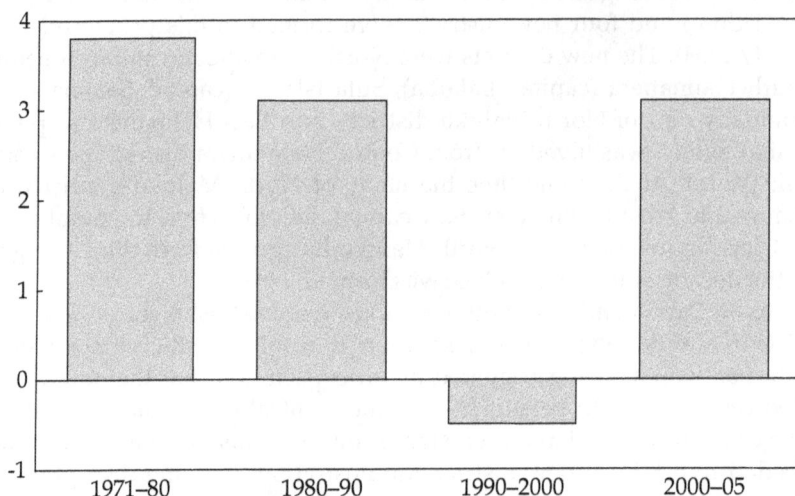

Source: BPS (1981, 1991, 2000, 2006a).

per cent), South Sulawesi (10 per cent) and North Sulawesi (9 per cent). In 2005, these five provinces still accounted for 80 per cent of migrants, but in a slightly different order: East Java (24 per cent), Southeast Sulawesi (17 per cent), Central Java (16 per cent), South Sulawesi (13 per cent) and North Sulawesi (10 per cent). Between 1990 and 2005, the number of migrants from Southeast Sulawesi fell from 51,000 to 21,000; the number from East Java from 43,000 to 30,000; the number from Central Java from 28,000 to 19,000; the number from South Sulawesi from 19,000 to 16,000; and the number from North Sulawesi from 16,000 to 13,000 (BPS 1991, 2006a). Among the migrants who chose to stay in Maluku, 41 per cent were living in urban areas in 2005: 42 per cent in new Maluku and 39 per cent in North Maluku (BPS 2006a).

Data on religion for the whole of Maluku show that in 2005, 58 per cent of the population was Muslim, 37 per cent Protestant, 4 per cent Catholic and 1 per cent other religions. However, there were marked differences between the provinces. In North Maluku, approximately 79 per cent of the population was Muslim, 20 per cent Protestant and 1 per cent Catholic. Most Protestants and Catholics resided in urban areas; their share of the total urban population was 32 per cent in the case of Protestants and 2 per cent in the case of Catholics. But in new Maluku, only 44 per cent of the population was Muslim, while 49 per cent were Protestant, 6 per cent were Catholic and 1 per cent belonged to other religions. Muslims made up 49 per cent of the urban population and Protestants 42 per cent. In rural areas, however, Protestants (58 per cent) significantly outnumbered Muslims (38 per cent).

Most migrants are Muslim. But if we recall that migrants comprise only 6 per cent of the Maluku population — not enough to skew the data strongly in their favour — the religious composition of the two provinces just described would seem to be a fair representation of the religious composition of the indigenous population of Maluku.

Social Conditions

Social indicators for Maluku improved slowly until 1999, then slid backwards. However, they have never been as bad as in some other regions, notably East and West Nusa Tenggara, West Kalimantan, Southeast Sulawesi and Papua. Maluku's score on the human development index (HDI) rose from 64.1 in 1990 to 67.2 in 1999 before falling back to 66.2 in 2002. In all three years its score was above the national average, of 63.4 in 1990, 64.3 in 1999 and 65.8 in 2002. In terms of its ranking among Indonesia's 26 provinces, Maluku advanced from thirteenth position in 1990 to fifth position in 1999, then fell back to thirteenth position in 2002 (BPS, Bappenas and UNDP 2001, 2004).[4] The main factor in these relatively good results was the outperformance of its education sector.

Education

Together with North Sumatra, West Sumatra and North Sulawesi, Maluku is one of the few regions outside Java to have had a relatively well-developed education sector since the Dutch colonial era (Meyer and Hardjodimedjo 1989). Its performance in education, particularly basic education, has been significantly above the national average for several decades.

In 1990, Maluku's adult literacy rate (literacy among those aged 15 and over) was 91.4 per cent and educational attainment among adults (measured by years of schooling) was 5.9 years. These were good results by Indonesian standards — better than those for West Java, for example. By 1999, the adult literacy rate had risen to 95.8 per cent (compared with a national average of 88.4 per cent) and educational attainment to 7.6 years (compared with a national average of 6.7 years). Among Indonesia's 26 provinces, Maluku ranked fourth in terms of literacy and sixth in terms of educational attainment in 1999. Even after the violence broke out, Maluku continued to notch up some of the best educational outcomes in the country: the adult literacy rate was 96.3 per cent in new Maluku and 95.6 per cent in North Maluku in 2002, while educational

---

4   Figures for the provinces of new Maluku and North Maluku have been aggregated to allow for comparisons between the pre- and post-1999 data.

attainment was 8.0 years in the former province and 8.4 years in the latter province. Moreover, adult literacy and educational attainment did not vary much across districts, with the usual exception of above-average figures for the capital, Ambon. Across islands within a district, however, variations in adult literacy and educational attainment are suspected to be relatively high. Most schools are located on the bigger islands, out of reach of the children living on smaller islands where transport links are poor (BPS 1996; BPS, Bappenas and UNDP 2004).

In higher education as well, Maluku has performed reasonably well. For example, in 2002, 22 per cent of adults aged 15 and over had at least a high school degree (compared with a national average of 20 per cent) and 1.9 per cent had a tertiary degree (compared with a national average of 2.2 per cent) (BPS 2006a).

Employment

The Maluku workforce grew at an average annual rate of 2.2 per cent between 1980 and 1999, faster than the national average of 1.8 per cent, before slowing to 1.3 per cent in 2000–02. The total workforce increased from approximately 597,000 people in 1980 to 1,514,000 people in 2002, 92 per cent of them working and the rest either unemployed or looking for work. The main source of employment was agriculture (including forestry and fisheries), which soaked up about 57 per cent of the workforce in 2002. This was followed by community, social and personal services (12 per cent) and trade, hotels and restaurants (12 per cent). The composition of the workforce differed between new Maluku and North Maluku. In new Maluku, around 66 per cent of the workforce was employed in the agricultural sector, 11 per cent in community, social and personal services, and 8 per cent in trade, hotels and restaurants. The figures for North Maluku were 42 per cent, 15 per cent and 18 per cent respectively (BPS 2003; BPS, Bappenas and UNDP 2004).

Health

Maluku has performed below the national average on health indicators. In 1996 life expectancy was 63.1 years, a little below the national average of 64.4 years. In 2002, life expectancy was 65.5 years in new Maluku and 63.0 years in North Maluku, compared with 66.2 years for the nation as a whole. The infant mortality rate in new Maluku and North Maluku combined was 66 deaths per 1,000 live births in 2000, well above the national figure of 47.[5]

---

5   There are no infant mortality data for the individual provinces as yet.

Maluku's relatively poor performance in health can be attributed to its lack of health infrastructure. In 2002, 26.1 per cent of the population of new Maluku and 42.2 per cent of the population of North Maluku had no ready access to a health care facility, compared with 23.1 per cent for Indonesia as a whole (BPS, Bappenas and UNDP 2004). Fixing this deficit clearly requires urgent attention.

3 THE ECONOMY

Growth

Since its dominance of the spice trade ended, Maluku has struggled to find other sectors to compensate. The agricultural sector, particularly forestry and fisheries, continues to play a major part in the economy, but its performance has not been impressive. Between 1975 and 1996, for example, the sector grew at only 3 per cent per annum, below the national figure of 4 per cent (BPS, various years).

Services, particularly trade services, contributed around 31 per cent of Maluku's gross domestic product (GDP) in 1975. The sector grew at an average annual rate of 13.6 per cent between 1975 and 1983, driving provincial GDP growth of 8.1 per cent (compared with 7.3 per cent for the whole of Indonesia) (BPS, various years). Although the services sector continued to grow at the respectable rate of 6.6 per cent per annum between 1984 and 1996, the main driver of GDP growth during this latter period was industry.

Industry (mining, manufacturing, utilities and construction) was the fastest growing sector between 1975 and 1996; the fastest growing industrial subsectors were the fish-processing, sawmill and plywood industries.[6] The industrial sector grew at close to 20.5 per cent per annum between 1975 and 1983, but this was from a very low base. Between 1975 and 1983, its share of provincial GDP increased from 5 per cent to 18 per cent. The sector continued to record strong growth of 15.7 per cent per annum between 1984 and 1996. The momentum in the sector during this period pushed Maluku's annual rate of GDP growth to 7.5 per cent, above the national average of 7 per cent (BPS, various years).

Thus, in the mid-1990s Maluku appeared to be making significant progress towards shifting from an agriculture-dominated economy to a more broadly based economy in which industry and services played a larger role. The share of the agricultural sector fell to just 26 per cent in

---

6 Based on information provided by Mukhtar A. Adam, lecturer, Khairun University, Ternate.

Figure 4.2   Maluku: Growth in GDP, 1994–2003 (%)[a]

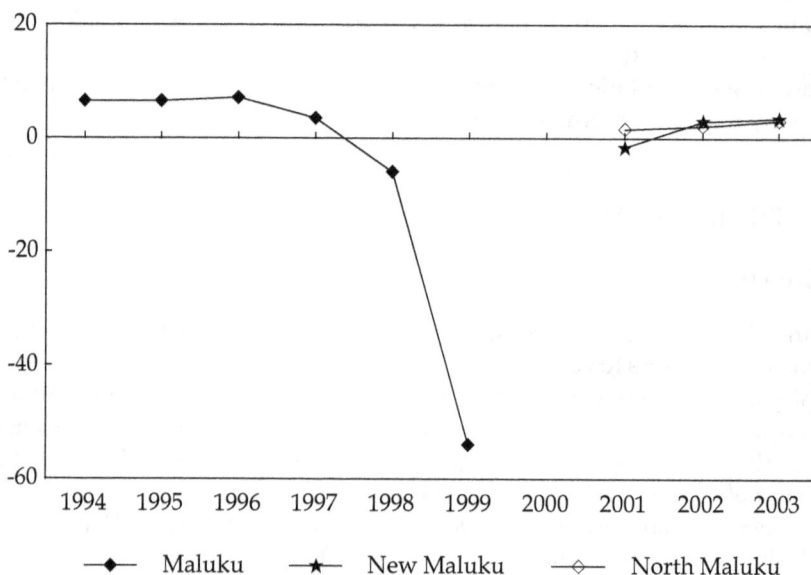

a   In 1993 constant prices.
Source: BPS (various years).

1996 – a significant reduction from 63 per cent in 1975 – while the shares of industry and services rose to 32 per cent and 42 per cent respectively (BPS, various years).

The 1997-98 Asian economic crisis and the 1999–2003 conflict in Maluku put an end to this progress. From 7.1 per cent in 1996, annual growth in GDP slowed to 3.5 per cent in 1997 and slid further to –3.5 per cent in 1998, mainly because of the crisis (Figure 4.2). Maluku's industrial sector was the hardest hit; its contribution to GDP halved from 32 per cent in 1996 to just 16 per cent in 1998. At the peak of the conflict in 1999, the GDP growth rate collapsed to –54 per cent. No other province in Indonesia has ever experienced an economic collapse on this scale – not even Aceh after the 2004 tsunami.

In 2001 (after Maluku was divided into two provinces), North Maluku recorded positive growth in GDP, while new Maluku had to wait another year to enter positive territory (Figure 4.2). Clearly this was because new Maluku (especially Ambon) was the locus of discontent during the extended period of unrest. In 2003, the GDP growth rates of both provinces stood at about 3.5 per cent, still well below the rates recorded before 1997.

Structural Change

Nearly all sectors were negatively affected by the 1997–98 economic crisis, but the situation was made much worse by the ensuing socio-political conflict. During this period activity fell in every sector. However, because most of the violence occurred in urban areas, industry and services were particularly badly affected. The speed of recovery has varied across sectors, changing the structure of Maluku's economy (Table 4.1). In 2004, the contribution of the industrial sector to provincial GDP was just 13 per cent (less than half its share in 1996), while the contribution of agriculture had increased significantly to 37 per cent.

Construction was the industrial subsector that bore the brunt of the contraction between 1996 and 2004: the economic crisis slowed activity, then the outbreak of conflict brought it to a halt. Because of the widespread damage caused by the unrest, one might have expected this subsector to recover quickly in the post-conflict period. Between 2002 and 2004, however, growth in the construction subsector was at best moderate. This suggests that the reconstruction effort is making only slow progress. Good infrastructure underpins the health of all sectors of the economy. It is therefore important that the province's damaged infrastructure be fixed as quickly as possible.

Mining was the next worst-hit subsector, as investor confidence plummeted. In addition to the national economic crisis and the unstable local conditions, investors had to cope with the regulatory uncertainties caused by the rapid shift from a centralized to a decentralized system of government in 2001. Signs of improvement can be seen in new Maluku, where growth in mining averaged 3.3 per cent in 2002–04. However, North Maluku may not experience a sustained recovery until BHP Billiton and the Indonesian company Antam are ready to develop the Buli nickel deposit on the island of Halmahera.

Manufacturing also took a pummelling as business confidence nosedived. It recorded growth of only 1.9 per cent in new Maluku and 3.4 per cent in North Maluku in 2002–04. Problems with infrastructure undoubtedly contributed to the subsector's difficulties; the reconstruction of markets, electricity, roads and telecommunications has been slow in many districts.

As one would expect, Maluku's troubles hit capital investment as well as both exports and imports (Table 4.2). As a result, the expenditure side of the economy became dominated by household and government consumption; the former expanded from 41.9 per cent in 1996 to 71.3 per cent in 2004, while the latter increased from 13.5 per cent to 25.0 per cent. After the conflict, capital investment appeared to recover faster in new Maluku than in North Maluku, growing by 11.6 per cent in 2002–04. Most of the expenditure was directed towards replacing old or dam-

Table 4.1   Maluku: Composition of GDP by Sector, 1996–2004 (%)[a]

	Maluku				New Maluku		North Maluku	
	1996	2001	2004[b]	Growth, 1997–2004	2004	Growth, 2002–04	2004	Growth, 2002–04
Agriculture	**25.7**	**36.1**	**36.5**	**−0.9**	**35.7**	**1.9**	**37.7**	**3.6**
Food crops	5.8	9.4	9.5	1.5	9.1	2.4	10.2	2.5
Estate crops	4.4	11.7	10.7	3.6	7.3	−0.8	16.5	4.5
Livestock	1.0	1.4	1.5	2.7	1.2	2.3	1.9	2.7
Forestry	6.3	2.0	2.3	−16.3	1.7	3.4	3.2	3.8
Fisheries	8.3	11.7	12.5	1.8	16.3	2.7	6.0	2.7
Mining	**6.5**	**2.7**	**2.3**	**−12.3**	**0.9**	**3.3**	**4.6**	**1.4**
Oil & gas	0.5	0.3	0.3	−7.8	0.5	2.2	n.a	n.a
Mining	4.5	1.9	1.5	−11.4	n.a	n.a	4.1	1.0
Quarrying	1.5	0.5	0.5	−18.2	0.5	4.7	0.5	6.3
Manufacturing	**17.5**	**9.2**	**8.1**	**−9.0**	**4.6**	**1.9**	**14.1**	**3.4**
Electricity & water	**0.7**	**0.6**	**0.7**	**−0.6**	**0.7**	**−0.2**	**0.6**	**12.7**
Electricity	0.6	0.5	0.6	−2.5	0.7	0.2	0.3	8.1
Clean water	0.1	0.1	0.1	6.0	0.1	−3.2	0.3	19.1
Construction	**7.8**	**1.4**	**1.5**	**−26.0**	**1.2**	**5.5**	**1.9**	**2.6**
Trade, hotels & restaurants	**19.2**	**23.5**	**24.3**	**0.0**	**25.4**	**4.9**	**22.4**	**4.3**
Trade	18.6	22.7	23.4	−0.2	24.3	4.9	22.0	4.2
Hotels & restaurants	0.7	0.8	0.9	3.0	1.1	5.5	0.4	7.3
Transport & communications	**6.0**	**7.2**	**8.4**	**3.0**	**8.7**	**11.0**	**7.8**	**3.9**
Transport	4.8	6.1	7.0	4.7	8.0	11.2	5.3	3.5
Communications	1.2	1.0	1.4	−4.4	0.7	7.6	2.5	5.2
Financial, rental & corporate services	**5.9**	**4.5**	**4.5**	**−1.9**	**5.3**	**5.2**	**3.2**	**4.7**
Banking	1.6	1.0	1.1	−2.6	1.4	5.6	0.5	5.0
Non-bank financial institutions	0.5	0.6	0.7	2.9	0.9	6.7	0.4	16.2
Rental services	3.6	2.8	2.7	−2.6	2.9	4.7	2.2	3.0
Corporate services	0.1	0.1	0.0	1.2	0.0	5.7	0.1	1.5
Other services	**10.7**	**14.9**	**13.8**	**2.8**	**17.5**	**3.3**	**7.6**	**3.1**
Government	9.4	12.9	11.9	2.7	15.6	3.3	5.6	2.9
Private	1.3	2.0	1.9	3.3	1.9	3.2	2.0	3.6
Total	**100.0**	**100.0**	**100.0**	**−2.7**	**100.0**	**3.9**	**100.0**	**3.7**

a   Sectoral composition is in current prices; growth rates are in constant 1993 prices.
b   New Maluku and North Maluku combined.
Source: BPS (various years).

Table 4.2 Maluku: GDP by Expenditure, 1996–2004 (%) [a]

	Maluku				New Maluku		North Maluku	
	1996	2001	2004[b]	Growth, 1997–2004	2004	Growth, 2002–04	2004	Growth, 2002–04
Household consumption	41.9	76.6	71.3	1.9	74.3	1.9	66.1	4.1
Non-profit organization consumption	1.1	1.8	1.7	3.8	2.1	2.7	1.0	-4.1
Government consumption	13.5	24.8	25.0	6.3	23.3	3.3	28.0	2.6
Capital investment	27.9	3.2	4.3	-28.0	4.7	11.6	3.5	2.8
Exports	47.5	29.0	33.1	-8.2	29.0	3.4	40.3	0.3
Imports	29.7	26.4	31.0	-6.8	36.4	1.2	21.8	7.9
Change in stock	-2.2	-9.0	-4.4	n.a.	3.0	n.a.	-17.1	n.a
Total	100.0	100.0	100.0		100.0		100.0	
GDP including mining (Rp billion, in current prices)[c]	3,634	4,959	6,417	-2.7%	4,048	3.9%	2,368	3.7%
GDP per capita including mining (Rp million, in current prices)[c]	1.7	2.2	3.2	-2.1%	3.3	1.7%	2.7	1.3%
GDP per capita excluding mining (Rp million, in current prices)[c]	1.6	2.1	3.1	-1.6%	3.2	1.7%	2.6	1.5%

n.a. = not available.

a Expenditure composition is in current prices; growth rates are in constant 1993 prices.

b Note that although GDP and per capita GDP increased between 1996 and 2004 in current prices, they declined in real terms.

c New Maluku and North Maluku combined.

Source: BPS (various years).

aged equipment. The fact that exports grew at a rate of 3.4 per cent in new Maluku, but just 0.3 per cent in North Maluku, supports the view that the recovery of capital investment was faster in new Maluku than in North Maluku.

The main exports from both provinces were frozen fish and plantation products such as copra and cloves. During the period of conflict, the fishery and estate-crop processing industries were hit particularly hard. Exports from these sectors dropped sharply and have been slow to recover.

4 POVERTY

The respectable performance of the Maluku economy until the mid-1990s translated into a significant reduction in the proportion of people living in poverty. In 1980, about 50 per cent of the population was assessed as being poor (that is, living below the BPS poverty line) but by 1996 this had fallen to 21 per cent (Figure 4.3). The development of small and household industries such as fish processing and sawmills seems to have been a major factor in the decline in poverty (Meyer and Hardjodimedjo 1989).

When Maluku was divided into two provinces in 1999, new Maluku was left with a far higher proportion of poor people than North Maluku. If we combine the figures for the two provinces, we find that the proportion of poor people in the whole of Maluku was 27 per cent in 2002, as the effects of the crisis and conflict were beginning to ease. That is, the proportion of poor people in the region had increased, but not by much.

In both new Maluku and North Maluku, the proportion of poor people in the large cities is typically low (Table 4.3). In 2004, 6 per cent of the Ambon population was classified as poor, and just 4 per cent in Ternate. This is low by Indonesian standards. But with the exception of Ambon, the proportion of poor people in new Maluku is consistently above 30 per cent, with the highest level occurring in the district of West Southeast Maluku (43 per cent). In contrast, the poverty rates in North Maluku are consistently *below* 30 per cent. The district of Central Halmahera had the highest rate in 2004, at just under 30 per cent.

Somewhat surprisingly, a relatively high proportion of the poor have a primary or even a secondary education (Table 4.3). This seems to contravene the conventional wisdom that increasing the number of children enrolled in primary school necessarily reduces the level of poverty. Maluku's net enrolment ratios in primary and secondary education are very high. In 2004, the ratio for primary education (number of children attending primary school to total number of children aged 7–12) was 97

Figure 4.3   Maluku: Poor People as a Share of the Total Population, 1980–2004 (%)

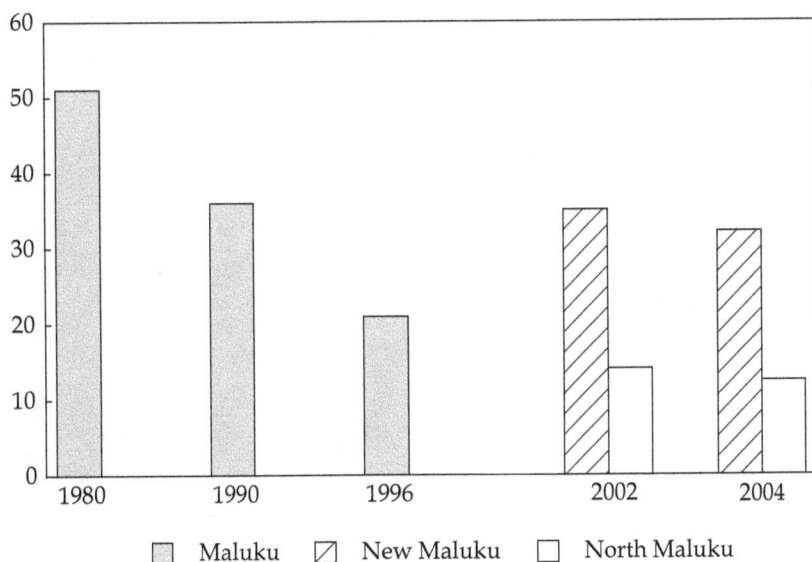

Source: BPS (various years).

per cent in new Maluku and 98 per cent in North Maluku, while the ratio for secondary education (number of children attending junior high school to total number of children aged 13–15) was 92 per cent in new Maluku and 88 per cent in North Maluku. Recall that the national averages were 93 per cent for primary education and just 60 per cent for secondary education.

Table 4.3 indicates that a large majority of poor people are working in the agricultural sector. In regions with a higher prevalence of poverty, such as Southeast Maluku and West Southeast Maluku, the proportion of poor people employed in the agricultural sector is correspondingly higher. This suggests the need for policies to assist farmers to participate in the non-farming economy, namely rural industries and services. Given the anticipated low rates of growth in the agricultural sector, this will be an important means of improving farmers' incomes and alleviating poverty.

4 FISCAL POLICY

In a region with challenging geographical conditions such as Maluku, prudent fiscal policy is critical. In particular, government spending needs

Table 4.3   *Maluku: Total Population, Proportion of Poor People and Characteristics of Poor People, 2004*

	Total Population (thousand)	Share of Poor People (%)	Educational Background of Poor			Field of Work of Poor		
			Less than Primary (%)	Primary or High School (%)	Tertiary (%)	Not Working (%)	Agriculture (%)	Non-Agriculture (%)
Maluku	**1,237**	**32.13**	**37.93**	**52.90**	**9.17**	**16.78**	**68.96**	**14.26**
West Southeast Maluku	144	43.30	37.56	49.87	12.57	15.15	74.01	10.84
Southeast Maluku	192	37.68	46.23	48.56	5.21	14.51	80.01	5.48
Central Maluku	553	38.05	33.58	57.64	8.78	18.55	65.48	15.97
Buru	121	31.55	50.62	43.42	5.96	13.50	70.64	15.86
City of Ambon	227	6.24	30.78	41.32	27.90	22.33	25.73	51.94
North Maluku	**868**	**12.42**	**47.20**	**45.89**	**6.91**	**10.20**	**69.70**	**20.10**
West Halmahera	96	15.51	52.61[a]	42.27[a]	5.12[a]	9.75[a]	64.86[a]	25.39[a]
North Halmahera	171	10.41						
South Halmahera	168	12.97						
Sula Islands	118	14.77						
Central Halmahera	32	29.61	37.36[b]	52.83[b]	9.81[b]	9.48[b]	83.62[b]	6.90[b]
East Halmahera	54	22.39						
City of Tidore	79	10.68						
City of Ternate	151	3.99	32.40	53.75	13.85	19.34	54.55	26.11

a   Includes West Halmahera, North Halmahera, South Halmahera and Sula Islands.
b   Includes Central Halmahera, East Halmahera and Tidore.
Source: BPS (2005).

to be directed at developing the basic infrastructure and human capital
needed to attract private investment. The main obstacles to developing
such a policy are two-fold. First, regional governments are spending a
higher proportion of their budgets on civil servant salaries, administration and other routine expenditures, and less on human and physical
infrastructure development. And second, a significant proportion of the
funds allocated to development is evaporating due to corruption.

The implementation of decentralization in 2001 gave regional governments far greater freedom to develop their own fiscal policies, but
also much heavier responsibilities to develop their regions. They have
been assisted in their task by higher transfers from the central government, from which they must pay the salaries of the huge number of civil
servants transferred to them from central government departments.
Naturally, routine expenditure has had to increase. But instead of limiting the size of their administrative structures to keep them small but
efficient, many local governments have unnecessarily expanded them,
typically to include the friends and families of local government officials.
The increased powers and budgets available to regional governments
are exacerbating the tendency towards corrupt behaviour. Together with
the blowout in the routine portion of the budget, this is sapping sorely
needed funds from the development budget.[7]

Table 4.4 compares government revenue in Maluku in 1999/2000 (the
financial year preceding decentralization) with that in 2001 and 2002 (the
two years after decentralization was implemented). It can be seen that
the income of new Maluku and North Maluku combined tripled between
1999/2000 and 2001. Most of the new revenue came from an expansion
of the program of block grants from the central government, channelled
through the General Purpose Fund (DAU).

In 2002, the DAU of new Maluku increased again by almost 90 per
cent, while that of North Maluku went up by only 40 per cent. The difference is attributable to the change in formula for calculating the DAU,
to place a higher weight on poverty and other indicators of development
needs. Own-source revenue increased sharply in both new Maluku and
North Maluku as their governments sought to impose new taxes. Both
provinces need to be careful: if they continue to add to the taxation burden on business, business activity will decline and their own revenues
will suffer. It is also important to note that whereas conflict-ridden provinces such as Aceh and Papua benefited from significant increases in targeted grants under the Specific Purpose Fund (DAK), Maluku did not.
That is, despite the destruction delivered on the local economy by the

---

7 Similar problems are identified in the chapters on Papua in this book and in
 Resosudarmo and Kuncoro (2006).

Table 4.4   *Maluku: Government Budget, 1999/2000, 2001 and 2002*
           (Rp billion)

	Maluku 1999/ 2000	New Maluku		North Maluku	
		2001	2002	2001	2002
TOTAL INCOME	**435.1**	**645.9**	**1,325.1**	**664.0**	**934.7**
Transfer from previous year	**6.0**	**30.0**	**180.6**	**16.1**	**75.7**
Own revenue	**15.6**	**13.8**	**43.1**	**16.1**	**30.1**
Regional tax	6.8	1.9	16.4	5.4	12.0
Levies & other income	8.8	11.9	26.7	10.7	18.1
Transfer from the centre	**405.4**	**566.8**	**1,081.0**	**568.7**	**799.2**
Tax revenue sharing	41.7	30.7	61.5	33.7	47.4
Non-tax revenue sharing	12.5	3.1	17.8	35.8	69.5
SDO/DAU[a]	182.9	528.7	992.4	476.7	668.6
Inpres/DAK[a]	168.3	4.3	9.3	22.5	13.8
Other	**8.1**	**35.3**	**20.4**	**63.1**	**29.7**
TOTAL EXPENDITURE	**407.3**	**587.7**	**1,147.4**	**585.5**	**835.0**
Routine expenditure	**232.5**	**496.7**	**820.6**	**350.7**	**517.7**
Development expenditure	**174.8**	**91.0**	**326.8**	**234.8**	**317.3**
Industry	0.2	0.8	4.4	0.7	2.7
Agriculture	4.8	4.5	31.7	12.5	35.5
Irrigation	0.3	2.2	3.8	0.2	1.2
Trade	5.6	6.0	8.8	6.3	10.6
Mining	0.3	0.5	4.3	1.1	4.9
Telecommunications	0.5	0.6	2.4	0.6	2.1
Transport	43.5	19.1	90.3	40.2	46.9
Regional development	42.7	5.1	29.1	16.2	18.0
Environment	1.2	1.3	12.1	2.5	16.0
Education	25.1	16.8	34.3	27.7	40.9
Health	13.2	7.9	16.5	33.6	28.2
Housing	14.2	15.5	33.0	49.0	46.6
Science	11.3	1.0	4.3	1.9	2.2
Judicative apparatus	0.1	0.5	1.6	0.5	1.3
Government apparatus	9.8	6.6	40.8	32.6	45.3
Security	0.7	0.8	2.3	2.3	6.2
Other	1.3	1.8	7.1	6.9	8.7

a   Figures for 1999/2000 are Autonomous Regional Subsidy (SDO) or Presidential Instruc-
    tion (Inpres) grants; figures for 2001 and 2002 are General Purpose Fund (DAU) or Spe-
    cific Purpose Fund (DAK) grants.

Source: Department of Finance (http://www.sikd.djapk.go.id/).

conflict, it appears that Maluku did not receive any special compensatory treatment from the central government.

Both new Maluku and North Maluku spent a significant proportion of their income on routine expenditure, that is, on civil servant salaries and local government administration (Table 4.4). Expenditure on government administration was of course inflated by the division of Maluku into two provinces (ICG 2007).

New Maluku was the region most affected by the unrest, and consequently the one most in need of higher than usual development allocations. Nevertheless, it allocated only 15 per cent of its total expenditure to development in 2001, rising to 28 per cent in 2002. This was far less than North Maluku, which allocated 40 per cent to development in 2001 and 38 per cent in 2002. The higher spending on development in North Maluku is likely to induce a faster recovery there than in new Maluku.

The breakdown shown in Table 4.4 indicates that both provinces spent similar proportions on the various components of the development budget. The large expenditures on government apparatus (mainly buildings) provide another indication of the expansion in the size of the civil services and administrative activities of both provinces.

Both new Maluku and North Maluku need to reel back their routine expenditures and spend more on development. Developing and maintaining infrastructure such as roads, ports, markets and utilities should be the main priority. At the same time, when implementing infrastructure projects, both provincial governments need to ensure that administrative costs and losses due to corruption are minimized.

5 CONCLUDING REMARKS

Maluku continues to be counted among Indonesia's backward regions. However, this does not mean that there has been no progress. In fact, from the mid-1970s until the mid-1990s, Maluku progressed quite well on several fronts: GDP grew at an average rate of 7.5–8 per cent per annum; the proportion of poor people declined from 50 per cent in 1980 to 20 per cent in 1996; and at the end of the 1990s Maluku ranked fifth among Indonesia's 26 provinces on the HDI.

The main engines of growth from the mid-1970s through mid-1990s were the industrial and service sectors. During that period Maluku made steady progress in shifting its economy from agriculture to industry and services—a pattern typical of a successful region (Hill 1989). Nevertheless, in 1996 Maluku was still categorized as a backward region.

In the late 1990s the direction of progress suddenly reversed as Maluku experienced its share of the chaos created by the Asian economic crisis, then succumbed to socio-political unrest. When the conflict of 1999–2003 finally receded, Maluku's economy was in a state of near-collapse: the industrial sector had been destroyed and much of the region's basic infrastructure was defunct. In 1999, Maluku was split into two provinces: 'new' Maluku and North Maluku.

There is reason to hope that new Maluku and North Maluku will get back on track. First, government transfers to the region have increased significantly. These funds need to be spent wisely and efficiently, particularly on the infrastructure needed for the economy to function well, such as transport, markets and utilities. Second, conflict resolution has been progressing (see Chapter 12). And third, Maluku has relatively well-developed human capital, better than in many other regions in Indonesia.

But Maluku also faces several challenges. First, despite being a post-conflict region like Papua and Aceh, Maluku has not received extra assistance from the national government in the form of increased central government transfers. Second, both Maluku governments still spend a large proportion of their budgets on salaries and administration rather than development. Third, repairing and replacing damaged infrastructure will take time, and restoring investor confidence will take even longer. Fourth, the creation of additional districts has been costly in terms of absorbing government funds that could have been used to provide badly needed infrastructure, and has disrupted existing development programs. Hence, it will be some time yet before Maluku returns to its former growth trajectory.

ACKNOWLEDGMENTS

The author would like to thank Mukhtar A. Adam of Khairun University, Ternate, and Craig Thorburn of Monash University, Melbourne, for their useful suggestions and comments, and Ditya A. Nurdianto and Yogi Vidyattama for their research assistance. Any mistakes remain the author's responsibility.

REFERENCES

BPS (Badan Pusat Statistik) (various years), *Statistik Indonesia* [Statistics of Indonesia], Jakarta.
BPS (Badan Pusat Statistik) (1981), *Penduduk Indonesia: Hasil Sensus Penduduk Tahun 1980* [Population of Indonesia: Results of the 1980 Population Census], Jakarta.

BPS (Badan Pusat Statistik) (1991), *Penduduk Indonesia: Hasil Sensus Penduduk Tahun 1990* [Population of Indonesia: Results of the 1990 Population Census], Jakarta.

BPS (Badan Pusat Statistik) (1996), *Laporan Indeks Pembangunan Manusia 1996* [Report on the 1996 Human Development Index], Jakarta.

BPS (Badan Pusat Statistik) (2001), *Penduduk Indonesia: Hasil Sensus Penduduk Tahun 2000* [Population of Indonesia: Results of the 2000 Population Census], Jakarta.

BPS (Badan Pusat Statistik) (2003), *Keadaan Angkatan Kerja Indonesia 2002* [The Labour Force Situation in Indonesia, 2002], Jakarta.

BPS (Badan Pusat Statistik) (2005), *Data dan Informasi Kemiskinan Tahun 2004* [Data and Information on Poverty, 2004], Jakarta.

BPS (Badan Pusat Statistik) (2006a), *Penduduk Indonesia: Hasil Survei Penduduk Antara Sensus Tahun 2005* [Population of Indonesia: Results of the 2005 Inter-censal Survey], Jakarta.

BPS (Badan Pusat Statistik) (2006b), *Statistik Indonesia* [Statistics of Indonesia], Jakarta.

BPS, Bappenas and UNDP (Badan Pusat Statistik, Badan Perencanaan Pembangunan Nasional and United Nations Development Programme) (2001), *Indonesia Human Development Report 2001. Towards a New Consensus: Democracy and Human Development in Indonesia*, Jakarta.

BPS, Bappenas and UNDP (Badan Pusat Statistik, Badan Perencanaan Pembangunan Nasional and United Nations Development Programme) (2004), *Indonesia Human Development Report 2004. The Economics of Democracy: Financing Human Development in Indonesia*, Jakarta.

Brown, G., C. Wilson and S. Hadi (2003), *Overcoming Violent Conflict: Peace and Development Analysis in Maluku and North Maluku*, CPRU-UNDP, LIPI and Bappenas, Jakarta.

Duncan, C.R. (2005a), 'The Other Maluku: Chronologies of Conflict in North Maluku, Eastern Indonesia', *Indonesia*, 80: 53–80.

Duncan, C.R. (2005b), 'Unwelcome Guests: Relations between Internally Displaced Persons and Their Hosts in North Sulawesi, Indonesia', *Journal of Refugee Studies*, 18(1): 25–46.

Hill, H. (ed.) (1989), *Unity and Diversity: Regional Economic Development in Indonesia since 1970*, Oxford University Press, Oxford and Singapore.

ICG (International Crisis Group) (2007), 'Indonesia: Decentralisation and Local Power Struggles in Maluku', Asia Briefing No. 64, Brussels.

Meyer, P.A. and M. Hardjodimedjo (1989), 'Maluku: The Modernization of the Spice Islands', in H. Hill (ed.), *Unity and Diversity: Regional Economic Development in Indonesia since 1970*, Oxford University Press, Oxford and Singapore, pp. 548–65.

Monk, K.A., Y. de Fretes and G. Reksodiharjo-Lilley (1997), *The Ecology of Nusa Tenggara and Maluku*, Periplus Editions, Singapore.

Pariela, T.D. (2007), 'Political Process, Public Policy, and Peace Building Process: Case of Ambon City, Maluku', in K. Matsui (ed.), *Regional Development Policy and Direct Local-Head Election in Democratizing East Indonesia*, ASEDP No. 76, IDE-JETRO, Chiba, pp. 101–23.

Resosudarmo, B.P. and A. Kuncoro (2006), 'The Political Economy of Indonesian Economic Reform: 1983–2000', *Oxford Development Studies*, 34(3): 341–55.

van Klinken, G. (2001), 'The Maluku Wars', *Indonesia*, 71: 1–26.

5 SOCIO-ECONOMIC CONDITIONS AND POVERTY ALLEVIATION IN EAST NUSA TENGGARA

Colin Barlow and Ria Gondowarsito

East Nusa Tenggara (Nusa Tenggara Timur, or NTT) is the poorest province in Indonesia and one of the poorest regions of the world. Situated far from the main centres of national economic activity, its economy is based on subsistence agriculture. In 2004 it had 17 districts (*kabupaten*), 194 subdistricts (*kecamatan*) and 2,599 villages (*desa*), each with 4–5 hamlets (*dusun*) (BPS NTT 2008); Map 5.1 shows the major divisions. The province encapsulates major variations in culture between its different regions. Since poverty is concentrated in the rural areas where most people live, efforts to improve living standards must focus there.

This chapter first reviews the economic, social, political, geographical and agricultural circumstances of East Nusa Tenggara, concentrating on rural areas. It highlights key features in each sphere and their implications for further development. It then turns to poverty alleviation, discussing approaches to socio-economic improvement and how the latter might best be achieved.

1 THE ECONOMY AND RELATED ASPECTS

In 2003, East Nusa Tenggara had the lowest gross domestic product (GDP) of all eastern Indonesian provinces except North Maluku and Maluku, despite growing at the relatively high real rate of 5.1 per cent per annum over the two decades to 2003 (Table 5.1). Growth in GDP was set back only slightly by the 1997 crisis, owing to the dominance of agriculture. The province's GDP per capita of Rp 2,626,200 (in current prices) in 2003

Map 5.1   East Nusa Tenggara

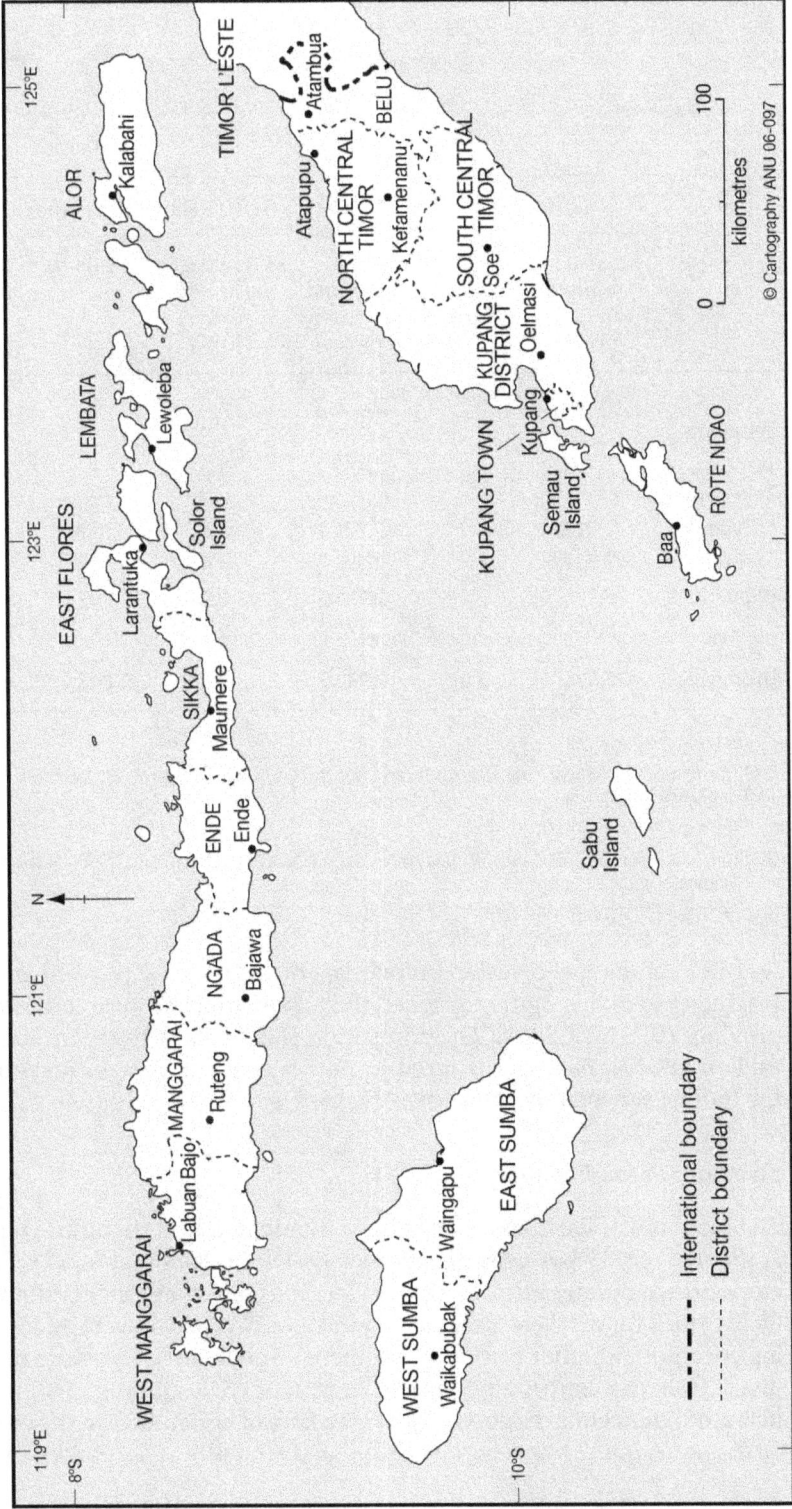

WEST MANGGARAI

Labuan Bajo

MANGGARAI

Ruteng

NGADA

Bajawa

ENDE

Ende

SIKKA

Maumere

EAST FLORES

Larantuka

Solor Island

LEMBATA

Lewoleba

ALOR

Kalabahi

TIMOR L'ESTE

Atapupu

Atambua

BELU

NORTH CENTRAL TIMOR

Kefamenanu

SOUTH CENTRAL TIMOR

Soe

KUPANG DISTRICT

Oelmasi

KUPANG TOWN

Kupang

Semau Island

ROTE NDAO

Baa

Sabu Island

WEST SUMBA

Waikabubak

Waingapu

EAST SUMBA

N

8°S

10°S

119°E   121°E   123°E   125°E

International boundary

District boundary

0   100

kilometres

© Cartography ANU 06-097

Table 5.1   East Nusa Tenggara and Selected Provinces: GDP,[a] per Capita GDP and Population

Province	GDP (2003)		Per Capita GDP (2003)		Population (2004)	
	(Rp million, in 1993 prices)	Growth rate (% p.a.)[b]	(Rp thousand, in current prices)	Growth rate (in 1993 prices) (% p.a.)[c]	(million)	Growth rate (% p.a.)[d]
E. Nusa Tenggara	3,480.9	5.1	2,626.2	4.2	4.1	1.6
W. Nusa Tenggara	5,104.3	5.3	3,959.2	1.3	4.3	1.8
N. Maluku	918.6	2.2	2,776.4	2.6	0.8	2.0
Maluku	1,361.6	1.7	3,099.2	3.4	1.2	1.8
Papua	9,179.8	3.2	1,818.5	–0.2	2.4	3.0
Bali	8,314.5	3.3	8,172.7	2.4	3.3	1.2
Indonesia	**412,696.7**	**3.0**	**7,942.7**	**2.8**	**217.8**	**1.6**

a   Including oil and gas.
b   Figures are for 2000–03 for all provinces except East Nusa Tenggara, and 1980–2003 for East Nusa Tenggara.
c   Figures are for 2000–03.
d   Figures are for 1980–2004 for all provinces except North Maluku, and 2000–04 for North Maluku.
Source: BPS NTT (2004); BPS (2005).

was also among the lowest in Indonesia, although the 4.2 per cent annual real increase in this figure exceeded that of any other eastern Indonesian province (BPS NTT 2004). The population of East Nusa Tenggara was 4.1 million in 2004, having advanced at 1.6 per cent per year, or just above the Indonesian average, since 1980 (Table 5.1).

Structure of the Economy

The economy of East Nusa Tenggara is dominated by agriculture, which accounted for 35 per cent of provincial GDP in 2003 (Table 5.2). Food crops grown mainly for subsistence were the chief component, followed by livestock for markets elsewhere in Indonesia. Non-food crops, including coconut and other tree and fruit crops, were among the more minor items. Fisheries contributed only 3 per cent of GDP, although fish products are significant in exports. While the share of agriculture in provincial GDP has declined, this sector has expanded annually at 3.2 per cent, with

*Table 5.2   East Nusa Tenggara: Composition of GDP, 1993 and 2003
           (% of total)*

Sector	1993	2003	Average Annual Growth Rate, 1993–2003 (in 1993 prices)
Agriculture	40.4	34.8	3.2
Food crops	22.3	18.8	3.3
Non-food crops	4.2	3.8	3.6
Livestock	9.5	8.6	4.0
Forestry	1.0	0.4	0.8
Fisheries	3.5	3.2	3.7
Mining	1.9	1.1	1.9
Manufacturing	2.4	2.3	4.4
Electricity & water	1.6	1.0	7.5
Construction	8.0	5.8	2.0
Trade	12.4	14.3	6.5
Transport	9.1	10.9	7.0
Banking & business	4.4	3.8	3.8
Services	19.8	26.0	8.0

Source: BPS NTT (2004).

livestock growing the fastest. Almost all of those enaged in agriculture are smallholders.

Agriculture is followed in importance by services, which accounted for 26 per cent of GDP in 2003. The services sector has advanced faster than other sectors, and its share has risen substantially. Most services are provided by government, with only 5–6 per cent being of private origin. Trade in agricultural crops follows services in importance. It comprised 14 per cent of provincial GDP in 2003, and is again growing in share. Transport, with 11 per cent of GDP, is also expanding, while the share of construction, with 6 per cent in 2003, tends to vary depending on economic conditions. The biggest single item in construction is roads and bridges, followed by non-residential works.

Manufacturing comprises only 2 per cent of GDP but is advancing steadily. It is concentrated in metal products, plastics, printing and other items for the local market. It also includes the weaving of cloth (*tenun ikat*) by village women—an important rural activity and in some cases a major source of revenue. There is a small and declining mining sector, involving the quarrying of sand, marble and other items. There is no oil and gas in the province, which plays no part in exploiting the Timor Sea reserves between Indonesia and Australia.

East Nusa Tenggara is a typical remote economy dependent on primary production. Although insulated against global market pressures by subsistence farming, it is vulnerable to fluctuating prices for cattle, coffee, other tree products and fish. Efforts at improvement must necessarily focus on agriculture and associated aspects, and especially on improving yields and marketing. There is considerable potential for advances in these areas, as will be explored below.

Trade and Prices

Trade revolves around agriculture, and at the most basic level is concentrated in small regional and often periodic markets. These in turn are linked to markets in bigger centres, such as Atambua, Soe, Kefamenanu, Waingapu, Waikabubak, Maumere, Ende, Bajawa, Ruteng and Larantuka (see Map 5.1). Goods going to and coming from these places pass through adjacent ports with connections to Surabaya, Makassar, Jakarta and overseas venues. The ports of Tenau near Kupang, Atapupu near Atambua and Ende in eastern Flores handle most exports and imports of goods (BPS NTT 2008), while produce emanating from or destined for Timor-Leste (East Timor) passes by road through Atambua.

The bigger markets sometimes carry out further processing of items for final consumers, but most products exported from the province are barely modified after leaving the farm. Hence fat cattle are despatched live so that they may be slaughtered according to *halal* rites in Java and elsewhere. Coconut is largely consigned as copra after being dried at the production site. Much trade takes place within the province, with rice from Kupang or Belu, for example, going to other destinations in West Timor. At the village level, and especially in remote locations, trade may be by barter, where small sellers exchange goods in kind. Kupang handles most non-agricultural trade, including trade in manufactured goods.

Exports from East Nusa Tenggara to foreign countries are exceedingly small. In total they were worth around US$17 million in 2005 (BPS NTT 2008), which was just below the average for the previous two decades. The major component in 2005 was mineral fuels and oil products going to East Timor, which earned US$14 million. These items were transshipped through West Timor from elsewhere in Indonesia. The other chief export destinations in 2005 were China, Japan and Australia, with exports comprising metals, metal articles, fish and other seafood.

Imports are even smaller than exports. They amounted to US$2.1 million in 2005 (BPS NTT 2008), under half the long-term average. They chiefly included manufactures from Japan, wheat from Australia and rice from Vietnam. But imports comprise a minor portion of the many consumer products traded in East Nusa Tenggara. Indeed, a marked change observed by the authors since they first entered the province in the late 1980s is the arrival of products from elsewhere in Indonesia. Whereas small, remote village kiosks previously sold only rice, kerosene, sugar, coffee, tea, candles and matches, by 2008 they were offering several hundred items, and sometimes even a choice of brands.

Trade in East Nusa Tenggara is generally competitive, and except in isolated places there are usually several separate dealers or players. Subject to taxes by local authorities, farm-level producer and consumer prices appear broadly fair. Considering onward transport and marketing charges, the price spread between point of production and point of consignment from East Nusa Tenggara may be considered reasonable. There is still room, however, to raise local prices through producer alliances and further processing, as argued below. The domination of trade by persons of Chinese origin is not ideal, and should be addressed by measures to open the field to others.

East Nusa Tenggara has experienced price inflation along with the rest of Indonesia. In the early 2000s the mean annual inflation rate was 13 per cent (BPS 2005), but the rate is slowing, with the year-on-year figure in 2007 being just under 10 per cent (BPS NTT 2008). Transport costs are rising at almost double the national average, while education and health cost increases are well below it. Rice prices in Kupang are the highest in Indonesia but meat prices are among the lowest.

Investment and Lending

Large Indonesian commercial groups have little interest in East Nusa Tenggara (Table 5.3). The only significant recent domestic investment, amounting to Rp 133 billion, occurred in 2004 and 2005 when a large shopping mall, an extension to the cement factory and several office and housing ventures went ahead in Kupang. These developments could presage a more active future, however, since construction appears to have been active again in 2008. Foreign investment has been minor and sporadic (Table 5.3). Small local business investment in urban centres is substantial, and with lower bank interest rates of 15–20 per cent per annum, is expanding slowly but steadily (Bank NTT 2006). Formal banking is well established in the major urban centres, and Bank Rakyat Indonesia and Bank NTT operate in the smaller market towns.

But investment in rural areas is minimal: entrepreneurs wanting to sink money in small businesses in these areas must pay at least 5 per cent *per month*. Lenders face uncertainty over outcomes, under conditions of poor information, low skill levels, high administrative costs and doubts

Table 5.3   *East Nusa Tenggara: Domestic and Foreign Investment,*
              1997–2005

Year	Domestic Investment (Rp billion)	Foreign Investment (US$ million)
1997	–	1.8
1998	–	–
1999	–	–
2000	–	6.1
2001	–	5.3
2002	–	–
2003	–	–
2004	114.3	2.4
2005	19.0	1.5[a]

a   About Rp 13.5 billion at an exchange rate of Rp 9,000/US$, the average prevailing between 1997 and 2005.

Source: BPS NTT (2008).

over repayment. The banks generally find they cannot operate profitably in the countryside. Rural finance is consequently almost entirely confined to small private lenders, credit unions and microcredit agencies operated by non-government organizations (NGOs).

Private lenders tend to restrict their investments to projects where the likelihood of failure can be minimized. Chinese investors, for example, select accessible groups of local farmers and supply them with cattle for fattening. They collect and sell the animals when they reach the right weight, paying the farmers a small proportion of the final price. They only do this in places where they are able to exercise control and maximize the prospect of a good return. Other Chinese lend selected local fishermen boats and equipment, on condition that the fishermen hand over their catch in return for a share of the proceeds. Wealthy schoolteachers, officials and businesspeople with the ability to monitor ventures may also sponsor small enterprises.

Some credit unions secure capital from the national agencies to which they are affiliated and lend it to local societies that support small enterprises. This is especially the case in Flores. The purpose of these partly voluntary organizations is social as well as commercial; they provide training in accountancy and loan management together with their other services. However, all these approaches, including those of private lenders, have only a minor impact on rural development.

Table 5.4   East Nusa Tenggara: Government Budget, 2002

Revenue/Expenditure	Rp billion
Total revenue	**3,835.76**
Transfer from the 2001 budget	714.63
Revenue derived from within East Nusa Tenggara	223.98
Transfers from the centre[a]	2,833.60
Other official revenue[b]	63.55
Total expenditure	**2,428.87**
Routine expenditure	1,890.28
Development expenditure	538.59
Industry	6.60
Agriculture & forestry	52.45
Trade	76.32
Transport	116.78
Regional development	30.59
Education	36.63
Health	34.48
Housing & settlements	32.81
Government	77.41
Other[c]	74.52

a   Almost all block grants distributed through the General Purpose Fund (DAU).
b   Comprises a mix of central and provincial sources.
c   That is, irrigation, labour, mining and energy, tourism, environment, family planning, religion, technology, law, politics and security.
Source: Bappeda NTT (2005).

Government Income and Expenditure

Total government income in East Nusa Tenggara in 2002 was Rp 3,835.8 billion (Table 5.4). Over 70 per cent comprised transfers from the centre, highlighting the reliance of the province on outside help. This income is crucial to maintaining the province's administrative apparatus, and to promoting economic and social development.

Around 78 per cent of the province's total expenditure of Rp 2,428.9 billion in 2002 was routine spending directed to maintaining the various arms of government (Table 5.4). The balance of Rp 538.6 billion was spent on development, mainly transport, government, trade, and agriculture and forestry. Smaller yet sizeable amounts were allocated to education, health, housing and settlements, and regional development. Govern-

Table 5.5   East Nusa Tenggara; Total Government Budget, 2000–03
(Rp billion)

Year	Revenue	Expenditure		
		Routine	Development	Total
2000	801.27	485.36	275.65	761.01
2001	2,215.81	1,325.97	668.98	1,994.95
2002	2,575.65	1,547.50	743.88	2,291.39
2003	2,985.20	2,100.12	885.08	2,985.20

Source: BPS (2007).

ment development expenditure dwarfed commercial investment (Table 5.3) and far exceeded financial help from other agencies (Table 5.6). It is by far the most significant element in efforts to promote poverty alleviation and economic improvement in the province. The nominal revenues and expenditures of government almost trebled between 2000 and 2001 (Table 5.5), increasing thereafter at about 10 per cent per year.

Since the implementation of decentralization in 2001, patterns of official spending in East Nusa Tenggara have largely been determined by the districts, with many transfers from the centre being made directly to this level of government. The spending patterns of districts vary depending on their socio-economic conditions and political circumstances. But in broad terms the authors judge that decentralization has benefited the province, with local governments proving better at delivering good results than the centralized New Order regime. The advantages of this big change have been offset by corruption and inexperience, however. The short-term costs of hiring new staff and building offices must also be considered. The costs of the change have been swelled by the rush to establish many new subdistricts and villages, and a few new districts. The higher costs are reflected in the sizeable figure for government expenditure shown in Table 5.4.

Other Financial Contributions

National and international NGOs, UN bodies and other official foreign entities spend substantial amounts to effect improvements in East Nusa Tenggara. Details of their contributions are given in Table 5.6. In 2004 these amounted to Rp 122.7 billion, but if contributions by other NGOs, the Churches and credit unions (for which no data are available) were included, the total would exceed Rp 160 billion. All agencies work

*Table 5.6   East Nusa Tenggara: Expenditure by Other Agencies, 2004
(Rp million)*

Agency	Annual Expenditure
International NGOs[a]	
World Vision Indonesia	55,000
CARE International	18,250
Catholic Relief Service	8,828
CCF Indonesia	8,645
Oxfam Great Britain	4,300
Global Fund	2,249
Subtotal	**97,272**
Local NGOs[a]	
Alfa Omega	607
Increase	82
Subtotal	**689**
UN bodies	
United Nations Population Fund (UNFPA)	3,000
United Nations Children's Fund (UNICEF)	1,869
United Nations High Commissioner for Refugees (UNHCR)	750
International Labour Organization (ILO)	400
Subtotal	**6,019**
Other foreign entities	
GTZ Health	6,300
GTZ Water	3,000
Australian Agency for International Development (AusAID) Schools	6,234
Australian Agency for International Development (AusAID) Access	898
Post-Crisis Program for Participatory Integrated Development in Rainfed Areas (PIDRA)[b]	1,344
World Bank[c]	960
Subtotal	**18,736**
Total (all agencies)	**122,716**

a   The figures exclude expenditures by some prominent international NGOs (notably Plan International and Swiss Contact), all small international NGOs, many local NGOs, the Churches and credit unions. The contributions of these agencies would add at least Rp 40 billion to the total.

b   Largely financed by the International Fund for Agricultural Development.

c   Mainly for the Kecamatan Development Program.

Source: Bappeda NTT (2005).

mainly in rural areas, undertaking small-scale developments in health, education, income-earning projects and trade.

International NGOs make by far the biggest single contribution in this category. Among them, World Vision Indonesia (WVI) and CARE International are easily the most prominent. The United Nations Children's Fund (UNICEF) and the United Nations Population Fund (UNFPA) have the largest budgets among the UN bodies, while the German and Australian aid agencies, GTZ and AusAID, are important among foreign government entities. Although comprehensive details for earlier years are not available, the 2004 expenditure levels can be considered typical of those in the 2000s. The total expenditure by all these agencies in 1983–2004 is estimated to be Rp 1,371 billion in 2004 prices (Bappeda NTT 2005), giving an average of Rp 54.8 billion per year.

Population and Workforce

The province's low population density, of just 87 persons per square kilometre in 2003, reflects the vast areas of widely scattered villages where most people live. The density varies between districts, and ranges from 28 persons per square kilometre in infertile East Sumba to 169 in Sikka with its productive volcanic soils. The average household consists of 4.6 persons, a decline from 5.3 persons in 1990 but still the highest of any province in Indonesia. These and other population and income statistics are derived from BPS NTT (2004, 2008) and BPS (2005).

In 2004, almost half of East Nusa Tenggara's population of 4.1 million persons was recorded as having worked during the previous week: 73 per cent in agriculture, forestry and fisheries, 11 per cent in trade, hotels and restaurants and 7 per cent in public services. Indeed, in that year 77 per cent of the working population was classed as economically active, a higher proportion than in any other Indonesian province and above the national average of 67 per cent. This situation reflects the employment opportunities presented by large areas of land, as well as the constant pressure to maintain basic subsistence levels. Wage rates in agriculture are low – Rp 8,000–9,000 per day in the areas studied by the authors in 2008. The average household spent Rp 100,000–200,000 per month in 2003. However, there was a substantial group with far lower expenditure, reflecting widespread poverty.

Many younger workers seek jobs elsewhere in Indonesia, as well as in Malaysia, Singapore and other overseas locations. This is particularly true of people from Flores, who mainly go to Sarawak and Sabah. The men tend to work in plantations, construction, industry and services such as restaurants and security. The women are usually employed as domestic servants, including as nannies and housekeepers. While people going to other parts of Indonesia may settle and never come back, those proceeding overseas normally stay for a series of periods, returning several times prior to their final homecoming.

Comprehensive statistics on migration are not available, partly because of the high levels of illegal migration to Malaysia in particular. But 170,000 individuals are recorded as having left East Nusa Tenggara in 2000, with 106,000 returning (BPS NTT 2008). Both the numbers leaving the province and the numbers remaining outside the province have risen since 2000. Most migrants send remittances back home, and this generates substantial revenue. Further background on migration from Flores is given in Mantra (1998) and Williams (2005).

Infrastructure

Despite steady improvements, infrastructure and services outside the chief municipalities remain poor. The road system is among the worst in Indonesia, although it is being improved slowly. The big highway from Kupang to Atambua on the border of East Timor is well maintained. But interior roads are frequently unsealed, irregularly serviced, and often impassable during the annual 3–4-month rainy season. Indeed, most locations off the Kupang–Atambua highway, and a few other main routes, can only be accessed by four-wheel drive or motorcycle, even in dry weather.

With the exception of Kupang, Atapupu and Ende, the ports are barely developed; even the largest one in Kupang is not properly equipped to handle containers, although facilities are being constructed. These three ports, along with Waingapu in East Sumba, Larantuka in East Flores and Maumere in Sikka, are equipped to service passengers using interisland ferries; there were 1.7 million such passengers in 2005 (BPS NTT 2008). However, ferry use is dropping as people take advantage of the lower air fares accompanying the entry of new airlines.

As elsewhere in Indonesia, telecommunications have improved vastly with the arrival of mobile phones, and many repeater stations are being erected. Most people now have some access to a phone, although in general inhabitants of rural areas still would not own a mobile. Electricity generation and supply also have far to go. In 2003 only 33 per cent of the province's 812,200 households were connected to the electricity grid (BPS NTT 2004), and the city of Kupang and its environs consumed 40 per cent of all electricity produced. The districts of South Central Timor, North Central Timor and Alor in particular had low rates of electricity connection. Again, the fact that a village has an electricity connection does not mean that all households have access to it. The authors observe from extensive travel throughout the province that only 15–20 per cent of richer families in connected villages actually use electricity. Others rely primarily on small lamps comprising a wick dipped in kerosene. Although many villagers own bigger lamps with pumps, these are luxuries used only on special occasions.

The absence of water facilities is a major problem for those living outside the major centres. In 2003 only 17 per cent of households in East Nusa Tenggara, mainly those in towns, had access to piped water, while a further 27 per cent had access to a nearby well. The remaining 56 per cent had to walk to the nearest spring or river, which was often several kilometres away. Many wells dry up late in the dry season, which runs from August to October. The problem of water scarcity is particularly acute in the districts of Belu, Kupang, South Central Timor, North Central Timor and Lembata.

Education and Health

Over 79 per cent of the province's 806,000 school students were attending primary school in 2003, with the balance attending junior or senior high school (BPS NTT 2004). But in the same year, 43 per cent of the 3 million persons aged 10 years and over had either not attended or not completed primary school. A further 34 per cent had completed primary school only, while 21 per cent had finished high school and the remaining 2 per cent had attended a tertiary institution. The lack of schooling is reflected in the authors' experience; during our vists we usually find that only two or three of the 15–20 persons in each small cooperative can read and write, especially in upland West Timor.

Yet education is improving steadily, with local communities and government establishing new kindergartens, primary schools and high schools in many places. The situation in rural areas is again far worse than in the towns, especially in certain districts. Thus, 41 per cent of people in West Sumba, and almost as high a proportion in South Central Timor, North Central Timor and Kupang, were illiterate in 2003. An appraisal of primary schooling in East Nusa Tenggara is presented by Daliyo et al. (1999).

Health services are poor but improving. While each district has a general hospital and there are a few private and army hospitals, in 2003 the province had only 1,994 beds for over 4 million people (BPS NTT 2004). In addition there were 222 community health centres (*puskesmas*), 765 sub-*puskesmas* and 139 mobile health centres. Most main *puskesmas* had an attending doctor, albeit not always full-time. The authors have observed that the sub-*puskesmas* are often short of drugs and understaffed in rural areas, although personnel clearly do their best. Finally, in 2003 there were 6,951 integrated health posts (*posyandu*), catering especially for nursing mothers and children and sometimes numbering several in each village. These are run by trained volunteers and have proved very effective at providing maternal and child health services.

East Nusa Tenggara has one of the highest incidences of illness in Indonesia. In 2004, 37 per cent of the population had experienced one or more health problems during the previous month, compared with a national average of 27 per cent (BPS 2005). The proportion varied greatly between areas, from only 17 per cent in Kupang to a high of 54 per cent in Manggarai. Life expectancy is low; the provincial average is 57 years.

Health services may nonetheless be seen as advancing slowly under generally good management. This matches the comments of Mboi (1996) that 'trends in a number of critical fields are promising' (p. 189) despite 'daunting ... complications of logistics' (p. 191). Indeed, the problems of poor access and manifold other difficulties apply to all areas of development in East Nusa Tenggara, and should be recalled in discussions of improvement. Appropriate measures to improve public infrastructure and services will always be a key part of any poverty alleviation policy.

2 SOCIAL AND POLITICAL ASPECTS

East Nusa Tenggara is one of the most ethnically plural provinces in Indonesia. Its many ethnic groups include two in West Timor, five on the islands of Sumba, Sabu, Alor, Rote and Semau, and eight in Flores. These groups arrived from disparate parts of eastern Asia and the Pacific islands in migrations over several thousand years. Most people are farmers, although those from Rote, Sabu and Flores have done well in government and the bureaucracy, and tend to dominate public affairs. There are also small groups of Chinese. These include the 'black' Chinese or *Cina hitam*, who arrived centuries ago and were absorbed into local communities, and the Chinese traders in urban centres who arrived in the early twentieth century. There are, too, Bugis from Sulawesi, who are active in trading and often maintain connections with their places of origin.

Each ethnic group has a separate language (Ethnologue 2007). Dawan is spoken by the largest group in East Nusa Tenggara, the Atoni in South and North Central Timor. Tetun is used by the people of Belu and many residents of East Timor. People in eastern Sumba speak Kambera; those on the southwest coast of the island employ Anakalangu; and those in the western interior use Wejewa. Manggarai is spoken by a large number of people in western Flores, and Riung is the medium on the north coast of eastern Flores.

Many of the languages are similar but not mutually comprehensible. For example, Anakalangu is 'close to, but unintelligible to speakers of Wejewa' (Ethnologue 2007). Most languages have many dialects, and these are comprehended by nearly all in the language group. Hence Manggarai has 43 dialects and Tetun 19. Sometimes different languages are spoken in adjacent places, and the people living in the area master both. This is true, for example, of the Helongese in north Semau and the Rotinese in the south of that island. Nearly everyone under 50–60 years of age is fluent in Bahasa Indonesia, and this is the primary language of communication with outsiders. Yet because language is so vital to understanding, it is highly advantageous for outsiders to be able to speak both Indonesian and the local dialect. A comprehensive atlas covering the more than 40 languages in East Nusa Tenggara has been produced by Asher and Moseley (2007).

These ethnic and linguistic differences are paralleled by societal and cultural differences. Yet the fundamental socio-cultural characteristics of all the province's societies are essentially similar, with traditional leadership primarily defined by genealogical territory. First-comers to a location possess key land rights, while more recent arrivals have less entitlement. The social arrangements in each village revolve around kinship groups that govern day-to-day affairs, and traditional life is regulated by customary laws (*adat*). While *adat* has lost ground under the influence of government and the Church, it is still important. But the distinctions that used to exist between aristocrats, commoners and slaves were chiefly lost in the twentieth century, especially following independence.

The principal kinship group in East Nusa Tenggara is the clan. Together with older kinspersons, the head of the clan manages traditional activities. Each group has rites and procedures involving land, marriage, burial, inheritance, labour exchange, environmental management and other key functions, and it is in these aspects that divergences arise. While clans in a village or adjacent villages usually operate similarly, those in different regions do not. Fox (1977), for instance, compares the ecologically balanced and stable farming systems involving lontar palm on the islands of Sabu and Rote, with the exploitative shifting cultivation arrangements of mainland Timor. And Vel (1994) scrutinizes the distinctive organization of activity in Lawonda in north Sumba, noting the considerable differences from other locations with respect to land tenure, land use and work patterns.

All clans in East Nusa Tenggara practise extensive cooperation, forming groups (*kelompok*) of 10–15 families to undertake farming and household tasks. But the authors have observed that the nature of cooperation varies from place to place. For example, local clan members in the subdistrict of Kewapante (in Sikka) strongly emphasize combining in *kelompok* to undertake joint improvements. They always attend meetings to discuss what needs to be done, and an active community view prevails. In contrast, clan members in the subdistrict of South Amanaban (in South Central Timor) are less concerned with group decision making. While they do patronize *kelompok* meetings, these tend to be dominated by a few persons who essentially determine what will be done. People on Semau island are even more individualistic, with only those directly concerned attending discussions of new initiatives, and many farmers operating largely on their own account. The Semau people are the best informed of all the communities mentioned; nearly everyone is literate, and they also benefit from their island's closeness to Kupang. Such differences in behaviour need to be carefully recognized by interveners in community development.

Religion

The institutions and observances of the Roman Catholic Church have slowly penetrated East Nusa Tenggara since Portuguese Dominicans first came to Solor island in 1561. The expansion of the Church initially accompanied trade, being facilitated first by the Portuguese and later by sympathetic Dutch authorities. The Protestant Church took longer to establish a foothold, but it advanced rapidly in the twentieth century as the mainstream Calvinist Church of Timor (GMIT) came to dominate southern West Timor and most islands except Flores and Solor. Pentecostal Protestantism spread quickly in the late twentieth century but is still not significant. Today, 55 per cent of the province's population is Roman Catholic, 32 per cent Protestant (largely GMIT) and 9 per cent Muslim, with the balance being Buddhist and Hindu (BPS NTT 2004). The adherents of these faiths are swelled by the edict that all Indonesians must have a religion, although a backlog of animistic beliefs continues to influence most people's behaviour.

The Churches are a major element of life in East Nusa Tenggara, and congregations put substantial personal resources into the big new buildings springing up throughout the province. The weekly services and other activities of the pastors (the Catholic *romo* and Protestant *pendeta*) play a major role in people's lives. The Churches run some 30 per cent of all schools, although in the last few decades the resources for these schools have increasingly come from government. Many NGOs involved in development activities in East Nusa Tenggara have religious connections, and the largest NGO of all, World Vision Indonesia, is strongly Protestant. The religiosity of local communities certainly facilitates the work of such NGOs, while assisting their overseas fundraising. Webb (1986) appraises the role of the Churches in socio-economic development in East Nusa Tenggara.

Politics and Government

Provincial, district and subdistrict politics and government have changed dramatically since the advent of democracy in the late 1990s and the implementation of decentralization in the early 2000s. Throughout Indonesia, the centralized and autocratic system of the New Order has largely been dismantled, reducing the power of central and provincial authorities and increasing that of the district head (*bupati*) and district officials. The change has not been as dramatic in East Nusa Tenggara as in the richer provinces, however, due to continuing high remittances from the centre (Table 5.4). Thus, in East Nusa Tenggara the provincial government is still important in formulating overall development policies and in transmitting initiatives from Jakarta. The *bupati* is nevertheless a key figure, especially because he or she usually heads the dominant party in the local legislature and is directly elected. The office and staff of the *bupati* are important in determining the nature of government improvements in their districts, and NGOs and others delivering development assistance rely heavily on their approval and assent.

The activities of politicians, especially those belonging to the major parties, are a significant new influence on provincial and district affairs. East Nusa Tenggara's provincial and local parliaments, as well as its national representatives, are dominated by Golkar and the Indonesian Democratic Party of Struggle (PDI-P). The former secured slightly more votes in the 1999 and 2004 elections and has a majority both provincially and in the districts of West Timor, but PDI-P usually leads strongly in Flores. In some cases minor parties have provided critical support for particular candidates as *bupati*, and accordingly can get them to pursue special policies.

Government institutions operate alongside the traditional arrangements and activities of the Churches at the village level, and are usually the primary influence on village affairs. Indeed, the standard formats of the government and the Church impose a uniformity on village affairs, in contrast to the more variable traditional structures. The village and *dusun* heads are elected democratically by villagers for five years, along with secretaries and treasurers. Together with members of such bodies as the village development committee, they tend to be the main decision makers in village socio-economic activity. These officials have connections with their subdistrict and district superiors, hence securing new ideas about how village affairs should be organized. In the judgment of the authors, village government complements rather than competes with the traditional and religious elements of village society, with the same leaders sometimes involved in all spheres. Village government is rarely connected with provincial politics, and officials are generally chosen on merit based on village issues. Non-government interveners in development certainly need to work with these people, and at least secure their blessing for what is being proposed.

3   GEOGRAPHY AND AGRICULTURE

The extensive mountain spines and foothills of West Timor, Flores and other islands make agriculture difficult, and complicate the provision of infrastructure and services. Most areas are 'upland', although there are also quite extensive coastal plains. Much of the province experiences four months of rainfall between December and March, and a long dry season in the remaining months. Annual precipitation ranges from 1,000 millimetres in Belu to 4,000 millimetres in Manggarai, but there are large fluctuations in each region and big differences between low and high altitudes. These fluctuations often cause disastrously low crop yields; food shortages were experienced in 2003, 2005 and 2006.

But in cultivated areas the soils are often good, and given periodic fallows and organic farming, can produce well in the wet season. The soils can also support excellent dry season crops where water is available. Some regions are favoured by particularly fertile soils and beneficial microclimates. These places include the rice-growing plains of Belu, the cocoa-planted hillsides of Sikka and Ngada, the garlic-growing areas along the Timor coast, the cattle-fattening locations in Kupang district and elsewhere, and the vegetable and citrus-producing localities of upland West Timor. Details of the geography and environment of Timor are provided in the classic book by Ormeling (1956) and in the more recent volume by Monk, de Freitas and Reksodihardjo-Lilley (1997).

East Nusa Tenggara had 571,900 hectares under annual crops in 2003 (Table 5.7), most of it devoted to subsistence production. Maize is cultivated by nearly all farmers and is the staple food occupying the single largest area. Next in importance come wetland rice, cassava and dryland rice, which are also staples. Rice has grown more popular as a food in recent years, and cassava is a backstop during periods of low rainfall. Other food crops include dry season vegetables, which do well in much of the province. All these items are sold for cash once domestic food and other needs are met.

Tree crops covered 636,000 hectares in 2003. The main items were coconut, cashew nut, candlenut and coffee. Coconut is grown partly for subsistence, including to produce cooking oil, while the produce of all other trees is for sale. The areas under both annual and tree crops vary little from year to year. In 2006, for example, food crops covered 579,200 hectares (BPS NTT 2008). Tree crops are less susceptible than annuals or

Table 5.7   East Nusa Tenggara: Crop and Livestock Statistics, 2003

	Harvest Area (thousand hectares)	Yield per Hectare (tonnes)[a]
Total food crops	**571.9**	
Wetland rice	118.0	3.3
Dryland rice	58.4	2.1
Maize	257.7	2.3
Cassava	80.3	10.7
Green peas	24.6	0.8
Peanuts	13.0	1.0
Sweet potatoes	10.9	7.8
Other[b]	9.0	–
Total tree crops	**636.0**[d]	
Coconut	163.7	0.55
Cashew nut	153.2	0.39
Candlenut	85.0	0.53
Coffee	68.0	0.49
Fruit trees	44.2	–
Areca nut	38.2	0.35
Cocoa	37.2	0.71
Kapok	31.8	0.28
Cloves	11.4	0.36
Other[c]	3.3	–
Forestry	**1,809.0**	

	No. (thousand)	No. Slaughtered (thousand)
Livestock & poultry		
Cattle	513	26
Pigs	1,225	98
Goats	435	35
Buffalo	135	4
Horses	95	–
Sheep	56	5
Poultry & ducks	10,648	–

a   Of the area in production.
b   Soybeans and sorghum.
c   Vanilla, nutmeg, castor oil and pepper.
d   Excluding a large area of tamarind, for which details are not available.
Source: BPS NTT (2004).

animals to fluctuations in rainfall, and barring pests, disease and price changes, can be counted on to provide a more stable source of income. But average yields per hectare are low for both food and tree crops, leaving considerable room for the introduction of better production techniques.

Forests covered an extensive 1.8 million hectares in 2003, but they grow sparsely because of the province's dry climate. They are mainly contained in reserves for purposes of conservation.

Livestock are an important resource for the province, and cattle, pigs, goats and poultry are all widespread. The cattle are farmed for cash, with 25,000–30,000 fattened animals being consigned live to Java and elsewhere each year. Other livestock are mainly kept for domestic purposes. Because production efficiency is low, there is considerable potential for improvement. In much of East Nusa Tenggara, annual and tree crops are produced side by side with livestock, raising household returns through complementary effects and providing ecological stability. A fascinating account of the integrated agricultural system in use in the district of Sikka is provided by Metzner (1982).

Virtually all agriculture in the province is based on owner-occupied farms, each covering a few hectares with additional access to common pasture. Big enterprises occupying larger areas are rare, and the predominance of traditional tenure means that there is little opportunity for the expansion of such units. But in the authors' view, most production improvements can be realized within the framework of small farms, given adequate extension services.

Many crops are sold at local markets that can be hard to access. Barter is common, with farmers exchanging corn for chickens, for instance. But specialized marketing facilities have been established for each of the key cash crops, including rice, copra, cashew nut, coffee, cocoa, tamarind and cattle. While competitive pricing often prevails, there is still room to increase producers' market returns and this is an important thrust for developers.

4   POVERTY ALLEVIATION

Within East Nusa Tenggara, per capita GDP varies greatly between jurisdictions. In the municipality of Kupang and several other towns, it was over three times the average for other districts in 2003 (Table 5.8). It was especially low in districts with a high share of population in poverty, defined as entailing an average monthly income below Rp 100,000 per person (see also Appendix A2.1, Chapter 2). These poor districts included West Sumba, the district of Kupang, South Central Timor, North Central

Table 5.8   East Nusa Tenggara: Per Capita GDP, Population and the Extent of Poverty by District, 2003

District	Average per Capita GDP[a] (Rp thousand)	Population (thousand)	Share of Population in Poverty[b] (%)
West Sumba	1,487.2	383.2	44
East Sumba	2,411.1	195.3	12
Kupang district	1,785.5	430.2	35
South Central Timor	1,682.6	395.7	37
North Central Timor	1,807.5	201.2	30
Belu	1,883.4	334.4	21
Alor	2,078.8	165.6	28
Lembata	1,485.5	96.6	33
East Flores	2,370.9	213.6	16
Sikka	2,150.2	274.5	20
Ende	2,372.3	236.6	22
Ngada	2,237.9	237.2	15
Manggarai	1,571.7	653.3	33
West Manggarai	1,942.9	–[c]	30
Rote and Ndao	2,074.7	–[d]	29
Kupang municipality	6,373.9	255.5	11
Total	**2,248.3[f]**	**4,073.2[e]**	**29**

a In current prices.
b Percentage of persons with an income below Rp 100,000 per month (in 2003 prices).
c Included in Manggarai.
d Included in Kupang district.
e These totals do not exactly match those in Table 5.1, but are the figures presented in the quoted source.
Source: BPS NTT (2004).

Timor, Lembata and Manggarai, whose combined population in 2003 was 2.2 million or over half the provincial total. In these districts, the weighted average proportion of population in poverty was 35 per cent. They are mostly remote and highly dependent on subsistence activities. They are certainly areas to emphasize when devising poverty alleviation strategies, although there are also difficult locations elsewhere.

There are two main routes to poverty alleviation in rural East Nusa Tenggara. One is to improve infrastructure and services, and the other is to introduce improved production and marketing techniques. These routes are complementary and should be followed in parallel. They need to be undertaken in economically appropriate ways, meaning that they should be sustainable and give the best possible returns to those involved. They should also be socially pertinent to communities, relating effectively to local cultures and institutions and stimulating people to participate in change. Again, the two routes should be implemented in such a way that their impact is distributed as widely as possible, both to maximize spread effects and achieve greater equity.

These desirable features are easy to state but hard to implement. Indeed, the chequered history of efforts to secure higher living standards in East Nusa Tenggara and elsewhere (see Barlow and Gondowarsito 2006) is ample testament to the complexity of the task. On the other hand, there are numerous ways of effecting improvements in the province that would, if properly executed, greatly benefit local populations.

Infrastructure and Services

The betterment of roads, ports, the electricity grid, telecommunications and water infrastructure is a specialist task requiring professional attention. It is also important that each project should be of reasonable size, so as to secure adequate economies of scale. Accordingly, in East Nusa Tenggara as elsewhere, there is an element of infrastructure 'lumpiness', where a minimum package must be executed in each situation. This exacerbates the problem of choice in allocating scarce staff and funds among many needs, in the presence of diverse political pressures. Dealing with this problem is hard, leading sometimes to decisions that have less than optimal outcomes. For example, the official controlling rural road development in South Central Timor, the district with the worst communications in the province, told the authors that with repairs costing Rp 50–60 million per kilometre, he could only apply his upgrade package to 100–120 kilometres of roads per year. This was in circumstances where 2,000–3,000 kilometres of roads were in need of major repairs. He had in practice to choose three projects from 70 of roughly equal merit. Similar problems arose with other infrastructure.

Education and health present similar problems of choice. Although school teachers can generally be assigned where they are needed most, school buildings and materials cannot be redistributed so easily. Thousands of primary schools have deficient classrooms, furniture, toilets, wells and other facilities, and would benefit hugely from upgrading. But in practice this is undertaken in relatively few schools, where packages of funds are released for complete reconstruction and refurbishing. The same is true of health amenities. In contrast, smaller items like wells, water tanks and water reticulation systems are not as subject to lumpiness. Since less money is involved each time, these items can be distributed more widely among those in need.

With all infrastructure and services, it is advantageous to enlist community participation to ensure that the initiatives are appropriate for local circumstances. This increases the likelihood of local help and cooperation, substantially reduces costs and enhances long-run sustainability. However, the level of participation necessarily varies according to circumstances, with large specialized facilities normally entailing less community involvement than smaller ones.

Production and Marketing

With the appropriate technology, yields from subsistence maize and root crops as well as coconut, cashew nut, cocoa and other tree products can be doubled or even tripled, and the growth rates and quality of cash-earning cattle much increased. The standard of products can also be increased through better processing. Alliances among producers are a good way of achieving marketing effectiveness and raising farm-level prices. Such changes can be expected to lift both farm and provincial revenues substantially.

But because these improvements involve the deployment not only of finance but also of extension, training and technical staff, problems of lumpiness and choice arise once again. There are numerous locations and communities in East Nusa Tenggara where a good return on investment in new initiatives could be achieved, but not all can be helped. Unfortunately, only certain places can be targeted by government and other agencies.

It has been found through long experience in the social setting of East Nusa Tenggara that production and marketing improvements are best undertaken by *kelompok* consisting of 10–15 families. These manage and operate the new activities themselves under the guidance of extension officers and other interveners. As well as securing economies of scale, this mode of community interaction and participation has been shown to enhance the sustainability of projects. This is good for the wider community — because when a project becomes self-sufficient, extension staff can move on to a new group and replicate the improvement.

Approaches to Development

Approaches to development have evolved substantially over recent decades as government and other interveners have learned how best to assist rural households. In general, growing emphasis has been placed on community interaction, especially with respect to training, consultation and participation. At the same time, the volume of resources available for development has increased, and the quality and experience of government staff have improved greatly. More organizations have entered the development field, as denoted in Table 5.6. Finally, greater regional autonomy has enabled interesting experiments by particular district offices. These have sometimes led to the introduction of effective new means of intervention, replicable on a wider scale. Despite all such advances, however, the resources to back up development efforts remain grossly inadequate.

The various groups currently working to alleviate poverty in East Nusa Tenggara may be seen to have assumed distinct roles. Government, especially at the district level, has the largest resources and is therefore the most important player. It is best equipped to supply hard infrastructure and to provide education and health facilities and services. It is also well placed to assist in implementing improved production and marketing techniques, through the agricultural and technological research centres controlled by the Agricultural Development Board (Litbang Pertanian) in Jakarta and through the supply of technical staff from local Agriculture Offices (Dinas Pertanian). Government has also done a good job of promoting handicraft industries through the Industry Offices (Dinas Perindustrian). Yet it has not proved effective in general agricultural extension, partly because its resources have been insufficient to finance the necessary deployment of officers.

National and international NGOs have recently assumed a useful role in extension and training, while private credit unions are making an impact by providing funds. The substantial financial commitment of NGOs (Table 5.6), and their effectiveness in working with communities, has enabled them to sponsor many successful small improvements. UN bodies and other international government entities with less funding have also been able to contribute in specialist spheres, ranging from work on particular infrastructure projects to initiatives in education and health. The latter usually involve spheres where their expertise can back up the existing programs of the East Nusa Tenggara government.

Examples

A few examples may bring to life the contributions and adjustments to reality of these diverse groups. First, education in East Nusa Tenggara is largely in the hands of government education departments at the district and subdistrict levels. They work with the Churches to manage the province's primary and secondary schools, which cater for over 800,000 children. They are responsible both for constructing and maintaining infrastructure and for arranging teaching of the national curriculum.

However, the approaches of the various education departments frequently differ, due to the divergent attitudes of *bupati* and other local factors. Thus, while all departments face the problem of how to achieve the maximum benefit from limited funds, some have proved more effective than others. The more effective departments have allocated smaller amounts of money to given endeavours, harnessing community participation to make up the shortfall. Parents are encouraged to carry out the work themselves, using cement and other materials purchased by the school. Indeed, they have sometimes been responsible for constructing entire new schools, receiving some help from the local government but also committing substantial resources of their own. Again, certain departments have promoted far more imaginative approaches to teaching than others, building constructively on the national curriculum handed down by Jakarta.

Turning to the non-government sphere, World Vision Indonesia has generated many production and marketing improvements through its area development groups, each consisting of some 20 staff (mainly extension workers). In one region suitable for vegetable growing, for instance, it successfully introduced high-quality vegetables grown with animal compost (WVI 2002). These were sold in a neighbouring municipality through a producers' marketing group. This venture involved several years of preliminary training and extensive extension accompanied by credit, and was based on active local participation. It is now a successful commercial venture that has spread autonomously, and that is financing its activities from private sources.

Finally, the Kecamatan Development Program, a joint initiative of the World Bank and the Indonesian government, finances small village infrastructure projects, particularly rural roads, water supply facilities and educational and health facilities, in many subdistricts of East Nusa Tenggara (KDP 2007). It cooperates with other official bodies, emphasizing consultation with and active participation by local villagers through a group consultation (*musyawarah*) process. Its relatively small program in East Nusa Tenggara (Table 5.6) has tackled projects that would be too restricted for regular government agencies, again allowing small packages of improvement to be implemented in a more equitable and sustainable manner.

Not all initiatives involving community participation are successful and many problems are encountered along the way. Nevertheless, the efforts described represent a more flexible and less centralist approach to development. This approach has been adopted in light of experience, and has been facilitated by new agencies bringing fresh insights to the problems of development.

5 CONCLUSIONS

The province of East Nusa Tenggara has grown slowly over recent decades and is likely to continue to make gradual progress. Yet its basic infrastructure and education and health facilities remain poor, leading to high transport costs, widespread illiteracy and major health problems. The economy continues to be dominated by agriculture, followed by government services and trade. Some parts of the province are especially poor, and deserve particular attention. The province represents a classic case of the difficulties caused by remoteness, including lagging socio-economic development and lack of integration into the wider national economy.

East Nusa Tenggara is ethnically and culturally diverse, with many different ethnic groups and local languages. It remains a traditional society in which religion, as expressed through the Catholic and Protestant Churches, is a significant factor governing behaviour. But the institutions of tradition, government and Church appear to work together quite well at the village level, and outside organizations have found they are most effective where they adjust their activities to this structure. Much of the province is hilly upland country and East Nusa Tenggara has a long dry season. Yields and quality are poor, for both crops and animals. But there is good potential to improve this situation, especially through the application of new technologies and by teaching farmers new skills.

Government activity in the province is still largely dependent on finance from the centre. Outside investors display little interest in the region, but NGOs and various foreign agencies are supplying development assistance in increasing amounts. Like other parts of Indonesia, East Nusa Tenggara has been greatly influenced by the advent of democracy and regional autonomy, which have imparted new vigour to the conduct of local affairs.

The twin routes to economic and social advancement are better infrastructure and services and improved agricultural production and marketing techniques. But the limited resources available for development, along with the difficulty of mounting improvement packages below a certain size, mean that progress can only be slow. There are, however, ways of introducing more flexibility into development efforts, so as to accelerate the rate of advancement and attract further investment. All agencies involved in developing East Nusa Tenggara have found greater community involvement to be effective, and this has become more common in recent years. While the chief architect and implementer of development in the province is necessarily the government, because it has the most resources, other development agencies, including national and international NGOs and UN bodies, can make a useful contribution.

Looking to the future, there is a clear and urgent need to commit more resources to development in East Nusa Tenggara. This is especially necessary in poorer districts, where over half the population lives. Manifestly, infrastructure, education and health require substantial help, partly from the government but also by enlisting more aid from foreign sources. Production and marketing, too, need far more assistance. Here, NGOs working with credit agencies have the potential to expand the useful programs that are already in place.

Given proper management of change and appropriate coordination by government, the province can expect to see an improvement in the socio-economic returns on expenditure, and in the effectiveness of development programs. East Nusa Tenggara is inhabited by robust peoples from many ethnic groups, and many of them have demonstrated the ability to respond vigorously to change. Ultimately, this should assist this remote and backward province to catch up with the more advanced regions of Indonesia.

REFERENCES

Asher, R.E. and C. Moseley (eds) (2007), *Atlas of the World's Languages*, Routledge, New York NY.

Bank NTT (2006), *Laporan Tahunan* [Annual Report], Kupang.

Bappeda NTT (Badan Perencanaan Pembangunan Daerah Nusa Tenggara Timur) (2005), *Selayang Pandang Kegiatan Bantuan Luar Negeri di Propinsi Nusa Tenggara Timur* [A Brief Outline of External Project Assistance in East Nusa Tenggara], Kupang.

Barlow, Colin and Ria Gondowarsito (2006), 'Economic Development and Poverty Alleviation in Indonesia; The Case of Nusa Tenggara Timur', Working Paper No. 18, Institut Kajian Malaysia dan Antarabangsa, Universiti Kebangsaan Malaysia, Bangi.

BPS (Badan Pusat Statistik) (2005), *Statistik Indonesia* [Statistics of Indonesia], Jakarta.

BPS (Badan Pusat Statistik) (2007), *Statistik Indonesia* [Statistics of Indonesia], Jakarta.

BPS NTT (Badan Pusat Statistik Nusa Tenggara Timur) (2004), *Nusa Tenggara Timur dalam Angka, 2003* [East Nusa Tenggara in Figures, 2003], Kupang.

BPS NTT (Badan Pusat Statistik Nusa Tenggara Timur) (2008), *Nusa Tenggara Timur dalam Angka 2007* [East Nusa Tenggara in Figures, 2007], Kupang.

Daliyo, Philip Guest, Marian May and Riwanto Tirtosudarmo (1999), *Child Labour and Education Planning in Nusa Tenggara Barat and Nusa Tenggara Timur*, Center for Population and Manpower Studies, Jakarta.

Ethnologue (2007), 'A Language of Indonesia (Nusa Tenggara)', available at <www.ethnologue.com/show_language.asp?code=akg>.

Fox, James J. (1977), *The Harvest of the Palm: Ecological Change in Eastern Indonesia*, Harvard University Press, Cambridge MA.

KDP (Kecamatan Development Program) (2007), 'Indonesia Kecamatan Development Program', World Bank, Washington DC, available at <http://www.worldbank.org/id/kdp>.

Mantra, Ida Bagoes (1998), 'Indonesian Labour Mobility to Malaysia. A Case Study: East Flores, West Lombok and the Island of Bawean', paper presented to the National Workshop on International Migration, Population Studies Centre, Gadjah Mada University, Yogjakarta.

Mboi, Nafsiah (1996), 'Health and Poverty: A Look at Eastern Indonesia', in C. Barlow and J. Hardjono (eds), *Development in Eastern Indonesia*, Institute of Southeast Asian Studies, Singapore, pp. 175–97.

Metzner, J.K. (1982), *Agriculture and Population Pressure in Sikka, Isle of Flores*, Development Studies Centre Monograph No 28, Australian National University, Canberra.

Monk, K.A, Yance de Freitas and Gayatri Reksodihardjo-Lilley (1997), *The Geography of Nusa Tenggara and Maluku*, Periplus Editions, Hong Kong.

Ormeling F.J. (1956), *The Timor Problem: A Geographical Interpretation of an Underdeveloped Island*, J.P. Wolters, Groningen.

Vel, Jacqueline (1994), *Indigenous Economics and Development Work in Lawonda, Sumba (Eastern-Indonesia)*, University of Wageningen, Wageningen.

Webb, Paul (1986), *Palms and the Cross: Socio-economic Development in Nusatenggara, 1930–1975*, Centre for Southeast Asian Studies, James Cook University of North Queensland, Townsville.

Williams, Catharina (2005), '"Knowing One's Place": Gender, Mobility and Shifting Subjectivity in Eastern Indonesia', *Global Networks*, 5(4): 401–17.

WVI (Wahana Visi Indonesia) (2002), *ADP Kupang, 1997–2001* [Agricultural Development Project Kupang], Kupang.

PART II

Natural Resources
and the Environment

6　BALANCING BIODIVERSITY CONSERVATION AND DEVELOPMENT IN EASTERN INDONESIA

Ian M. Dutton, Rili Djohani, Setijati D. Sastrapradja and Karla M. Dutton

---

The biodiversity of eastern Indonesia is globally important from both an evolutionary biology and a socio-political perspective. An estimated 12 million Indonesians east of the Wallace line depend directly on biodiversity and ecosystem services for their livelihoods and well-being. Those resources are under increasing pressure as global demand increases, as comparable resources in western and central Indonesia are depleted and as population expands due to in-migration and local economic and population growth. In order to protect food security, sustain livelihoods and conserve critical biodiversity habitat such as coral reefs and forests, we must plan for appropriate use and conservation of biodiversity. In this chapter, we describe some of the challenges to biodiversity conservation in eastern Indonesia, and the innovative approaches being used in North and Central Sulawesi, Komodo and West Papua to conserve biodiversity and secure sustainable livelihoods for local communities.

1　INTRODUCTION

In this archipelago there are two distinct faunas rigidly circumscribed which differ as much as do those of Africa and South America and more than those of Europe and North America: yet there is nothing on the map or on the face of the islands to mark their limits (Alfred Russell Wallace 1869: 340).

Eastern Indonesia is remarkable for its biological differences to western Indonesia. The line that Wallace drew between the islands of Bali and

Lombok, continuing between Borneo and Celebes (now Sulawesi), has become a hallmark of modern biogeography. While there has been much debate subsequently about where that line ought to be drawn and why (Wickramanayake et al. 2002), recent analyses of terrestrial and marine biogeographical patterns (Briggs 2005) have confirmed that, from an evolutionary biology perspective, there is clearly something very special about the flora and fauna of eastern Indonesia.

The so-called Coral Triangle (Djohani et al. 2003) that represents the global epicentre of marine biodiversity covers a larger area than just eastern Indonesia, but the centre of that marine diversity stretches from the Banda Sea to Papua New Guinea, as indicated in Figure 6.1. This vast area is characterized by complex and dynamic geological and oceanographic processes that nurture evolution. Much of the biodiversity of the area is still relatively intact, and ecologically functional.

This also represents an important difference between the terrestrial ecosystems of eastern Indonesia and those of western and central Indonesia. In the more populated central and western provinces of Indonesia, centuries of unregulated and inappropriate exploitation have reduced natural systems to isolated and often non-viable fragments. Rapidly growing population and development pressures in recent decades (Cribb 2000) have further impaired the processes that would enable those systems to survive and recover. For example, in Java and Sumatra, as a result of mangrove clearing and pond aquaculture construction (*tambak*), there are very few intact coastal wetlands that can support native birds, fish or other fauna. As a consequence, previously widespread species are now locally extinct or critically endangered. Equally significantly, because of inappropriate fisheries development policy and lack of control of destructive fishing and overharvesting, there are very few functional fisheries (Yowono 1998; Mous et al. 2005).

Some areas of eastern Indonesia, notably the longer-settled areas of Sulawesi, Ambon and West Papua, have also begun to experience the ravages of overexploitation of natural resources. Coral reefs in Southeast Sulawesi are heavily damaged by bomb fishing and many economically important species such as trepang, clams and sharks are now locally extinct. Buginese and Makassan fishers now roam throughout eastern Indonesia and even into northern Australian and Papua New Guinean waters to obtain these resources. Illegal loggers and miners are increasingly active throughout the Moluccan and Raja Ampat islands of West Papua, areas once remote from commercial-scale exploitation. In 2005, before the Indonesian government's crackdown on illegal logging, it is estimated that some 300,000 cubic metres of logs were being smuggled out of West Papua each month (Nakashima 2006).

Figure 6.1   Ecoregions of the Coral Triangle[a]

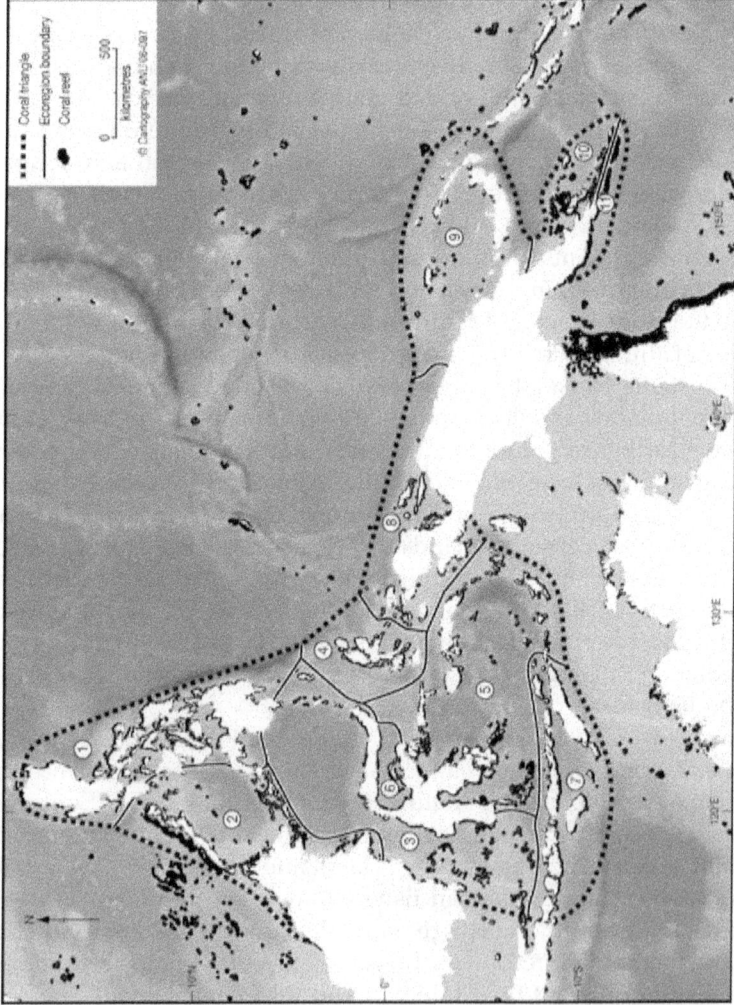

a   Boundaries of the ecoregions within the Coral Triangle: 1 = eastern Philippines; 2 = Palawan/North Borneo; 3 = Sulawesi Sea/Makassar Strait; 4 = Halmahera; 5 = Banda Sea = Northeast Sulawesi; 7 = Lesser Sunda; 8 = Papua; 9 = Bismarck Sea; 10 = Milne Bay Area; 11 = Southeast Papua New Guinea.

Source: Green and Mous (2005).

The 2001 decentralization of governance has empowered district-level administrations to generate income for development from local resources, including the forests and seas. While such empowerment may have short-term benefits, it also has typically underrecognized and largely unregulated negative impacts on both terrestrial and marine systems (Dutton 2005). There is also increasing evidence of conflict between indigenous communities and 'outsiders'. Local communities are unable to protect in-shore reef fisheries and island forests from commercial and external interests and thus obtain little or no revenue from resource exploitation by others. Even where self-regulation or traditional management is practised, few species are managed to address the cumulative impacts of harvesting at different lifecycle stages by all exploiters.

Despite these challenges, for most terrestrial and marine systems in eastern Indonesia, there is still the opportunity to protect intact ecosystems and to maintain the ecosystem services that provide livelihoods for communities and protect them from natural disasters such as flooding, landslides and tsunamis. This chapter reviews four case studies of conservation implementation on the ground and in the seas of eastern Indonesia over the past decade. They were chosen because of the diversity of contexts they represent and for the insights they provide for future conservation planning and management. All emphasize the critical importance of involving local communities and governments in conservation and reinforce the importance of greater national and global support for conservation.

2   THE GLOBAL SIGNIFICANCE OF THE BIODIVERSITY OF EASTERN INDONESIA

Indonesia is arguably the most important nation for global conservation and is second only to Brazil in terms of terrestrial biodiversity. Although it occupies less than 1.3 per cent of the land area of the world, it is home to some 17 per cent of all species and contains:

- 515 species of mammals (39 per cent endemic), ranked second in the world;
- 511 species of reptiles (29 per cent endemic), ranked fourth in the world;
- 1,531 species of birds (26 per cent endemic), ranked fifth in the world;
- 270 species of amphibians (37 per cent endemic), ranked sixth in the world;
- 35 species of primates (18 per cent endemic), ranked fourth in the world;

- 121 species of butterflies (44 per cent endemic);
- 1,400 species of fish, ranked third in world; and
- 38,000 species of plants (55 per cent endemic) (Bappenas 2003: 20).

As with any data on biodiversity, these figures tend to mask the lack of systematic study of the flora and fauna of Indonesia. New species are constantly being discovered and many species are not adequately described. However, even with these qualifications, Indonesia emerges in all global analyses as one of the 10 terrestrial megadiverse countries.

Within Indonesia, because of the dynamic and diverse geological and climatic conditions that shape their evolution, eastern Indonesian ecosystems tend to be the most diverse. Because of their remoteness, they also tend to be less well studied. For example, during a survey of the Tangguh liquefied natural gas (LNG) site in West Papua some nine new species were identified (PT Hatfindo 2003). Supriatna (1999) estimates that the number of plant species in West Papua may triple from the current known base to an estimated 20,000–25,000 once more detailed studies have been completed. That prediction was borne out in reports of a survey of the Foja Mountains of West Papua in which a new bird species (the first in 60 years), 20 new frog species, four new butterflies and a new mammal (the golden mantled tree kangaroo) were recorded (Shatwell 2005).

The significance of Indonesia to global conservation is even more pronounced when marine biodiversity is considered. Indonesia contains 38 per cent of all marine fish species and some 78 per cent of the world's corals. While Wallace was able to discern different patterns of speciation between terrestrial animals in western and eastern Indonesia, only recently have we been able to detect similar patterns in marine species (Barber et al. 2000). Allen and Adrim (2003), for example, reported 1,111 fish species from a single bay in Flores — more than from the entire tropical Atlantic Ocean. Similar diversity has been reported for corals (Connolly, Bellwood and Hughes 2003), prompting Briggs (2005: 301) to describe the East Indies as:

> … an area of evolutionary origin where dominant species are being produced. That is, the evolutionary process concentrated in the East Indies has the function of supplying species that help to maintain the diversity patterns in the rest of the Indo-Pacific.

These discoveries have prompted increased interest in conservation in eastern Indonesia. For example, a recent analysis of global conservation priorities identified all the major island groups of eastern Indonesia as having significant potential to avoid extinctions of non-marine mammals (Cardillo et al. 2006). That is a most significant finding in the context of the Convention on Biological Diversity commitment to a significant reduction in the current rate of biodiversity loss at the global, regional and local levels by 2010 (Secretariat of the CBD 2004). It also justifies the emphasis in the national Indonesian Biodiversity Strategy and Action Plan on improved conservation efforts in Sulawesi, West Papua, West and East Nusa Tenggara and the Maluku islands (Bappenas 2003).

3   HEADING TOWARDS A BIODIVERSITY CRISIS IN EASTERN INDONESIA

Much has been written about the destruction of Indonesia's forests and coral reefs, particularly in western and central Indonesia where there are generally more obvious and longer-established patterns of harvesting, both legal and illegal. Whitten, Holmes and MacKinnon (2001) paint a bleak picture of how much Sumatra has changed in the past 30 years. The Environmental Investigation Agency (2005), Burke, Selig and Spalding (2002) and Mous et al. (2005) provide detailed evidence of forest and fisheries systems in decline near centres of population, or where road or vessel access makes exploitation possible, or where policy makers have little understanding of the true condition of stocks.

Key threats to biodiversity include overexploitation or overharvesting (beyond sustainable limits), destructive harvesting (such as blast fishing or the inappropriate use of fire) and habitat conversion (to, for example, agriculture). They in turn are greatly influenced by the nature of government and community control or oversight, by the extent of corruption, by the market value or level of commercialization of the resource and by the quality of management. Rarely is one single factor the root cause of biodiversity degradation and many factors will change over the lifecycle of exploitation of a natural resource. Situation analyses of biodiversity exploitation in Komodo National Park provide an example of this complexity. Using the example of fisheries exploitation in the national park, Mous (2001) demonstrates the diversity of local and external factors that must be considered when developing a management system, and the importance of a holistic approach.

It seems that there is an unwavering cycle of resource exploitation that is moving from west to east, from island to island, pursuing timber and fish with little thought for sustainability and community well-being once commercial enterprises have removed the available resources. That cycle further diminishes the prospects of local communities for sustainable livelihoods and this contributes to increased poverty (Leisher and Peters 2004). Even those areas that have been set aside for conservation generally offer little promise. Most protected areas in Indonesia are underfunded and exist on paper only. There is little active management within the park borders and even less effort to harmonize conservation with surrounding land and sea uses. As a consequence, there is both little substantive protection from encroachment, hunting and illegal harvesting of resources and little incentive for park neighbours to manage adjacent lands and seas in ways that are compatible with nature conservation.

4 BIODIVERSITY AND DEVELOPMENT IN EASTERN INDONESIA

It has been more than a decade since Indonesia ratified the Convention on Biological Diversity in 1994. However, as noted in the Indonesian Biodiversity Strategy and Action Plan, biodiversity is still not in the mainstream of national, far less regional and local, development (Bappenas 2003). The strategy proposes detailed action plans, but given the recent history of such efforts, and the natural resource management challenges being faced in all regions, one questions their ultimate impact. It seems that far more effort is being expended on planning than on action on the ground.

The Indonesian government and the global donor community have made efforts to address biodiversity conservation and related issues. The most significant of these were the integrated conservation and development projects (ICDPs) that were funded to the tune of US$150 million by multilateral organizations from the mid-1980s in an attempt to better manage protected areas in Indonesia in harmony with adjacent communities. These have proven to be largely ineffective in western and central Indonesia for a variety of reasons. According to Wells et al. (1999: 45):

> ... direct threats from local communities ranked well behind road construction, mining, logging concessions, and sponsored immigration. While ICDPs can address threats posed by local communities, such threats are better addressed through mechanisms such as spatial planning, involvement of PA [protected area] managers in public investment decisions, and improved development coordination, rather than investments in community economic development.

The study did, however, suggest that ICDPs may potentially be more effective in eastern Indonesia where community-based management capacity is stronger.

Decentralization has provided significant challenges and opportunities for new approaches to development in eastern Indonesia. Since the downfall of the Soeharto regime, local governments have been empowered to play a greater role in land use decision making (Alm and Bahl 1999). In many cases they are ill-equipped to implement the mandates of decentralization; very few of the provincial or district-level staff now responsible for permitting or regulating development have any technical expertise and they are subject to increasing political pressure. Provincial and local officials have increasingly requested direct external assistance (domestic and international) to develop more effective land and sea use plans.

For example, led by a steering committee comprising local government leaders and academics and supported by international conservation organizations, in the mid-2000s researchers finished a complete ecoregional assessment of the island of Sulawesi (Gunawan, Summers and Salim 2005). As a result of that process, each of the island's provinces is proposing to set aside some 30 per cent of its land area for conservation and ecosystem services protection.

Given the richness and uniqueness of the biological diversity in eastern Indonesia, it is not surprising to observe the variable responses of policy makers and implementing agencies to the guidance provided in the national and regional Indonesian Biodiversity Strategy and Action Plans (Bappenas 2003), AGENDA 21-Indonesia (Bappenas 1997), the National Consensus on Sustainable Development, the Millennium Ecosystem Assessment (MEA 2005) and a multitude of other 'policy instruments' that have emerged from the national government in recent years.

At a March 2006 meeting in Jakarta on science and technology for development, it was noted that the government faces many problems in delivering on its national and international commitments to sustainable development (Sastrapradja, personal communication). From a political perspective, the government needs quick and tangible solutions that address the immediate needs of Indonesian society for food, income and so on. But that perspective is typically in conflict with the needs of biodiversity conservation, where the results of conservation efforts are not always immediately evident, or able to satisfy more immediate needs beyond the scale of a small community. The question therefore arose as to whether scientists and technologists could offer meaningful options to the government on how to manage biodiversity to meet short-term needs while encouraging sustainable use over the long term.

To answer that vexing question, we postulate that scientists and decision makers need to develop a shared vision for development in eastern Indonesia. Specifically, scientists must help decision makers and communities better understand the role of biodiversity conservation in supporting sustainable utilization of natural resources, and in maintaining (and even restoring) ecosystem services. As Figure 6.2 indicates, we clearly need to put in place a process of development that takes a long-term view.

As the figure indicates, a critical but increasingly overlooked first step in this process is to better understand the nature of Indonesia. Unlike

Figure 6.2   Moving beyond the Traditional Development Cycle

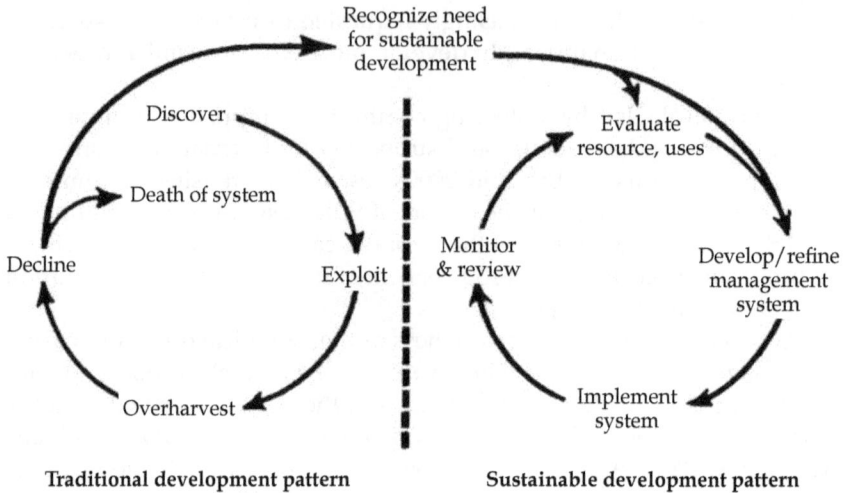

Traditional development pattern   Sustainable development pattern

Source: Hotta and Dutton (1995).

the remaining areas of native plant and animal resources in western and central Indonesia, the biodiversity resources of eastern Indonesia have not been systematically inventoried or assessed to determine their distribution, abundance and sustainable economic potential. This is true for widely exploited species like sandalwood in East Nusa Tenggara, the Sago forests in West Papua or the clams and other target fisheries of the Banda Sea as well as for species that may have little direct economic value but which play a key role in maintaining ecosystem processes (for example, mangroves).

An equally significant need relates to the institutional capacity to formulate and implement effective natural resource management plans. Eastern Indonesia has very few trained ecologists, regional planners or protected-area managers. The capacity of most academic institutions to provide the blend of skills and training needed to sustain development trails behind that of the longer-established and better-funded universities in Java and Sumatra. As a consequence, eastern Indonesia suffers from the dual malaise of increasingly complex development decisions and a lack of capable decision makers. The failure to address fundamental human resource development needs and build the capacity of eastern Indonesian scientists and decision makers exacerbates the inappropriate use of biodiversity resources. Building the expertise and institutional capacity for sustainable development is thus a high priority for regional development.

5   OPPORTUNITIES FOR CONSERVATION

> If there is to be any hope from the growing body of conservation biologists (at home and abroad) now focusing their attention on Indonesia, they will have to move away from priority setting exercises, scientific studies and theoretical modeling to on-the-ground management and policy decisions (Whitten, Holmes and MacKinnon 2001: 2).

The relative intactness of the ecosystems of eastern Indonesia, but increasing urgency for conservation action in parallel with expanding timber, agricultural, mining and fisheries exploitation, has prompted significant investments by multilateral organizations and international conservation organizations in the region. Most perceive that there is still time to undertake conservation activities in a range of eastern Indonesian ecosystems, although the window for meaningful impact is closing rapidly.

Concurrent with local action has been an increased level of global analysis of conservation options and priorities in eastern Indonesia. For example, a recent analysis of the relative costs and benefits of terrestrial conservation investments in Indonesia suggested that Sulawesi is potentially a more cost-effective location for conservation investment than the other large islands that comprise the Sundaland and Wallacea bioregions (Wilson et al. 2006).

All major conservation organizations have now identified global priority areas for action in eastern Indonesia and most have at least some on-the-ground projects in several key ecoregions and hot spots. However, with a few notable exceptions, there is a relative paucity of conservation investment that is commensurate with the scale of the needs. There are also significant strategic gaps that cannot be addressed by action in any one area (large areas of the Moluccas and East Nusa Tenggara, for example, where there are no active conservation projects) or investment in any single strategy (the need to build indigenous capacity to undertake conservation, for example).

Some programs, such as the Western Pacific program of the David and Lucille Packard Foundation, have given priority attention to marine conservation in this region, and others, such as the Regional Natural Heritage Program of the Australian government, represent a pioneering effort to expand the horizons of traditional aid. But much more is needed if Indonesia is to be in a position to avert the loss of species, habitats and ecosystem services that has occurred in other parts of Indonesia in recent decades.

In that context, it is increasingly evident that conservation for conservation's sake is not an attractive proposition for donors or the communities they target. As the Millennium Ecosystem Assessment demonstrated, the interdependence of human well-being and natural systems must now be a more prominent component of all conservation and development efforts (MEA 2005). That need is clearly evident in natural resource-dependent communities such as the coastal villages of eastern Indonesia where fish is the main source of protein (Dutton 2005). It is also evident in the wake of the 2004 Asian tsunami where it has been demonstrated that coastal communities with intact mangroves and coral reefs were less affected (UNEP-WCMC 2006). However, as Whitten et al. (2001) argue, we need examples that show the value of conservation at all scales.

The following four case studies describe work in progress that exemplifies the kinds of challenges to be addressed, and some of the types of innovations that will be required if Indonesia is ultimately to be successful in conserving the biodiversity of eastern Indonesia.

6   CONSERVATION IN PRACTICE: LESSONS FROM ONGOING PROGRAMS

Case 1: The Ecosystem Services of Lore Lindu National Park

Lore Lindu National Park is a UNESCO-designated Biosphere Reserve with significant natural and cultural values. It covers some 220,000 hectares in the province of Central Sulawesi. The province is mostly covered in montane and sub-montane moist tropical forest, but other vegetation types include rare cloud forest, heath forest, monsoon forest, marsh and small amounts of lowland forest. Among the threatened and endemic species found in the province are the anoa, babirusa, Sulawesi hornbill, maleo, Sulawesi palm civet and Tonkean macaque.

The capital of Central Sulawesi, Palu, is reputed to be one of the driest places in Indonesia, as the steep mountains to the east and west of the city divert and trap most of the rainfall, leaving the valley in a rain shadow. Even so, the Palu valley supports an extensive wet rice and mixed agriculture system, most of it irrigated by extraction from the Gumbasa River, which drains from Lore Lindu National Park. Urban water is generally supplied by shallow or artesian wells. The Municipal Water Authority estimates that it supplies 3.8 million cubic metres of water to homes and industry in the city, but supplies less than 20 per cent of homes, which mainly rely on shallow wells.

Between 1991 and 2001, the rate of clearing of forest inside the park boundaries was still relatively modest (compared with other Indonesian protected areas) — less than 1 per cent had been altered. However, with the acceleration of decentralization efforts and due to the lack of support for enforcement of park boundaries, local squatters seized the opportunity to begin clearing a forest block in the Dongi Dongi area inside the national park. This land grab quickly threatened to escalate into a large-scale clearing of forest by new immigrants eager to acquire land to harvest timber and plant crops such as cacao and coffee (ESG International 2001).

In 2001, the Lore Lindu National Park management agency, working with provincial agencies and with strong support from The Nature Conservancy, initiated a three-part strategy. The first was to assist the provincial planning agency (Bappeda) to evaluate options for resettlement of the squatters outside the national park. The second was to accelerate participatory management of the park. By involving the 65 villages that border the park and formalizing rights of use and protection between the park authority and those communities, it was hoped that local communities would assist the authority to protect the park's resources. The third was to build a coalition of stakeholders from the local to the provincial level who understood the values of the park and why it was in their collective interest to protect the park in perpetuity.

All three strategies were ultimately significant in protecting the park, but the last was especially important in bringing new champions to the management table. In December 2001, a study of the value of the water resources of Lore Lindu commissioned by The Nature Conservancy concluded that the park provides services worth some US$8.9 million per year (ESG International 2001). This value mostly accrues to the agriculture sector (US$5.94 million), with livestock (US$1.64 million) and urban/industrial consumption (US$1.41 million) also important. The total does not include the value of protection against flooding and erosion; this is considerable, as the steep topography of the mountains around Palu and the relatively short length of the rivers contribute to common flooding events and high levels of erosion.

This study turned out to be one of the key elements in being able to implement the third strategy of building a stronger coalition of stakeholders. Previously, a seven-year management partnership by Indonesia's Forest Protection and Nature Conservation agency (PHKA), The Nature Conservancy and local NGOs had led to only lukewarm support for the park. It was only when the values of the park beyond the boundaries were documented that agricultural users (previously a threat to the park) and the local government (a key management stakeholder in the new era of decentralization) began actively to unite as park supporters. The economic and social values of water production now form an integral part of the management effectiveness assessment of Lore Lindu National Park.

The park continues to face a range of development pressures, with the specific threats changing as cycles of development occur. For example, with increased global demand for cacao and the lack of effective disease control in crops elsewhere in Sulawesi, there has been pressure to open up accessible areas of the park to cacao production. The Nature Conservancy has responded by assisting farmers to improve pest and disease management in existing cacao plantations while working with the 65 villages that border the park to codify rights of access and management responsibilities. Such challenges are a constant reminder of the need for vigilance and flexibility in managing large natural areas, but also of the importance of building a constituency of local support for the services and values that such areas provide. Park neighbours now play a key role in regulating access and resource extraction—a role that cannot be undertaken unilaterally by a national parks agency.

Case 2: Community-based Marine Protected Areas in North Sulawesi

Indonesia's seas have long been perceived as an endless source of marine riches. There has been massive investment over the past 30 years in fisheries development projects, resulting in massively increased local and international fishing capacity. There has been little corollary investment in effective stock management or species/area conservation: less than 1 per cent of Indonesia's seas are now within marine protected areas (MPAs) and even the areas that have been declared are not effectively managed for fisheries or habitat conservation (Dutton 2005).

There is a rapidly growing body of evidence to show how efficient and effective MPAs can be in both the conservation of a wide range of fish stocks and the generation of spillover effects beyond the borders of MPAs. Roberts et al. (2001) note that species as diverse as molluscs and crustaceans as well as fish from a wide range of life histories and mobilities benefit measurably from reserve establishment and other fisheries restriction practices. Such benefits typically occur within two to five years of reserve establishment and continue for decades. One of the most dramatic examples of spillover benefits the authors cite is the case of Apo Island in the Philippines, where catch per unit effort in the waters around Apo increased tenfold over 20 years of protection! The benefits of such conservation efforts are not just biological and economic; they also provide a strong basis for improved village and district-level governance as well as a host of intangible benefits such as food security.

It is fitting, therefore, that Apo Island was the inspiration for the establishment of the first community-based MPA in North Sulawesi. The idea of turning six hectares of coastal waters containing a mangrove forest and part of a fringing reef into a marine sanctuary came about after a field visit by Blongko villagers to the Apo Island marine sanctuary, and a return visit by the Apo Island village chief and members of the women's cooperative to observe Blongko and exchange ideas (Dutton and

Crawford 1998). Blongko is a small village with a population of 1,250. Its approximately 6.5 kilometres of coastline is intact and productive, bordered by relatively thick and vigorous mangroves. Most of the villagers live along the water and the majority are fishers, although almost all residents both fish and farm. The fishery, both offshore and on the local coral reef, plays a significant role in the livelihood of the community.

The village head of Blongko and the community quickly understood the Apo islanders' description of how they had developed and implemented their community-driven marine sanctuary effort. Realizing the value of the local fishery, and seeing a way to protect it as a valuable nursery for fish that could help feed future generations, community members worked with the staff of Proyek Pesisir — the Indonesia Coastal Resources Management Project implemented by the Coastal Resources Center of the University of Rhode Island — to collect data, identify an appropriate site and develop a local ordinance to regulate the proposed protected area. The village government also received support from the regional and national governments for the ordinance that the villagers had crafted. In October 1998 the area was officially designated a marine sanctuary. An information/meeting centre was constructed, boundary markers installed and information signs created. Within two years, fish numbers within the reserve had increased, with fishers also reporting increased catches in adjacent waters.

By promoting the community-based marine sanctuary, Blongko's residents now have responsibility for and a more active role in protecting and sustaining the marine resources that directly affect their day-to-day lives. The resource users in Blongko are now informed resource managers. Importantly, Blongko has inspired other communities, government and academic organizations, and NGOs to establish similar sanctuaries elsewhere. Some 1,500 people from other parts of Indonesia have now visited Blongko to learn from the community, and 26 similar community-managed reserves have been established in North Sulawesi and a further 20 in other Indonesian provinces (Crawford et al. 2003). The minister of marine affairs and fisheries gave the Blongko community a national coastal award in May 2000 in recognition of its pioneering efforts in coral reef management.

While one small sanctuary may not seem like much, it could provide a model for the 6,000+ other coastal villages of Indonesia and, if replicated, add greatly to the area of coral reef protected within the nation. In tandem with larger, well-managed MPAs, such reserves could provide the basis for an integrated national marine conservation network that underpins sustainable fisheries production and other processes, such as increasing resilience to climate change (Djohani et al. 2003; SEACMPA 2003).

Case 3: Sustaining Komodo National Park

Komodo National Park is famous for its Komodo Dragon (*Varanus komodoensis*), and the Komodo Dragon is the reason that the area has enjoyed some form of protected status over many centuries. In 1980 the national park was gazetted in such a way that, perhaps unintentionally, 1,214 square kilometres of highly diverse marine habitat were included in the park besides the 603 square kilometres of land. In 1986, UNESCO declared the park a World Heritage Site and a Man and Biosphere Reserve.

The four villages inside the park are inhabited by approximately 3,000 people who mostly depend on fishing for their livelihood. Another 17,000 people live in the direct surroundings of the park (PKA and TNC 2000: 55). In 1995 the Indonesian park authority invited The Nature Conservancy to help implement a conservation program for coastal and marine conservation targets. The Nature Conservancy conducted a Rapid Ecological Assessment that confirmed the high biodiversity of marine biota. Early appraisals also confirmed that, as in many other areas in Indonesia, destructive fishing practices such as blast fishing and cyanide fishing, as well as overexploitation, were severely threatening the coral reef communities in the park. It was clear that alongside the *opportunity* provided by a supportive government and a high biodiversity value, there was also the *need* for a comprehensive coastal and marine conservation program (Mous 2001).

Together with the national parks agency and with local government support, in 1996 The Nature Conservancy opened a Komodo Field Office to implement a comprehensive conservation program. Some activities, such as awareness raising, constituency building, and monitoring and enforcing the ban on blast fishing, could be implemented immediately. As indicated in Figure 6.3, once the park authority implemented routine patrols, the incidence of blast fishing in the park decreased almost immediately, with a massive 80 per cent reduction in blasting within two months. As a result of this reduced destruction, coral cover improved by 60 per cent between 1996 and 2000.

For other activities, a more comprehensive planning process was necessary. A 25-year master plan for the management of the park was endorsed by the national park authority and the district government of Manggarai on 4 July 2000 (PKA and TNC 2000). The master plan was the precursor for the endorsement of a zoning plan (October 2001) and for the district decree that provided the legal basis for the zoning plan. Now that the zoning plan and the decree have come into effect, there is a transparent and systematic basis for the regulation of overexploitation and the development of sustainable financing and livelihood development projects.

*Figure 6.3   Reduction of Blast Fishing in Komodo National Park after
            Initiating Patrols in 1996 (no. of incidents)*

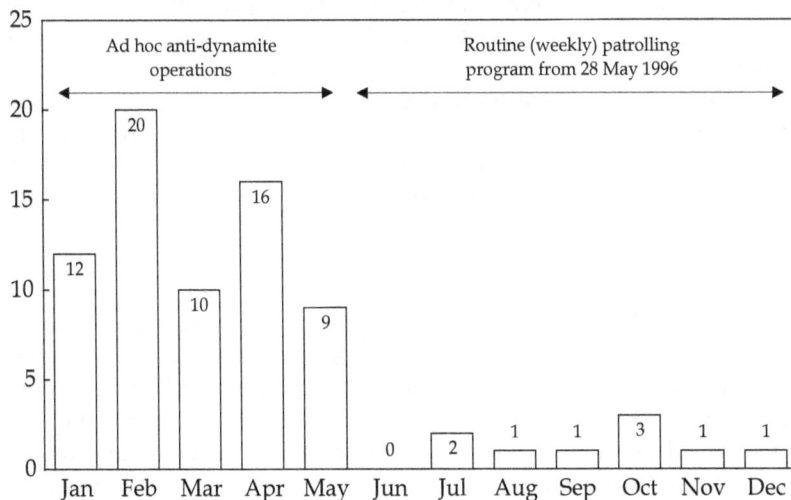

Source: Mous (2001).

The root of the problem for many protected areas in Indonesia is the
lack of adequate and predictable recurrent funding. It has been estimated
that protected areas in Indonesia face an annual shortfall in funding of
US$97 million (TNC 2006). The international conservation community
currently provides US$15 million per year to meet that need, but clearly
innovative and new long-term or sustainable sources of national funding
are urgently required.

In Komodo, the park authority, the local government, The Nature
Conservancy and a private sector partner are engaged in one of the most
innovative protected-area financing programs ever attempted in Indonesia. The program seeks gradually to introduce visitor fees that will
ultimately cover the cost of park operations (and hence reduce the need
for external assistance) and supplement the livelihoods of local communities. In the seven-year period before this funding level is reached, The
Nature Conservancy is committed to providing bridging funds to support both park management and local communities.

There have been considerable political, legal and economic challenges
in developing this collaborative management model, requiring great
patience and commitment by all parties. The nature of the issues to be
addressed will continue to evolve; rebuilding international confidence in
Indonesia as a safe destination for tourism since the Bali bombings has
required a coordinated response well beyond Komodo National Park,
for example.

There are also fundamental challenges in meeting the expectations of all stakeholders as the transition to sustainable funding begins; for example, not all anticipated beneficiaries will receive sufficient funding to provide them with a viable alternative to destructive fishing practices in the short term. However, there is tremendous momentum towards making Komodo a model for a self-funding protected area that benefits local people directly, and there is a strong commitment by local government and resource users to break the cycle of unsustainable fishing threatening all coastal fishers in Indonesia (Yowono 1998).

Case 4: Towards Integrated Management of Bintuni Bay

Berau–Bintuni Bay is a vast area of lowland rainforest, nipa palm and mangrove forming the base of the Bird's Head region of West Papua. The bay is about 200 kilometres long and 70 kilometres wide at its mouth. Bintuni Bay is home to one of the largest contiguous mangrove forests in the world (450,000 hectares) and most coastal residents are directly dependent on coastal and watershed resources for their livelihoods. The bay has now become the focus of development of a major LNG project by BP and BPMigas. The area is expected to experience significant and rapidly increasing development pressures as a result of the construction of the BP Tangguh LNG facility in the bay.

As part of a global commitment to have a positive impact on biodiversity in the places in which it operates, BP developed the company's first regional Biodiversity Action Plan (BP 2003). As well as constituting a written commitment to conservation, the plan committed BP to implementing key biodiversity conservation strategies in cooperation with local, regional and national partners. These were in addition to the company's existing regulatory commitments at each of its facilities worldwide. Under the plan, BP proposed to:

- support more detailed analyses of the biodiversity of the bay, including a baseline flora and fauna survey of the Tangguh LNG site (PT Hatfindo 2003), a regional land use atlas (Pemerintah Provinsi Papua et al. 2003) and a management plan for the Bintuni Bay Nature Reserve (Suartana et al. 2003; Sihite et al. 2006);
- provide founding support for the Papua Conservation Fund and support the development of a volume of the *Ecology of Indonesia* series on Papua (the one island not yet covered by the series), to be managed by Conservation International;
- provide founding support for the development of a national Conservation Training and Resource Centre in partnership with four government agencies — PHKA, the National Development Planning Agency

(Bappenas), the Bogor Agricultural Institute (IPB) and the Southeast Asian Regional Centre for Tropical Biology (SEAMEO Biotrop) – and six NGOs (Sudibyo, Boreri and Pieter 2003);

- undertake testing of metric guidelines in Tangguh as part of a global Energy and Biodiversity Initiative (see <http://www.theebi.org/>); and
- fund a bay fisheries health assessment led by the University of Papua at Manokwari and the World Wide Fund for Nature.

All these activities have now been implemented, providing an interesting insight into how biodiversity can be integrated with industrial and regional development. The Bintuni Bay coastal resources atlas now provides a starting point for all stakeholders to engage in discussions on the management of the watershed and coastal resources of Bintuni Bay. Over 1,000 copies of the atlas and 5,000 summary brochures were distributed to key stakeholders in the bay and to provincial organizations. The atlas contributes significantly to ongoing discussions on how to sustainably manage the development resulting from BP-generated revenues and the pressures of both upstream and downstream development.

The various studies and related activities (such as training programs for local university staff on mangrove survey methods) have raised the bar for biodiversity conservation activities involving the private sector in eastern Indonesia. The partnerships between aid organizations and research institutions (such as that between Proyek Pesisir and the University of Papua to develop and distribute the atlas), between local university and government partners to develop management plans, and between NGOs at the local, national and international levels have both increased project transparency and led to more informed decision making that allows biodiversity values to be incorporated into local and regional planning. Additionally, more than 300 eastern Indonesian conservation professionals and related decision makers have now been trained and are applying that learning to conservation action projects, inside and outside traditional protected areas.

The ultimate outcomes of these investments may not be realized until the project matures, but early indications are promising. For example, as a result of the focus on the value of the fisheries of Bintuni Bay, greater emphasis is being given to protection of the nurseries found in the upper bay mangroves. The Bintuni project also stands in stark contrast to other large-scale development projects that have occurred in eastern Indonesia over the past 50 years, in that social, economic and environmental concerns are being proactively and transparently addressed in the project design and inception process.

CONCLUSION

Each of the four case studies presented above describes action on the ground that has been tailored to the rapidly changing circumstances and needs for biodiversity conservation of eastern Indonesia. Together they demonstrate that while there is no fixed model for biodiversity conservation that is preferable to another, there are four key principles that must be addressed in the design of conservation projects in eastern Indonesia.

1 Biodiversity conservation must be made relevant to the lives and livelihoods of communities. There is little interest in the non-use values of nature. Therefore, conservation proponents must demonstrate the value of conservation in terms of either the benefits provided (as per the water example in Lore Lindu National Park) or the damages avoided (as in the case of sustainable fishing in Komodo).
2 Biodiversity conservation cannot be the sole domain of conservation organizations. Effective partnership with government, communities, the private sector and other institutions in civil society is critical to success.
3 Biodiversity conservation is best implemented and sustained by eastern Indonesians themselves. As the case studies exemplify through their engagement of local and national research and training institutions, it is essential to invest in building the capacity of local institutions to act as agents of change in biodiversity management, as well as to engage in wider outreach to all sectors of civil society to share knowledge and build a constituency for conservation.
4 Conservation projects must be designed as 'learning experiments'. All the projects described had clear goals and a strong emphasis on measurement, learning and adaptation. These are key components of effective conservation and critical to being able to demonstrate to others whether an approach works (or not) and why. The extra expenditure on monitoring is well worth the cost!

Above all, the examples show the value of taking action before a threat reaches the point where action is no longer meaningful to the viability of biodiversity or to the livelihoods of the communities that depend on healthy biodiversity and healthy ecosystems. Much of the biodiversity of eastern Indonesia is still in better than 'half-full' condition. For the sake of the communities of eastern Indonesia and the world at large, we ought not to wait until it reaches 'half-empty' before we assist eastern Indonesians to take action on the ground to conserve it.

ACKNOWLEDGMENTS

The authors are grateful to all those who have collaborated closely with us in the design and development of the projects described in this chapter, including the Indonesian Institute of Sciences (LIPI), The Nature Conservancy, the USAID–Bappenas Coastal Resources Management Project, local government, NGOs, BP Berau Ltd, and local communities and research institutions, particularly IPB. We especially appreciate the support and encouragement of Dr Budy Resosudarmo, Dr Frank Jotzo, Ms Lydia Napitupulu and staff of the Indonesia Project at the Australian National University, Canberra.

REFERENCES

Allen, G.R. and M. Adrim (2003), 'Coral Reef Fishes of Indonesia', *Zoological Studies*, 42: 1–72.

Alm, J. and R. Bahl (1999), 'Decentralization in Indonesia: Prospects and Problems', discussion paper prepared for the United States Agency for International Development (USAID), Jakarta, June.

Barber, P.H., S.R. Palumbi, M.V. Erdmann and M. Kasim Moosa (2000), 'A Marine Wallace's Line?', *Nature*, 406: 692–3.

Bappenas (1997), 'A National Strategy for Sustainable Development-Agenda 21 Indonesia', March, available at <http://www.searo.who.int/en/Section23/Section1318/Section1792.htm.>, accessed 24 August 2007.

Bappenas (2003), 'Indonesian Biodiversity Strategy and Action Plan 2003–2020', Jakarta.

BP Indonesia (2003), 'BP Indonesia Biodiversity Action Plan', BP Tangguh LNG, Jakarta.

Briggs, J.C. (2005), 'The Marine East Indies: Diversity and Speciation', *Journal of Biogeography*, 32: 1,517–22.

Burke, L., E. Selig and M. Spalding (2002), *Reefs at Risk in Southeast Asia*, World Resources Institute in collaboration with the United Nations Environment Programme's World Conservation Monitoring Centre, World Fish Center and International Coral Reef Action Network, World Resources Institute, Washington DC, available at <http://pdf.wri.org/rrseasia_full.pdf>.

Cardillo, M., G.M. Mace, J.L. Gittleman and A. Purvis (2006), 'Latent Extinction Risk and the Future Battlegrounds of Mammal Conservation', *Proceedings of the National Academy of Sciences*, 103(11): 4,157–61.

Connolly, S.R., D.R. Bellwood and T.P. Hughes (2003), 'Indo-Pacific Biodiversity of Coral Reefs: Deviations from a Mid Domain Model', *Ecology*, 84: 2,178–90.

Crawford, B.R. et al. (2003), 'Navigating a Course for ICM in Indonesia: The Indonesia Coastal Resources Management Project (1997–2003)', in S.B. Olsen (ed.), *Crafting Coastal Governance in a Changing World*, CRC/USAID Coastal Management Report No. 2241, University of Rhode Island, Kingston RI, pp. 205–41.

Cribb, R. (2000), *Historical Atlas of Indonesia*, Curzon Press, London.

Djohani, R., P. Mous, J. Pet, J. Subijanto, I.M. Dutton, B. Wiryawan and R. Salm (2003), 'SEACMPA: Strengthening Resilient Networks of MPAs Designed to

Survive, Managed to Last and Connected like Strings of Pearls across the Seas of Southeast Asia', paper presented to the Global Marine Initiative Conference, Asilomar CA, 7–10 October.

Dutton, I.M. (2005), 'If Only Fish Could Vote: The Enduring Challenges of Coastal and Marine Resources Management in Post-*reformasi* Indonesia', in B. Resosudarmo (ed.), *The Politics and Economics of Indonesia's Natural Resources*, Institute of Southeast Asian Studies, Singapore, pp. 162–78.

Dutton, I.M. and B. Crawford (1998), 'Villagers Keep the Seas Alive', *Inside Indonesia*, July–September, pp. 24–5.

Environmental Investigation Agency (2005), 'The Politics of Extinction', available at <http://www.eia-international.org>, accessed 26 March 2006.

ESG International (2001), 'The Value of Water Resources in Lore Lindu National Park, Central Sulawesi, Indonesia', report to The Nature Conservancy, Guelph.

Green, A. and P.J. Mous (2004), *Delineating the Coral Triangle, Its Ecoregions and Functional Seascapes: Report on an Expert Workshop, Held at the Southeast Asia Center for Marine Protected Areas, Bali, Indonesia (April 30 – May 2, 2003)*, The Nature Conservancy, Southeast Asia Center for Marine Protected Areas, Bali.

Gunawan, T., M. Summers and A. Salim (2005), 'Konservasi Keanekaragaman Hayati: Perlindungan bagi Warisan Alam Sulawesi' [Conservation of Biodiversity: Protection of the Natural Heritage of Sulawesi], report prepared for the Sulawesi ECA, The Nature Conservancy, Bogor.

Hotta, K. and I.M. Dutton (eds) (1995), *Coastal Management in the Asia–Pacific Region*, JIMSTEF, Tokyo.

Leisher, C. and J. Peters (2004), *Direct Benefits to Poor People from Biodiversity Conservation*, The Nature Conservancy, Brisbane.

MEA (Millennium Ecosystem Assessment) (2005), 'Ecosystems and Human Wellbeing', available at <http://www.millenniumassessment.org/en/index.aspx>, accessed 28 March 2006.

Mous, P.J. (2001), 'Programmatic Audit of the Coastal and Marine Conservation Program in Komodo National Park, Indonesia', available at <http://www.komodonationalpark.org>, accessed 20 March 2006.

Mous, P., J. Pet, R. Djohani, M.V. Erdmann, A. Halim, M. Knight, L. Pet-Soede and G. Wiadnya (2005), 'Policy Needs to Improve Marine Capture Fisheries Management and to Define a Role for Marine Protected Areas in Indonesia', *Fisheries Management and Ecology*, 12: 259–68.

Nakashima, E. (2006), 'Floorboards Put the Finishing Touch on Forests', *Washington Post*, 22 March.

Pemerintah Propinsi Papua, Permerintah Kabupaten Manokwari, Universitas Negeri Papua and Proyek Pesisir (2003), *Atlas Sumberdaya Pesisir Kawasan Teluk Bintuni*, BP, Jakarta.

PKA and TNC (Perlindungan dan Konservasi Alam and The Nature Conservancy) (2000), '25 Year Master Plan for Management: Komodo National Park, Book 2, Data and Analysis', available at <http://www.komodonationalpark.org/downloads/Management%20Plan%20Book%202.pdf>.

PT Hatfindo (2003), 'Flora and Fauna Survey of the Tangguh LNG Site Papua Province: Executive Summary, Indonesia', BP and Pertamina, Jakarta.

Roberts, C.M., J.A. Bohnsack, F. Gell, J.P. Hawkins and R. Goodridge (2001), 'Effects of Marine Reserves on Adjacent Fisheries', *Science*, 294: 1,920–23.

SEACMPA (Southeast Asian Centre for Marine Protected Areas) (2003), *Strings of Pearls*, The Nature Conservancy, Bali.

Secretariat of the CBD (Convention on Biological Diversity) (2004), 'The 2010 Biodiversity Target: A Framework for Evaluation of Progress', available at <www.biodiv.org>, accessed 20 March 2006.

Shatwell, J. (2005), 'Mysterious Bird of Paradise: Lost and Found', available at <http://www.conservation.org/xp/frontlines/species>, accessed 17 March 2006.

Sihite, J., O.N. Lense, Surarti, C. Gustiar and S. Kosamah (2005), 'Bintuni Bay Nature Reserve Management Plan 2006–2030', The Nature Conservancy, Bali.

Suartana K.G., M. Mirino, S. Kosamah, Y. Ramba, N. Kadam and D. Neville (2003), 'Participatory Conservation Planning at Kampung Pasamai Bintuni Nature Reserve', The Nature Conservancy, Conservation Training and Resource Centre and BKSDA, Sorong.

Sudibyo, K.M. Boreri and T. Pieter (2003), 'Conservation Training and Resource Centre: A Practical Approach to Building Capacity for Biodiversity Conservation in Indonesia', paper presented to the World Parks Congress, Durban, 11–13 September.

Supriatna, J. (1999), 'The Irian Jaya Biodiversity Conservation Priority-setting Workshop, Final Report', Conservation International, Washington DC.

TNC (The Nature Conservancy) (2006), *An Effective Protected Area System: How Much Will It Cost Indonesia?*, Jakarta.

UNEP-WCMC (United Nations Environment Programme's World Conservation Monitoring Centre) (2006), *In the Front Line: Shoreline Protection and Other Ecosystem Services from Mangroves and Coral Reefs*, UNEP-WCMC Series No. 24, Cambridge.

Wallace, A.R. (1869), *The Malay Archipelago*, reprinted by Periplus in 2000, Singapore.

Wells, M., S. Guggenheim, A. Khan, W. Wardojo and P. Jepson (1999), *Investing in Biodiversity: A Review of Indonesia's Conservation and Development Projects*, World Bank, Washington DC.

Whitten, T., D. Holmes and K. MacKinnon (2001), 'Conservation Biology: A Displacement Behavior for Academia?', *Conservation Biology*, 15(1): 1–3.

Wickramanayake, E. Dinerstein, D. Olsen and C. Loucks (eds) (2002), *Terrestrial Ecoregions of the Indo-Pacific: A Conservation Assessment*, Island Press, Washington DC.

Wilson, K.A., M.F. McBride, M. Bode and H.P. Possingham (2006), 'Prioritizing Global Conservation Efforts', *Nature*, 440: 37–340.

Yowono, F.D.H. (1998), 'Community-based Fishery Management', in D. Bengen (ed.), *Proceedings of the First National Coastal Conference*, 19–20 March, Institut Pertanian Bogor, Bogor, pp. C68–C85.

7 BETWEEN A ROCK AND A HARD PLACE: CORPORATE STRATEGY AT THE FREEPORT MINE IN PAPUA, 2001–2006

Chris Ballard and Glenn Banks

1 'THE COMPANY THAT EVERYBODY LOVES TO HATE'

In certain respects, Freeport's Grasberg mine in the province of Papua (Figure 7.1) is now more accessible to a global audience than ever before. For anyone with internet access, Google Earth provides immediate (if delayed) satellite imagery of the mine and surrounds. Other free sites (such as the University of Maryland's Global Land Cover Facility) provide detailed Landsat satellite imagery showing the four-kilometre-wide open pit where the vast Grasberg or Grass Mountain once stood, and the sprawl of overburden dumped on every side of the pit (Figure 7.2). Google Earth's web address for this particular image is fast becoming a must-visit site for virtual tourists, assisted by its advertisement in a *New York Times* article (Perlez and Bonner 2005); even NASA has identified the Grasberg pit as worthy of particular focus on its Earth Observatory site (Earth Observatory 2005). It is no small irony, then, that despite this novel form of scrutiny by satellite, access to Freeport and to knowledge about its operations in Papua has actually become increasingly constrained over the past five years.

Freeport's Grasberg mine complex is one of the world's richest mining operations, with an annual revenue for 2005 of US$4.2 billion (Morrison 2006). Recent estimates suggest that the mine has both the second largest reserves of copper, and the largest reserves of gold, in the world. With much of the necessary infrastructure already in place when construction began in 1967, production costs are exceptionally low and profit margins are correspondingly high. In addition, the unknown potential of the larg-

Figure 7.1 Freeport's Original Contract of Work Area (Block A), and Its Location in Papua Province

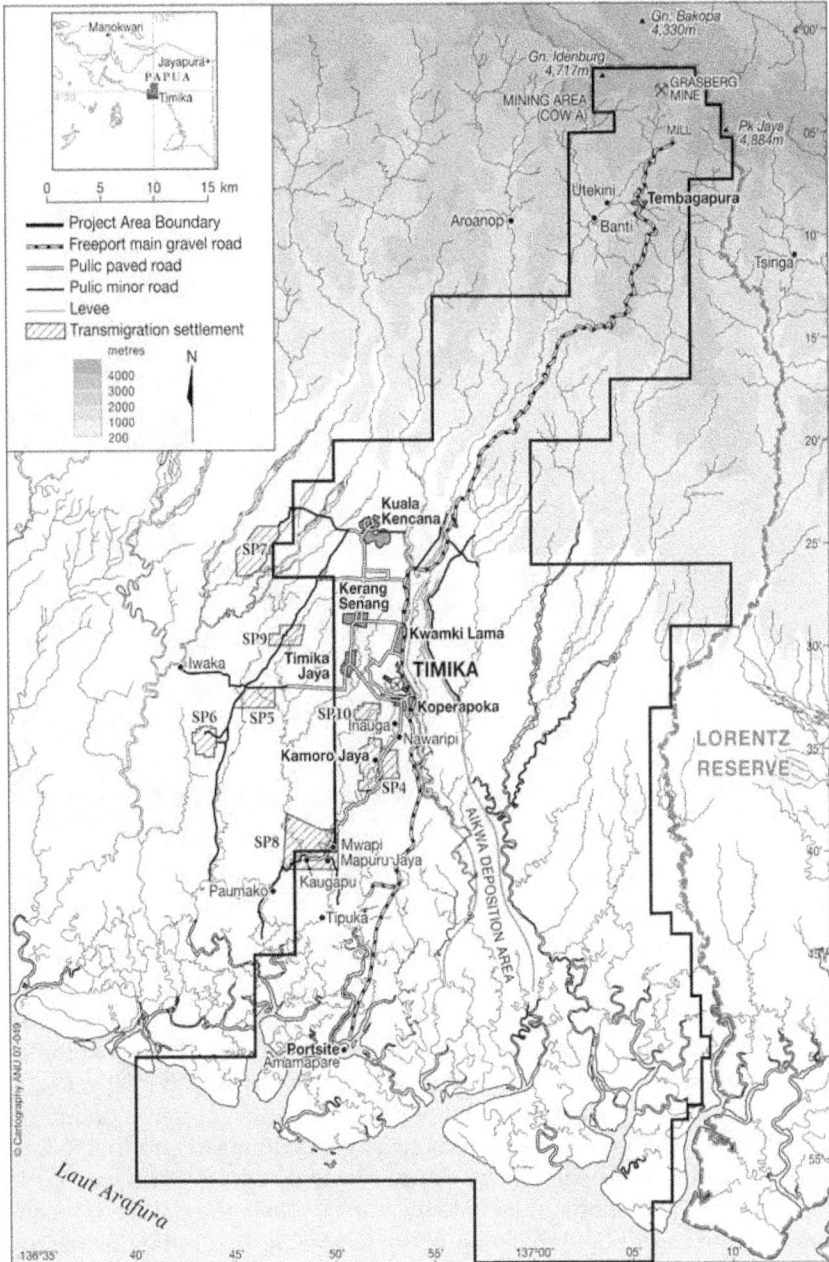

Figure 7.2   Satellite Image of Grasberg Mine, 29 May 2003

Source: Global Land Cover Facility, University of Maryland.

est ore body, the Grasberg, where the base of the ore deposit has yet to be identified, and of several additional ore bodies currently being explored, suggests that the mine's life could extend for at least another 30 years.

It is hard to overstate the value of Freeport to the Papuan economy: it contributes over 50 per cent of provincial gross domestic product (GDP) and accounts for 90 per cent of the province's exports. But even these figures almost certainly understate the mine's role in the provincial economy, as the multiplier effects on other sectors, such as manufacturing, construction, electricity, water, trade, hotels and restaurants, are presumably considerable. Freeport's value to Indonesia is also significant, as the nation's single largest taxpayer (paying US$1.09 billion to the government in 2005) and, with over 18,000 employees directly involved in its operations, one of the larger private sector employers in the country. Freeport claims to have contributed an estimated US$33 billion to the national economy during its time of operation and, citing a University of Indonesia report on its economic impact, to have generated an estimated 2.4 per cent of national GDP and 58 per cent of provincial GDP in 2005 – up from 1.6 per cent and 50 per cent respectively in 2003 on the back of inflated metal prices (Freeport McMoRan 2006: 5; Investor Daily 2005). However, Freeport's strategic importance to the state appears to exceed even its monetary value. In recognition of both its wealth and its status as the earliest symbol of foreign investment confidence in the New Order government, the Freeport mine was one of the first 10 sites in Indonesia to be declared a 'national asset', requiring particular state attention and special security measures.[1]

While multinational resource companies have an unenviable record of being able to operate in the most chaotic and violent of political landscapes, Freeport's achievement in this regard must still be considered extraordinary. Prospecting of the original ore body was conducted during the final years of the Dutch administration of what was then Netherlands New Guinea, and the initial 1967 Contract of Work (CoW) was the first such contract negotiated under the new Soeharto regime. Production has continued essentially unbroken since 1972, surviving the Papuan uprisings of 1977 and 1984 and riding out the titanic upheavals of the late 1990s in Indonesia, including the economic crisis, Soeharto's downfall and the ensuing period of political and social reform (*reformasi*). Freeport has emerged as one of the key elements of stability in the provincial and national landscape.

Internationally, the mine and the company have had to endure a high degree of critical scrutiny from a wide range of stakeholders, including environmental and human rights organizations, ethical shareholders, the US Overseas Private Investment Corporation (OPIC) and the United States Securities and Exchange Commission. Over time, whether deservedly or not, Freeport has attracted a reputation as 'the company that everybody loves to hate' (ICG 2006) or the 'poster child for all that is wrong with mining in Indonesia' (McBeth 2006).

In this chapter we seek to explore how Freeport's strategies have evolved in response to changes in the political and industrial context since 2000. A brief summary of the mine's history up to 2000 is followed

---

1 There are now an estimated 270 such 'vital national objects' in Indonesia, but Freeport remains the most heavily guarded of them all (Rukmantara 2006).

by a review of post-2000 developments in global, national and local conditions. The focus then turns to Freeport's mining, political and environmental strategies, its often fraught relations with indigenous Papuan communities and its reliance on national security forces in the vicinity of the mine. We conclude with some reflections on the role of Freeport in the past and future of Papua, and on the extent to which the capital-intensive operations of global corporations such as Freeport are able to remain impervious to dramatic transformations at the national and provincial levels.

The authors have been monitoring events at the Freeport mine since 1994, when we were both initially invited to visit the mine by Freeport's newly formed Community Affairs Department. The fact that such a department had only just been set up in about 1990, more than 20 years after construction began at the site, provides some indication of the neglect of the relationship between company and community, unthinkable in neighbouring Papua New Guinea during the same period (Filer 1996). We returned in 1996 and worked until 1998 with colleagues from the local University of Cenderawasih in Jayapura, establishing a baseline account of the living conditions and aspirations of the indigenous landowning Amungme and Kamoro communities against which subsequent progress in their status could be gauged — a project known as the UNCEN–ANU Baseline Studies Project (UABS 1998; Banks 2000). Inevitably, much of our work also involved documentation of events over the 30 years since 1967. Although neither of us has had access to the Timika area since 2002 (foreign journalists and researchers have generally been discouraged from entering Papua since about 2000 and were formally banned between 2003 and 2005), we have read the available reports on subsequent events and attempt to interpret them in the light of our earlier experience of the political complexities attending all matters involving Freeport.

2   THE FREEPORT OPERATION (1967–2000)

Freeport is the term used almost universally to refer both to the parent company, Freeport McMoRan Inc., based in New Orleans, Louisiana, and to its principal revenue-generating operation, the Grasberg mine complex in Papua, which is operated by an Indonesian subsidiary, PT Freeport Indonesia. This apparent conflation of the parent and subsidiary companies together with the location of their mine in fact captures fairly accurately the close integration and mutual dependence of all three elements, none of which would exist without the others. References in this chapter to 'the company' thus identify the parent and its subsidiary as a single entity. Freeport McMoRan Inc. and PT Freeport Indonesia are also essentially single-mine corporations[2] in which substantial decisions taken about the operation of the mine emanate almost entirely from New Orleans, while the fate of the mine, which generates approximately 90 per cent of Freeport McMoRan's revenues, is central to that of the parent company.

The corporate histories of the mine and the two companies are relatively well documented, by Indonesian standards (Wilson 1981; Mealey 1996; Leith 2003). The brief summary below of events prior to 2000 reviews some of the challenges that have confronted the mine's operators, distinguishing between two broad periods: the first, from 1967 to about 1995, in which Freeport operated largely free of external and international attention, and the second, more tempestuous period from 1995 to about 2000 during which the mine and its operators came under intense scrutiny and pressure for change. The question then posed is whether that scrutiny has in fact generated more than cosmetic change in corporate outlook and practice in New Orleans and on the ground in Papua.

Under the Radar (1967–95)

The original ore body in Freeport's Papuan mine complex, the Ertsberg, was first identified in 1936 by a Dutch geologist on a mountaineering expedition. His published report of the find was the stimulus for a second expedition in 1960, conducted jointly by a Dutch mining company, Oost Borneo Maatschappij, and Freeport Sulphur, an American company then scouting for nickel prospects in Indonesia. The results of this second expedition were sufficiently promising for Freeport to pursue its option on the deposit, but the takeover of Dutch New Guinea by Indonesia in 1962 forced a delay in further development. Following the accession to power of Soeharto's New Order regime, Freeport was awarded the first mining CoW in 1967, operating through its local subsidiary, PT Freeport Indonesia. Construction began on-site almost immediately and production commenced in 1972. After an initial profit windfall in the early 1970s, riding on the back of high copper prices, Freeport's CoW was renegotiated on less generous terms in 1976. Copper prices promptly dived and by 1977–78 Freeport was experiencing difficulty servicing its debt repayments. Only when metal prices recovered at the end of the decade did Freeport begin to rise above the status of a marginal enterprise (Mealey 1996).

---

2 Or at least they were until Freeport McMoRan's US$26 billion friendly takeover of Phelps Dodge in 2007, which created the world's largest publicly listed copper company (Mandaro 2007).

During the 1970s, a series of additional ore bodies adjacent to the original Ertsberg find had extended initial estimates of the mine's life into the late 1980s, but it was the discovery of the massive Grasberg ore body in 1987, just as the Ertsberg approached exhaustion, that saw Freeport gain its current position as an industry giant. Freeport currently holds a 1991 extension to its CoW that is valid for the next 50 years. Under the 1991 agreement, Freeport also secured a new exploration concession area of 4.8 million acres, known as Block B; the original Block A, by comparison, covered a mere 24,700 acres. To finance the considerable cost of exploration over such a vast area, Freeport accepted a US$1.7 billion offer from Rio Tinto Zinc (now Rio Tinto), which saw Rio acquire just over 10 per cent of Freeport Indonesia's parent company, Freeport McMoRan, together with a 40 per cent beneficial interest in the Block B concession (Mealey 1996).

Changes in the volume of mill throughput are a useful index of developments in mining activity at Freeport. There was a sharp increase in mill throughput following the discovery of Grasberg, from 7,500 metric tonnes per day (mtd) in 1972, to 66,000 mtd in 1993, to 220,000 mtd in 1998. Mill waste is dumped directly into the Agabagong River, which disgorges into the Aikwa River and thence into the Arafura Sea (Figure 7.1). Freeport underwent a process of environmental evaluation, monitored by the government, which has allowed for an increase in daily throughput to a maximum of 300,000 mtd. By way of comparison with mines in neighbouring Papua New Guinea, Ok Tedi, which is also a copper and gold project, has an average mill throughput of about 80,000 mtd and the Porgera gold mine an average of only 17,000 mtd. Until 1995, what external scrutiny there was of Freeport's operations focused largely on environmental impacts, particularly in the aftermath of a large overbank event at the Aikwa River in 1990 which saw tailings disgorged over a 30-square-kilometre area of lowland forest (Mealey 1996: 266).

This earlier period was characterized by very successful management of the mine's relatively low national and international profile, despite numerous problems with protests from local communities about the lack of compensation or consultation for use of their land, and a 1977 province-wide uprising in which the mine was directly attacked as a symbol of the Soeharto regime (see below).

In the Spotlight (1995–2000)

The scale of the 1987 Grasberg discovery, and the dramatic increase in activity at the mine site from about 1990, inevitably brought Freeport to greater national and international attention. This process culminated in a five-year period, from 1995 until about 2000, during which Freeport was exposed to near-continuous scrutiny and criticism, albeit largely from a distance. Although the scale of the project, and of foreign direct investment, demanded some level of media attention, access to the mine site has been very closely controlled by both the company and the state: foreign visas for the Timika district are rarely given for activities other than employment by Freeport or its contractors, and access to the CoW area is controlled by the company, which owns most of the transport and infrastructure beyond the township of Timika.

With the 1991 renegotiation of Freeport Indonesia's CoW, the mine attracted increased scrutiny from national and international environmental and human rights organizations, US regulators and the media. A group of international environmental non-government organizations (NGOs) had already written to Freeport in 1990 to express their concerns about the forthcoming environmental impact assessment (EIA) to be undertaken as a provision of the new CoW. The Indonesian environmental umbrella NGO, WALHI, began to monitor the mine's impacts in 1991. A series of flood events between 1990 and 1994 considerably enlarged the lowland area affected by tailings and began to threaten the township of Timika, raising questions about the wisdom of Freeport's strategy of dumping tailings in the river system (WALHI–YPMD 1991). An independent environmental field study of the mine's operations was conducted by EnviroSearch International on behalf of OPIC, which had underwritten the mine's risk insurance policy (Emel 2002: 835–6). OPIC's 1995 decision to cancel Freeport's policy on the basis of its failure to adequately disclose its environmental performance was Freeport's first truly stern external test, but the manner in which it dealt with this challenge, and with the threat posed by WALHI's constant attention, served to set in place some basic strategic precepts for the company. These included aggressive and often intimidating responses to challenges, coupled with a massive public relations campaign, complete with full-page advertisements in US and Indonesian newspapers, and a tactic of hiring or in other ways suborning its critics (Bryce 2005). As Freeport McMoRan's larger than life Texan CEO, Jim-Bob Moffett, described it, this was a 'new cold war' (McBeth 1996).

While this strategy proved effective in dealing with local NGOs and distant critics, new methods were required to deal with the outbursts of extreme violence around the mine concession area between 1994 and 1997. Public rallies towards the end of 1994 in support of political independence and the armed independence movement, the Free Papua Movement (OPM), were ruthlessly suppressed by the military, with loss of life and incidents of torture in which Freeport company equipment was reportedly used. When news of these events and of further killings of refugees who had fled into the forest leaked out in 1995 (Munninghoff

1995), Freeport came under intense international pressure and scrutiny. A hostage-taking incident in early 1996 in the Lorentz National Park, immediately abutting Freeport's CoW area, led to a dramatic increase in military presence and activity in the Timika region, and to yet more reports of human rights abuses into 1997. At the same time, in March 1996, a large-scale riot directed against Freeport installations spread from Tembagapura down to the Timika lowlands, and was halted only by the neatly timed arrival of fresh troops led by Lieutenant-General Prabowo, a son-in-law of President Soeharto (Ballard 1997). The net effect of the period of extreme violence from 1994 to 1997 was an unfortunate cementing of the relationship between Freeport and the military, coinciding with an increase in international scrutiny of the company and of events generally in Indonesia and Irian Jaya.

Jim-Bob Moffett contributed substantially to this new focus on Freeport by building a four-star Sheraton hotel in the Timika lowlands and developing a grandiose US-style company town, Kuala Kencana, complete with an 18-hole golf course and club house. Kuala Kencana was formally inaugurated in December 1995 by President Soeharto, reflecting the company's careful cultivation of ties with the Soeharto family and administration. The fall of Soeharto in May 1998 appeared ominous for Freeport, given the company's close identification with the president and the subsequent push for increased transparency in the nationwide post-Soeharto process of *reformasi*. The goal of this chapter is to understand how Freeport survived the post-Soeharto transformations at the national and provincial levels, to emerge — in defiance of all expectations — in a position that is possibly even stronger than it was before 1998.

3   THE CHANGING CONTEXT (2001–06)

The Changing Global Environment for Corporations

Changes in Freeport's Indonesian operations are inevitably shaped to some degree by recent shifts in international attitudes towards mining operations elsewhere, and by the various initiatives adopted by the global mining industry. Various high-profile 'disasters' and exposés in the 1980s and early 1990s, along with far greater mobilization of and scrutiny by international NGO networks, led to a period of self-reflection and examination by the industry (see the papers in Denoon et al. 1996 and Ballard and Banks 2003). This strategic repositioning and, to be fair, reshaping and redefinition of stakeholder relationships, has exposed the industry to a far greater degree of external relationship building and re-examination of practices — in relation to environmental and human rights issues in particular—than for any other industry. Critics observe that mining has had further to go than many other industries.

Two recent initiatives have crystallized industry thinking and approaches to 'sustainability' generally. These are the industry-funded Mining, Minerals and Sustainable Development (MMSD) report of 2002 and the World Bank's Extractive Industry Review (EIR) of 2003. While it might be assumed that these exercises were initiated in the spirit of the Johannesburg 'Rio+10' Summit push for greater corporate involvement in improving social and economic conditions, the primary motivation for both relates more directly to corporate concerns about public image and the 'social licence to operate'—issues that are increasingly seen as being connected to profitability (Stanwick and Stanwick 1998; Vogel 2005). Whatever the ironies of a resource extraction industry apparently embracing and championing 'sustainability', one of the results of this discursive shift has been to bring to the foreground issues of the relationship between companies and communities in the developing world. In particular, the MMSD process provided an important stimulus for the industry to come to terms with changing international community expectations in relation to its role in protecting and securing the human rights of communities in the areas in which mines operate.

Freeport, with its past record of human rights and environmental problems, and an element of secrecy attached to its remote and relatively inaccessible location, has been an obvious target for international scrutiny, and indeed was featured at a number of points in the MMSD process (see, for example, Handelsman 2002; Ballard 2002a). The recent growth of international attention reflects the scale and breadth of the Freeport project and its myriad and complex relationships with an increasingly broad range of actors, interests and issues. The evolution of the company's corporate strategies has been directly influenced by the often unwelcome attention of this new constituency of external stakeholders.

An important element in Freeport's profile over the past decade was the buy-in of Rio Tinto to the broader project. At the time this generated two apparently contradictory tendencies, with Freeport increasingly coming to the attention of longstanding NGO critics of Rio Tinto as the industry giant (such as MineWatch), while at the same time becoming exposed to a more stringent set of corporate controls in relation to a wide range of issues—everything from financial reporting standards and reserve estimation to Rio Tinto's code of conduct in relation to human rights. There is certainly anecdotal evidence to suggest that the entry of Rio Tinto imposed new limits (in relation to exploration programs and the worst excesses of Freeport's infrastructure expenditure in and around Timika) and offered new insights and perspectives for a company that had previously had no active corporate partners and just the one mine and jurisdiction within which to learn and transfer lessons. The reputational slur now works in the other direction, with Rio Tinto's involvement in Freeport continuing to dog it even though it sold its direct stake in Freeport McMoRan in 2004 (Freed 2005).[3] Freeport was also linked to the Bre-X or Busang fiasco of the late 1990s, although the company's corporate reputation actually improved as a result of its role in bringing this sham to an end (Francis 1997; Goold and Wills 1997; Tsing 2000).

The influence of fluctuating metal prices on global markets has obvious financial effects on the industry: it affects the stock prices of resource stocks as well as the profitability of companies and operations. Metal prices also shape the outlook and attitudes of the industry itself. Like a manic depressive, the mining industry experiences periods of intense gloom followed regularly by periods of euphoria. The relationship between these swings and attention to concerns of corporate social responsibility is not as simple. Forcing industry and operator attention to the so-called 'soft' issues is usually easier during the good times, but boom times may also obscure the need for attention to non-core business. In other cases, corporate social responsibility is turned to as a panacea or smokescreen precisely when financial performance has weakened or environmental or social issues have come under scrutiny (Banks 2006). Regardless of the circumstances that lead companies into the discursive world of corporate social responsibility, there is a danger that when the industry equivalent of the 'black dog' lingers, notions of broader responsibility are rapidly shed. We should not assume, in other words, that value change and the confrontation of past practices will result in enduring changes. A poor corporate memory and regular personnel changes in key positions can also quickly shift the diagnosis to one of amnesia.

National and Provincial Transformation since 1998

The broader context of change at the national and provincial Papuan levels is set out in Chapters 2 and 3 of this book; the summary here focuses on those issues that bear most directly on the case of Freeport. A nationwide process of political and fiscal decentralization initiated as a central component of the post-Soeharto *reformasi* process was embodied in the Regional Autonomy Law (Law No. 22/1999) and the Fiscal Decentralization Law (Law No. 25/1999) — since replaced by Law No. 32/2004 and Law No. 33/2004 respectively. This legal reform required further elaboration in the case of Papua province, through the instrument of a Special Autonomy Law (Law No. 21/2001).

---

3 Rio Tinto retains a 40 per cent interest in any copper and gold reserves discovered after 1994.

Table 7.1   *Allocation of Mining (Non-oil and Gas) Royalties and Land Rent under Law No. 25/1999*

Source of Revenue	Central Government	Provincial Government	Producing District	Other Districts
Land rent	20	16	64	–
Royalties	20	16	32	32

Source: Mollet (2001).

The offer of a special level of the general autonomy being granted to regional authorities elsewhere in Indonesia was regarded by Jakarta as a useful means of countering the calls for political independence that were being made in Papua during the short-lived 'Papuan Spring', between 1998 and 2001 (ICG 2001). Under the nationalist administration of President Megawati, the temporary political freedoms experienced in Papua under the Habibie and Wahid administrations were sharply revoked. The ensuing crackdown placed strong limits on political organization within Papua. In addition, the restrictions on access to the province for media and foreigners that had characterized some of the worst periods of the Soeharto era were restored. This has had direct implications for national and international scrutiny of Freeport's operations in Papua, as Freeport has essentially been able to select for site visits only those journalists who were deemed worthy of particular support and facilitation in terms of the company's interests.

The special autonomy legislation can be said to have created two broad sets of new conditions for Freeport's operations: new political conditions, and new revenue conditions. The devolution of powers from the national centre to the provincial periphery includes a further devolution to the district (*kabupaten*) and subdistrict (*kecamatan*) levels. In the Timika area, the creation of new administrative entities has generated novel vectors for competition and thus conflict. A heavy-handed attempt by Jakarta to create a new province, Central Irian Jaya, centred administratively and financially on Timika, led to open and fatal conflict in 2003 (Timmer 2004). Plans for the new province have since been shelved, at least for the present.

Under the terms of the Fiscal Decentralization Law, provincial and local governments throughout Indonesia are to receive up to 80 per cent of general mining revenues, and have gained the authority to issue mining permits — terms which apply equally to the special autonomy provisions for Papua (Dwiyana 2001; Mollet 2001). Table 7.1 illustrates the breakdown of mining royalties and land rents between the central government in Jakarta, the provincial government, and resource-producing and other districts. One probable consequence of this redirection of royalties may be to strengthen the bond between Freeport and the local provincial and district administrations, a situation that could work to the company's advantage in terms of an increased scope for political influence. The decentralization laws also include provisions for improved environmental protection standards and an increase in the permit holder's responsibility for local community development. The regulations governing the implementation of these modifications, which have not yet been elaborated, will obviously be crucial to their success.

4   FREEPORT'S MANAGEMENT OF CHANGE

Corporate strategies put in place to manage Freeport's image and its Indonesian operation are more prominent and subject to greater scrutiny than those of virtually any other mining company.[4] This is partly a response to its high profile, and partly a consequence of the nature of the operation itself. In this section we review strategies adopted by Freeport in four areas: mining and finance, politics, environment, and community relations.

'Hunker Down and Go': Mining Strategies

Freeport has a reputation within the global mining industry for being less concerned with production efficiency than most other contemporary operations. The nature and grades of the ore bodies allow for higher cut-off grades than virtually anywhere else, and the focus on getting the 'rocks in the box' (a phrase that we frequently encountered at Freeport in the late 1990s) allowed rumours to surface within the company and among its industry partners of a relative neglect of maintenance, environment, costs and safety. More recently, with the widely reported failures in its waste dumps and the landslips in the pit over the last five years, one of which was fatal, concern has been raised about the operation's safety and engineering standards, and particularly bench maintenance within the open pit (Freeport McMoRan 2005). This relatively cavalier strategy might be regarded as the sign of a company that has the economic and regulatory luxury of operating away from North American industry standards, although it is also symptomatic of mining industry strategies of high grading in the face of longer-term uncertainty. This

---

4   Freeport's former minority shareholder, Rio Tinto, would be the one possible rival in this regard.

Figure 7.3   Freeport McMoRan Share Price and Cash Copper Price on the London Metal Exchange, 1995–2006

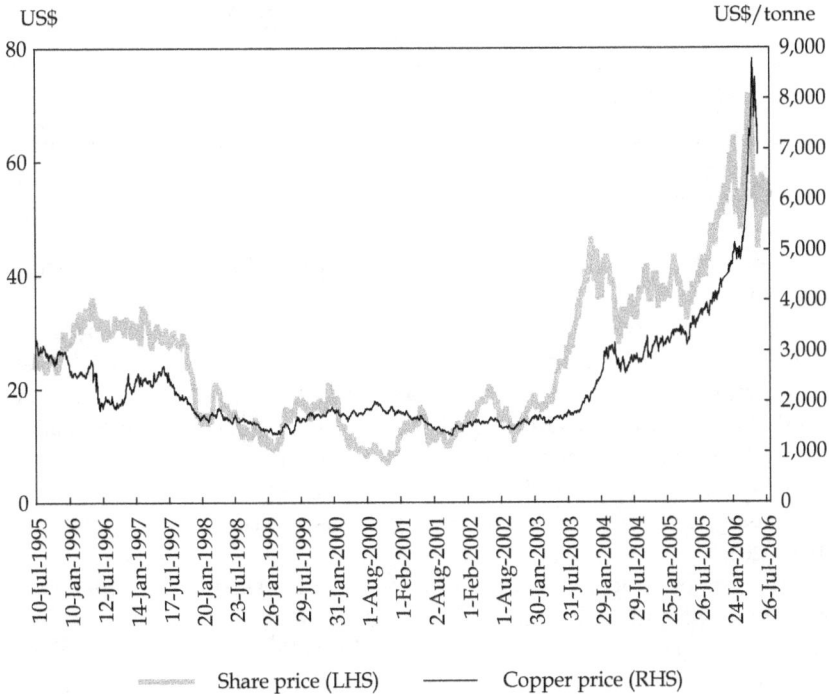

Share price (LHS) ——— Copper price (RHS)

Source: Publicly available data.

uncertainty — particularly political uncertainty — has shaped Freeport's political engagements with successive Indonesian regimes and domestic politics (Leith 2003) and the extreme bottom-line focus of its operational management, with damaging consequences for both the environment and local communities (see below).

Since 2003, Freeport's approach has seen it well positioned to take advantage of copper and gold prices at 25-year highs, to the extent that revenues topped US$4 billion for the first time in 2005 on the back of these elevated commodity prices. Freeport's share price has likewise climbed from a low in 2001, when it traded at around US$10, to sustained levels of over US$50, with peaks of over US$70. Figure 7.3 shows the Freeport McMoRan Copper & Gold share price against prices for its primary commodity, cash copper, during the period 1995–2006. What the graph strongly suggests is that Freeport's fortunes have reflected very closely the value of its principal product, and have seldom been deflected by other issues; Freeport, like most other large mining houses, has been able

Table 7.2   *Freeport Senior Executive Salary Packages and Share Sales, 2005*

Executive	Salary Package	Share Sales	Total
Jim-Bob Moffett (chairman)	$47 million	$88 million	$135 million
Richard C. Adkerson (CEO)	$36 million	$42 million	$78 million

Source: Freed (2006).

to ride out temporary slumps in the copper price through its program of hedging.

Senior executives have translated these returns into huge personal gain (Table 7.2). Jim-Bob Moffett (chairman) and Richard C. Adkerson (president and CEO) netted salary and Freeport share sale receipts totalling more than $200 million between them in 2005 (Donnan 2006a; Freed 2006). Moffett has always been very well compensated for his role at Freeport, having been described in 1997 as 'easily the most overpaid chief executive officer in the mining industry' (Project Underground 1998: 20).

The rise of ethical investment funds and increased shareholder pressure have provided an additional point of attack for critics, and Freeport's response to this is noteworthy. The *Risky Business* alternative report for Freeport shareholders (Project Underground 1998) argued that, for financial reasons if nothing else, shareholders would be wise either to pressure Freeport to address the issues of human rights and complicity with the Indonesian military, or to divest their shares in the company. At about the same time, the Seattle Mennonite Church used its status as a shareholder to raise questions about Freeport McMoRan's activities at its annual general meetings. In recent times, similar strategies have been pursued at Rio Tinto shareholder meetings. Most recently, the Norwegian government's oil fund blacklisted Freeport (Vaporean 2006).

Two broad, if partly contradictory, approaches have framed Freeport's response to such attacks. The first is the tried and true Freeport tactic of aggressive or dismissive denial. For example, the recent exclusion of Freeport shares from the US$240 billion Norwegian oil fund elicited the response that the tailings were simply 'natural rock', that operations were conducted 'with the least environmental impact possible' and that the whole fuss was a 'misunderstanding' (Vaporean 2006). Second, there has been a concerted attempt by Freeport to reduce the scope for influence of these 'fringe' shareholders. It is no coincidence that Freeport began an extensive program of buying back its shares in 1995, at the height of international scrutiny and criticism of its Papua operation. The company has since expended at least US$1.1 billion in reducing by 25 per cent the number of common shares available. One of the goals of this strategy, so Emel (2002: 840) claims, is to 'relieve [Freeport] of shareholder and other pressure', although given the presence of the large mutual funds among Freeport's shareholders, activist pressure is more likely to occur through these funds rather than directly.[5]

'No Tall Trees': Political Strategies

Freeport's core political strategy under the leadership of CEO Jim-Bob Moffett (since 1984) has been to service key political relationships, especially with successive US administrations, as well as in Jakarta and with the military, and to engage with critics either briefly and sharply or as little as possible. The conventional mining industry goal of avoiding scrutiny has been greatly assisted in Freeport's case by the limits placed by the state on access to Papua, and by Freeport's control of much of the infrastructure and means of access within its CoW area. The motto promulgated by Moffett at Freeport is 'No tall trees' (Perlez and Bonner 2005; McBeth 2006), symbolizing a strategy which the company hopes will return it to the pre-Grasberg era when the company was largely able to fly under the radar.

Internationally, Freeport has enjoyed exceptional support from successive US administrations and agencies. Its board members have included Henry Kissinger and former US ambassadors to Indonesia such as Stapleton Roy. At arbitration with OPIC in 1995–96, Freeport's interests were represented by R. James Woolsey, a former director of the CIA. Ex-CIA officers and former US military attaches to Jakarta have been hired to head company security. Freeport's ties with the US military have been particularly close; on several occasions since the mid-1990s the company has hosted low-profile meetings at Timika between high-level officers of the US, Indonesian and Australian security forces (TAPOL 2006). Freeport also acts as one of the two principal coordinators (along with Exxon-Mobil) of the US–Indonesia Business Council, sponsoring numerous exchanges and cultural events that serve to cement business ties between the two countries.

Freeport's strong Jakarta connections have enabled the company to ride out most political storms at the national level. The company's Jakarta connections suffered a blow with the resignation of President Soeharto in 1998, as the company had carefully nurtured close connections with the president, his family and their immediate business partners; but Freeport still boasts an impressive array of contacts and a remarkable degree of

---

5   We are obliged to Chakriya Bowman for this insight.

influence in Jakarta, among civilian politicians and government officials, and at the highest levels of the security forces.

Reflecting its economic weight, within Papua the company has enormous influence over the provincial and district-level political and administrative environments. As indicated by the distribution of Freeport funds documented in a report by Global Witness (2005), Freeport also maintains strong links with the provincial security forces at all levels, and at almost all locations throughout the province.

Not all of Freeport's political alliances in Indonesia have been judicious. An early attempt to curry favour on both sides of the autonomy/independence debate by part funding the Second Papua Congress, held in Jayapura in 2000, proved to be a strategic mistake, and the company is now much more cautious in its direct dealings with Papuan politics. Opposition to Freeport at the national level—from the mercurial Amien Rais, Sonny Keraf (former minister for the environment and currently chair of the Parliamentary Commission on the Environment) and others—has the potential to create awkward moments for Freeport. During the Soeharto era, Freeport's tactic of sidelining its partner ministries in Jakarta and making direct representations to the president created a legacy of opposition to the company within several key ministries. But this opposition is not coordinated in exerting pressure, and individual opponents of the company are seldom in positions of real executive power for long enough to see their criticisms take effect.

One of the more successful internal initiatives adopted by Freeport to reduce unnecessary exposure to critical media or observers has been to sharply curtail the public appearances and pronouncements of the gaffe-prone Jim-Bob Moffett. On occasion, Moffett has slipped the leash and broken the tenets of this strategy, but Freeport's public statements are now much more measured in tone than they were during the heady days of the 'cold war' of the 1990s.

'Speeding up Geological Time': Environmental Strategies

One of the most controversial elements of the Freeport operation, and a major lever in terms of international scrutiny, has been the environmental impact of the mine. As with other elements of the operation, little attention was given to the environmental impact of the mine prior to Grasberg's discovery in 1988, and it was still largely unexamined in 1994 when Freeport established an environmental laboratory close to Timika airport (Leith 2003). The Indonesian government has taken a far more active interest in the environmental aspects of the mine in the last decade, approving the first EIA (or AMDAL in the Indonesian regulatory context) in 1995. A subsequent AMDAL to approve the mill expansion to

300,000 mtd was approved in 1997, and the mine operation was reviewed critically by the Indonesian Environmental Impact Management Agency (Bapedal) in 1999. Despite several written reports and letters from various government agencies pointing out breaches of government regulations, Freeport has consistently stated that it complies in all material respects with Indonesian law in terms of its operation. As a recent report by WALHI (2006) notes, many of these breaches have never been satisfactorily addressed but in the absence of strong political or civil society support for action, and given its financial significance and political connections, Freeport has been able to continue operating. In 1996 and again in 1999, Freeport commissioned and published two environmental audits of its operation (Dames & Moore 1996; Montgomery Watson Indonesia 1999). They confirmed Freeport's material compliance with Indonesian law, although both raised some concerns about the scale and nature of the impacts. Leith (2003: 183) notes concerns about the independence and subsequent selective use by Freeport of these audits. It is significant that no external environmental audits have been commissioned since.

The environmental impacts of the Freeport operation are similar to those of many other mines in the region, and revolve around management of the waste generated by mining activities (Banks 2001). This waste takes one of two primary forms: overburden or waste rock, and tailings. The former is material that is moved to access the metal-bearing ore. The Freeport operation typically moves 500,000 tonnes of overburden per day. It is stored in a stable waste dump in the headwaters of the Wanagon River, itself part of the Aikwa (or Ajkwa) River catchment. Tailings are the finely ground residue of the milling and extraction process. At Freeport they typically make up 97 per cent of the ore that is processed; that is, only the 3 per cent copper and gold in the ore that enters the mill complex is extracted. A recent report published by the company provides a description of the tailings disposal system, noting that the company:

> ... uses the Ajkwa River system for tailings transport to a designated area in the lowlands and coastal zone, called the Modified Ajkwa Deposition Area (ModADA) which is an engineered, managed system for the deposition and control of tailings (Freeport McMoRan 2004: 4).

The benign language of this statement conceals a dramatic set of physically extensive changes to the landscape, resource base and ecology of the floodplain area, as shown in the images published in Paull et al. (2006). From this work it is clear that the affected area (the ModADA) covered 167 square kilometres in 2004 and will continue to grow: indeed, the issue of how Freeport intends to manage the more than 3 billion tonnes of waste material still to be produced is unclear.

In the absence of transparent company or government data on the impact of the mine, satellite imagery is as close as most outside observers can get to the affected area or communities, as Perlez and Bonner (2005) have observed. As noted in our introduction, the ability to access and use such imagery has certainly become more widely available – due to the sheer scale of the operation, Freeport has nowhere to hide. Such imagery does allow for a limited analysis of the impact of the mine, but detailed material on, for example, the likely future effect of the build-up of copper in the tailings containment area comes from leaked reports commissioned by the company.

A significant aspect of the company's strategic ability to regulate concerns about the environmental aspects of its operation rests on its control over access to the area. In such a context, reliable, independent monitoring of impacts is nonexistent. A recent report by WALHI (2006) – perhaps the most comprehensive public environmental review of Freeport – had to rely heavily on leaked internal Freeport reports such as the Parametrix Ecological and Health Assessments of 2002. This unsanctioned flow of information is revealing of Freeport's inability to assert full control over the very data that it commissions to try and defend its environmental record. The WALHI report notes a long list of serious environmental concerns, including the long-term future of the tailings disposal area and the true impact on the ecosystems and communities in the area.

The recent sustained attention of the Indonesian parliament to environmental aspects of the mine (of which the March 2006 visit and subsequent report by the Ministry of Environment is the most high profile) represents a new development. Whereas in the past national attention was cursory and fleeting (usually in response to a particular event or international report), and easily weathered or deflected by Freeport, the current politically driven campaign appears more serious and sustained. This is probably because it is framed as a political rather than simply environmental concern – the extensive environmental impacts are as much a political tool for critics as they are an environmental liability for Freeport.

'Pacts with the Devil': Papuan Communities, the Security Forces and Human Rights

Papuan Communities

At the time of Freeport's arrival in the Timika area in 1967, the total population of the CoW area was no more than 3,000, consisting largely of communities of the two indigenous landowning language groups, the highland Amungme in the vicinity of Tembagapura (Cook 1995) and the lowland Kamoro, distributed along the coast and riverine plains (Harple 2000; Pickell and Muller 2001). Since the development of the mine, and particularly since 1988, there has been significant migration to the CoW and surrounding area. The migrants include official government-sponsored transmigrants, mine employees and their families, members of the Kamoro and Amungme or related tribal groups from outside the CoW area, and so-called 'spontaneous migrants' from other parts of Papua and Indonesia. Precise figures for the various types of migrants are not available but the total population within the CoW area has increased from less than 3,000 in 1967 to more than 120,000 (Ballard 2002b). This figure is also significant in terms of the provincial total, which is currently estimated at about 2.5 million.

The impact of Freeport's arrival, of the loss of land to the mines and to mining infrastructure, and of this influx of migrants, has been severe for both of the local landowning groups. A long sequence of protests against these impositions, especially on the part of the Amungme, has led to an enduring environment of enmity and distrust between Freeport and the indigenous landowners. The company's recourse to the protection of the national security forces has resulted in an appalling history of gross human rights abuses and intimidation, further alienating the communities.[6] At least 160 people, mostly Amungme, Nduga and Lani highlanders, have been killed by the security forces since the mid-1970s. Many more have been tortured, raped or illegally detained, or have spent years in refuge in remote forests.

After earlier province-wide uprisings in 1977–78 and 1983–84, which also involved loss of life in the Timika region, local protests in the Tembagapura area in 1994, associated with rising activity on the part of OPM, were brutally crushed. An extended period of terror ensued, lasting until at least 1999 and involving a massive build-up in troop numbers. The role of elements within the security forces in orchestrating or exacerbating many of the events used to justify this build-up—including roadside shootings in 1994, large-scale riots in March 1996 and a hostage crisis in Lorentz National Park in 1996—remains uncertain, but Freeport acquiesced in the process and committed itself to supporting and largely funding the long-term presence of the security forces. In so doing, the company perhaps irreparably damaged its chances of ever achieving a profound reconciliation with the Amungme and other indigenous communities (Perlez 2006).

Indigenous ownership of land at the mine site and in the Tembagapura and Timika areas has never been formally acknowledged, and its use by Freeport was neither negotiated nor compensated. An early attempt in 1974 to arrive at a belated settlement of compensation claims was poorly handled and resulted in a heightened sense of grievance on the part of the Amungme (Ballard 2002a). Following the discovery of the

---

6 See Ballard (2002a, 2002b, 2002c) for details.

Grasberg ore body, Freeport made a concerted attempt to re-engage with the Amungme and Kamoro by establishing a Community Affairs Department and putting in motion plans to reserve 1 per cent of the profits of PT Freeport Indonesia for community development. This initiative was effectively hijacked by the security forces, which insisted that the fund be disbursed among all of the neighbouring ethnic groups, the so-called 'seven *suku*'. By putting forward their own clients as leaders of these groups, individual security units were able to siphon off the lion's share of the benefits earmarked for the indigenous communities.

Opposition to the continuing presence of the company and the military was led by Tom Beanal, the chair of the Amungme Traditional Council (LEMASA), who lodged a high-profile lawsuit in Louisiana against Freeport for cultural genocide and environmental damages (Jessup 1999). Following the failure of the lawsuit, Beanal was recruited to the board of PT Freeport Indonesia, a move that effectively negated his capacity for opposition. In similar fashion, other community leaders have been hired by Freeport or appointed to run foundations sponsored by the company (Lowry and Miller n.d.; Freeport McMoRan 2006). These seemingly beneficent initiatives have had the effect of dividing opposition and limiting the capacity of the communities to articulate positions that are distinct from those of the company.

In reflecting publicly on its relationship with the indigenous communities, Freeport focuses firmly on the scale of its 1 per cent and other financial contributions, trumpeting its own philanthropy: '*Business Week* magazine ... named [Freeport] as America's most philanthropic company in terms of cash given as a percentage of revenues' (Collier 2005). Yet the company remains profoundly reluctant to explore the impact of its presence, or to cede any real authority or control to indigenous communities (Soares 2004). As Michelle Chan-Fishel, a Friends of the Earth campaign manager, has observed, the community and its external NGO supporters have found limited success in influencing the core issues: 'peripherals, like clinics and social services, are okay, but the center, the cake [that is, power sharing], is out of bounds' (cited in Emel 2002: 841).

The Security Forces

Freeport's relationship with the security forces is underpinned by an excessively generous interpretation of a commitment in the original 1967 CoW to support government officials in the vicinity of the mining project (Leith 2003: 233–4). The rise in the number of security forces in the Timika area indicates something of the extent of this generosity, from about 100 police and troops during the 1970s, to 1,800 after the 'security crises' of the mid-1990s, to a current figure approaching 3,000 (Matthew

Davies, personal communication, 2006). Most of the different elements of the national security forces are represented, including elite Kopassus and Kostrad troops, organic army units, elements of the navy, air force and coast guard and, rather bizarrely given the limited road network, an armoured car unit. Freeport's support for these units has taken the form of construction of barracks and other facilities, provision of meals, transport, fuel and vehicles, and direct payments to individual units as well as to senior officers.

Unhappy about rising costs and aware of the scope for scrutiny by the US Justice Department, Freeport has made efforts to wean the security forces off this corporate largesse. One early attempt to do so may have contributed to the most spectacular act of violence in the Freeport CoW area since 2000: the August 2002 ambush of a convoy of Freeport teachers on the road between Tembagapura and Timika, which left one Indonesian and two American teachers dead and others wounded. An initial assessment by the highly respected provincial police commander, I Made Pastika, pointed strongly to military involvement in the shootings, which had involved two former OPM fighters in an attempt to divert the blame to OPM. The killings had major international consequences, including delaying the restoration of training and other military links between the United States and Indonesia until 2006. Repeated visits to Timika by FBI agents, ostensibly to determine the true identity of the perpetrators, appear to have been as much a means of exerting pressure on senior Indonesian military commanders to rein in their troops (Radio Australia 2003; McBeth 2003), and no such incidents have taken place since.

Following the shootings, in 2003 Freeport began to declare its total payments to the Indonesian security forces in filings to the US Securities and Exchange Commission. In a report entitled *Paying for Protection*, Global Witness (2005) dug a little deeper to find that Freeport had been making direct payments to individual officers, including almost $250,000 between 2001 and 2003 to the provincial army (TNI) commander at the time, Major-General Mahidin Simbolon. As much as $342,000 was apparently paid to the TNI for its work on unspecified community development programs. Recent increases in these payments, and the cost of running PT Freeport Indonesia's own internal security department, are shown in Table 7.3. Freeport's payments to the security forces are currently under scrutiny from the US Securities and Exchange Commission and the Justice Department. In Indonesia as well, the long-term consequences of the army's mercenary tendencies have been the subject of considerable debate; as an editorial in the *Jakarta Post* (20 March 2003) observed, 'For $5.6 million a year, soldiers deployed around Freeport may as well call themselves the Freeport Army'.

Although Freeport declares that there is 'no alternative' to its arrangement with the security forces, the contrast with the large BP-operated

Table 7.3   Freeport Indonesia's Security Expenditure, 2001–04 (US$ million)

Year	PT Freeport Indonesia Security	TNI/ Police
2001	6.8	4.7
2002	n.a.	5.6
2004	13.4	7.5

Source: Global Witness (2005); Metal Bulletin News (2006).

natural gas project at Tangguh in West Papua, where a program of community policing is being developed, is striking (ICG 2002). However, Freeport's assessment of its own situation may be correct, insofar as the political and other costs of attempting to divorce itself completely from the security forces are now likely to outweigh purely financial considerations. The process of the 'billeting' and 'billing' of Freeport by Indonesia's security forces is thus likely to persist well into the future.

Human Rights

Questions about the particularly poor human rights record in and around the Freeport CoW area have dogged the company since the 1970s (Ballard 2002a). Until 1999, Freeport made little attempt to address these claims, either through investigation or by attempting to exploit its political connections to limit the violence. To some extent the payments to the security forces have enabled the company to exercise some influence over their worst excesses — but this elides the company's responsibility for introducing those forces to its CoW area in the first instance. Freeport also tends to define the scope of its responsibility for human rights issues rather narrowly as 'the area of company operations', electing to disassociate itself from the operations beyond this area of those security forces quartered at Timika, and to claim no role in the frequent violence between different ethnic communities in the Timika area, even though much of this conflict centres on the distribution of benefits from the company's activities.

In step with changing attitudes within the mineral resources industry, Freeport announced in 1999 that it was adopting a social and human rights policy.[7] It sets out guidelines for staff conduct, requires annual

---

7 The current version of this policy is reproduced as Appendix C in Freeport McMoRan (2006).

compliance reports and mandates regular training for staff. Crucially, Freeport stated in the original policy that:

> It is the company's policy to immediately report any credible accusation of a human rights violation to the appropriate government authorities, to provide the company's full cooperation with any responsible human rights investigation and to support appropriate punishment for any proven violations.

In addition, in 2000 Freeport McMoRan and its Grasberg partner Rio Tinto signed the UK–USA Voluntary Statement of Principles on Human Rights and Security,[8] which sets a high standard for corporate observance of basic human rights, although as voluntary principles they are not enforceable. In 1999, Freeport appointed Judge Gabrielle Kirk McDonald, formerly a judge at the International Criminal Tribunal for the Former Yugoslavia in The Hague, as a member of the board of directors and special counsel to the chairman on human rights. Her human rights work for Freeport is not exactly *pro bono* — she has been well rewarded for her role, reportedly selling company stock worth $6.3 million during 2005 alone (Bryce 2005).

In 2005 Freeport commissioned an independent audit of its human rights performance from the International Center for Corporate Accountability (ICCA) of Baruch College in New York (ICCA 2005). The centre, which was able to conduct independent enquiries (within certain constraints), found in its first report that almost 60 per cent of Freeport's Security Department personnel were unfamiliar with the company's own human rights policy. The report was also critical of various aspects of community development, especially the failings in the education sector of the semi-independent Amungme and Kamoro Community Development Institution (LPMAK). The audit was definitely a bold move on Freeport's part, and was lauded by *Business Week* as a new industry standard (Bernstein 2005). But it is also evident that the audit has been restricted thus far to discussion of recent events, and barred from enquiring about certain topics, such as the 2002 teacher killings.

Judge McDonald has been quoted as saying:

> Those [incidents of the past around Freeport] have been investigated, but there isn't really any closure to it yet. Let's end it. And whatever shows up, let it show up (Ballard 2002a).

Whether Freeport will ever be able to meet Judge McDonald's challenge remains to be seen. For many critics, Freeport's newfound human rights awareness is little more than further evidence of the company's ability to pay lip service to corporate social responsibility and human rights prin-

---

8   This is reproduced as Appendix D in Freeport McMoRan (2006).

ciples without seeking to bring about real change. The various initiatives, from this perspective, are designed primarily to deflect criticism from Freeport, and only secondarily to address human rights abuses, actively promote respect for human rights among its partners or address the company's part in the root causes of local conflict. As Global Witness (2005: 33) concludes:

> [I]t seems that a company can endorse the Voluntary Principles, and draw the reputational benefits, without providing any information to the public about any payments that it makes to armed parties to a conflict.

5   THE LIGHTNING ROD

The quixotically erratic spotlight of global media attention has recently returned to Freeport, led on this occasion by a major article in the *New York Times* on 27 December 2005 (Perlez and Bonner 2005). In an overview of the usual topics associated with Freeport—human rights, transparency, environmental impacts, local community relations—Perlez and Bonner gave prominence to the questions raised by the Global Witness report on Freeport's payments to the security forces. However, events in the months following the appearance of the article indicated something of the true scope and complexity of the challenges confronting Freeport, and the extent to which the company and its Papua operation have become a lightning rod for much broader issues and conflicts (Dow Jones 2006).

In February 2006, 400 'illegal' alluvial miners, mostly non-landowning Western Dani, protested after being denied access to pan for gold in Freeport's tailings waste, downstream from the mill. The protest turned violent, leading to the closure of the mine for four days (Donnan 2006b). Ironically, such access has long been controlled and run as a business by the security forces (Mellish 2006). Freeport's reported claim that the removal of the alluvial miners was intended to ensure their own health due to the 'negative impacts of chemicals in the tailings' (Antara News 2006) sits oddly with the company's usual statements about the quality of its processed mine waste. On this occasion, however, the alluvial miners' cause was adopted by protest rallies already planned by activists in Jayapura and Jakarta in order to highlight more general Papuan grievances. Some of these activists formed a 'Freeport Closure Action Front', and the Jayapura protests in particular resulted in violence and loss of life. The logic apparently linking these broader protests to Freeport was articulated by a student activist in the following terms:

> [Protestors believe that] if they shut down Freeport-McMoRan there will be no money to support the military to enable all the other mining and human rights abuses (Cordell 2006).

The arrest in January 2006 of Anton Wamang, one of the self-confessed 'OPM' perpetrators of the August 2002 teacher killings, along with a group of his associates, might appear to have capped this unfortunate episode. However, the likelihood is that the forthcoming trial will generate uncomfortable and potentially embarrassing revelations for both the security forces and Freeport (Bonner 2006). Meanwhile, a planned gradual replacement of military by police as general security in the Timika area (Somba 2006) appears to have resulted in a rise in both police and military numbers, and has either coincided with or provoked otherwise rare attacks on the security forces by OPM units and yet another mysterious shooting incident involving Freeport vehicles (Reuters 2006b). Whoever the perpetrators of this last incident might be, the historical link between troop build-ups and increased violence at Timika appears to have been confirmed once more.

Finally, criticism of Freeport from politicians and ministry officials is on the rise again. Vice-President Jusuf Kalla has established an interdepartmental team to conduct a government audit of Freeport's Indonesian operations; the House of Representatives (DPR) has set up a working committee on Freeport; Amien Rais has once again led the push to renegotiate Freeport's CoW; and the minister for the environment, Rachmat Witoelar, has commissioned an investigation into Freeport's environmental performance. Yet within weeks Witoelar was declaring Freeport's sheet to be clean; this suggests that the company can still counter or dismiss criticism from Jakarta with relative ease.

For if Freeport is a lightning rod for Papuan protest on a host of other issues, and an 'irresistible piece of chocolate cake' for politicians (Iskandar 2006), it is also an important bellwether for the investment climate in Indonesia. It is unlikely that a serious challenge will be posed to the company's CoW, for fear of the signal this would send to foreign investment in Indonesia. President Susilo Bambang Yudhoyono has attempted to intercede in order to rally investor confidence in the integrity of the CoW system (Forbes 2006), and accordingly, Vice-President Kalla has been careful to restrict his criticism of Freeport to questions about 'the implementation of the contract' (Reuters 2006a).

Freeport's critics have expressed cautious optimism about these recent events, seeing in them the signs of a potential downturn in the company's political fortunes (Abrash Walton and Meek 2006). But are we witnessing the gathering of a 'perfect storm' of crises for Freeport, or simply another hiccup along the company's seemingly irresistible progress towards new heights of profitability? Freeport appears to have ridden out the storm of the late 1990s as well as the potentially more damaging slump in metal prices. It was with no small pride that Freeport CEO Adkerson reviewed this achievement: 'We worked through the change of government in 1998

... the Asian financial crisis, the telecom bust, and through times of very low metals prices' (Morrison 2006). Copper prices had returned to highs, Freeport shares were once again highly prized and the company was now more profitable and seemingly more impregnable than ever. Investment analysts continued to express a very high level of confidence in Freeport:

> [P]eople talk about country and mine risk but there's absolutely no discount applied to Freeport stock ... The stock price seems to tell me there is zero chance of secession, therefore zero chance of change of rules, therefore zero chance of closure (Attwood 2006).

In the course of its 'cold war' conflict with its critics during the 1990s, Freeport committed some strategic errors, perhaps most notably in the blank cheque approach it took to its relationship with the security forces. Freeport also took to heart some invaluable lessons about the limited capacity of its external critics, and about the company's own ability, founded on its sheer size and the remoteness of its operations, to outstay them. Like all actors in a complex transnational field, Freeport can control only certain portions of its environment and influence only some stakeholders. Given these restrictions, and with the exceptions of events such as the 2002 teacher killings and the landslips of 2003, Freeport has been remarkably successful at managing its political environment while scarcely wavering from its essential objectives, or modifying its basic strategies.

As Emel (2002: 842) concludes, for all the critical pressure exerted on Freeport over the past decade, 'the mountain is still coming down' and nothing is likely to prevent the continuing operation of the mine. There are very real limits to the 'green disciplining of capital' and the effects of national or international scrutiny by NGOs and other industry critics. Freeport's momentum and the breadth of its influence are such that the most that we can safely anticipate by way of change in the future is simply further modification and refinement of the strategies that have served the company so well in the past.

REFERENCES

Abrash Walton, Abigail and David Meek 2006), 'Freeport Mine Faces Investigations and Divestment', *Tok Blong Pasifik*, Summer: pp. 4–5.

Antara News (2006), 'AMPI Condemns PT Freeport Incident', 25 February.

Attwood, James (2006), 'Deadly Protests Highlight Grasberg Mine's Risks', Dow Jones, 17 March.

Ballard, Chris (1997), 'Melanesia in Review, Issues and Events, 1996: Irian Jaya', *Contemporary Pacific*, 9(2): 468–74.

Ballard, Chris (2002a), 'Human Rights and the Mining Industry in Indonesia: A Baseline Study', MMSD Working Paper No. 182, Mining, Minerals and Sustainable Development, London.

Ballard, Chris (2002b), 'The Denial of Traditional Land Rights in West Papua', *Cultural Survival Quarterly*, 26(3): 39–43.

Ballard, Chris (2002c), 'The Signature of Terror: Violence, Memory and Landscape at Freeport', in Bruno David and Meredith Wilson (eds), *Inscribed Landscapes: Marking and Making Place*, University of Hawaii Press, Honolulu, pp. 13–26.

Ballard, Chris and Glenn Banks (2003), 'Resource Wars: The Anthropology of Mining', *Annual Review of Anthropology*, 32: 287–313.

Banks, Glenn (2000), 'Social Impact Assessment Monitoring and Household Surveys', in Laurence Goldman (ed.), *Social Impact Analysis: An Applied Anthropology Manual*, Berg, Oxford, pp. 297–343.

Banks, Glenn (2001), 'Mining and Environment in Melanesia: Contemporary Debates Reviewed', *Contemporary Pacific*, 14(1): 39–67.

Banks, Glenn (2006), 'Mining, Social Change and Corporate Social Responsibility: Drawing Lines in the Papua New Guinea Mud', in S. Firth (ed.), *Globalisation, Governance and the Pacific Islands*, ANU E Press, Canberra, pp. 259–74, available at <http://epress.anu.edu.au/ssgm/global_gov/pdf_instructions. html>.

Bernstein, Aaron (2005), 'Freeport's Hard Look at Itself', *Business Week Online*, 24 October.

Bonner, Raymond (2006), 'New Twist in Deaths of Americans in Indonesia', *International Herald Tribune*, 13 January 2006.

Bryce, Robert (2005), 'Written in Stone', *Austin Chronicle*, 23 September.

Collier, William L. III (2005), Letter, *Financial Times* (London), 28 February, p. 20.

Cook, Carolyn Diane Turinsky (1995), 'The Amung Way: The Subsistence Strategies, the Knowledge and the Dilemma of the Tsinga Valley People in Irian Jaya, Indonesia', PhD thesis, University of Hawaii, Honolulu.

Cordell, Marni (2006), 'West Papua: The Act of No Choice', <http://www.new matilda.com/home/articledetail.asp?ArticleID=1468>, 29 March.

Dames & Moore (1996), 'PTFI Environmental Audit Report'/'Laporan Audit Lingkungan PTFI', Jakarta.

Denoon, D., C. Ballard, G. Banks and P. Hancock (eds) (1996), *Conference Proceedings: Mining and Mineral Resource Policy Issues in Asia Pacific: Prospects for the 21st Century*, Division of Pacific and Asian History, Research School of Pacific and Asian Studies, Australian National University, Canberra.

Donnan, Shawn (2006a), 'Freeport Chiefs Cash in 130m Options', *Financial Times*, 11 April.

Donnan, Shawn (2006b), 'Plant's Shutdown Adds Pressure on Freeport', *Financial Times*, 28 February.

Dow Jones (2006), 'Freeport's Indonesia Ops Not Powering Papua Unrest— Expert', 11 April.

Dwiyana, Agus (2001), 'Oil, Gas and Mining Development and Decision Making Process in Irian Jaya', Issue Paper on District Budget Collection prepared for Rapid Assessment of Conservation Economy (RACE), Conservation International Indonesia, Irian Jaya Program, Jayapura.

Earth Observatory (2005), 'Grasberg Mine, Indonesia', Earth Observatory, NASA, available at <http://earthobservatory.nasa.gov/Newsroom/NewImages/ images.php3?img_id=16988>, accessed 17 January 2006.

EIR (Extractive Industries Review) (2003), *Striking a Better Balance: The Final Report of the Extractive Industries Review*, Jakarta and Washington DC.

Emel, Jody (2002), 'An Inquiry into the Green Disciplining of Capital', *Environment and Planning A*, 34: 827–43.
Filer, Colin (1996), 'The Melanesian Way of Menacing the Mining Industry', in B. Burt and C. Clerk (eds), *Environment and Development in the Pacific*, Australian National University and University of Papua New Guinea Press, Canberra and Port Moresby, pp. 91–122.
Forbes, Mark (2006), 'Investment Fears over Mine Protest', *Sydney Morning Herald*, 4 March.
Francis, Diane (1997), *Bre-X: The Inside Story*, Key Porter Books, Toronto.
Freed, Jamie (2005), 'Rio Tinto Tarred with Freeport Brush', *Sydney Morning Herald*, 28 December.
Freed, Jamie (2006), 'Jim Bob Rakes in Millions from Papua Goldmine', *Sydney Morning Herald*, 24 March.
Freeport McMoRan (2004), *Riverine Tailings Transport by PT Freeport Indonesia*, New Orleans LA.
Freeport McMoRan (2005), *Annual Report 2004: Making the Grade*, New Orleans LA.
Freeport McMoRan (2006), *The Elements of Sustainable Development 2005: Working toward Sustainable Development Report*, New Orleans LA.
Global Witness (2005), *Paying for Protection: The Freeport Mine and the Indonesian Security Forces*, Washington DC.
Goold, Douglas and Andrew Willis (1997), *The Bre-X Fraud*, McLelland & Stewart, Toronto.
Handelsman, Simon D. (2002), 'Human Rights in the Mineral Industry', MMSD Working Paper No. 9, Mining, Minerals and Sustainable Development, London.
Harple, Todd S. (2000), 'Controlling the Dragon: An Ethno-historical Analysis of Social Engagement among the Kamoro of South-west New Guinea (Indonesian Papua/Irian Jaya)', unpublished PhD thesis, Australian National University, Canberra.
ICCA (International Center for Corporate Accountability) (2005), 'Human Rights, Employment and Social Development of Papuan People in Indonesia', audit report for Freeport McMoRan Copper & Gold, Inc. and PT Freeport Indonesia, New York NY.
ICG (International Crisis Group) (2001), 'Indonesia: Ending Repression in Irian Jaya', Asia Report No. 23, Jakarta and Brussels.
ICG (International Crisis Group) (2002), 'Indonesia: Resources and Conflict in Papua', Asia Report No. 39, Jakarta and Brussels.
ICG (International Crisis Group) (2006), Papua: The Dangers of Shutting Down Dialogue', Asia Briefing No. 47, Jakarta and Brussels.
Investor Daily (2005), 'The House Unwilling to Let Freeport's Shares Go to a Private Enterprise', internet communication, 21 June.
Iskandar, Israr (2006), 'Freeport and the Suffering of the Papuans', *Jakarta Post*, 21 March.
Jessup, Ethan (1999), 'Beanal v. Freeport-McMoran, Inc.: Anatomy of an International Environmental Tort Case', *New England International and Comparative Law Annual*, 5, <http://www.nesl.edu/intljournal/VOL5/jessup.htm>.
Leith, Denise (2003), *The Politics of Power: Freeport in Suharto's Indonesia*, University of Hawaii Press, Honolulu.
Lowry, David B. and D. James Miller (n.d.), 'Response from Freeport-McMoRan Copper & Gold Inc. to the Draft Report of Minerals, Mining and Sustainable

Development (MMSD) Inc.', <http://www.iied.org/mmsd/mmsd_pdfs/comments_freeport.pdf>.

Mandaro, Laura (2007), Freeport-McMoRan Gauges Earnings after Phelps Dodge Merger, *Marketwatch*, 1 March, <http://www.marketwatch.com>.

McBeth, John (1996), 'Company under Siege: Mining Firm Freeport Indonesia Hits Back at Critics', *Far Eastern Economic Review*, 25 January.

McBeth, John (2003), 'FBI Faces Tough Task with Murder Probe in Papua', *Far Eastern Economic Review*, 13 March.

McBeth, John (2006), 'Freeport in Indonesia: Filling in the Holes', *Asia Times*, 22 February.

Mealey, George A. (1996), *Grasberg: Mining the Richest and Most Remote Deposit of Copper and Gold in the World, in the Mountains of Irian Jaya, Indonesia*, Freeport-McMoRan Copper & Gold, New Orleans LA.

Mellish, Morgan (2006), 'Indonesia's River of Gold Makes Its Own Rules', *Australian Financial Review*, 5 January.

Metal Bulletin News (2006), 'Freeport Defends Payouts Made to "Support" Indonesia's Military', Joyo Indonesia News Service, internet communication, 4 January.

MMSD (2002), *Breaking New Ground: Mining, Minerals and Sustainable Development*, Earthscan Publications, London.

Mollet, Julius Ary (2001), 'District Budget Collection under Decentralization and the Impacts to the Natural Resource in Irian Jaya', Issue Paper on District Budget Collection prepared for Rapid Assessment of Conservation and Economy (RACE), Conservation International Indonesia, Irian Jaya Program, Jayapura.

Montgomery Watson Indonesia (1999), '1999 External Environmental Audit, PT Freeport Indonesia Operations, Irian Jaya, Indonesia', Jakarta.

Morrison, Mark (2006), 'So Much Gold, So Much Risk', *Business Week*, 29 May.

Munninghoff, H.F.M. (1995), *Violations of Human Rights in the Timika Area of Irian Jaya, Indonesia: A Report by the Catholic Church of Jayapura*, ACFOA, Melbourne, August.

Paull, David, Glenn Banks, Chris Ballard and David Gillieson (2006), 'Monitoring the Environmental Impact of Mining in Remote Locations through Remotely Sensed Data', *Geocarto International*, 21(1): 33–42.

Perlez, Jane (2006), 'Letter from Indonesia: No Longer Can a Hammer Trade for Mining Rights', *International Herald Tribune*, 31 March.

Perlez, Jane and Raymond Bonner (2005), 'Below a Mountain of Wealth, a River of Waste', *New York Times*, 27 December.

Pickell, David and Kal Muller (2001), *Kamoro: Between the Tides in Irian Jaya*, Aopao Productions, Jakarta.

Project Underground (1998), *Risky Business. The Grasberg Gold Mine: An Independent Annual Report on P.T. Freeport Indonesia, 1998*, Berkeley CA.

Radio Australia (2003), 'Papua: US FBI Tries to Uncover Truth on Freeport Killings', transcript, 22 January.

Reuters (2006a), 'Indonesia Evaluating Freeport Contract—Kalla', 30 March.

Reuters (2006b), 'Extra Indonesian Police Sent to Papua Violence', 4 September.

Rukmantara, Arie (2006), 'Military to Stay at Freeport', *Jakarta Post*, 19 June.

Soares, Adérito de Jesus (2004), 'The Impact of Corporate Strategy on Community Dynamics: A Case Study of the Freeport Mining Company in West Papua, Indonesia', *International Journal on Minority and Group Rights*, 11: 115–42.

Somba, Nethy Dharma (2006), 'Police to Take Control of Security at Freeport', *Jakarta Post*, 26 June.

Stanwick, Peter A. and Sarah D. Stanwick (1998), 'The Relationship between Corporate Social Performance, and Organizational Size, Financial Performance, and Environmental Performance: An Empirical Examination', *Journal of Business Ethics*, 17: 195–204.

TAPOL (2006), '21 Defence Attaches Visit Timika', TAPOL internet communication, 25 January.

Timmer, Jaap (2004), 'West Papua', *Contemporary Pacific*, 16(2): 409–19.

Tsing, Anna (2000), 'Inside the Economy of Appearances', *Public Culture*, 12(1): 115–44.

UABS (UNCEN–ANU Baseline Studies) (1998), 'UNCEN–ANU Baseline Studies Final Report', unpublished report to PT Freeport Indonesia, Canberra.

Vaporean, Carol (2006), 'Freeport Objects to Exclusion from Norway Fund', Reuters, 6 June.

Vogel, David (2005), *The Market for Virtue: The Potential and Limits of Corporate Social Responsibility*, Brookings Institution, Washington DC.

WALHI (Wahana Lingkungan Hidup Indonesia) (2006), 'The Environmental Impacts of Freeport–Rio Tinto's Copper and Gold Mining Operation', Jakarta.

WALHI-YPMD (Wahana Lingkungan Hidup Indonesia and Yayasan Pengembangan Masyarakat Desa) (1991), 'Laporan Kunjungan WALHI-YPMD ke Freeport Indonesia di Tembagapura' [Report on the WALHI-YPMD Trip to Freeport Indonesia at Tembagapura], unpublished report, Jakarta.

Wilson, Forbes K. (1981), *The Conquest of Copper Mountain*, Atheneum, New York NY.

8   ILLEGAL FISHING IN THE ARAFURA SEA

Budy P. Resosudarmo, Lydia Napitupulu and David Campbell

The Arafura Sea forms part of the Sahul Continental Shelf and covers an area of 650,000 square kilometres. It is bordered to the north by the southern coast of Papua, to the west and southwest by the Banda and Timor Seas, and to the south and southeast by the Gulf of Carpentaria and the Torres Strait (Map 8.1). In most parts, the shallow sea floor consists of a vast sand and mud bank ranging from 50 to 80 metres in depth (Tomascik et al. 1997).

As the Arafura Sea is one of Indonesia's most productive commercial fisheries, it is sometimes referred to as one of the nation's 'golden fishing grounds'. In addition to its shallow depth, this productivity is the result of a system of southward-flowing rivers originating in the central dividing mountain range that forms an east to west cordillera through central Papua. These rivers deposit a heavy load of nutrient-rich sediment in the thriving coastal mangrove forests along the south coast of Papua from Kimaam Island to the Mimika River. The mangrove forests, in turn, provide spawning grounds and sources of food for various fish and shrimp[1] species and other biota (Petocz 1987; Sadhotomo, Rahardjo

---

1   In Indonesia, 'shrimp' is the default common English translation of *udang* (order *Decapoda Crustacea*, suborder *Natantia*), to which all species of shrimps and prawns belong (Sumiono and Priyono 1998). The main species harvested commercially in the Arafura Sea is the *Penaeidae* family, to which the well-known banana prawn (*Penaeus merguiensis de Man*) belongs (Holthuis 1980). In this chapter, the term 'shrimp' is used in reference to the shrimp and prawn category, while 'prawn' is used if it is a more common name for a particular species.

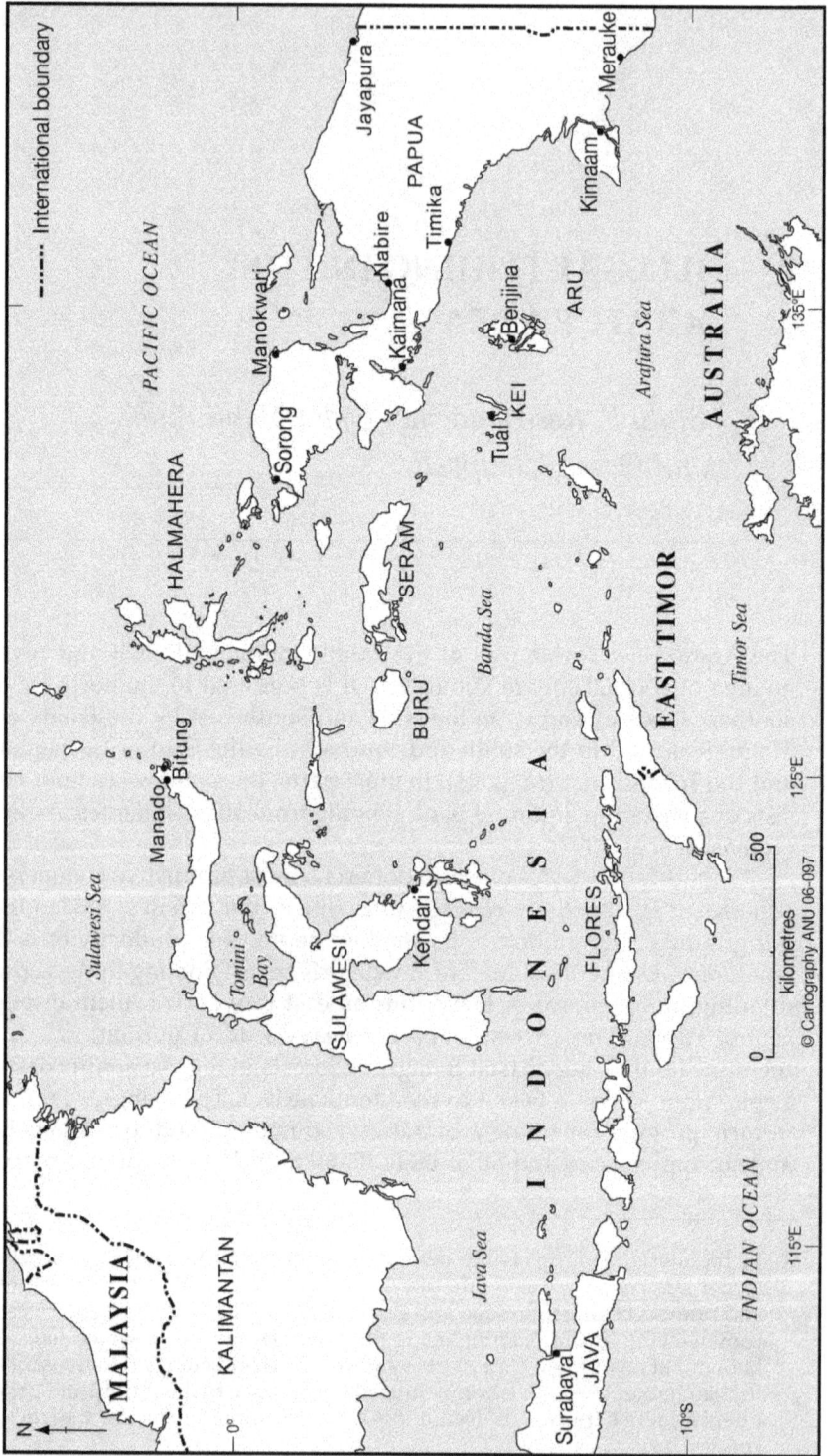

Map 8.1   The Arafura Sea and Surrounding Areas

and Wedjatmiko 2003). Despite the Arafura Sea's productivity, however, the widespread incidence of illegal fishing — especially by large vessels — raises questions about the real benefits of the fishery for Indonesia.

Illegal fishing leads to socio-economic losses through overfishing, the transfer of benefits overseas, ineffective public spending on fishery management and administration, and the undermining of Indonesian administrative bodies and institutions. In this chapter we review the nature of illegal fishing in the Arafura Sea, its national and local effects, the consequences of decentralization and regional autonomy for illegal fishing, and ongoing policies for its prevention and mitigation.

1   DEVELOPMENT OF A CONCEPTUAL FRAMEWORK

Consideration of the loss of social benefits from illegal fishing includes factors such as market failure and agency failure. Here we set out the principles by which these possible sources of net social loss due to illegal fishing in the Arafura Sea fishery can be examined.

Market Failure

When individual rights to units of fish are inappropriate or are inadequately enforced, profit-maximizing fishers will race each other to maximize their harvest of the available fish stocks. Although it may be socially preferable to forgo some of the catch so that fish stocks and fish biomass can increase, without effective rights to the resource, fishers will be uncertain as to whether they will be able to harvest the future benefit of forgoing current catches. As a result, they will ignore the effect of their harvesting activities on fish biomass, including higher unit costs of harvest due to reduced fish stocks, lower future catch rates and increased operational costs due to the crowding of fishing boats and fishing gear while fishing. These costs to society are referred to as negative externalities because they are external to the fishers' cost accounting, and are an example of market failure.

The direct economic consequences of market failure are the inefficient use of factor inputs and low returns from the fish resource. The first is caused by the use of more effort — labour, equipment, fuel, supplies — than necessary to catch a given harvest. Such excessive use of scarce resources has a cost to society as a whole, as these resources could have provided a greater social benefit were they used elsewhere. Low returns from the fish resource are a consequence of overharvesting of the fish stock and fish being taken at a non-optimal age class (catch size). Returns are also affected by the competitive race among fishers to maximize their share of the catch, which results in poor-quality catches and the dumping of peak loads onto the market. If rights to the resource were more appropriate and secure, fishers would have an incentive to concentrate on the most economic means of catching fish, thus maximizing the prices received through better timing of catch onto the market, and improving catch quality.

To understand the overharvesting of fish stocks, it is useful to recognize that fish biomass or fish stocks can be described as 'flow' resources — that is, different units of the resource become available at different times (as such, fish stocks are a form of natural capital), and for each fish age class, there are annual changes in biomass due to natural growth, natural death and predation (including disease and harvesting). For the younger age classes, growth in biomass will exceed the natural loss in biomass through natural causes. These two biological variables will affect the rate (or flow) of the harvestable fish biomass and, therefore, the sustainable yield. In addition, the unit cost of harvest will increase with decreasing stock size. That is, the fewer fish there are, the harder fish are to locate and the lower the catch per unit of fishing effort will be.

The biological nature of fish resources and the unit cost of harvest determine the economically optimal sustainable yield of the fishery. When stocks fall below the optimal size due to too much effort being expended, *stock overfishing* occurs; when a fish age class is harvested to the point that expected biomass growth exceeds the social discount rate, *growth overfishing* occurs. Both causes of overfishing result in economic losses and decreased benefits to society (see Clark 1985; Anderson 1986; Grafton et al. 2006).

Agency Failure

The role of fishery managers is to maximize the socio-economic benefits from fish resources in a sustainable way. In this role, both government and fishery managers act as agents for the Indonesian public, who are the owners of the resource and who fund the fishery management agency. Under the limitations and constraints of international law, and the restraints imposed by the rights and interests of traditional owners and regional groups, a necessary condition is that the marginal return from public investment in fishery management at least equals the marginal cost of management. If this is not the case, management costs will be an additional source of social loss and a burden on the public, in addition to the loss from overfishing.

Agency failure occurs when agency members carry out their functions according to their own interests rather than the interests of the public (Campbell and Haynes 1990; Mueller 2003; Weimer and Vining

2005). This leads to failures in fishery management. For example, monitoring and control procedures may be lacking or inadequately enforced, and fishery management tools may be inappropriate or inappropriately applied.

Agency failure is relevant in accounting for the level of illegal fishing in the Arafura Sea fishery. Wasted public expenditure, overfishing and non-productive investment in self-seeking behaviour by government and agency bureaucrats result in agency failure and social loss.

2   MANAGEMENT OF THE ARAFURA SEA FISHERY

The Indonesian maritime jurisdiction extends to the margin of Indonesia's exclusive economic zone (EEZ), that is, all waters within 200 nautical miles of the Indonesian islands, as regulated by Law No. 5/1983 on Indonesia's Exclusive Economic Zone and Law No. 17/1985 on the Ratification of the United Nations Convention on the Law of the Sea. Under the Constitution, the main principle guiding resource utilization is that: 'The land, the waters and the natural riches contained therein shall be controlled by the State and exploited to the greatest benefit of the people' (article 33, paragraph 3). This article guides all laws and regulations relating to natural resource utilization, including marine resources.

Indonesian laws and regulations form a hierarchy under the Constitution in order of decreasing importance, as set out in Law No. 10/2004 on the Establishment of Laws. This hierarchy is as follows.

1 Laws or Acts (Undang-Undang) or Government Regulations in Lieu of an Act (Peraturan Pemerintah Pengganti Undang-Undang).
2 Government Regulations (Peraturan Pemerintah).
3 Presidential Regulations (Peraturan Presiden), formerly Presidential Decrees (Keputusan Presiden).
4 Regional Regulations (Peraturan Daerah), consisting of Provincial Regulations (Peraturan Daerah Provinsi), District/Municipality[2] Regulations (Peraturan Daerah Kabupaten/Kota) and Village Regulations (Peraturan Daerah Desa).

The laws and regulations governing marine resource utilization can be grouped into the following categories (Rudiyanto 2002).

1 Marine spatial regulations on the geographic extent of the oceans and maritime zones.

---

2 Henceforth called 'districts' for simplicity.

2   Environmental regulations relating to environmental protection and
    natural resource conservation.
3   Maritime regulations regarding the sectoral use of ocean resources.
4   Terrestrial spatial regulations relating to general planning of coastal
    areas.
5   Terrestrial sectoral regulations relating to coastal resource utilization.
6   Decentralization regulations relating to the division of authority for
    the management of Indonesian waters between the central govern-
    ment and local governments, and to revenue sharing between the
    central, provincial and district levels of government.

Although there is no mention in this hierarchy of Ministerial Decrees
(Keputusan Menteri) or Ministerial Regulations (Peraturan Menteri), and
their status is therefore unclear, they continue to be an important tool in
fishery management. For example, Agriculture Ministerial Decree No.
607/1976 on Fishing Zones reserved coastal areas for small fishing vessels, thus giving coastal communities restricted access to fish resources,
protecting the spawning grounds of fish stocks and providing protection
for juvenile fish against overfishing.

This decree has been renewed several times, the latest being Agriculture Ministerial Decree No. 392/1999. It established three fishing zones
based on distance from the shoreline at low tide, boat size and gear type.
Zone I is comprised of two parts: Zone Ia extending out to three nautical
miles and Zone Ib extending 3–6 nautical miles. Zone Ia is for non-motorized vessels of up to 5 gross tonnes and less than 10 metres in length
fitted with stationary gear or unmodified non-stationary gear. Zone Ib
is for vessels of less than 12 metres in length fitted with non-stationary
fishing gear (purse seine to a maximum head rope length of 150 metres
or drift gill nets to a maximum length of 1,000 metres). Zone II extends
6–12 nautical miles from the shoreline. It is for motorized vessels of up to
60 gross tonnes fitted with purse seine to a maximum head rope length
of 600 metres if operated from one boat and 1,000 metres if operated from
two boats, or with drift nets to a maximum length of 2,500 metres, or
with tuna longlines with a maximum of 1,200 hooks. Zone III extends
from 12 nautical miles to the EEZ boundary. It is for vessels of up to 350
gross tonnes, except in the Malacca Strait, where the maximum vessel
size is 200 gross tonnes. There are no restrictions on gear used, except
that the use of purse seine nets to take large pelagic fish is forbidden
in Tomini Bay and in the Maluku, Seram, Banda, Flores and Savu Seas.
Except in the Malacca Strait, vessels of 350–800 gross tonnes using purse
seine nets are permitted if they operate at least 100 nautical miles from
the shoreline.

An important national institutional change was the shift in 1999 of
responsibility for marine resource management from a directorate-

general in the Ministry of Agriculture to a newly created ministry, the Ministry of Marine Affairs and Fisheries (MMAF).[3] This upgrade enabled national fishery-related issues to be fully represented at the presidential cabinet level for the first time, and to be more closely integrated with other national policy issues (Dutton 2005).

3   UNDERSTANDING ILLEGAL FISHING IN THE ARAFURA SEA

Observed Forms of Illegal Fishing

Illegal fishing in the Arafura Sea takes several forms. The most conspicuous is fishing without an entitlement or licence to fish — that is, poaching. This was a common practice up to the late 1990s. Indonesia's vast seas, coupled with lax patrolling, meant that the risk of being caught was low compared with the benefits received. According to the MMAF, in 2001 about 85 per cent of all vessels over 50 gross tonnes (about 7,000 vessels) were operating without a licence (*Kompas*, 9 June 2003; *Tempo Interaktif*, 30 February 2003).

A second form of illegal fishing is the use of falsified or forged documents, either the supporting documents required when applying for a fishing licence or the fishing licence itself. Forgery of supporting documents was made possible by the government's weak licensing process, whereby licence applications were not thoroughly checked. Fegan (2003) found that some applicants were even able to get away with providing a false address. Since 2001, the MMAF has been conducting checks of suspicious supporting documents submitted for licence applications. At least up until 2004, it found that a large proportion of these documents were either forged or unrecognized by the (supposed) issuing authority (MMAF press release, 5 May 2004).

Forgery of fishing licences has a number of variants. Some licences look completely authentic, yet are not formally registered with the licensing authority. This indicates weaknesses in the MMAF's licensing procedures as well as the willingness of some MMAF staff to accept inducements, a problem acknowledged by the former minister, Sarwono Kusumaatmadja (*Business News*, 10 March 2000). It has been reported that a fake licence costs US$10,000–20,000, whereas an official (legal) one costs US$25,000–55,000 (Charoenpo 2002; Sitathan 2003). Official licences may also be copied, made to look authentic, then used by other vessels of a similar type (*Kompas*, 17 March 2005). The cost of duplication is cer-

---

3   When established in 1999, this institution was called the Ministry of Marine Exploration and Fisheries. The change in name occurred in 2000.

tainly trivial compared with the cost of obtaining a licence. The benefits
of forged licences are clear: operators can avoid arrest when stopped by
law enforcement authorities, while the vessel owners can avoid paying
taxes.

A third form of illegal fishing is fishing in violation of fishing licence
conditions with respect to vessel size and gear type, fishing ground, fishing zone, home port or crew. Fishing vessels are considered to be operating illegally when they violate any of these particulars. While many
violations can only be detected by well-equipped patrols, it is not difficult to detect many other forms of violations without actually inspecting
a vessel's documentation — by comparing the vessel size with its location
of operation, for example. During a field trip conducted for this research
in 2004, one of the authors observed a large vessel in excess of 200 gross
tonnes trawling less than one mile from shore a half-hour from the town
of Kaimana, a small Papuan town on the Arafura Sea; at least three others could be seen on the horizon. According to a local fisherman in the
area, this is a regular occurrence. Large vessels have also been observed
operating closer than a mile from shore, including entering estuaries
along the Merauke coast.[4]

A fourth type of illegal fishing, and probably the most common, is
underreporting or misreporting of catch. This occurs when vessels report
lower than actual catch volumes, or document only a few species rather
than the actual species composition of the catch, categorizing the rest as
'mixed fish'. Based on research conducted between 1998 and 2000 in eastern Indonesia, Fegan (2005) concluded that, on average, operators report
only 30 per cent of their catch.

The Actors: Foreign Vessels

While both foreign and Indonesian fishers are involved in illegal fishing
in Indonesia, it is the foreign fishers that have the greatest impact. Illegal
foreign fishers originating from Thailand, Taiwan, South Korea, China,
the Philippines and Japan have been fishing in Indonesian waters without permits since the 1960s (Fegan 2005). During the 1980s and 1990s,
illegal fishing by Thai-based operators was reportedly responsible for
the biggest loss of earnings (60 per cent) in the form of forgone revenues
(Charoenpo 2002). Most of these Thai trawlers were fishing in the Java
Sea. By the end of the 1990s, it appears that at least 3,000 Thai vessels were
operating in an area extending from the South China Sea to the Java and
Arafura Seas (Heazle and Butcher 2007). In the Arafura Sea, large shrimp

---

4 Personal communication with several local leaders in Merauke, 20 August
   2004.

trawlers have dominated illegal fishing activities since the early 1970s. Vessels from Thailand, South Korea and other Southeast Asia countries appear to have been particularly prevalent since the early 1990s (*Kompas*, 17 March 2005; *Kompas Cyber Media*, 5 March 2005).

In the new millennium, illegal fishing by Chinese operators has increased in prominence. In 2003, 23 Chinese-flagged purse seiners, reportedly on their way to the Arafura Sea, were caught fishing without permits around Tomini Bay in Sulawesi (*Republika Online*, 9 June 2003). In August 2005, the navy patrol chief for eastern Indonesia reported that in January–August 2005, most of the vessels apprehended for illegal fishing in the Arafura Sea were from China or Thailand (*Tempo Interactive*, 30 August 2005).

Most illegal foreign fishing vessels operating in the Arafura Sea have bases in Indonesian ports, such as Surabaya (East Java), Manado and Bitung (North Sulawesi), Kendari (Southeast Sulawesi), Benjina and Tual (Maluku), Sorong (West Papua) and Kimaam and Merauke (Papua) (see Map 8.1) (*Kompas*, 17 March 2005).

The Actors: Indonesian Middlemen

The 'conventional' form of illegal fishing, practised by both Indonesian and foreign vessels, was to operate in the Arafura Sea without the necessary documentation. But as illegal fishing came under increased scrutiny in the 1990s, most foreign operators chose to reflag their vessels as 'Indonesian' by registering them as being owned in a joint venture with an Indonesian entity, or as being chartered from an Indonesian company. In both cases, the Indonesian company only had to provide the vessel licence and, in a few instances, port services (such as arranging papers for the crew, providing domestic supplies of fuel, food and water, and dealing with or bribing officials). Although they received a fee for their services, they had no ownership in the vessel, gear or catch and no share in the profit or loss. Inkopal, the cooperative owned and run by the Indonesian navy, held many of these 'joint venture' licences (Fegan 2003, 2005; Heazle and Butcher 2007). This constitutes a conflict of interest, as the Indonesian navy is also involved in enforcement.

With the advent of licensing reforms and increased surveillance since 2001, new actors have surfaced, and the role of Indonesian licensing agents, especially those with high-level political connections and capital, has become more important. Previously, the main role of Indonesian partners was to obtain forged licences, but since 2001 they have had the more sophisticated task of obtaining both forged licences and the information needed for illegal fishers to avoid surveillance activities. These new actors do not wait to be approached by foreign companies but actively seek out and resell licences to foreign operators (*Jakarta Post*, 26 September 2001). They are not just middlemen but often the part or full owners of one or more fishing vessels.

A recent investigative study by an Indonesian environmental non-government organization (NGO) highlights the significance of Indonesian businessmen in illegal fishing activities.[5] The most important of them is a businessman based in Surabaya since at least 2002. While he keeps a very low profile in Indonesia, in mainland China he is known as the 'King of Arafura'.

The King allegedly started his business by obtaining introductions from high-ranking Indonesian navy officers. He has expanded his operations by distributing leaflets advertising his services throughout Chinese ports. He is said to own around 60 fishing vessels and to have part owner-ship of hundreds of others. Most of the fish harvested by his vessels is shipped directly to China, since he does not own any land-based process-ing plants in Indonesia.

In the past, it is believed that the King's illegally operating ships were able to avoid apprehension by obtaining inside information on details of navy patrols. In 2005, however, four of his ships were apprehended for illegal fishing in the Arafura Sea, resulting in one case in the death of a crew member. The captains and crew members later received very lenient sentences, indicating a possible close relationship with local offi-cials, including those within the judicial system (*Kompas Cyber Media*, 21 September 2005).

According to the NGO, a second prominent player is a Jakarta-based gang leader with close connections to the military. In 2006 he is reported to have obtained a large number of fishing licences on the basis of a prom-ise to build processing plants in eastern Indonesia; since the mid-2000s, having or intending to build a processing plant has been an important requirement to obtain a fishing licence. Yet another large player is 'Uncle T', a Semarang-based businessman who is alleged to have the backing of the family of former president Soeharto (*Kompas*, 16 February 2003).

Decentralization

In 2001 the central government introduced a decentralization policy aimed at devolving some of its decision-making and fiscal powers to the provincial and district levels of government. The policy was imple-mented through Law No. 22/1999 on Regional Government and Law No. 25/1999 on Fiscal Balancing between the Central Government and Regional Governments, later amended as Law No. 32/2004 and Law No.

---

5 Personal communication with staff member, Jakarta, 14 March 2006.

33/2004 respectively. These laws contain administrative inconsistencies, raising questions about how the decentralization policy is to be applied at the local level.

Law No. 32/2004 delegates responsibility for managing marine territories to the relevant provincial and district governments. This includes exploration, exploitation, conservation, spatial planning, administration, law enforcement, contribution to defence and maintenance of national integrity (Law 32/2004, article 18). District governments are responsible for the marine territory extending 0–4 nautical miles out from the shoreline; provincial governments for the marine territory extending 4–12 nautical miles; and the central government for the marine territory extending 12–200 nautical miles. Consequently, jurisdiction over the Arafura Sea is now shared between the three provincial governments of West Papua, Papua and Maluku, several district governments and the central government.

To further complicate the situation, the local governments' territorial jurisdiction is not consistent with their authority for vessel licensing. As noted earlier, Agriculture Ministerial Decree No. 392/1999 states that vessels of up to 5 gross tonnes can operate in Zone I; vessels of up to 60 gross tonnes in Zone II; and vessels of up to 350 gross tonnes in Zone III. However, Government Regulation No. 54/2002 on Fisheries Business gives district governments the authority to license vessels of up to 10 gross tonnes; provincial governments the authority to license vessels of 10–30 gross tonnes; and the central government the authority to license vessels of over 30 gross tonnes (Table 8.1). Clearly there are jurisdictional inconsistencies between the fishing and licensing regulations, as the following three examples demonstrate.

First, the licence for a fishing vessel of 30–60 gross tonnes would be issued by the central government, but the fishing zone regulations would allow it to operate in the provincial zone, 6–12 nautical miles from shore. Thus, vessels of this type would operate under the jurisdiction of both the central and provincial governments. Provincial governments are not happy with this situation, especially as they receive no revenue from licensing while still incurring management and enforcement costs.[6] Should such a vessel enter the provincial jurisdiction, it is clear that there would be an incentive for the provincial government to argue that the vessel was fishing illegally. Second, a motorized vessel of 5–10

6   Under Law No. 25/1999 (as well as Law No. 33/2004), 20 per cent of the revenue from fishery-related charges is allocated to the central government, with the remainder distributed equally among all district governments. Importantly, there is no mention of any required allocation for provincial governments (Alisjahbana 2005).

Table 8.1   *Jurisdictional Inconsistencies between Fishing and Licensing Regulations*

	Zone I		Zone II	Zone III
	Zone Ia	Zone Ib		
Fishing zone regulations (Ministry of Agriculture Decree No. 392/1999)				
Distance from low-tide mark (nautical miles)	0–3	3–6	6–12	12–200
Vessel size (gross tonnes)	≤5	≤5	≤60	≤350

	District Governments	Provincial Governments	Central Government
Marine territorial jurisdiction (Law No. 32/2004)			
Distance from low-tide mark (nautical miles)	0–4	4–12	12–200
Vessel licensing authority (Government Regulation No. 54/2002)			
Licensing authority (gross tonnes)	≤10	10–30	30+

gross tonnes would obtain its licence from the district government but operate in provincial waters where the issuing district had no authority. And third, zone violations would occur when a vessel that had received its permit from one district or province operated within the jurisdiction of another district or province. A zone violation of this kind occurred in 2003 when the Merauke Fisheries Service apprehended 30 vessels in Merauke waters whose licences had been issued by the Manokwari Fisheries Service.[7]

These jurisdictional inconsistencies have created a 'new game in town' whereby government agencies provide fishing licences for vessels that operate outside their jurisdictional control, thus gaining access to a lucrative source of locally derived revenue without having to incur any

---

7   Personal communication with an officer of the Merauke Fishery Service, August 2004.

management costs. This creates interagency conflicts and undermines efforts to prevent illegal fishing.

4   THE IMPACT OF ILLEGAL FISHING

The effects of illegal fishing are felt at the national, regional and local levels. They include direct financial losses and indirect non-financial losses. The latter are not easily observed but can be substantial. Such impacts occur as a result of the direct theft of fishery resources, the mismanagement of biological capital, increased operational costs and the misallocation of resources through self-seeking behaviour. This leads to social mistrust of policing and enforcement as well as negative social interactions between illegal fishers and local communities.

Direct Financial Losses

The national annual financial loss from illegal fishing in 2002–03 has been estimated at roughly US$2.1 billion. This comprised around US$1.2 billion in lost fish exports, US$0.6 billion in forgone licensing fees, US$0.2 billion in unwarranted fuel subsidies[8] and US$0.1 billion in the loss of royalties and other fees (*Tempo Interaktif*, 19 February 2003). In September 2006 the fisheries minister, Freddy Numbery, said that the annual financial loss due to illegal fishing was about US$3 billion (*Suara Pembaruan*, 29 September 2006). Though these figures are rough estimates, they are consistent with the estimate above that about 7,000 vessels of 50 gross tonnes and over are engaged in some form of illegal fishing.

Biological Capital and Operational Costs

Excess fishing effort and the mismanagement of fish stocks (which are a form of natural capital) affect both current operational costs and future returns. In 2001, the MMAF's Centre for Research on Fish Capture found that the stock of large pelagic, demersal and shrimp species in the Arafura Sea had been overexploited (Fox, Adhuri and Resosudarmo 2005). There is ample evidence to suggest both stock and growth overfishing, leading to suboptimal stock levels and increased cost per unit of catch.

Table 8.2 shows that there was a large increase in the number of licensed trawlers operating in the Arafura Sea fishery in the 1990s. Between 1992

---

8   This was from the consumption of domestic fuel by illegal fishers. Before the reduction in fuel subsidies in October 2005, the domestic price of fuel was much lower than the world price.

Table 8.2   Licensed Vessels Operating in the Arafura Sea by Gross Tonnage, 1992–2001 (no.)

Vessel Type	<50 GT	51–100 GT	101–200 GT	200+ GT	Total
Shrimp trawlers					
1992			198	59	257
1996	39	59	280	53	431
2000	70	207	198	51	526
Fish trawlers					
1992					222
1996	13	116	250	209	588
2000	1	65	346	367	779
2001[a]	1	67	351	376	795
Bottom trawlers					
2001	7	9	16	1	33

GT = gross tonnes.

a   As of September 2001.

Source: Sadhotomo, Rahardjo and Wedjatmiko (2003).

and 2000, the number of shrimp trawlers doubled while the number of fish trawlers more than tripled. During the same period, total recorded annual landings from the Arafura Sea rose from around 18,000 to 25,000 tonnes for shrimp and from 170,000 to 262,000 tonnes for fish (Table 8.3). The fact that the annual recorded landings for shrimp and fish did not increase in line with the increase in the number of licensed vessels provides further evidence of overfishing.

A number of other studies support the increasing concern about overfishing. Evans and Wahju (1996) observed a 50 per cent reduction in the average catch per unit of effort between 1970 and 1990 for shrimp trawlers owned by an Ambon-based firm operating in the Arafura Sea. Iskandar, Sumiono and Sarjana (1993) found that there had been a decline in the size composition of the shrimp catch between 1985 and 1990, indicating size overfishing.

Sumiono and Priyono (1998) estimated the sustainable annual yield of shrimp in the Arafura Sea to be about 17,200–21,700 tonnes per year. The data in Table 8.3 indicate that, even without taking illegal fishing into account, total shrimp landings were already at the top of this range in 1996 and had exceeded it by 2000. The high incidence of illegal fishing in the Arafura Sea further compounds the problems of excess fishing effort and excess harvesting of shrimp.

*Table 8.3   Reported Annual Shrimp and Fish Landings in the Arafura Sea,
1992–2005 (thousand tonnes)*

	1992	1996	2000	2003	2005
Shrimp	18	21	25	21	22
Fish	170	216	262	273	273
Total	**188**	**237**	**287**	**294**	**294**

Source: MMAF (2002, 2005a).

Overfishing — including illegal fishing — in the Arafura Sea fishery
affects not only Indonesian landings but the health of adjoining national
fisheries. For instance, collaborative research by Australia's Commonwealth Scientific and Research Organization (CSIRO) and the MMAF's
Centre for Research on Fish Capture showed that red snapper stocks
(*Lutjanus erythropertus* and *Lutjanus malabaricus*) in the neighbouring
sea waters of eastern Indonesia and northern Australia had declined to
10–20 per cent of their 1971 level by the early 2000s (Badrudin and Blaber
2003). If current levels of fishing activity continued, it was predicted that
red snapper stocks would collapse by 2007 in both the Indonesian and
Australian fisheries (Blaber et al. 2005).

Allocative and Distributional Effects

In recent years small-scale fishers, particularly traditional indigenous
fishers in places like Merauke, have experienced a decline in both catch
sizes and the size of the fish caught. They attribute this to illegal inshore
fishing by large vessels. For fishers and their families, the lower yields
lead to decreased fish consumption and lower fishery earnings. For
the broader coastal community, the main impact comes from the likely
increase in the price of fish. It is important to recognize that the decrease
in the supply of fish also has secondary budgetary effects, in terms of
reduced earning opportunities for those who handle the catch onshore
(Vieira 2004).

As a result, many traditional fishers have been faced with the choice
of either fishing further out to sea or switching to farming. In both cases,
they encounter the problems of lack of capital and lack of know-how
(that is, how to operate motorized boats or cultivate crops). Some of
the increase in offshore fishing by small-scale vessels is observable in
the increase in the number of small Indonesian fishing vessels operating illegally in the Australian EEZ (see Chapter 9). Disenfranchised by

what they perceive to be unfair enforcement, and unable to compete with illegal operators, some inshore communities resort to destructive (and illegal) fishing practices such as the use of explosives or cyanide to kill fish (Erdman 2000; Apituley and Hiariey 2004). Such practices affect fish stock recruitment and destroy the inshore environment important to fish spawning, thus further reducing future catches, future returns and social well-being.

Important to any consideration of illegal fishing is the perceptions of those who do — or would like to — comply with fishing regulations. Any perceived lack of transparency, reliability or equity of enforcement is likely to reduce their acceptance of and compliance with fishery regulations (Dahuri and Dutton 2000). Non-compliance with fishing regulations works to the relative financial disadvantage of complying fishers, giving them an incentive not to comply.

At present, compliant fishers are subject to higher marketing and taxation costs than illegal fishers, who are able to achieve operational and other advantages by ignoring the restrictive requirements of their licences or by not paying licence fees and other fees and charges. The illegal operators of large boats are also able to pay higher prices for fish at sea than their onshore competitors. Operators of small and medium-sized vessels have a financial incentive to participate in these at-sea sales, both because of the higher prices paid and because the income from these sales is easier to protect from port charges and taxes.

Social Effects

The broad social implications of illegal fishing are often observed at the local level. In Merauke, for instance, illegal fishers provide markets for the products of local communities, thus implicating them in illegal fishing. The lack of a developed market for fish in the coastal areas of the district, far from the city of Merauke, is a major reason for sales at sea by small-scale and artisanal fishers. However, the volumes involved are small, since foreign operators prefer deep sea (demersal) species such as pomfret. Some foreign operators barter for the fish provided by artisanal fishers, especially as they may not have any local currency. Bartering can be advantageous for local fishers, since there is a dearth of goods such as clothes and other household items in many rural areas of Merauke. In addition, local fishers are able to trade fish for foodstuffs such as coconuts and other fresh fruits.

At times, illegal fishers come into conflict with small local communities and small-scale or artisanal fishers, especially when large and medium-sized vessels breach their zoning and gear regulations. In retaliation, local Merauke and Kaimana fishers have been known to destroy or cut the nets of illegal operators, sometimes sharing the nets among themselves.

The presence of foreign fishers also raises concerns about the transmission of human (and fish) diseases. For instance, while it is unclear how much illegal fishers have contributed to the spread of HIV/AIDS in Merauke, it is generally believed that the disease was introduced by Thai ship crews in the 1980s. Merauke has the highest incidence of HIV/AIDS in Indonesia, but other coastal Papuan cities such as Timika, Sorong, Jayapura and Nabire also report high incidences of the disease (*Kompas*, 5 June 2000). According to a local organization in Merauke that cares for HIV/AIDS sufferers, between 1992 and March 2006, 827 people were infected and 197 people died from HIV/AIDS (*Media Indonesia Online*, 8 April 2006).

5   EFFORTS TO COMBAT ILLEGAL FISHING

The MMAF has initiated a number of actions to reduce the extent of illegal fishing in Indonesian waters. These can be grouped into three broad types of activities: regulatory reform, strengthened law enforcement, and improved fishery information and management systems. All have been applied in the Arafura Sea fishery.

Regulatory Reform

Following its establishment in 1999, the MMAF streamlined and improved the licensing system in order to combat illegal fishing. Through Government Regulation No. 54/2002 on Fisheries Business, the ministry reduced the number of different types of fishing licences from around 15 (13 from the Ministry of Transportation and two from the Ministry of Agriculture) to three, consisting of an overall commercial licence for firms involved in fishing (SIUP), a fishing vessel licence for Indonesian and foreign operators (SPI) and a separate licence for vessels transporting fish (SIKPI). The regulation also changed the basis for vessel licensing from type of fish harvested (large pelagic, small pelagic or demersal) to type of gear used. Under this regulation, foreign vessels were allowed to operate in Indonesian waters through joint ventures between Indonesian and foreign entities, by chartering a vessel from an Indonesian company or by operating in the central government's zone, 12–200 nautical miles offshore.

Foreign entities wishing to operate within the Indonesian EEZ must obtain a foreign fishing allocation or quota (APIA) before being allowed to apply for the required licences (*Kompas*, 9 June 2003). The allocations are set out in bilateral agreements between the Indonesian and a number of foreign governments. The agreements place limits on the number of fishing vessels from the country concerned and require the foreign government to ensure that its vessels comply with Indonesian regulations (Tribawono 2002).

The MMAF has also tried to reduce the number of vessels licensed to operate in Indonesian waters. Between 2001 and 2003, it reduced the number of centrally licensed vessels operating in the four fishery management areas surrounding Papua from around 3,700 to 2,600 vessels, or by 39 per cent (MMAF 2005a). Over the same period, however, the number of vessels licensed by district and provincial governments to operate in the Arafura Sea with inboard motors increased from around 1,000 to 2,200 vessels, or by 105 per cent (MMAF 2005b).

In October 2004, Law No. 31/2004 on Fisheries was enacted to replace Law No. 9/1985. It regulates fishing effort, including providing for the establishment of specialist courts with sole responsibility to try suspected violators. Under the new law, the severity of the penalties for violations varies according to the role of the perpetrator. As a result, criminal activities[9] are dealt with more severely than violations,[10] and vessel or business owners face more severe penalties than captains or crew. Importantly, by focusing on the vessel or business owner, the new law targets the primary beneficiary of illegal fishing and the person best placed to ensure compliance with fisheries legislation and management practices (Agoes 2005).

Law Enforcement

Since the early 2000s, the Indonesian government has taken a number of steps to strengthen the fisheries monitoring, control and surveillance system at the national, regional and local levels. One component of this system was the plan to have 1,500 of the 2,350 fishing vessels of 100 gross tonnes and above fitted with satellite tracking devices by 2004. How-

---

9 Criminal activities include gear violations; deliberate pollution and/or destruction of fish resources and/or the environment; deliberately catching, cultivating, transporting, processing or marketing fish without a fishery business licence (SIUP); and owning or operating a fishing or fish-transport vessel without the appropriate licence. These criminal acts are punishable by imprisonment of 5–10 years and/or a fine of Rp 1.5–20 billion.

10 Violations include the construction, importation or modification of a fishing vessel without the consent of the relevant authorities; operating an unregistered vessel; and violating the code of conduct for foreign vessels, such as not stowing away fishing gear when traversing Indonesian waters without a permit. These violations are punishable by a maximum of one year's imprisonment and/or a fine of Rp 0.2–1 billion.

ever, by mid-2004 less than half the planned number of vessels had been equipped with such devices.[11]

To further strengthen compliance, the MMAF has instituted a number of measures to support local jurisdictions in carrying out surveillance and enforcement activities, under Ministerial Decree No. 58/2001. These include the introduction of civil fishery officers to investigate and prepare cases against illegal fishers and bring them before the new fishery courts. The officers have been provided with improved fishery monitoring vessels and are equipped with firearms and other self-defence equipment.

Improvements in Information and Management Systems

In 2005 the MMAF began publishing official statistics detailing the number of vessels holding central government licences by size, home port and gear type. The first of these reports provided data on licences issued between 2001 and 2003 (MMAF 2005b). To overcome some of the earlier difficulties in enforcing licensing requirements, the MMAF is setting up a data exchange system that will connect the ministry with its regional offices. This will allow quick and accurate exchange of data among fishery offices and agencies, and should prove a boon for efficient licensing and enforcement.

6 FINAL REMARKS AND CHALLENGES

The overall challenge for the Indonesian government in marine resource management is to optimize the socio-economic benefit from the resource. An ongoing impediment to achieving an optimal outcome in the Arafura Sea has been the level of illegal fishing. In this chapter we have described the forms of illegal fishing, the actors involved and the significant socio-economic losses caused by illegal fishing. We have also discussed the problems of market and agency failure contributing to illegal fishing, and described the bio-economic and agency requirements to address them.

The first challenge is to overcome institutional and agency failure with regard to illegal fishing. This will require the synchronization of laws and regulations across governmental levels to meet the common goal of maximizing the socio-economic benefit from the country's fisheries. For example, action is needed to synchronize Law No. 32/2004, Agriculture Ministerial Decree No. 392/1999 and Government Regulation No. 54/2002 to obtain a consistent licensing regime across the different

---

11 Personal communication with staff of the MMAF's monitoring, control and surveillance team, August 2004.

zones and territories. In parallel, laws and regulations need to be strictly enforced, particularly in relation to large, organized foreign and local players with links to local fishery management and enforcement bodies. Agency failure, which occurs when some members of the respective agencies exhibit self-seeking behaviour rather than acting in the public interest, must be eliminated. Independent investigations are needed to bring such officials before the courts.

The second set of challenges is to overcome the problems of market failure that are currently causing overinvestment in fishing effort, overharvesting of fish stocks, and crowding or gear conflict among fishers. In broad terms, this can be dealt with by putting either input or output controls in place. Input controls rely on the use of technical constraints to overcome excess fishing effort, overharvesting and the harvesting of fish at too small an age class. While input controls have a long history, they have had at best limited success, because they fail to take into account the behaviour of fishers and the incentives they face to continue overfishing (Grafton et al. 2006). One of the most commonly discussed output (or yield) controls is the use of the individual transferable catch quota (ITCQ). While the ITCQ has had mixed success, it does address the question of inadequate rights to fish resources by giving individual fishers specific rights to a proportion of the allowable catch.[12] Also relevant to this set of challenges is the possible establishment of a system of marine protected areas. This might help to protect fish stocks and maintain fish yields over the longer term. It would also be easier to administer and ensure greater compliance than other management options.

Ideally, individual jurisdictions would choose the mix of management options best suited to their local circumstances, rather than it being a question of one approach versus another. That is, different components of an 'optimal' management structure would be introduced, depending on their suitability, the likely level of acceptance and the capacity to ensure compliance. But regardless of the form of management, strengthening fisheries surveillance and enforcement is a matter of urgency. This

---

12 The application of the ITCQ depends on identifying the annual total allowable catch, where this is set at a level to achieve the maximum economic benefit. The total allowable catch is shared among the fishers licensed to operate in a fishery, so that the actual allowable catch for each vessel will vary from year to year depending on the level of the total allowable catch. Under the ITCQ, fishers are free to sell or lease their quotas or, in the case of a fleet owner, consolidate them across a number of vessels. Where quotas are applied and compliance is enforced, both improvements in profits (as a result of lower harvesting costs) and improvements in prices (as fishers concentrate on quality rather than quantity) have been observed. An example of this outcome is observable in the Australian southern bluefin tuna fishery (Campbell, Brown and Battaglene 2000).

could be facilitated by collaboration between Indonesia and neighbouring countries, particularly Australia, to monitor fishing activities in
the Arafura Sea. Also important is developing a good data set, a better
appreciation of fisher behaviour and a better understanding of the nature
of the fishery, including both its biological and economic aspects.

The Indonesian government has taken a number of steps to mitigate
illegal fishing in the Arafura Sea. These include the creation of a separate
ministry for marine territories and fisheries, the establishment of a new
legislative and judicial framework, and a greater emphasis on monitoring and control. However, the effectiveness of the various measures is not
known; they may have resulted merely in a change of players or changes
in the ways illegal fishing is carried out. At least until the mid-2000s, illegal fishing in the Arafura Sea fishery continued to be an important issue
compounding the problem of non-optimal harvesting of fish stocks, with
the accompanying loss of social well-being. It is important to note that
the consequences of illegal fishing are not limited to Indonesia, but are
shared worldwide.

REFERENCES

Agoes, E.R. (2005), 'Adequacy of Indonesian Laws and Regulations to Combat
    IUU Fishing: An Evaluation of the New Law on Fisheries', paper presented
    to the National Workshop on IUU Fishing in Indonesia, Ministry of Marine
    Affairs and Fisheries (Indonesia) and Centre for Maritime Policy (University
    of Wollongong), Jakarta, 28 April.
Alisjahbana, A.S. (2005), 'Does Indonesia Have the Balance Right on Natural
    Resource Revenue Sharing?', in B.P. Resosudarmo (ed.), *The Politics and Eco-
    nomics of Indonesia's Natural Resources*, Institute of Southeast Asian Studies,
    Singapore, pp. 109–24.
Anderson, L. (1986), *The Economics of Fisheries Management*, Johns Hopkins Uni-
    versity Press, Baltimore MD.
Apituley, T.M.T.N. and J. Hiariey (2004), 'Sasi Laut as a Community-based Fish-
    ery Resources Management in Maluku', in Y. Matsuda and T. Yamamoto
    (eds), *Proceedings of the Twelfth Biennial Conference of the International Institute
    of Fisheries Economics and Trade*, International Institute of Fisheries Economics
    and Trade, Corvallis OR.
Badrudin and S.J. Blaber (2003), 'Pengkajian Stok Sumber Daya Ikan Kakap
    Merah di Perairan Laut Arafura dan Laut Timor' [Stock Analysis of Red
    Snapper Fisheries in the Arafura Sea and the Timor Sea], in J. Widodo, N.N.
    Wiadnyana and D. Nugroho (eds), *Prosiding Forum Pengkajian Stok Ikan Laut
    2003, Jakarta, 23–24 Juli 2003* [Proceedings of the Fishery Stock Analysis
    Forum, Jakarta, 23–24 July 2003], PUSRIPT-BRKP, Ministry of Marine Affairs
    and Fisheries, Jakarta, pp. 47–56.
Blaber, S., C. Dichmont, R. Buckworth, Badrudin, B. Sumiono, S. Nurhakim, B.
    Iskandar, B. Fegan, D. Ramm and J. Salini (2005), 'Shared Stocks of Snap-
    pers (*Lutjanidae*) in Australia and Indonesia: Integrating Biology, Population

Dynamics and Socio-economics to Examine Management Scenarios', *Review in Fish Biology and Fisheries*, 15(1–2): 111–27.

Campbell, David and Jos Haynes (1990), 'Resource Rent in Fisheries', ABARE Discussion Paper 90.10, Australian Bureau of Agricultural and Resource Economics, Canberra.

Campbell, David, Debbie Brown and Tony Battaglene (2000), 'Individual Transferable Catch Quotas: Australian Experience in the Southern Bluefin Tuna Fishery', *Marine Policy*, 24(2): 109–17.

Charoenpo, A. (2002), 'Illegal Thai Fishing Robbed Indonesia of Billions of Catches and Cash', Southeast Asian Press Alliance, available at <http://www.seapabkk.org/fellowships/2002/anucha.html>.

Clark, C. (1985), *Bioeconomic Modelling and Fisheries Management*, John Wiley and Sons, New York NY.

Dahuri, R. and J.M. Dutton (2000), 'Integrated Coastal and Marine Management Enters a New Era in Indonesia', *Integrated Coastal Zone Management*, 1: 11–16.

Dutton, I.M. (2005), 'If Only Fish Could Vote: The Enduring Challenges of Coastal and Marine Resources Management in Post-*reformasi* Indonesia', in B.P. Resosudarmo (ed.), *The Politics and Economics of Indonesia's Natural Resources*, Institute of Southeast Asian Studies, Singapore, pp. 162–78.

Erdmann, Mark V. (2000), 'Leave Indonesia's Fisheries to Indonesians!', *Inside Indonesia*, 63(July–September), available at <http://insideindonesia.org/content/view/547/29/>.

Evans, S.M. and R.I. Wahju (1996), 'The Shrimp Fishery of the Arafura Sea (Eastern Indonesia)', *Fishery Research*, 26: 365–71.

Fegan, B. (2003), 'Plundering the Sea', *Inside Indonesia*, 73(January–March): 21–3, available at <http://insideindonesia.org/content/view/339/29/>.

Fegan, B. (2005), 'Box 10.1: Offshore Fishing', in B.P. Resosudarmo (ed.), *The Politics and Economics of Indonesia's Natural Resources*, Institute of Southeast Asian Studies, Singapore, pp. 168–9.

Fox, J.J., D.S. Adhuri and I.A.P. Resosudarmo (2005), 'Unfinished Edifice or Pandora's Box? Decentralisation and Resource Management in Indonesia', in B.P. Resosudarmo (ed.), *The Politics and Economics of Indonesia's Natural Resources*, Institute of Southeast Asian Studies, Singapore, pp. 92–108.

Grafton, R. Quentin et al. (2006), 'Incentive-based Approaches to Sustainable Fisheries', *Canadian Journal of Fisheries and Aquatic Science*, 63: 699–710.

Heazle, M. and J.G. Butcher (2007), 'Fisheries Depletion and the State in Indonesia: Towards a Regional Regulatory Regime', *Marine Policy*, 31: 276–86.

Holthuis, L.B. (1980), *Shrimps and Prawns of the World*, Food and Agriculture Organization (FAO) Species Catalogue Vol. 1, Rome, available at <http://www.fao.org/docrep/009/ac477e/ac477e00.htm>.

Iskandar, B., B. Sumiono and Sarjana (1993), 'Penelitian Potensi Udang dan Hasil Tangkap Sampingan di Perairan Maluku dan Irian Jaya' [Research on the Potential of the Shrimp and By-catch in the Waters of Maluku and Irian Jaya], Laporan Penelitian Balitkanlut, Jakarta.

MMAF (Ministry of Marine Affairs and Fisheries) (2002), *Statistik Perikanan Tangkap Indonesia 2000* [Statistics of Capture Fisheries 2000], Jakarta.

MMAF (Ministry of Marine Affairs and Fisheries) (2005a), *Statistik Perikanan Tangkap Indonesia 2003* [Statistics of Capture Fisheries 2003], Jakarta.

MMAF (Ministry of Marine Affairs and Fisheries) (2005b), *Statistik Perikanan Laut Izin Pusat 2001–2003* [Statistics of Centrally Licensed Vessels 2001–2003], Jakarta.

Mueller, Dennis C. (2003), *Public Choice III*, Cambridge University Press, Cambridge.

Petocz, R.G. (1987), *Konservasi Alam dan Pembangunan di Irian Jaya: Strategi Pemanfaatan Sumber Daya Alam Secara Rasional* [Conservation and Development in Irian Jaya: Rational Strategy in Utilizing Natural Resources], Grafitipers, Jakarta.

Rudiyanto, A. (2002), 'A Critical Appraisal of Marine and Coastal Policy in Indonesia including Comparative Issues and Lesson Learnt from Australia', PhD thesis, University of Wollongong, Wollongong.

Sadhotomo, B., P. Rahardjo and Wedjatmiko (2003), 'Pengkajian Kelimpahan dan Distribusi Sumber Daya Demersal dan Udang di Perairan Laut Arafura [Review of the Abundance and Distribution of Demersal Fish and Shrimp Stocks in the Arafura Sea], in J. Widodo, N.N. Wiadnyana and D. Nugroho (eds), *Prosiding Forum Pengkajian Stok Ikan Laut 2003, Jakarta, 23–24 Juli 2003* [Proceedings of the Fishery Stock Assessment Forum, Jakarta, 23–24 July 2003], PUSRIPT-BRKP, Ministry of Marine Affairs and Fisheries, Jakarta.

Sitathan, T. (2003), 'Illegal Fishing Hurts Indonesia's Net Income', *Asia Times Online*, 29 April.

Sumiono, B. and B.E. Priyono (1998), 'Sumber Daya Udang Paneid dan Krustasea Lainnya' [Stocks of Paneid and other Crustacea Shrimps], in J. Widodo et al. (eds), *Potensi dan Penyebaran Sumber Daya Ikan Laut di Perairan Indonesia* [The Potential and Distribution of Fish Stocks in Indonesian Waters], Komisi Nasional Pengkajian Stok Sumber Daya Ikan Laut LIPI, Jakarta.

Tomascik, T., A.J. Mah, A. Nontji and M.K. Moosa (1997), *The Ecology of the Indonesian Seas, Part Two*, Periplus, Hong Kong.

Tribawono, H.D.T. (2002), *Hukum Perikanan Indonesia* [Indonesian Fishery Laws], PT Citra Aditya Bakti, Bandung.

Vieira, S. (2004), 'The Potential Management Impacts on the Incomes and Welfare of Artisanal Fishers in Indonesian Shark and Ray Fisheries: A Case Study of Cilacap', Bachelor of Economics Honours thesis, Murdoch University, Perth.

Weimer, David L. and Aidan R. Vining (2005), *Policy Analysis: Concepts and Practice*, Pearson, Prentice Hall, Upper Saddle River NJ.

9 SEARCHING FOR A LIVELIHOOD: THE DILEMMA OF SMALL-BOAT FISHERMEN IN EASTERN INDONESIA

James J. Fox, Dedi S. Adhuri, Tom Therik and Michelle Carnegie

1 INTRODUCTION

Nowhere on earth is there a greater disparity in maritime environments than between northern Australia and the southern regions of Indonesia. Northern Australia's historically low population and its regulated fisheries management have — until now — provided relatively good protection for the rich and diverse marine resources of the Timor Sea. By contrast, the Arafura Sea, directly to the north of Australia, is among the most heavily fished regions in the world. As the marine resources of other Indonesian regions have progressively been overexploited, fishing vessels — both local and foreign — have shifted operations eastward. Under a ruling of the Soeharto period, trawlers banned elsewhere in Indonesian waters are allowed to operate legally in the Arafura Sea. A plethora of these fishing vessels, some legal and others illegal, vie with each other to exploit available resources. The increasingly sophisticated operations of these large fishing fleets have disrupted and diminished the opportunities for the small-boat fishermen of eastern Indonesia to derive a living from the sea. As these fishermen have seen their capacity to operate curtailed, they, too, have been forced to extend their voyaging.

Many of these small-boat fishermen, especially from South and Southeast Sulawesi where pressures on sea resources are particularly acute, have shifted, either permanently or on a seasonal basis, to strategic locations along the coasts of the southern islands of eastern Indonesia.

Limited by commercial vessels operating in the Arafura Sea, they have increasingly looked to Australian waters for key commodities that were previously plentiful in their own seas, particularly shark but also trepang and trochus.

As the number of small-boat fishermen has multiplied and the resources they seek in their own waters have diminished, the problem of illegal fishing in Australia's northern waters has become ever more acute. Under a memorandum of understanding (MOU) concluded with Indonesia in 1974, Australia permitted 'traditional fishermen' — those who relied exclusively on sail power — to fish within a demarcated sea area known as the MOU (or MOU74) Box. Until recently, however, the majority of small-boat fishermen have utilized motorized craft of various sizes to fish across the entire northern region of Australia and along the northern reaches of both the western and eastern coasts of the continent.

In response, Australia has mounted larger and more effective surveillance and apprehension operations. In 2004/05, these led to the apprehension of over 200 illegal vessels.[1] Australia's largest ever air and sea effort targeting incursions by foreign fishing vessels in northern waters, known as Operation Clearwater, was conducted in April 2005, and a similar operation, Operation Breakwater, was carried out in 2006.

In this chapter we look at specific aspects of this considerable problem.[2] We concentrate primarily on the small-boat fishermen who fish for shark, taking fin to feed an almost insatiable Chinese market. We begin by considering the conditions in the Arafura Sea, which is one of the most overfished areas in the world, and Australian arrangements with regard to the 'traditional' Indonesian fishermen who are allowed to sail into Australian waters.

We then focus on the four small ports — Pepela, Saumlaki, Dobo and Merauke — from which most small-boat fishermen depart (see Map 9.1). Pepela is located on the eastern end of the small island of Rote just to the west of Timor in the province of East Nusa Tenggara. Saumlaki is situated at the southern end of the island of Tanimbar, and Dobo on the western coast of the island of Aru. Both of these islands are part of the province of Maluku. Merauke, on the southern Papuan coast, belongs to the province

---

1 There were 202 apprehensions, 176 legislative forfeitures and 1,480 persons detained between 1 July 2004 and 30 June 2005 (AFMA 2005: 97).

2 This chapter was originally prepared in 2006 when this problem was particularly acute. It describes fishing practices in 2004–05, prior to the Australian naval and customs operations that substantially reduced small-boat shark-fishing incursions into Australian waters.

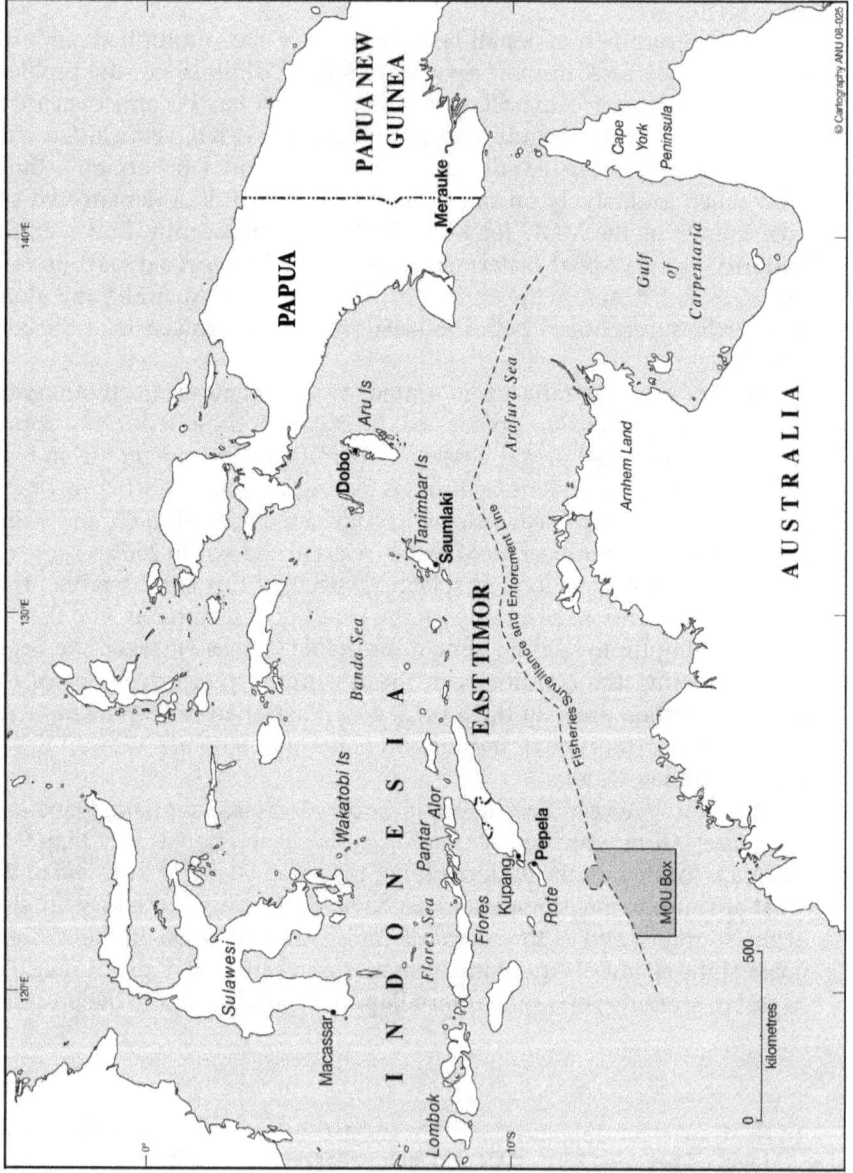

Map 9.1 The Southern Ports of the Shark Fishermen of Eastern Indonesia

of Papua.[3] Under Indonesia's new regime of local autonomy, jurisdiction over these ports is vested in three different provincial governments.

Although these fishermen sail from just a few ports, most of them come from other islands in eastern Indonesia. In discussing differences among these ports, we set out to identify some of the home islands from which the fishermen originate. We then examine the distinguishing features of the vessels and technologies used in these ports; the changing patterns involved in this fishing; and the variety of on-shore owners, outfitters and local traders who provide the capital and equipment for voyages and then purchase the catch supplied by the fishermen. We consider the prices paid to fishermen for their efforts and the situation of debt that often ties them to particular traders. Finally, we attempt to give some indication of the size of this fishery.

It should be emphasized that small-boat shark fishermen represent only one of the groups of illegal fishermen now entering Australian waters. Other small-boat fishermen target trepang or trochus and fleets of larger vessels have begun to penetrate deep into Australian waters to fish for red snapper and other valuable species.

2   CONDITIONS IN THE ARAFURA, BANDA AND FLORES SEAS

The Indonesian government divides its national waters into nine separate regional fisheries. What in Australia is often referred to as a single region — the Arafura Sea — is considered by Indonesia to be two maritime zones: the Arafura Sea and the Banda Sea. The Arafura Sea extends around Papua/Irian Jaya. The island of Aru is considered part of the Arafura Sea, as is all of Papua. Thus, the ports of Dobo and Merauke belong to this zone. Tanimbar, however, is considered part of the Banda Sea, so Saumlaki belongs to the Banda Sea zone. The islands of Timor and Rote are included in the Indian Ocean; Pepela belongs in this zone. Official Indonesian information and statistics are organized according to these regional categories.

For each of these fishing areas, the Indonesian Ministry of Marine Affairs and Fisheries tries to conduct regular assessments of stock capacities.[4] However, because of the high level of illegal fishing and the signifi-

---

3   To this list one could add various other fishing settlements: those in the vicinity of Merauke; those on other islands of Maluku, such as the tiny port of Tepa on the island of Babar; and, most significantly, various ports on the Bay of Kupang (Tablolong, Oesapa and Sulamu).

4   These surveys are carried out by the ministry's Research Centre for Capture Fisheries (Pusat Riset Perikanan Tangkap), often in cooperation with LIPI's Research Centre for Oceanography (Pusat Penelitian Oseanografi).

cant tendency to underreport the level of catch to avoid taxes and fees (see Fegan 2003 and Chapter 8, this volume), these assessments depend upon independent research and oceanographic surveys to bolster their accuracy.

Despite the limitations faced in conducting these assessments, the scientific results of this research provide a sobering contrast to the general, often official, rhetoric about the enormous untapped potential of Indonesia's seas, particularly its eastern seas. Thus, for example, the stock assessment report for 2001 prepared in cooperation with the Indonesian Institute of Sciences (LIPI) indicated that there was little opportunity for a significant expansion of fishing in any of Indonesia's nine fishing areas, and instead called for the establishment of management strategies to set limits on fishing activities (MMAF and LIPI 2001; Fox, Adhuri and Resosudarmo 2005: 96–7). A similar statement is found in the conclusion to the ministry's technical report for 2003: 'A majority of fish resources in Indonesia's various fishing areas have experienced exploitation pressures that are beyond long-term sustainability' (MMAF 2004: 83).

For the Arafura Sea, the 2001 report called for limits on all large pelagic and demersal fish as well as shrimp. For the Banda Sea, it called for limits on all small pelagic and demersal fish. And for the Flores Sea, it called for limits on demersal fish and shrimp (MMAF and LIPI 2001: 192). A technical report for 2002 focusing specifically on the Arafura Sea noted indications of a continuing reduction in stocks, which it attributed to a combination of fishing vessels of under 150 gross tonnes operating directly along the shore and pair-trawling by a fleet of mainly Thai boats (MMAF 2003: 129–72).

Indonesia has taken steps to address its problems of illegal, unreported and unregulated fishing. In 1999, the Ministry of Marine Affairs and Fisheries was established by presidential decree to separate fisheries from the Ministry of Agriculture and provide it with a wider mandate.[5] The ministry initiated a program of re-registering fishing vessels and re-flagging foreign vessels. But even as it carried out this new program to reduce and eventually eliminate foreign fishing fleets, new joint venture arrangements were put in place to allow the re-entry of many foreign vessels under the guise of domestic economic cooperation. A new law passed in 2004 (Law No. 31/2004 on Fisheries) increased the penalties for all fisheries violations, provided new investigatory powers and procedures for officials to deal with such offences and established local fisheries tribunals to hear cases and make judgments (see also Chapter 8).

---

5 Initially called the Ministry of Marine Exploration and Fisheries, its name was changed in 2000 to the Ministry of Marine Affairs and Fisheries (Departemen Kelautan dan Perikanan).

Table 9.1   Registered Fishing Vessels in the Arafura Sea by Gross Tonnage, 2000

	30–50 GT	51–100 GT	101–200 GT	201–300 GT	>300 GT	Total
No. of vessels	158	312	582	284	186	1,522

GT = gross tonnes.
Source: MMAF (2003: 139).

The new law has yet to be fully implemented, and in the meantime large-scale fishing continues to build up in the Arafura Sea. Various estimates exist as to the extent of this fishing. For example, the ministry's technical report for 2002 shows that 1,522 registered fishing vessels were operating in the Arafura Sea in 2000, many of them well above 200 gross tonnes (Table 9.1). These figures date from the period prior to the re-registration initiative but are nevertheless indicative of the levels of fishing in the Arafura Sea.

In contrast to these official figures for 2000, the head of the Marine Affairs and Fisheries Office of the province of Maluku estimated that in 2005 there were at least 1,400 illegal fishing vessels operating in the Arafura Sea (*Suara Merdeka*, 17 March 2005). On the basis of extensive field research carried out between 1998 and 2001, Fegan (2003: 21) estimated that there were '700–750 trawlers operating in the Arafura Sea'.

Whatever the number of vessels involved, all indications are that the level of overfishing in the Arafura and adjoining seas remains substantial. Small-boat fishermen repeatedly bemoan the fact that they can rarely put out their fishing lines without them being ripped away by larger vessels. In the face of such constraints, they have increasingly turned to fishing in Australian waters. Fishing by small-boat fishermen in traditional sailing boats is permitted within the area demarcated by the 1974 MOU, but from 2000 to 2006 the majority of small-boat fishing in Australian waters was carried out in motorized vessels, many of them specially designed to avoid apprehension. It is important to recognize the developments that occurred in the 1990s leading to these new forms of illegal fishing.

3   ASHMORE REEF AND THE AUSTRALIAN MOU

The MOU concluded between the Australian and Indonesian governments in 1974 identified five small areas on the northwest Australian continental shelf to which 'traditional' Indonesian fishermen would be given access. These areas were Ashmore Reef, Cartier Islet, Scott Reef, Seringapatam Reef and Browse Islet. The MOU allowed the fishermen to take trepang, trochus, abalone, green snail, sponges and all molluscs on the seabed adjacent to these areas, but not turtles of any species. It also permitted landings to obtain fresh water at two points on Ashmore Reef and allowed boats to shelter within the group without landing.

This simple document consisting of three pages plus a map provided the basis for traditional Indonesian fishing in Australian waters. It came into effect on 1 February 1975. However, the use of the term 'traditional' in the original document was considered ambiguous. Eventually, in 1988, both Indonesia and Australia agreed to a further advisory clarification that 'traditional' referred to fishermen who used non-motorized sailing vessels, generally *lambo perahu*, to access the MOU Box.[6] At the same time, Australia committed itself to work with Indonesia to provide assistance to fishermen in eastern Indonesia.

Ashmore Reef is the largest and most important of the five tiny areas designated in the MOU. It is a raised platform reef near the edge of the Sahul Shelf, approximately 120 kilometres directly south of the island of Rote. In 1983 the Australian government declared Ashmore Reef a National Nature Reserve, because of its remarkable biodiversity and because it is a staging point for migratory birds and a breeding ground for dugong and several types of turtles. This declaration banned the removal of all fauna and flora to a depth of 50 metres.

By the time the ban came into effect, trepang stocks were already depleted near all the reefs and islets identified by the MOU. A stock assessment undertaken by CSIRO Marine Research in 1998 reported that 'high-value species were either absent or at low abundances on all reefs' covered by the MOU and that local gathering efforts had switched to medium and low-value species — but even these were at low densities on most reefs (Skewes et al. 1999).[7]

By the mid-1990s, voyages to Ashmore and other reefs in the Australian Fishing Zone for the purpose of gathering trepang had already begun to decline. Only fishermen from Oelaba and Hundi Huk, the two neighbouring settlements located at the western end of the island of Rote, along with fishermen from the small islands of Tonduk and Raas

---

6   For a discussion of the MOU, its modification and the consequences of Australian policy, see Fox (1995, 1998).

7   The report by Skewes et al. (1999) and subsequent surveys by Smith et al. (2000, 2002) provided data for the preparation of the Commonwealth Management Plans for the Ashmore Reef National Nature Reserve and the Cartier Island Marine Reserve, published in 2001 (DEH 2001). The latest survey was conducted in 2005 (see Kospartov et al. 2006).

to the east of Madura, continued regular voyaging to gather trepang. Beginning in the early 1990s, fishermen from the port of Pepela shifted from trepang and trochus gathering to intensive shark fishing.[8] Joined by fishermen from other areas, they relied on access to the waters of the MOU Box to fish for shark fin.

As the price of fin rose and more vessels entered Australian waters in search of shark, fishermen inevitably began to venture beyond the permitted sea boundaries into better shark-fishing grounds. This resulted in a steady increase in the apprehension of vessels for illegal fishing in the Australian Fishing Zone and closer to the Australian coast. Beginning in 2001, fishermen in Pepela began to rely on the small, fast motorized vessels known as *bodi* to avoid apprehension while they continued their pursuit of shark. The number of *bodi* rose rapidly, with their area of operation extending well beyond the MOU Box area.

At the time that Pepela fishermen were shifting to shark fishing, other eastern Indonesian fishermen were doing much the same. An important fishing port for these initial changes was Dobo on the island of Aru, but other ports, particularly Merauke, were drawn into shark-fishing activities and have continued to develop their capacity to take shark.

4   THE FOUR SOUTHERN PORTS FOR INDONESIAN SHARK FISHING

The four ports from which the bulk of small-boat shark fishermen sailed into Australian waters — Pepela, Saumlaki, Dobo and Merauke — form an arc that extends from the western tip of the island of Timor across the Arafura Sea to the south Papuan coast (Map 9.1). Each of these ports has distinguishing features, including differences in the number of boats that utilize each one. The situation is a dynamic one. Conditions among and within these ports do not remain constant.

There are broad similarities in the arrangements between fishermen and their local outfitters, but there are also notable variations in specific

---

8   In the late 1980s, Bajau from Mola on Wanci Island began to move to Pepela, where they were given an area to settle. They used this as their base for shark fishing further to the south. The local fishermen in Pepela then began to learn shark fishing from the Bajau. Initially they did this by assigning young men from Pepela to *perahu* with Bajau captains and crew. By 1996–97, all *perahu* sailing from Pepela were targeting shark. Local Pepela fishermen quickly — and somewhat contemptuously — discarded the traditional Bajau methods and accompanying taboos and adopted more effective longline technology. Within five years they saw themselves as better shark fishers than their teachers. See Fox (1998, 2005: 48–53) for further discussion.

arrangements, and even differences from port to port in the prices paid for shark fin. These differences reflect the fact that the fishermen tend to access different fishing areas with varying species of shark, whose fins attract different prices. Another important difference between ports lies in the history of their involvement in shark fishing in Australian waters.

Dobo

Dobo is an 'old' port town. In the nineteenth century, it was the chief emporium for the trade in exotic commodities from the Papuan coast to Makassar. Alfred Russel Wallace sailed in a Bugis prau (*perahu*) from Makassar to Dobo in December 1856 and wrote a brief description of the trade at that time:

> More important than all of these [commodities from other parts of eastern Indonesia] is the trade to Aru, a group of islands situated on the southwest coast of New Guinea, and of which almost the whole of the produce comes to Makassar in native vessels. These islands [are] out of the track of all European trade … Pearls, mother-of-pearl, and tortoiseshell, find their way to Europe, while edible birds' nests and 'tripang' or sea-slug are obtained by shiploads for the gastronomic enjoyment of the Chinese (Wallace 1869, Vol. II: 158).[9]

Although Dobo has since declined in importance as a trading port, it has retained its position as a local fishing port and as a key node in the network of fishing communities across eastern Indonesia. According to its fishermen, Dobo has a local fleet of 100–125 boats. In addition, the port is used seasonally as a staging point for small boats from other parts of Indonesia and thus the number of boats increases as the main fishing season progresses.

The diverse origins of the fishermen now living in Dobo reflect the importance of this port and its established social network within eastern Indonesia. One can find individual fishermen from all over eastern Indonesia in Dobo, as well as a number of established local communities from other islands. There are, for example, separate communities of fishermen from Bone Rate and from Batu Ata, tiny islands in the sea between Flores and Sulawesi, as well as a small community of fishermen who have come from the Bay of Maumere on the north Flores coast.

The first substantial wave of shark fishers from Dobo began to sail into Australian waters in the early 1990s (Fox 1992). Fishermen from Dobo constitute a substantial number of the illegal fishermen who are

---

9 For an extended discussion of the history of various maritime communities in eastern Indonesia, see Fox (2000).

regularly apprehended. Many fishermen who previously sailed from Dobo are, however, now shifting to Merauke.

Merauke

The port of Merauke is used by large commercial fishing vessels as well as small-boat fishermen. In recent years it has taken the 'spillover' of small fishermen from Dobo; many of the community of fishermen from the Bay of Maumere have moved to Merauke, for example. In the words of one fisherman from Dobo: 'Merauke is where our young men go if they can't make a living in Dobo'.

As a result, Merauke has a mix of fishermen from all over eastern Indonesia. A majority of them come from different parts of Buton in Southeast Sulawesi. As a port for small-boat fishermen, Merauke is growing rapidly and has — or may soon have — more shark-fishing boats than Dobo. Since 2004 the shift of boats from Dobo to Merauke has increased, and a number of boats, financed from Dobo, now prefer to sail from Merauke. Local fishermen estimated that in 2005, 150–200 shark-fishing boats were based in the Pintu Air area of Merauke.[10] According to them, their fishing endeavours had been concentrated in Australian waters for the past five years.

Merauke is located in relatively close proximity to a productive boat-building industry at Kumbe, about 60 kilometres from the town. Between 2003 and 2006 Kumbe is reported to have produced 30–50 boats of various sizes each year (Adhuri 2006).

Saumlaki

Saumlaki on the island of Tanimbar is a far smaller port than either Dobo or Merauke. Local fishermen claim that Saumlaki harbours approximately 30 boats capable of shark fishing but other estimates indicate there may be 50 such boats. For part of the year, many of these boats fish in nearby waters to supply the local market with fish. There is also a traditional fishing village on Tanimbar called Namtabung. Boats from Namtabung sail from Saumlaki to fish for shark and young men from the village join the Saumlaki boats as crew members. Whereas most of the fishermen in Saumlaki are Muslims who have come from elsewhere in eastern Indonesia, many of the fishermen from Namtabung are Christians.

---

10 In addition, they estimated that there were as many as 50 larger boats (up to 60 gross tonnes) based in Merauke that regularly fished for shark using extensive nets rather than longlines.

Pepela

Pepela is located at the southeastern 'neck' of the island of Rote on a wide, protected bay that opens to the Timor Sea. The setting is beautiful but the settlement itself, built on limestone and coral sediment, is crowded, somewhat squalid and lacks a good source of water, particularly in the dry season. It is not clear when Pepela was founded. Local traditions recount the arrival and settlement of Muslim immigrants, on coastal land granted to them by the Rotinese *raja* of the domain of Ringgou, around the end of the nineteenth century or beginning of the twentieth century. These initial settlers are said to have come from Southeast Sulawesi, but over time they were joined by settlers from other islands in eastern Indonesia and Madura along with a number of Arab families of Haudramaut origin. The most recent arrivals have been Bajau from the Tukang Besi (Wakatobi) Islands, particularly Wanci, and fishermen from the Barnusa area of Alor and Pantar. The original settlement of Pepela was built near the sea and is still marked today by an old mosque near the harbour. The main concentration of houses is now in the New Settlement (Kampung Baru) built further away from the sea.

Most household heads (82 per cent) identify their occupation as full-time fishing. As such, Pepela is the largest fishing village on the island of Rote and certainly one of the largest in the Timor area. It is one of the principal organizational centres for crew recruitment for voyages into Australian waters.[11] It is also the initial marketing centre for the marine products obtained on these voyages. In addition to drawing on its own local manpower and that of neighbouring Rotinese villages, Pepela recruits captains and crews from other fishing villages on Rote, Flores, Alor and Timor. Pepela is also the site of a Bajau settlement known as Tanjung Pasir. It is clearly identifiable as a Bajau settlement by its houses, which are raised on poles and constructed of woven palm leaf on simple wooden scaffolding, whereas most other dwellings in Pepela are at ground level and built of more durable materials. The number of Bajau families living in Tanjung Pasir has more than doubled in the past 10 years.[12] Most continue to maintain regular contacts with their home villages in the Tukang Besi Islands.

---

11 Based on data recorded at Ashmore Reef between 1986 and 1998, 85 per cent of all fishermen and 93 per cent of all vessels sailing to Ashmore came from small ports on the island of Rote. Most of the vessels came from just two ports on the island: Pepela (69 per cent of vessels) and Oelaba (Fox and Sen 2002: 18–19).

12 In September 1994, anthropologist Natasha Stacey conducted a survey of Bajau living in Pepela. At that time there were 42 Bajau houses in the settlement of Tanjung Pasir and '50 Bajo houses in all of Pepela, inhabited by at least 65 families or approximately 300 people' (Stacey 1999, cited in Stacey

Pepela has gone through successive transformations. In the 1990s, its fishermen changed over from trepang and trochus gathering to intensive shark fishing. Beginning around 2001, they adopted *bodi* to replace their traditional sailing *perahu* and used these boats to make more frequent incursions into Australian waters. As these changes occurred, the numbers involved in fishing increased, and the port of Pepela grew larger as a consequence. Official government statistics for 2000 listed 133 *lambo perahu* for Pepela plus a few motorized vessels (BPS 2001: Table V.5.3). By October 2005, Pepela was reported to have over 400 vessels, most of them fast *bodi*.

5   BOATS AND THEIR FISHING GROUNDS[13]

Pepela

In Pepela, sailing technology began to change rapidly in 2003 with the introduction of the *bodi*. These sleek, narrow vessels were equipped with high-powered engines. A smaller *bodi* could accommodate a crew of three or four and had either a 24-horsepower or a 33-horsepower engine. A somewhat larger version of the *bodi*, known as a *bodi susun*, could accommodate a crew of five or six and had two engines. These purpose-built, fast shark-fishing *bodi*, most of them constructed and brought to Rote from islands further to the north, quickly replaced Pepela's *lambo perahu* fleet for the purposes of shark fishing.[14]

Bodi were well designed for making quick incursions into Australian waters. During the first few years in which these boats operated, many boat captains relied on GPS for precise navigation, but as sailing patterns were regularized, less use was made of this technology. *Bodi* carried a full complement of lines (*tali*) and hooks (*mata*). The norm was 80 hooks, which generally meant five lines with 16 hooks each, although some *bodi susun* carried a sixth line or used longer lines with more hooks.

2007: 128). In May 2006, Tanjung Pasir was reported to have over 90 houses and 160–180 families. However, because so many of these families travel back and forth between Pepela and other Bajau settlements, it is difficult to put a number on how many families are actually 'settled' on the site.

13   The following sections describe fishing practices at the height of the shark-fishing incursions into Australian waters: 2003 to 2006.

14   The time and cost differences between building a *lambo perahu* and a *bodi* were considerable. A *bodi* could be built in just two months at a cost of less than Rp 10 million, including engine. For a *lambo perahu*, the building costs alone might run to Rp 21 million.

There were two patterns of sailing. The first involved shorter incursions into the region roughly coincident with the Timor Gap area, which fishermen refer to as the 'Enterprise' or 'Operations' (Perusahaan) area because of the presence of oil rigs. According to the fishermen, there is less Australian surveillance here than elsewhere. The second involved longer incursions beyond Scott Reef (Pulau Dato) to an area closer to the Australian coast, known as Bawa Pulau Dato. Some boats ventured even further south into waters near the Rowley Shoals and closer yet to the Australian coast.[15] This general area is referred to as Bawa Angin or Masor.

For shorter trips, *bodi* generally left in the morning planning to arrive on target around 10 pm. The fishermen then set out lines to catch bait, often in the vicinity of the oil rigs. By the next afternoon, they were able to bait their lines and set them for shark. Before dawn the next morning they would check their lines. If they had caught fewer than seven shark — the target for a profitable short trip — they set their lines again and would fish until they reached or exceeded their target. Generally a short trip required three to five days.

Longer trips might take from five to seven (possibly eight) days, because it took longer to reach the target area. The fishing target for these voyages was generally higher because of the need to cover the greater cost of fuel. The target might be set at 10 or more shark, but a lot of the profit came from the fact that, nearer to Australia, fishermen were able to catch a considerable number of the highest-value shark.

What made these *bodi* so effective was the quick turnaround time after each relatively brief incursion into Australian waters. Previously a sailing voyage might have taken two weeks or more. With *bodi* it was possible to make several voyages a month.

It was far more dangerous to serve as a crew member in a *bodi* than in a *lambo perahu*.[16] The fishermen referred to themselves as 'troops who brave death' (*pasukan berani mati*). Each year, particularly early in the season when cyclones occur, *bodi* were lost in rough weather. The cyclone

---

15 The Rowley Shoals are located on the eastern edge of the Australian continental shelf only 260 kilometres west of Broome. The area is remarkable for its high concentration of shark.

16 The boats from Pepela drew their crews from different groups of fishermen. Across all these groups, it was generally the younger men from Rote, along with more experienced Bajau and Alor fishermen, who ventured to sea in *bodi*. The *lambo perahu* fleet was more likely to be manned by older fishermen from nearby villages, such as Daiama on the eastern side of the Rotinese domain of Landu. Many of these fishermen continue to sail to the MOU Box area either to gather trepang and trochus or to engage in shark fishing. This complex situation has been studied by Lintje Pellu, a PhD student at the Research School of Pacific and Asian Studies, Australian National University (see Pellu 2006, 2008).

period was referred to locally as the 'widows' season' (*musim janda*) because of the mortality among married men. In 2005, according to local officials, over 40 fishermen who sailed from Pepela were lost at sea.

Dobo and Merauke

The boats departing from Dobo showed less innovation than those in either Pepela or Merauke. These motorized vessels of approximately 5–7+ gross tonnes, all with cabin superstructure, exhibited (with some variation) what might be regarded as the standard boat form that has been common throughout much of eastern Indonesia for decades. They had five to seven crew members and roughly the same number of lines and hooks as most Pepela *bodi*.

Many of the boats sailing from Merauke were similar to those from Dobo, but many others showed various innovations. Merauke with its local boat-building industry began to produce larger, more powerful boats using double (or even triple) 23-horsepower in-board engines.[17] These boats had a distinctive 'bow winch beam', because they combined longline fishing with net fishing for shark. The winch beam was needed to haul in the net, and to be effective, these boats needed to operate closer inshore.

The boats ranged across the southern Arafura Sea, targeting in particular the Arnhem Land coast, the Gulf of Carpentaria and both the western and eastern sides of Cape York Peninsula. The near-shore waters of the Gulf of Carpentaria, which are particularly rich in the highest-priced species of shark, were a prime area for the use of nets rather than lines. Merauke fishermen, like those from Pepela, favoured frequent voyages of a shorter duration. Fuel was a critical factor in determining how far the boats ventured from their home ports and how long they would remain at sea. This became even more critical when the Indonesian government reduced fuel subsidies in October 2005.[18]

Fuel has now become the single most important factor affecting the activities of small-boat fishermen from all the southern ports of Indonesia. Traders and outfitters in each of the ports have had to take steps to gain control of the fuel supplies necessary to continue voyaging. Because of the problems with fuel costs and supply, in 2006, for the first time

---

17 The cost of these new boats with their additional gear is reported to have been around Rp 40–50 million.

18 Before the price rises, one captain from Dobo estimated the cost of a voyage at Rp 6.7 million (A\$957) for fuel and supplies, while another captain from Merauke estimated it at about Rp 7.7 million (A\$1,100). After the fuel price increases in October 2005, the cost of a single voyage for the new, larger Merauke boats is said to have almost doubled to Rp 15 million.

in three years, there was a significant increase in the number of *lambo perahu*, in place of *bodi*, sailing from the port of Pepela to take part in shark fishing.

6   THE FINANCING OF VOYAGES: THE OWNERSHIP AND OUTFITTING OF BOATS

Each of the ports of Pepela, Dobo, Merauke and Saumlaki has a slightly different system of boat ownership and varying procedures for the out-fitting of boats and the division of catch shares. Each port has a small number of key middlemen who own or finance the ownership of the boats, outfit them with gear and supplies, and purchase the catch after each voyage. In 2005, there were roughly six prominent traders in Pepela, a similar number in Dobo, fewer in Saumlaki and as many as 18 in Merauke who owned or financed small boats and exported shark fin.

Most arrangements with the fishermen follow similar lines, with the boat owner's share and the operating costs of the voyage deducted from the value of the catch before the captain and crew are paid. The owner-trader determines the value (weight and quality) of the catch and the cost of all supplies including fuel.

In Pepela, for example, we found that 50 per cent of the return from the catch went to the owner of the *bodi*. The remaining half was divided equally among the crew, with an extra portion allocated to the supplier of the fishing lines, who was generally the owner/outfitter of the *bodi*. The crew then divided the cost of the diesel fuel with the owner who had supplied the fuel at a predetermined price. Thus the owner and the crew each paid half the cost of the fuel. From their individual portions, crew members paid for the supplies of food and cigarettes used on the voyage and any other supplies provided for their families before they left port. If for some reason a voyage did not return a profit, an appropriate portion of the debt was divided among the fishermen and added to the costs of the next voyage.

Dobo has what is called a *joki* (from the English word 'jockey') system of ownership. Simply put, a merchant or 'boss' provides the funds for someone (usually a trusted fisherman who becomes the captain) to buy a boat; that person is the 'jockey' until the boat is paid for. The boss also provides the funding for all supplies and fishing equipment (basically, lines, hooks and anchors) and he buys the entire catch when the boat returns to port. Expenses are deducted from the price of the catch and the remaining money is divided equally among the captain and crew, with the captain assigned two shares. If a boat is apprehended, the debt accrues to the captain as 'jockey', but the cost of the confiscated lines, hooks and anchors is borne by both captain and crew. This *joki* system thus transfers the risk of the loss of the boat from a boss to a particular fisherman. As a result, most of Dobo's *joki* fishermen are deeply in debt to their bosses and patrons: the captain of one boat calculated he had a debt of over Rp 37 million (about A$5,285), and another had debts amounting to over Rp 70 million.

While the *joki* system exists as a financing mechanism in Dobo, most boats are owned outright by traders. In this case, the owner is responsible if the boat is lost. Profits are divided in two: half to the owner and half to the captain and crew, with the captain receiving two shares, one from the owner's half and the other from the crew's half.

Beginning in 2006, some *bodi* owners in Pepela began transferring ownership of their boats to Bajau who worked for them, thus essentially instituting the same kind of *joki* system found on Dobo. These 'sales' were made possible by the creation of large debts owed to the original owners. Any loss of a *bodi* came at a cost to the Bajau owner, whose debt remained. Although the new owners gained a greater share in the value of the catch, they were obliged to sell their catch to the boss to whom they were deeply in debt.

In the last few years, financiers in Merauke have tried to offer a better share in the profits of a voyage as a means of attracting fishermen from Dobo and elsewhere to Merauke.

7   PRICES FOR SHARK FIN

The trader who finances a voyage is the person who judges the quality of the shark fin and sets its price. He also determines the cost of supplies, including fuel, and thus, in the end, controls what the fishermen receive for their efforts. Because of this, fishermen often complain that they have little control over their returns. In fact, though, they do have a means of redress, because they are the ones who unload and report the catch. Some fishermen have become quite adept at hiding a portion of their fin and selling it separately to trusted associates. There is considerable evidence of this secondary trade in Pepela, particularly among the Bajau.

In Pepela, the price of high-quality shark fin has risen dramatically. In 2002, about the time of the initial shift from *lambo perahu* to *bodi*, the price of the best grade of shark fin was reported to range from A$82 to A$125 per kilogram (dry weight) (Fox and Sen 2002: 33–4). By 2005, high-quality fin (much of it derived from areas close to the Australian mainland) could command prices up to A$171 per kilogram (Table 9.2). However, some caution is needed in considering these figures. Prices are negotiated based on local judgments. Both size and quality of fin are considered when determining the price paid to fishermen.

Table 9.2   The Price of Shark Fin in Rote and Kupang, 2005

	Rp per Kilogram	A$ per Kilogram[a]
Class I (> 60 cm)	1,200,000	171
Class II (40–60 cm)	800,000	114
Class III (< 40 cm)	200,000	29
Base (of shark tail)[b]	65,000	9

a   The figures are based on a 2005 conversion rate of Rp 7,000/A$1. All figures have been rounded to the nearest dollar.

b   All shark fin is exported but the base of the tail is used in the domestic market as a substitute for fin. The price of a bowl of 'shark fin' (alias shark tail) soup in Surabaya is Rp 300,000 (A$43).

Source: Authors' estimates, based on information provided by local traders on Rote.

By 2006, fishermen from Dobo claimed they no longer encountered the species of shark commanding the highest prices. The highest price offered to the fishermen of Dobo for the best quality shark fin was Rp 800,000 (A$114) per kilogram (dry weight). This was substantially below the prices paid on Rote. This may have reflected the lack of Class I shark fin or the lower prices set by traders in Dobo.[19] By contrast, in 2006, fishermen from Merauke operating in the Gulf of Carpentaria were still taking species of shark with high-value fin that had now become rare in other fishing areas.

8   CRITICAL VARIABILITY IN SMALL-BOAT SHARK FISHING

Hundreds of small-boat fishermen were involved in shark fishing in Australian waters until Australian naval efforts at interdiction began to take effect. They made voyages of varying duration, to a variety of fishing grounds, at different times of the year. They set out on vessels of all sizes with an assortment of equipment, either longlines or nets but

---

19   If one assumes an average price for shark fin on Dobo of Rp 600,000 per kilogram and costs of Rp 6–7 million per voyage, then it would take 10–11 kilograms of shark fin to cover the cost of a voyage. With a crew of six plus captain (a total of eight shares under the *joki* system, including two shares for the captain), 20 kilograms of shark fin should result in a profit of Rp 750,000 (A$107) per share. For those who divide shares with a boat owner, each share would be worth about Rp 425,000 (A$61), because the captain would take only one share from the crew's half (and another equivalent share from the owner). Thus a successful voyage for the fishermen would yield roughly A$60–100 per crew member.

sometimes a combination of both. The fishermen themselves had vary-ing levels of experience; some were far more knowledgeable and, on the whole, successful than many novice fishermen who set out with great hopes but limited sailing or fishing ability. All these fishermen targeted a variety of shark species with fin of differing value. On each voyage, the catch varied in size, number and mix of species. It is important — indeed essential — to emphasize this variability when attempting to make gener-alizations about the catch and consequences of shark fishing. It is best to begin by viewing this shark fishing in terms of some general patterns.

The captains on every boat set sail from port with specific targets. On each voyage, they sailed to one fishing ground where they concentrated their activities, hoping to catch enough shark to return a profit to all crew members. Thus the more crew members, the higher the target catch. Many species of shark aggregate, so coming upon the 'right spot' could yield considerable success. Every captain and most crew members could tell amazing tales about some remarkable catch of shark. These tales would fire the imagination of other fishermen, particularly new recruits, with the hope of great gains. But fishermen also told sad stories of unsuc-cessful voyages. Such voyages occurred more often than the highly suc-cessful ones. The sea is particularly rough from December to March and sometimes well into April. Most fishing decreases during January and February and increases again in March and April, even though cyclones during this period make voyaging hazardous. Strong, gusty east winds normally arise during July and August. For the past few years, these winds seem to have begun earlier and to have been unusually intense. Thus weather, luck and the increasing possibility of apprehension were all factors in fishing success.

Most fishermen would say that they set their target for a successful voyage at 10 sharks, although some experienced fishermen claimed that they regularly succeeded in catching more than this. The targeted shark species, however, varied in size and possessed fin of varying value. Ten small blacktip sharks might not be as valuable as one normal-size pigeye shark. Thus, for the fishermen, the species of shark caught could be more important than the number of shark taken.

Fishermen from Pepela who relied exclusively on longlines sailed mainly to two fishing grounds: Perusahaan (the waters south of the oil rigs) and Bawa Pulau Dato (the waters beyond Scott Reef). Their main target species were blacktip or spot tip shark (*rante kolo*) — which are more numerous but smaller in size in the vicinity of the oil rigs — sand-bar shark (*iu putih*) and hammerhead shark (*bingku*). Occasionally, if they were lucky, fishermen might take a good-size pig-eye shark.

Longline fishermen from Dobo and Merauke targeted the same spe-cies. However, they caught a greater number of high-value hammerhead sharks, particularly in the Gulf of Carpentaria. They were also able to take some shovelnose rays (*lontar* or *pandruk*) and sawfish shark (*iu gergaji*). Net fishermen from Merauke concentrated on catching shovelnose rays and sawfish sharks, whose fins commanded high prices.[20]

9   THE SIZE OF THE SMALL-BOAT SHARK FISHERY

It is virtually impossible to provide a reliable estimate of the size of the shark take by Indonesian fishermen. On the other hand, it is critical to make some attempt at estimation despite the difficulties of doing so.

Since much of the trade in shark fin goes unreported, local figures on interisland trade, even when available, tend to underrepresent the level of the catch. Nevertheless there are some figures for this trade: in 2005 Merauke is reported to have shipped, on average, 3 tonnes of shark fin per month, totalling 37,849 kilograms for the year (Adhuri 2006).[21] Although a portion of this came from Merauke's own—now declining—local fishery, the bulk of it (conservatively, 20–25 tonnes) is likely to have come from Australian waters. Anecdotal reports from Dobo's traders suggest that they may have shipped about one-third the amount that Merauke did, possibly 10–12 tonnes, while Saumlaki may have shipped about a third of Dobo's total, about 3–4 tonnes. (By 2005, however, some Dobo-based boats had begun using Merauke as their port of departure and return, and at least one trader carried out his operations in both ports.) Putting these various figures together to arrive at an approximate estimate, the shark fin catch by these small boats in Australian waters in 2005 would have been, at a minimum, 33–41 tonnes.

Translating these figures into numbers of sharks caught is even more uncertain because of the strikingly different conversion rates for different species of shark. Sandbar sharks, for example, are relatively small, so it may take two or more of this species to obtain a kilogram of fin. In contrast, just one hammerhead shark might yield a kilogram or two of fin and a pig-eye shark even more.

---

20   A study supported by the Australian Fisheries Management Agency (AFMA) aims to identify the shark species targeted by Indonesian fishermen in different fishing grounds. Research is at a preliminary stage and remains unpublished (Fox and Meekan 2006).

21   These data derive from the local Merauke Fishing Office (Dinas Perikanan Merauke). They were compiled by Dr Dedi Adhuri from the monthly reports on shark fin from Merauke destined for Jakarta, Surabaya, Makassar and Menado. Each month Merauke exported between 2,332 and 3,849 kilograms of shark fin in this interisland trade.

Table 9.3   Summary of Voyages and Catch Rates of Bodi from Pepela, 2004/05

Number of *Bodi*	Length of Voyage (no. of days)	No. of Voyages per Month	Months of Operation	Target Catch (no. of sharks)	Total Catch (no. of sharks)
125	4–5	4	6	5	15,000
100	5–7	3	6	8	14,400
Total					**29,400**

Source: Authors' estimates.

Estimating the shark catch from Pepela is a far more difficult task because of the lack of any official figures for this trade.[22] Nevertheless, it is possible to arrive at an estimate by taking account of the number of *bodi* in Pepela, the estimated number of voyages by these vessels during the course of a season, and fishermen's reports on their targets for voyages to particular areas within Australian waters.

In 2005, there was a progressive build-up of *bodi* registered by the port master of East Rote to well over 400 boats. However, problems with fuel began to arise even before the price rise in October because, for several months beforehand, local distributors attempted to restrict supplies or sell fuel at a premium in anticipation of a price rise. After October, fuel was available but its cost prompted many fishermen to reduce their more distant voyaging. Thus the months preceding the price rise may have represented the high point in the wave of *bodi* entering Australian waters.

For the purposes of estimation, one could conservatively set the number of *bodi* operating throughout the season at 225 (Table 9.3). Although some boats ventured to sea throughout the year, the normal shark-fishing season lasted for approximately eight months, from March/April to October/November. Conservatively for purposes of estimation, one could reduce operations to a six-month season because of the inevitable disruptions. Again conservatively, one could assume that a majority of *bodi* (125) were involved in shorter 4–5-day voyages rather than longer 5–7-day voyages, and that they spent at least three days in

---

22 No agency reports shark catches or keeps records of shark fin exports — not the provincial East Nusa Tenggara Fisheries Office (Dinas Perikanan dan Kelautan NTT), the equivalent district office, the Office of Maritime Industries (Perusahaan Daerah Kelautan), the Regional Development Planning Agency (Bappeda), its provincial Data Centre for Planning and Development Management (Pusat Data Perencanaan dan Pengendalian Pembangunan Daerah NTT), the Bureau of Statistics in Kupang or the Customs Office (Kantor Bea dan Cukai).

port before setting out again. This would allow for four short voyages a month and no more than three long voyages a month. Although fishermen claimed to set their target at 10 sharks per voyage, it might be better to assume a target of seven sharks for shorter voyages and nine for longer ones; or better still, to take account of the distinct probability of occasional lack of success, to reduce the target catch to five sharks for a short voyage and eight for a long voyage. We then have all the elements needed for a rough, but conservative, estimate of the number of sharks taken in Australian waters.

A single *bodi* making only short voyages over a six-month period would be able to catch at least 120 sharks. A *bodi* making longer voyages over the same period would be able to catch 144 sharks.[23]

The parameters of this simple model might be changed by altering the number of *bodi*, the success rate in achieving the target catch or the mix of vessels sailing to different fishing grounds. The present calculations do, however, indicate that the Pepela shark fishery was, before concerted Australian interdiction operations, at least of the same order as that of Merauke. Certainly, on existing evidence, the total catch of targeted shark species by small-boat fishermen from Pepela to Merauke was unsustainably high. The pursuit of shark for its fin was seriously depleting shark numbers and, in the process, had the capacity to alter the ecological conditions of Australia's northern waters.

10   WHY SHARK?

For small-boat fishermen, shark fishing would seem to offer the possibility of a considerable income. Yet most of these fishermen and their families remain poor — some desperately poor. While the fishermen provide their labour and risk their lives, a disproportionate share of the profits goes to the boat owners and outfitters who control the trade in shark fin. As a consequence, perhaps a majority of these fishermen remain in a state of continual debt, living in squalid, crowded settlements and unable to provide better prospects for their children. It is therefore not surprising to find that some eastern Indonesian fishing communities do not consider shark fishing to be an attractive alternative to other fishing activities.

A striking case in point can be found on the island of Rote, in the contrast in development between the villages of Pepela and Oelaba. Beginning in the early 1980s, the fishermen of Oelaba, located on the

---

23   To this total could be added the shark catch by *lambo perahu* from Pepela legitimately engaged in shark fishing in the MOU74 Box. A draft paper prepared by the Department of the Environment and Heritage estimates this at a minimum of 1.2 tonnes per annum.

northwestern coast of Rote, would regularly sail to the MOU Box area to gather trepang (and, to a lesser extent, trochus), first at Ashmore and later at Scott Reef. Other fishermen from the neighbouring settlement of Hundi Huk soon followed their lead. Unlike Pepela at the eastern end of the island, Oelaba (and Hundi Huk) did not undergo a transition to shark fishing. To begin with, Oelaba did not experience the migration and settlement of Bajau fishermen who led the way in this transition in Pepela. Although some Oelaba fishermen did engage in shark fishing in the 1990s, and some have occasionally joined Pepela shark boats as crew members, these efforts have been sporadic and unsustained. Instead, Oelaba fishermen continue to gather trepang and trochus, primarily from Scott Reef, in the MOU Box. Although the pressures on stocks have not abated and trepang continue to be overexploited, Oelaba fishermen have probably benefited in recent years from the shift of a large number of fishermen to the pursuit of shark.[24] Although trepang stocks have declined, the prices for the five main species that the fishermen gather have more than doubled since 2005, providing a better return than previously.

A host of other reasons can be cited for the different path taken by Oelaba. A key factor is its fishermen's deep involvement in interisland trade, buying products such as lontar syrup on Rote and selling them on other islands. Their voyages to Scott Reef must therefore be fitted into a three-month period within the cycle of other activities. Oelaba fishermen themselves cite other factors. Pepela has direct and open access to the Timor Sea, while the harbour of Oelaba, fronted by extensive mangrove stands and subject to strong tides, opens only periodically to the sea. Oelaba sailors also claim that they are unwilling to take the risks that Pepela crews take. They time their voyages to avoid storms and rough seas and they pride themselves on their village's record for following Australian regulations when accessing the MOU Box (Carnegie 2006, 2008). Oelaba has not suffered the death toll from boats lost at sea that is an annual feature of life in Pepela, nor are its young men detained in Australian jails for illegal fishing.[25] Oelaba has not grown to the same

---

24 Department of the Environment and Heritage data based on Australian Customs records from Ashmore Reef indicate a relatively steady number of vessels entering the MOU Box area from 2000 onwards, 57 per cent of them targeting shark, 22 per cent trepang and 12 per cent trochus. However, Coastwatch data indicate a significant number of vessels bypassing Ashmore and Cartier. Many of these vessels sail directly to Scott Reef where they are allowed to gather trepang (DEH 2006).

25 On the other hand, it is worth noting that it was adult men (and adolescents) from Oelaba that captained and crewed the boats that took refugees to Ashmore Reef between 1998 and 2001; the majority of them served prison terms as a result. So while Pepela successfully made the transition to shark fishing, Oelaba later developed its own niche in people smuggling.

extent as Pepela through the continuing semi-permanent migration of fishermen from other islands. Rather, it experiences short-term influxes of boat labour for the annual three-month trepang voyages. This labour supply is made possible by the historical relations of trade and inter-marriage established between residents of Oelaba and the populations from specific villages on the islands of Pantar, Pura and Tereweng in the district of Alor. Today, Oelaba exists as a small, relatively prosperous settlement without the extremes of wealth and poverty evident in Pepela.

11 CONCLUSION

The dilemma faced by small-boat shark fishermen is clear. As shark continues to be targeted for its fin and populations continue to decline, not just in Indonesian waters but worldwide, the price of fin will continue to rise. China's increasing prosperity — and that of Taiwan, Hong Kong and Singapore — has created an insatiable market for shark fin soup as a celebratory delicacy. But as surveillance and apprehension by Australian patrols increase — as has already occurred with the Clearwater and Breakwater operations — and the penalties for illegal fishing rise, the risks to fishermen for shark fishing in Australian waters will also increase significantly. Yet, however unequal the returns from these voyages may be, there will continue to be poor fishermen drawn into the business as long as there are so few other ways for them to make a living and support their families. On present evidence, it seems likely that such fishermen will come mainly from particular pockets of poverty in eastern Indonesia — from a number of small islands where population pressure and a lack of alternative employment combine to produce a migrant group of fishermen who have now positioned themselves in ports with direct access to Australian waters.

    While deterrence is essential to a policy to control and limit shark fishing, the targeted provision of alternative livelihoods for fishermen — though not a deterrent in itself — must be considered as part of any effective policy strategy. In its 1988 revision to the memorandum on the MOU Box, Australia committed itself to work with Indonesia on assistance to fishermen in eastern Indonesia. It is only in cooperation with Indonesia that such a program of assistance can be achieved.[26]

---

26 For the past several years, with grants from the Department of the Environment and Heritage, members of the Research School of Pacific and Asian Studies at the Australian National University have been involved in developing a small-scale experimental program of alternative livelihoods for fishermen on Rote and in the Bay of Kupang.

REFERENCES

Adhuri, Dedi S. (2006), 'Illegal Shark Fishing in Merauke', unpublished report, ANU Maritime Research Group, Resource Management in Asia–Pacific Program, Australian National University, Canberra.

AFMA (Australian Fisheries Management Authority) (2005), *Annual Report 2004–2005*, Canberra, available at <http://www.afma.gov.au/information/publications/corporate/annual/ar04_05/ar04_05_00.pdf>.

BPS (Biro Pusat Statistik) (2001), *Rote Timur dalam Angka 2000* [East Rote in Figures 2000], Kupang.

Carnegie, Michelle (2006), 'Why Not Shark? Discourses of Conformity of Oelaba Fishermen, Rote', unpublished paper, ANU Maritime Research Group, Resource Management in Asia–Pacific Program, Australian National University, Canberra.

Carnegie, Michelle (2008), 'Place-based Livelihoods and Post-development Challenges in Eastern Indonesia', unpublished PhD thesis, Australian National University, Canberra.

DEH (Department of the Environment and Heritage) (2001), *Ashmore Reef National Nature Reserve and Cartier Island Marine Reserve Management Plans*, Canberra.

DEH (Department of the Environment and Heritage) (2006), 'An Assessment of Traditional Fishing within the MoU74 Box', unpublished draft report, Canberra.

Fegan, Brian (2003), 'Plundering the Sea', *Inside Indonesia*, 73(January–March): 21-3, available at <http://insideindonesia.org/content/view/339/29/>.

Fox, James J. (1992), 'Report on Eastern Indonesia Fishermen in Darwin', in *Illegal Entry*, Occasional Paper Series No. 1, Centre for Southeast Asian Studies, Northern Territory University, Darwin, pp. 13–24.

Fox, James J. (1995), 'Fishing Resources and Marine Tenure: The Problems of Eastern Indonesian Fishermen', in C. Barlow and J. Hardjono (eds), *Indonesia Assessment 1995*, Research School of Pacific and Asian Studies and Institute of Southeast Asian Studies, Canberra and Singapore, pp. 163–74.

Fox, James J. (1998), 'Reefs and Shoals in Australia–Indonesia Relations: Traditional Indonesian Fishermen', in A. Milner and M. Quilty (eds), *Australia in Asia: Episodes*, Oxford University Press, Melbourne, pp. 111–39.

Fox, James J. (2000), 'Maritime Communities in the Timor and Arafura Region: Some Historical and Anthropological Perspectives', in S. O'Connor and P. Veth (eds), *East of Wallace's Line: Studies of Past and Present Maritime Cultures of the Indo-Pacific Region*, A.A. Balkema, Rotterdam, pp. 137–56.

Fox, James J. (2005), 'In a Single Generation: A Lament for the Forests and Seas of Indonesia', in P. Boomgaard, D. Henley and M. Osseweijer (eds), *Muddied Waters: Historical and Contemporary Perspectives on the Management of Forests and Fisheries in Island Southeast Asia*, KITLV Press, Leiden, pp. 43–60.

Fox, James J. and Mark Meekan (2006), 'Report to AFMA on the Shark Species Targeted and Caught by Indonesian Fishermen in Australian Waters', unpublished report, Australian Fisheries Management Agency, Canberra, 7 September.

Fox, James J. and Sevaly Sen (2002), 'A Study of Socio-economic Issues Facing Indonesian Fishers Who Access the MOU Box', report prepared for the Department of Environment and Heritage, Canberra, available at <http://rspas.anu.edu.au/people/personal/foxxj_rspas/recent_papers.php>.

Fox, James J., Dedi S. Adhuri and Ida Aju Pradnja Resosudarmo (2005), 'Unfinished Edifice or Pandora's Box? Decentralization and Resource Management in Indonesia', in B.P. Resosudarmo (ed.), *The Politics and Economics of Indonesia's Natural Resources*, Institute of Southeast Asian Studies, Singapore, pp. 92–108.

Kospartov, Marie, Maria Beger, Daniela Ceccarelli and Zoe Richards (2006), *An Assessment of the Distribution and Abundance of Sea Cucumbers, Trochus, Giant Clam, Fish and Invasive Species at Ashmore Reef National Nature Reserve and Cartier Island Marine Reserve, 2005*, report produced for the Department of the Environment and Heritage, Canberra, February, available at <http://www.uniquest.com.au/uploads/Feb%200602%20-%2013631.pdf>.

MMAF (Ministry of Marine Affairs and Fisheries) (2003), *Laporan Teknis, Bagian Proyek Riset, Perikanan Tangkap 2002* [Technical Report, Research Project Division, Fishery Catch 2002], Jakarta.

MMAF (Ministry of Marine Affairs and Fisheries) (2004), *Laporan Teknis, Bagian Proyek Riset, Perikanan Tangkap 2003* [Technical Report, Research Project Division, Fishery Catch 2003], Jakarta.

MMAF and LIPI (Ministry of Marine Affairs and Fisheries and Lembaga Ilmu Pengetahuan Indonesia) (2001), *Laporan Akhir Pengkajian Stok Ikan di Perairan Indonesia* [Final Report on the Assessment of Fish Stocks in Indonesian Waters], Jakarta.

Pellu, Lintje (2006), 'Illegal Fishing Activity of the People of Daiama Village 2004–2005', unpublished fieldwork report, Australian National University, Canberra.

Pellu, Lintje (2008), 'A Domain United, a Domain Divided: An Ethnographic Study of Social Relations and Social Change among the People of Landu, East Rote, Eastern Indonesia', unpublished PhD thesis, Australian National University, Canberra.

Skewes, T.D., D.M. Dennis, D.R. Jacobs, S.R. Gordon, T.J. Taranto, M. Haywood, C.R. Pitcher, G.P. Smith, D. Milton and I.R. Pointer (1999), *Survey and Stock Size Estimates of the Shallow Reef (0–15m Deep) and Shoal Area (15–50m Deep). Marine Resources and Habitat Mapping within the Timor Sea MOU74 Box. Volume 1: Stock Estimates and Stock Status*, report to the Department of the Environment and Heritage, CSIRO Division of Marine Research.

Smith, L., M. Rees, A. Heyward and J. Cloquhoun (2000), *Survey 2000: Beche-de-Mer and Trochus Populations at Ashmore Reef*, Australian Institute for Marine Science, Report to Environment Australia, Townsville.

Smith, L., M. Rees, A. Heyward and J. Cloquhoun (2002), *Stocks of Trochus and Beche-de-Mer at Cartier Reef: 2001 Surveys*, Australian Institute for Marine Science, Report to Environment Australia, Townsville.

Stacey, Natasha (1999), 'Boats to Burn: Bajo Fishing Activity in the Australian Fishing Zone', unpublished PhD thesis, Charles Darwin University, Darwin.

Stacey, Natasha (2007), *Boats to Burn: Bajo Fishing Activity in the Australian Fishing Zone*, Asia–Pacific Environment Monographs 2, ANU E Press, Canberra, available at <http://epress.anu.edu.au>.

Wallace, Alfred Russel (1869), *The Malay Archipelago*, 2 volumes, Macmillan, London, reprinted in 1986 by Oxford University Press.

10 FOREST MANAGEMENT AND CONFLICT: THE CASE OF THE RENDANI PROTECTION FOREST IN PAPUA

Hidayat Alhamid, Peter Kanowski and Chris Ballard

1 INTRODUCTION

Papua's biologically diverse forests serve a multiplicity of roles and functions for its people. Historically, they have provided Papuans with household needs for food and shelter, a resource base for gardening and products to trade, while also fulfilling a fundamentally important cultural role. Although products from Papua's forests have been exploited commercially and exported regionally for at least a thousand years, it is only in the past 25 years that forest degradation and loss associated with large-scale commercial timber harvesting, an expansion of agricultural cash crops and the growth of population centres have begun to threaten the survival of the forests and the communities that depend on them. This chapter presents a case study of a particular forest and community, exemplifying issues of forest management and conflict in Papua more widely.

Indonesia's New Order government asserted state ownership over the country's forests in 1967, denying customary (*adat*) ownership and rights. It began to exploit the forests by issuing large-scale timber harvesting concessions (HPHs).[1] Other pressures on Indonesia's forests have included those associated with the expansion of forest and palm oil

---

1 These arrangements and their largely adverse consequences are described by Brown (1999) and Dauvergne (2001) among others.

plantations and agricultural crops, and with transmigration.[2] In Papua, as elsewhere in Indonesia, forests were zoned into those intended for conservation and protection, those to be retained for wood production and those to be converted to plantations or agriculture. The respective proportions of Papua's 33 million hectares of forests in these three broad categories are 46 per cent (conservation), 31 per cent (wood production) and 23 per cent (conversion).

With minor exceptions, during the Dutch colonial period and for some time afterwards, Papua's forests remained under indigenous forest management. The first HPH over Papuan forests was issued in 1984. By 2000, there were 54 HPHs covering a total area of 13 million hectares, a further 10 industrial forest plantation concessions (HTIs) covering 1.6 million hectares and many small-scale concessions. Holmes (2000) has estimated that deforestation associated with forest harvesting, plantation conversion and other land uses accelerated from 150,000 hectares per year during the period 1985–96 to around 720,000 hectares per year in 1997–2001. Legal timber production in 2000 was around 1.5 million cubic metres; illegal timber production in 2002 has been estimated at 7.2 million cubic metres (*Bisnis Indonesia*, 5 and 6 September 2003). Despite this scale of exploitation of their forest resources, Papuans remain very poor in terms of the criteria assessed by the United Nations Development Programme for its human development index (see Chapter 2).

The longstanding political tensions between indigenous Papuans and the national government led, in January 2001, to the declaration of special autonomy arrangements for Papua (Sumule 2002). Among other objectives, these arrangements were supposed to enhance the extent to which local people controlled and derived benefits from the forests. The subsequent division — through a decree issued by former president Megawati Soekarnoputri in January 2003 — of the former province of Irian Jaya into three new provinces has added to the complexity of forest governance in Papua. In practice, neither the implementation nor the intention of the regional autonomy arrangements has been realized thus far, and illegal logging in Papua appears to have accelerated (Telapak and EIA 2005).

This chapter draws on field research conducted by Hidayat Alhamid in 2001 in and around the Rendani Protection Forest, adjacent to the town of Manokwari in Papua (Alhamid 2005). He investigated the indigenous forest management and forest utilization regimes in Rendani, focusing in particular on how the pressures on Papua's forests and people were playing out in the Rendani context. This chapter focuses on the history of conflict over forest access and use in Rendani; this may be seen as a

---

2   See, for example, FWI, WRI and GFW (2002), Sunderlin and Resosudarmo (1996) and Tacconi and Kurniawan (2006).

microcosm of such conflict in Papua more generally. The information on which this work is based derives principally from individual interviews in the field in 2001, with the Hatam people, with the non-Hatam residents of Rendani and with government officers. It also draws on secondary sources in the form of leaflets, letters and reports.

2   THE RESIDENTS AND MANAGEMENT OF THE FOREST

The area now known as the Rendani Protection Forest is 300 hectares in extent. It was declared a protection forest in 1969 in order to secure the water supply of the town of Manokwari. The forest is home both to Hatam-speaking people, who migrated there from the adjacent highlands in the late 1800s, and to other more recent immigrants. The forest is situated some 5 kilometres from Manokwari in the Bird's Head region of Papua. Starting from the coast, the forest rises through gentle hills to an elevation of about 200 metres inland. Average annual rainfall is around 2,500 millimetres. Two creeks, Kali Dingin and Kali Kentek, flow through the forest.

The types of vegetation found in the Rendani Protection Forest are presented schematically in Figure 10.1. Excluding a forest enclave and infrastructure, the land area associated with each type is: bush, secondary forest or fallow ground, 198 hectares (67 per cent of the total forest area); gardens, 70 hectares (23 per cent); old secondary forest, 30 hectares (10 per cent); and cocoa plantations, 2 hectares (less than 1 per cent).

In 2001, the Hatam population of Rendani numbered 247 people living in 38 households, most of them young or middle aged (Table 10.1). Around 70 per cent of the population had completed primary school but only five individuals had graduated from senior high school and no one was attending or had graduated from university.

Traditionally, the Rendani forest was divided among the Hatam's five kinship groups, reflecting the history of gardening in the forest by those groups. The current land ownership structure is shown in Figure 10.1, but is much more fragmented than the boundaries would suggest. There are a number of reasons for this. First, the introduction of perennial cash crops such as cocoa and cloves has effectively resulted in the privatization of much clan land. Normal garden ownership rules were applied to married couples who planted perennial crops, even though these crops took a decade or more to mature. After such long periods of continuous use, the farmers considered the land to belong to them, even though it was actually owned by the clan as a whole.

Second, the Hatam have sold parts of the forest to outsiders and government agencies. The transfer of land to immigrants and government institutions, usually in return for small payments, has been common

Figure 10.1 Vegetation Cover and Customary Land Ownership in the Rendani Protection Forest

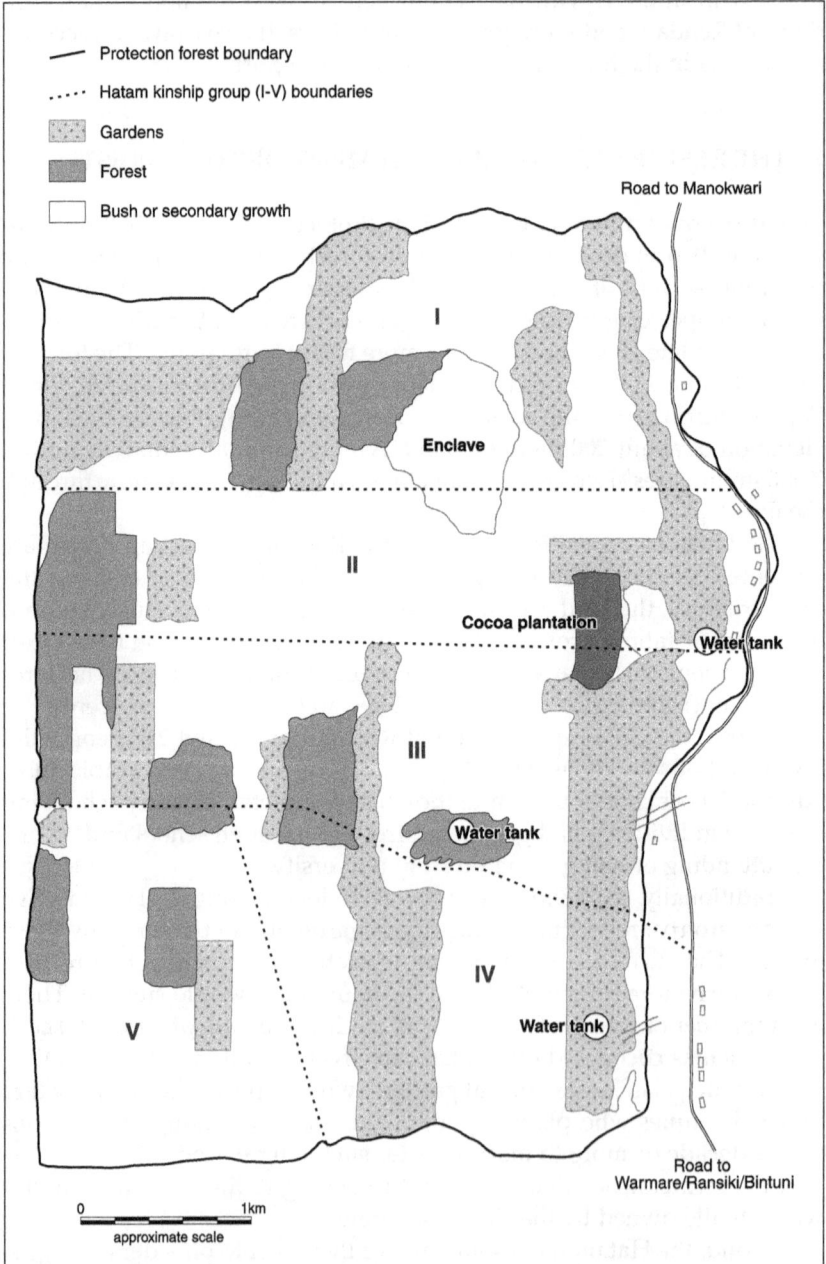

Source: Hidayat Alhamid, field notes, 2001.

Table 10.1   Distribution of Rendani Hatam by Age Group, 2001

Age Group	Hatam Population	
	(no.)	(%)
0–14	110	45
15–55	135	54
56+	2	1
Total	**247**	**100**

Source: BPS-Papua (2003).

since World War II. As discussed below, part of the Hatam's motivation for selling their land was to counter the government's assertion of control over the forest. But they have also been motivated by necessity — the rate of land sales accelerated greatly after the Indonesian economic crisis of the late 1990s. Whereas, in the past, land was most commonly exchanged for pigs or traditional textiles (*kain timur*), such transactions are now more likely to involve an exchange of money or of consumer goods such as televisions, video and DVD players, or motorbikes. Most land sales today are to non-Papuans. But whatever the circumstances of the sales, the Hatam have never considered the land as other than leased, to be restored to traditional ownership when the other party no longer requires it. As a result of these and other events described below, the Hatam people now form a minority of those residing in the Rendani forest (Table 10.2).

Table 10.2   Ownership of the Rendani Protection Forest by Ethnic Origin of Household, 2001

Ethnic Origin	Households	
	(no.)	(%)
Javanese	95	33
Buginese	82	29
Mixed tribes	61	21
Hatam	38	13
Ayamaru	10	4
Total	**286**	**100**

Source: Hidayat Alhamid, fieldwork.

Legal responsibility for managing the Rendani Protection Forest rests with the branch office of the Provincial Forestry Service (CDK), while responsibility for managing the water drawn from the forest lies with the Municipal Drinking Water Enterprise (PDAM), a state-owned enterprise. PDAM's responsibility is limited to selling the water; the maintenance of forest cover, which affects water yield and quality, is the responsibility of CDK and the Local Forestry Service (KPH). The Rendani Protection Forest is one of two main water supply catchments for the town of Manokwari, supplying around 50 per cent of its water. PDAM has built three water tanks in the forest: Rendani I, Rendani II and Kali Dingin. It paid some compensation to the Hatam when it installed these reservoirs but it does not make any ongoing payments to them for the water it draws from the forest. Neither does the local freshwater fishery service, which draws water from the reservoirs for its fishponds.

Hatam Leadership

As in most other Melanesian societies, community leadership among the Hatam was traditionally determined by competition on the basis of skills in warfare, oratory, accumulation of wealth and the arrangement of exchanges, or else the possession of special knowledge or personal qualities (Lederman 1990). As Langness (1972: 927) explains, this model of leadership was 'almost always achieved, almost never ascribed [inherited]'.

Leadership among the Hatam is now based primarily on wealth. A man who can accumulate significant wealth, especially in the form of pigs and *kain timur*, and who distributes that wealth by helping many people, creates indebtedness as well as dependency among his followers. Possession of land may also confer leadership, as may the capacity, usually dependent on wealth, to hire a *suanggi* – a person who can perform sorcery.

Two of the three recognized leaders of the Hatam are not tribal leaders in the traditional sense, but are treated as such because of their wealth and their use of it to help others (Peters 2001). However, as discussed further below, these leaders no longer enjoy uncontested authority over their people or the natural resources on Hatam land; instead, they must act in a broader political and economic arena in which their status and authority are not necessarily acknowledged, or acknowledged only when it is convenient for outsiders to do so.

Hatam Livelihoods

The Hatam have traditionally depended on subsistence agriculture and the sale or exchange of forest products and garden surpluses for their livelihoods. The valuable forest products that the Rendani Hatam cus-tomarily sold or exchanged included non-wood tree products such as resin (*kopal* or *damar*), massoy bark and aromatic oil (*minyak lawang*),[3] as well as animal products such as birds of paradise and their plum-age. These products are now rare, reflecting both the pressure human encroachment has placed on the forest and the limited area still approxi-mating natural forest (Figure 10.1).

Consequently, the primary products from which the Rendani Hatam now derive their livelihoods mainly come from their gardens. The Hatam still tend to think of their agricultural practices in terms of subsistence agriculture, with almost all villagers interviewed during fieldwork in 2001 stating that they worked in the gardens to satisfy their families' sub-sistence needs. Farmers who took all their agricultural products directly to market often carried back home whatever remained unsold. Surpluses were also sometimes distributed free to close family members such as par-ents, grandparents, brothers and sisters, and parents in-law.

The subsistence orientation of the Hatam is reflected in their choice of crops; they mainly cultivate traditional local varieties of vegetables, tubers and bananas. This is also the case for the neighbouring Biak people, who derive their livelihoods principally from fishing, and who mostly practise farming as a supplementary activity to meet their need for carbohydrates.

In contrast, the gardens established in Rendani by the immigrant Ayamaru people are more intensively farmed. Their crops are more mar-ket oriented, and include tomatoes, snake beans, Chinese cabbages, egg-plants and chillies. These are principally cash crops, grown from seed purchased from local wholesalers in Manokwari. The Ayamaru settlers apply fertilizers, pesticides and herbicides to their crops, in contrast to the Hatam and Biak, who continue to practise their traditional low-input farming methods. Clearly the Ayamaru – like the Javanese transmigrants who also farm the area – are more open to farming innovations intro-duced by agricultural extension workers than either the Hatam or the Biak, who tend to hold strongly to traditional practices.

The sale of agricultural commodities from Rendani takes place pri-marily at Wosi market, about 10 kilometres away. The cost of transport to and from the market is relatively high, at around Rp 1,000 per round trip. The Hatam take their produce to market two or three times a week,

---

3   The resin sold or bartered by the Hatam comes from the Western New Guinea Kauri (*Agathis labillardieri*), now a threatened species. Massoy bark (*Crypto-caria massoy* or *Cryptocaria aromatica*) is widely used in Indonesia in medicines, cosmetics and perfumes, as well as to fix dye and flavour food. The aromatic oil from a species of laurel (*Cinnamomum culilawan*) also has a multitude of uses.

mainly selling papaya flowers, chillies, cucumbers and tomatoes. Some of the fruit and vegetables they sell at the market does not come from their gardens but is collected from the forest; they also collect various types of mushroom from the forest floor for sale at Wosi. In addition, the Rendani Hatam produce home-brewed alcohol from the sap of the sugar palm (*Arenga pinnata*), both for their own consumption and for sale.

In general, marketing is the job of the Rendani women, who feel they have better marketing skills than the men. As one woman in her mid-30s commented: 'If buyers made a bargain to drop the price, they [the men] cannot negotiate to maintain it. They often sell at a cheap price because they want to go home early'. Her husband confirmed this, saying he would prefer to sell goods that had a fixed price, such as cocoa.

The Rendani earn more from selling garden produce than from the sale of forest products. Among those interviewed in 2001, the household income received from on-farm activities ranged from Rp 57,750 to Rp 114,000 per month (averaging Rp 80,000 per month), while the income from forest products was less than Rp 10,000 per month (Alhamid 2005). A few Rendani Hatam said that their total household income was less than Rp 50,000 per month. The only households that had significantly higher than average incomes were those containing civil servants, who were paid between Rp 600,000 and Rp 1 million per month, and those who owned grocery stores, who earned between Rp 300,000 and Rp 500,000 per month. The number of such households was very small indeed.

On the basis of these data, it appears that the average income of the Rendani Hatam is around half the Papuan average, which is itself very low. In 2001, around 42 per cent of Papua's 2.2 million people could be categorized as poor, most of them farmers with a household income of no more than Rp 106,312 per month (BPS 2002). Thus, most Rendani Hatam could be classified as living below the poverty line.

Pressures on Land

The land use patterns of the Hatam living in Rendani have gradually changed from temporary, short-term, kinship group-based uses such as swidden gardening, to longer-term, permanent, exclusive uses such as cocoa plantations. Market demand has accelerated the development of a cash economy, leading to an expansion of cash crop production and increased harvesting of forest products. This has led to enormous changes in the style of living of the Rendani Hatam, who now erect permanent houses (in place of their traditional longhouses) and own modern conveniences such as motorcycles and whitegoods. Such changes are welcomed by the Hatam themselves as bringing about an improvement in their standard of living. However, they have also exerted significant pressure on the viability and sustainability of the natural resource base, and the customary systems for its management.

With the incentives now in place for the Hatam to engage with the cash economy by working their land, it appears probable that more perennial cash crops will be established on customary land. The widespread adoption of perennial crops like cocoa or palm oil exacerbates pressure on the land, because of the long periods during which clan resources are effectively privatized. For example, cocoa continues to bear, and so occupies the ground, for over 30 years. Thus, if a kinship group grants a member permission to plant an area of land to cocoa, it is in effect giving that person exclusive use of the land for at least a 30-year period. Henceforth, the individual will virtually 'own' the block of customary land for private use for at least two generations, with the possibility of passing it down to a third generation. As long as the tree crops continue to grow there, then this customary land will not be available to other members of the landholding kinship group. This change in land use is creating dissatisfaction among the younger men of the Hatam community, who would like to gain access to clan land but are unable to do so because, in many instances, it is already being fully used by older members of their kinship group.

This pressure on the land is further exacerbated by the Hatam's sale of gardening rights to others and the sale of land to, or its resumption by, government agencies. But the Hatam feel they have no choice; they have to move from a purely subsistence economy and engage in the cash economy. Like anyone else, they need money to pay for social services such as health care and education, and to buy consumer goods. Money has now become central to the lives of the Hatam.

3   THE RENDANI FOREST: A HISTORY OF CONFLICT

Understanding the dimensions of the current conflict over the Rendani Protection Forest requires an understanding of its past history, which has also been beset by conflict. The first two phases of this history predate Indonesian rule, and are summarized briefly below. The most recent phase began with the end of Dutch colonial rule, and assertion of Indonesian rule, in 1963 (Vlasblom 2004).

Rendani before Indonesian Rule

The first phase of Rendani's history was that preceding the migration of the Hatam to the Rendani area in the late 1800s. Before this, the area was occupied by two lowland tribes, the Biak-Wandamen and the Mansim, who owned and managed the region's resources through communal arrangements. The internal bonds within the tribes were considerably stronger than the bonds between the tribes. Intertribal warfare was common, especially around Doreri Bay where Manokwari now stands (Kamma 1994). Tribal territory was limited and people were constrained by the tribal borders they had created. Papuans were strongly aware of the distinction between highlanders (Min) and lowlanders (Mam), and between Papuans and non-Papuans (Mbrey). Their belief systems did not separate humans from other parts of nature.[4] Animals and plants were incorporated within human social systems, and myths and taboos mediated people's relationships with nature. Traditional belief systems were challenged and changed by the arrival of Christian missionaries in the area in 1855, coinciding with the beginning of the colonial period (Kamma 1994). Changes in resource ownership due to warfare, combined with the challenge to traditional belief systems and related management practices, appear to have exacerbated resource exploitation during this early period.

The second phase of Rendani's history opened with the migration of the Hatam people from Bingrayut in the highlands to the coast, after their defeat of the lowland tribes around Manokwari in the late 1800s. This warfare was longstanding: when the English naturalist Alfred Russel Wallace visited Doreri Bay in April 1858, he reported seeing human skulls in many houses, 'the trophies of their battles with the savage Arfaks [including the Hatam] of the interior, who often come to attack them' (Wallace 1869: 496). Following their defeat, the Mansim moved to an adjacent coastal location, Arfai, and the area that is now the town of Manokwari was divided among three members of the Hatam.

One of these Hatam leaders, the grandfather of a present Rendani resident, was rewarded for his role in the war with the gift of a piece of what was then considered to be marginal land at Rendani. He established the first village (*kampong*), Kampong Syoribo, where around 100 inhabitants lived together in one longhouse. Migration from Bingrayut has continued ever since. During this period, the forest was collectively owned by the Hatam community, and managed principally according to traditional practices. The Hatam continued to sell non-wood forest products such as resin, massoy bark and aromatic oil, while the Dutch government set up a timber-logging and saw-milling company at Manokwari in 1956. At the end of Dutch colonial rule in 1963, a local Dutch rancher donated 30 head of cattle to the residents of Kampong Syoribo, who grazed them between the village and the coast.

---

4   Traditional Papuan belief systems and their relationship to resource management are described by Whittaker (1975), Craven and de Fretes (1987) and Kamma (1994) among others.

During this period, conflicts over resource use were usually resolved in traditional ways, within the Hatam community. Resolution was usually accomplished by the payment of an *adat* fine in the form of pigs, *kain timur* or women. At a special peace ceremony conducted by an honourable elder (*nekey*), the *nekey* would cut in two a length of bamboo held by the leaders of each kinship group, symbolizing that the conflict had been resolved. Intermarriage was another method used to resolve serious conflicts between tribes. This was known as *sob tai bouwa*, which literally means 'planting bamboo on a cliff in order to prevent a landslide'.

Rendani since the Assertion of Indonesian Rule

The most recent phase of conflict in Rendani began with the start of Indonesian rule in 1963. From the outset, relations between the Rendani Hatam and the Indonesian authorities were antagonistic. In 1965, many Hatam participated in the Free Papua Movement (OPM) revolt against the Indonesian government (Osborne 1985). When the uprising was crushed, most Hatam living in Rendani fled into the forest; the village and the possessions they left behind were burnt by the Indonesian army. On their return to Rendani in 1967, the Hatam built a new village closer to the beach called Kampong Kentek. The legacy of the Hatam's association with OPM has continued to shape their relations with the Indonesian authorities, as discussed below.

The Creation of the Rendani Protection Forest (1968–70)

As recounted by the Rendani Hatam themselves, in 1968 four of their elders were invited by a local forestry service staff member to discuss a planned change of function for the Rendani forest from a tribal forest to a protection forest. Without fully explaining its content and significance, the KPH staff member showed the elders a letter and asked them to endorse it with their thumbprints. Because the elders were illiterate, they did not understand that by endorsing the letter, they were signing away their traditional right of access to the forest. Moreover, according to one of the elders (still alive and interviewed in 2001), they misunderstood the meaning of the word 'protection', which they interpreted to mean protection of their livelihoods, including their tribal rights, by the state.

On 25 January 1969, the head of the subdistrict of Manokwari issued Regulation No. 03/KPS/1969 prohibiting the local Rendani people from cultivating gardens or collecting forest products inside the proposed protection forest. This came as a shock to the Hatam living in Rendani, who thereby lost legal right of access to their gardens and forest. In the words of one of those affected:

When we heard the story, we all felt as if we were already dead, because where would we go to find food, and where would we go to collect firewood? All of us were really angry with the old men, who [we thought] had sold this land.

On 17 February 1969, the government asked the village head (*kepala kampong*) to sign the letter confirming the transfer of control over the forest from the local people of Rendani to the head of KPH Manokwari, without reimbursement. For reasons that are not apparent, he did so, thus setting up a long-lasting conflict with members of his own family and with the community. Many Hatam were incensed by the government's failure to pay compensation for the use of the forest, but felt powerless to do anything about it. In part, this was because they were afraid that any protest would lead to them being labelled members of OPM, with adverse consequences for themselves and their community.

On 5 August 1969, the governor of West Irian (as Papua was then called) issued a legal instrument designating the Rendani forest a protection forest for its hydrological function (Letter of Instruction No. 118/ GIB/1969). This decree provided the legal basis for the government to take action against the local community.

Rather than fight the government directly for the restoration of their rights, the Rendani Hatam asserted their control over the forest in a different way. They gave the Biak, Serui and Wandamen people living in adjacent communities permission to make gardens inside the now-protected area, accepting payments of money, rice or machetes in return. Although KPH Manokwari tried to evict the illegal farmers, they kept returning to the gardens they now 'owned' on the basis that they had bought the land legitimately from the accepted legal owners, the Rendani Hatam. The entry of a third party into the conflict encouraged the Hatam to fight more strongly for their own rights.

By the early 1970s, direct conflict between the Rendani Hatam and the KPH could no longer be avoided. The forest rangers who had been given the task of maintaining the forest were chased away by the Hatam, who claimed that the government had not paid for the land. Conversely, the government argued that the Rendani Hatam had no legal right to claim that the forest still belonged to them, producing the thumb-printed letter releasing the land as evidence for their case.

Tree Planting and Infrastructure Development (1974–90)

In 1974, KPH Manokwari established a teak plantation inside the protection forest. The main intention appears to have been to strengthen the claim of the local government to the forest; as agents of the legal owners of the land, the forestry service asserted that it had the right to plant the trees. The head of forest conservation in KPH Manokwari also claimed that the planting was intended to improve the water-holding capacity of the forest, and to establish a trial site to assess the local environment's suitability for teak. In February 1976, rangers set about marking the boundaries of the protection forest with cement poles.

In 1977, KPH Manokwari built a forest ranger station close to the former Kampong Syoribo to prevent intruders from entering the protected area. This only increased the level of local protest, often leading to physical clashes. Also in 1977, to encourage local participation in protecting the forest, KPH Manokwari initiated a reforestation project inside the forest, planting several native Papuan commercial timber species. It invited the Hatam to participate, paying around 15 of them to take part in the project. This project had little effect on the views of the Rendani Hatam about their rights to the forest, however.

The nature of the conflict is exemplified by an exchange between a senior villager and forest rangers in mid-1986 over the matter of compensation for the land on which the forest ranger station stood. The villager first sought compensation of Rp 5 million from KPH Manokwari for the use of the land. In June 1986, the forestry service sent a letter to the local police office alleging that the villager had damaged the forest ranger station and describing him as 'non-cooperative' (*tidak mau bekerjasama*). In the prevailing political circumstances, this form of euphemism could have led to the individual being jailed or even killed. After failing to gain compensation from KPH Manokwari, in October 1988 the villager took his claim to the district head (*bupati*) of Manokwari district. But the claim was again rejected, on the grounds that the local government did not have sufficient resources to pay such compensation.

In 1990, the forest ranger station was completely destroyed by large numbers of Rendani Hatam. This was followed by the construction, from October 1990, of the Warmare–Sanggeng road, which split the protection forest into two parts. Almost all of the teak trees planted by KPH Manokwari, as well as any other trees that stood in the way of the new road, were logged by the Department of Public Works without any notification, or remuneration, being given to KPH Manokwari. From 1995, houses and businesses were built along the road, most of them owned by non-Papuan migrants from Makassar and Java. Many of the new owners had purchased certificates of land ownership from the National Land Agency (BPN), which issued them against the wishes of KPH Manokwari.

Gestures towards Sustainable Development (1998 – present)

In 1998, the Regional Forestry Office of Irian Jaya launched a protected areas management project in which the Rendani Hatam were again invited to participate. This time, instead of planting timber species, they were asked to plant cocoa as a cash crop. It was envisaged that the nine households that agreed to participate in the project would become the motivators for an expansion of cocoa farming around Rendani. The local community was initially quite enthusiastic about the project, because those who participated would be paid Rp 150,000 per month for their involvement. However, the intended 'snowball' effect of the pilot project never materialized, because the Rendani Hatam did not have the resources to continue farming after the project interventions ceased. Neither did they have the interest—most Rendani Hatam interviewed in 2001 said that they would have preferred to plant durian. As a result, the cocoa plantation did not expand beyond the demonstration plot of about 2 hectares, and has had minimal impact on the protected forest area.

The Hatam Perspective on Resource Conflicts

From a Hatam perspective, the conflicts associated with resource use in Rendani can be classified as (a) those occurring among the communities living in the Rendani area, and (b) those occurring between the state and local communities. These are discussed in turn below.

Conflicts among the Communities Living in Rendani

The Hatam divide people into three categories: those originally from Arfak (around Manokwari), comprising the Meyakh, Moskona, Sougb, Moile and Hatam, all of whom are called Min; Melanesians from other regions of Papua, called Mam; and people from outside Papua, the Mbrey. Thus, from a Hatam perspective, conflicts among the communities living in Rendani are of three types: conflicts among the Min; conflicts between the Hatam and the Mam; and conflicts between the Hatam and the Mbrey.

Traditionally, conflicts among the Hatam were resolved by customary means. The arrival among the Hatam of outsiders of Papuan (Mam) and non-Papuan (Mbrey) origin has dramatically affected the patterns of land use within and around the Rendani forest. As described above, many of the immigrants who use the forest for gardening—especially the Ayamaru—have been more commercially successful than the Hatam. With most of the stalls in the Wosi market now controlled by non-Papuan Mbrey, the Hatam have been pushed to the edges of the market to sell their agricultural products. Most of the conflicts between them and the Mbrey during the 1980s originated in the Hatam's feelings of being marginalized, alienated from their own land and treated as second-class citizens.

Many Mbrey from Makassar, Java and Manado operate non-agricultural commercial ventures near the Rendani Protection Forest, including hotels, hardware shops, vehicle sale and repair shops, and lime-burning and brick-manufacturing facilities. Very few Rendani are employed in these kinds of businesses — only two among those interviewed in 2001, for example. The low penetration of the Hatam into any non-agricultural business is connected to their low levels of formal education and limited business skills. Consequently, they must continue to depend on primary production to generate income. Very few have been able to gain employment in off-farm businesses to alleviate their dependence on income from their gardens and forest.

Conflict between the State and Local Communities

The declaration of the Rendani Protection Forest (under Regulation No. 03/KPS/1969) opened a new era of conflict between the Rendani Hatam and the Indonesian state. The Hatam recount a history of incidents, typically three or four annually since 1970, involving either the police or officers from KPH Manokwari.

The Hatam view, typical of those of indigenous Papuans elsewhere, is exemplified in the following complaint by an elder about the need for the traditional owners to seek official recognition of their residential status at Rendani:

> Who should acknowledge the Hatam and Meyakh as the landowners of Manokwari? That office [BPN]? Even the land to build their office was given by us, so why should they issue the paper for us? If you have already lived in your house for a long time and a newcomer comes and says that he wants to issue an official paper to acknowledge you as the owner of the house, what can you say? What is the purpose of a certificate? There is no need for it.

Like other indigenous Papuans, the Hatam consider rights to land to be determined by the customary first-settler principle: whoever comes first has the rights to the land. According to them, the government is a newcomer with no claim to the land. The Hatam know that their gardens are located within a protected area and they are aware of the forest's function to provide fresh water for the town of Manokwari. But they say that they have no alternative but to garden inside the forest, because that is where they have customary rights. For customary landowners, farming outside the boundaries of their customary land means an insecure and uncertain future, as they may be expelled by the owners and must pay a relatively high fee for the use of the land. They are also reluctant to cultivate other people's land, because this would imply acceptance of a change in status from landowners (*pemilik petuanan*) to newcomers (*pendatang*). Some Hatam say they would rather destroy the forest than give it to the government. They are also angry about the government attention being focused on forest sustainability at the expense of the sustainability of the traditional owners' livelihoods.

It is clear from discussions with the Rendani Hatam that the deforestation brought about by the Hatam themselves inside the Rendani Protection Forest has two dimensions. The first is the imperative to feed their families and generate an income, given the lack of alternative livelihood options. The second is the desire to demonstrate to the government that they are the rightful owners of the forest. Thus, the leasing of land inside the forest to the Biak and Ayamaru can be seen as part of their battle to assert their rights over the land. According to the Hatam, it is inconsistent and unjust for the government to refuse to recognize their claim over their traditional lands while according legal recognition, in the form of land certificates issued by BPN, to non-Papuans who have bought land on the periphery of the forest to set up non-farm businesses.

The State's Response

The government has taken a three-pronged approach to the management of the Rendani Protection Forest. First, it has used the agencies of the state—the KPH, the police and the military—to deal with disputes concerning the forest. Second, it has promoted forest conservation through extension and public awareness programs. And third, it has fostered 'sustainable' development in the forest. Each of these is considered below.

The Use of State Power

KPH Manokwari is the principal state agency responsible for the management of the Rendani Protection Forest. In addition to establishing a forest ranger station in the forest, it has progressively increased the number of rangers responsible for implementing regulations to protect the forests in the Manokwari district. This strategy has not been very effective, for reasons that are not unique to Rendani. The number of rangers is relatively small (16 for the entire Manokwari district in 2001) and they are poorly equipped (with only three two-way radios and one motorcycle in the same year). The rangers' low salaries and poor facilities mean that some are susceptible to corruption, while others must take second jobs—often for logging companies, usually in return for cash payments. Those who do try to carry out their duties conscientiously are often sidelined by their superiors, who turn a blind eye to illegal activity in return for payment or favours, or by corrupt members of the police or military, who stand to benefit from the illegal harvesting or sale of forest products. KPH Manokwari also faces direct resistance from the local people, as described above. As a consequence, it has seldom been effective in its role of forest protection.

KPH Manokwari often turns to the police for assistance in protecting the forest. It frequently forwards copies of forest management-related correspondence between itself and the Rendani Hatam to the local police office. The integral role of the police in resolving conflicts over resource management in the forest was formally acknowledged by the head of KPH Manokwari in a report dated 14 June 1986 (No. 358/IV/1986).

Although the army has not been directly involved in any conflict in Rendani since destroying Kampong Syoribo in 1965, the threat of being reported to the police and army as 'non-cooperative' is a powerful one given political sensitivities in Papua and the role of the army in suppressing dissent. The Rendani Hatam are keenly aware of the methods used to enforce local obedience, including torture and other physical and psychological abuse, the jailing of suspects and social stigmatization – by trying to link individuals to the separatist group OPM, for example.

Extension and Community Awareness

The government has implemented extension and community awareness campaigns to promote conservation of the Rendani Protection Forest. In 1999, a report prepared by the Regional Forestry Office of Irian Jaya in collaboration with the University of Papua at Manokwari identified the local people as the main agents of deforestation, and recommended a campaign of awareness raising (Dinas Pertanian 1999).

The local government responded by sending extension workers to Rendani to educate the local people about the importance of maintaining the forest. It erected many billboards and street banners exhorting the locals to increase their awareness of, and participate in, resource conservation. Both the extension and community awareness campaigns implicitly portrayed the inhabitants of the forest as the main actors in forest degradation. However, the campaigns had no discernible effect on the attitudes or behaviour of the Rendani Hatam, perhaps because they did not address the underlying causes of forest degradation and loss as perceived by the Hatam themsleves.

Sustainable Resource-based Development

Initiatives to encourage the Rendani Hatam to grow high-value tree crops – such as the reforestation project implemented by KPH Manokwari in 1977 and the cocoa-growing project implemented by the Regional Forestry Office of Irian Jaya in 1998 – have not been successful beyond the initial project stages. In part this was because they were very much 'top-down' rather than 'bottom-up' processes. For example, although the latter project involved a consultation process that was supposed to make it acceptable to the local community, this was essentially an exercise in rhetoric. In neither case did either forestry agency begin by simply asking the people what they wanted, and so involve them as true stakeholders. When interviewed, most Hatam said they would have preferred to plant species with valuable marketable fruit, such as durian, langsat and rambutan.

Nevertheless, the provincial government's cocoa initiative is noteworthy because it was at odds with the policy of the central government, which precluded any form of productive activity within a protection forest. It is likely that the initiative reflected, at least in part, the change in thinking that followed the fall of the Soeharto regime in favour of local interests and economic development rather than the suppression of those interests.

Towards Sustainable Management of the Rendani Protection Forest

The conflict between the Hatam and the state over the Rendani Protection Forest has had significant adverse consequences for the sustainability of forest resources and the water the forest is supposed to provide. The consequences for the forest are evident in Figure 10.1, which shows that around two-thirds of the forest is now secondary forest of various ages. Alhamid (2005) found that this secondary growth was relatively young and dominated by pioneer species, with an understorey of invasive plants.[5] Such species are indicative of a high level of disturbance. Active gardens occupy nearly a quarter of the forest area, while relatively old secondary forest exhibiting the species and structural complexity typical of Papuan primary forest occupies just 10 per cent. At the time of field research in 2001, a community logging cooperative had begun clear-cutting the remaining old secondary forest, ostensibly to establish a cocoa plantation. That plantation still had not been established in 2005.[6]

Since the official proclamation of the Rendani forest as a protected area, the government has proclaimed and sought to enforce severe restrictions on farming and the collection of forest products, to protect both the forest and the water supply. However, while the rules and regulations intended to effect protection of the forest have multiplied, the forest itself

---

5 These pioneer species were principally *Spathodea campanulata, Macaranga tanarius, Ficus* spp. and *Piper aduncum*; the understorey was composed mainly of *Nephrolepis exaltata* and *Imperata cylindrica*.

6 See Alhamid (2005) for details of the impact of such community logging initiatives in Papua.

has been degraded or destroyed. Although the government has the backing of the legal system to support its interests, the implementation of its policies, backed by police and the presence of the military, has been counterproductive to the stated objectives of those policies.

For example, when asked why he did not want to replant bushland with perennial crops, a 35-year-old Hatam farmer responded by asking why he should plant crops on land owned by the government (which he also claimed as part of his tribal land). If the government wanted the people to replant bushland inside the forest, he said, the government should pay them to do so, or at least provide the seed or seedlings to rehabilitate the land.

The outcome of the conflict for the environmental service for which the forest is reserved, water, has also been very adverse. PDAM now faces a serious decline in water yield from the Rendani forest, with a dramatic decline in flows into the Rendani I and Rendani II water tanks between 1988 and 2001. When PDAM was established in 1988, water flowed into the tanks at a rate of 20 litres per second; by February 2001 the rate of flow had decreased by more than 60 per cent to an average of 7.5 litres per second. The flow into the third tank (Kali Dingin) had also declined, by around 50 per cent, from 55 to 28 litres per second.[7] While the reasons for this decline in water yield have not been investigated, the results of studies conducted elsewhere suggest that it is consistent with a decrease in the extent of older forest and an increase in the proportion of other vegetation. This situation is exacerbated by loss of water through leakage and theft; in 2000, nearly 32 per cent of the total production of around 1.1 million cubic metres of water from the Rendani Protection Forest was lost prior to sale (although some of this could be attributed to non-payment of bills).

4   CONCLUSIONS

The conflict between the customary landowners and the state over the control and management of the Rendani Protection Forest is a microcosm of the larger conflict over resources throughout Papua. The perception by the Rendani Hatam that their traditional resources have been usurped by the Indonesian state is mirrored in the experiences of Papuan people elsewhere. Moreover, the government's denial of customary *adat* rights over the forest has disrupted the customary resource management system, which has progressively lost its practical value. Top-down govern-

---

7   Personal communication, manager of PDAM Manokwari, 2001, drawing on a
    PDAM technical information report issued in February 2001.

ment regulations that ignore the local social and cultural systems have degraded local knowledge and diminished the relevance of indigenous knowledge systems. Communities have been alienated from their own land, and have become dependent on foreign systems of exploitation and management.

It is interesting to contrast the acceptance of Hatam ownership of Rendani by the Biak and Mansim, whom they displaced in the late 1800s, with Hatam rejection of the rights asserted by the Indonesia state. Although the Hatam are relatively recent arrivals at Rendani, and secured it through warfare, other Papuans recognize the legitimacy of their ownership. No such recognition has been extended to the Indonesian state, which has also used the tools of warfare to secure its interests over the forest.

The intervention of the state in the management of the Rendani Protection Forest over the past 35 years has created a situation in which the traditional owners and residents of the forest have no incentive to cooperate with the state in achieving its management objectives. The income generated from water — the product for which the forest is formally managed — is captured entirely by PDAM and other beneficiaries such as the local freshwater fishery service. This has meant that the Hatam must continue to rely on gardening and forest products, and the 'sale' of their land to others, to meet their subsistence and livelihood needs. None of these uses is desirable in a forest managed for water production. It is not only the Rendani Hatam for whom this situation is a disincentive to management consistent with the production of drinking water; KPH Manokwari, which is responsible for the protection and management of the forest, also receives no income for this role. Thus, the economic signals associated with the state's forest management regime are counterproductive.

It would make far more sense if the rights and interests of the traditional owners of the Rendani Protection Forest were recognized by PDAM, the main beneficiary of the public-good water resources flowing through the forest. If PDAM shared its profits with the community that owns and resides in the forest, it and KPH Manokwari could expect a far greater level of cooperation from the Hatam in achieving their management objectives. This would simultaneously address PDAM's goal of maintaining or increasing current water flows; increase PDAM's profit; and improve the welfare of the Hatam, thus allowing them to reduce their dependence on other forms of forest use. Such management practices have been instituted elsewhere to good effect (see Landell-Mills and Porras 2002).

The experience of past reforestation initiatives suggests that the Rendani Hatam would be receptive to the establishment of those fruit tree species that the local people most appreciate, such as durian, langsat and rambutan. The establishment of such plantations would assist in improving the water-holding capacity of the forest and provide the Hatam with an income source that is more compatible with management for water production. PDAM may also need to consider sharing some of its profits with KPH Manokwari, both as an incentive to protect the catchment values of the forest and as a practical means of assisting it to fulfil its role in overseeing the management of the forest. While these changes may be seen as implying a fundamental shift in the attitude of state agencies to the ownership and management of forests — one that recognizes the rights and interests of the traditional owners — they may also be seen as simply pragmatic, given the poor outcomes of the prevailing management regime.

The situation that has arisen in the Rendani forest is an illustration of the vicious cycle of breakdown in resource management arrangements that follows the denial of local people's traditional rights and the imposition of a management regime that does not acknowledge the rights and interests of the traditional owners. What is needed in Rendani, as elsewhere in Papua, is a fundamental change in state thinking about resources and their ownership, to develop a partnership of interests between local and state actors for the mutually beneficial and sustainable management of those resources.

REFERENCES

Alhamid, H. (2005), 'Forest for the People? Indigenous Forest Management under Decentralisation: A Case Study of the Rendani Protection Forest, Papua, Indonesia', PhD thesis, Australian National University, Canberra.

BPS (Badan Pusat Statistik) (2002), *Statistik Indonesia* [Statistics of Indonesia], Jakarta.

BPS-Papua (Badan Pusat Statistik Provinsi Papua) (2003), *Statistik Papua* [Statistics of Papua], Jayapura.

Brown, D. (1999), 'Addicted to Rent: Corporate and Spatial Distribution of Forest Resources in Indonesia: Implications for Forest Sustainability and Government Policy', Report No. PFM/EC/99/06, Indonesia–UK Tropical Forestry Management Programme, Jakarta.

Craven, I. and Y. de Fretes (1987), 'Arfak Mountains Nature Conservation Area, Irian Jaya: Management Plan 1988–1992', WWF Project 3770, World Wildlife Fund, Bogor.

Dauvergne, P. (2001), *Loggers and Degradation in the Asia–Pacific: Corporations and Environmental Management*, Cambridge University Press, Cambridge.

Dinas Pertanian Tanaman Pangan Kabupaten Manokwari (1999), *Laporan Tahunan, Tahun Anggaran 1999–2000* [Annual Report, Financial Year 1999–2000], Manokwari.

FWI, WRI and GFW (Forest Watch Indonesia, World Resource Institute and Global Forest Watch) (2002), *State of the Forest: Indonesia*, World Resource Institute, Washington DC.

Holmes, D. (2000), *Deforestation in Indonesia: A Review of the Situation in Sumatra, Kalimantan and Sulawesi*, World Bank, Jakarta.

Kamma, F.C. (1994), *Ajaib di Mata Kita* [The Miracle before Our Eyes], BPK Gunung Mulia, Jakarta.

Landell-Mills, N. and I.T. Porras (2002), *Silver Bullet or Fools' Gold? A Global Review of Markets for Forest Environmental Services and Their Impacts on the Poor*, International Institute for Environment and Development, London.

Langness, L.L. (1972), 'Political Organization', in P. Ryan (ed.), *Encyclopaedia of Papua and New Guinea*, Melbourne University Press in association with the University of Papua New Guinea, Melbourne.

Lederman, R. (1990), 'Big Men, Large and Small? Towards a Comparative Perspective', *Ethnology*, 29: 3–15.

Osborne, R. (1985), *Indonesia's Secret War: The Guerilla Struggle in Irian Jaya*, Allen & Unwin, Sydney.

Peters, F. (2001), 'HPB di Manokwari: Menangani Segudang Tugas' [HPB at Manokwari: Handling Many Tasks], in P. Schoorl (ed.), *Belanda di Irian Jaya: Ambtenar di Masa Penuh Gejolak 1945–1962* [The Dutch in Irian Jaya: Officials in a Time of Flux, 1945–1962], KITLV Press and Garba Budaya, Leiden and Jakarta.

Sumule, A. (2002), 'Protection and Empowerment of the Rights of Indigenous People of Papua (Irian Jaya) over Natural Resources under Special Autonomy: From Legal Opportunities to Challenging Implementation', RMAP Working Paper No. 36, Resource Management in Asia–Pacific Program, Australian National University, Canberra.

Sunderlin, W. and I.A.P. Resosudarmo (1996), 'Rates and Causes of Deforestation in Indonesia: Towards a Resolution of the Ambiguities', CIFOR Occasional Paper No. 9, CIFOR, Bogor.

Tacconi, L. and I. Kurniawan (2006), 'Forests, Agriculture, Poverty and Land Reform: The Case of the Indonesian Outer Islands', Environmental Management and Development Occasional Paper No. 11, Crawford School of Economics and Government, Australian National University, Canberra.

Telapak and EIA (Environmental Investigation Agency) (2005), *The Last Frontier: Illegal Logging in Papua and China's Massive Timber Theft*, EIA, Washington DC.

Vlasblom, D. (2004), *Papoea: Een Geschiedenis* [Papua: A History], Mets and Schilt, Amsterdam.

Wallace, A.R. (1869), *The Malay Archipelago*, Macmillan, London.

Whittaker, J.L. (1975), *Documents and Readings in New Guinea History: Pre-history to 1889*, Jacaranda, Milton.

11 CLIMATE CHANGE AND DEVELOPMENT IN EASTERN INDONESIA

Frank Jotzo, Ida Aju Pradnja Resosudarmo,
Ditya A. Nurdianto and Agus P. Sari

Recent scientific findings show that climate change is already taking place and that there is the risk of severe impacts if emissions of greenhouse gases are not cut back (IPCC 2007). Climate change is no longer seen as 'just' an environmental problem, but as a threat to economic development and prosperity (Stern 2006; Garnaut 2008). This perspective has greatly elevated the issue among policy makers the world over. In Indonesia, climate change rose high on the public and policy agenda with the UN climate conference held in Bali in December 2007.

Indonesia faces a variety of impacts from climate change, from sea-level rise to a changing hydrological cycle and attendant droughts and floods, to greater stresses on public health. These will require attention and corrective action if development is to be safeguarded in the face of changes in the natural world. Indonesia itself is a significant emitter of greenhouse gases, especially connected to deforestation. Reducing these emissions creates its own challenges, but also brings opportunities.

This chapter summarizes the expected climate change impacts for Indonesia, and eastern Indonesia in particular. It discusses the main sources of emissions and options to reduce or avoid them. Climate change research on Indonesia is limited, and is especially patchy for eastern Indonesia. Nevertheless, enough information is available for us to sketch some options for climate change policies that would support development in eastern Indonesia.

1 CLIMATE CHANGE AND DEVELOPMENT: THE GLOBAL ISSUES

Causes and Impacts

Human-induced climate change occurs because of a build-up of greenhouse gases in the atmosphere, trapping the energy from the sun to a greater degree than previously. The main greenhouse gas from human activity is carbon dioxide, which is released in the combustion of fossil fuels (especially coal, oil and gas) and in the conversion of forests to other uses. Other greenhouse gases include methane, from sources such as agriculture and waste dumps, and nitrous oxide from agriculture and some industrial processes.

Warming is already evident, with 11 of the 12 years between 1995 and 2006 among the 12 warmest years since 1850. The average global temperature is now around 0.7 degrees higher than it was 100 years ago (IPCC 2007). Long time lags in the system mean that the earth is already committed to more warming, and feedback effects may amplify the effect of greenhouse gases on temperatures. Non-linearities in the climate system mean that changes could occur suddenly and in unanticipated ways.

Warming changes weather patterns, hydrological cycles and ocean currents. It causes thermal expansion of oceans, resulting in sea-level rise. Many of the expected impacts on people are to do with water: seawater inundation in coastal areas, especially during storm surges; flooding as a result of more rainfall in some regions or during some parts of the year; but also droughts as the flipside to these changes in rainfall. The frequency and intensity of tropical storms is also expected to increase.

Together with higher average temperatures and more extreme spikes in temperature during heatwaves, these changes are likely to have strong adverse impacts on settlements, economic activity (especially agriculture) and health. Many low-lying areas will be exposed to flooding, and freshwater will become scarcer in other places. The suitability of land for agriculture will change, depending on the changes in rainfall and temperature. That could affect food security. Higher temperatures will not only bring about greater heat stress but extend the spread of vector-borne diseases like malaria and dengue fever. Some changes will be positive: rainfall will increase in some previously drought-prone areas, and cold parts of the world may become warmer. However, most of the changes will be for the worse, if only because existing patterns of settlement and economic activity are not suited to the new conditions under climate change.

Climate change is also poised to have strong impacts on ecosystems and biodiversity. One-third or more of global species is at risk of extinction even at moderate temperature increases over this century (IPCC 2007). And oceans are increasingly turning acidic as a result of more carbon dioxide uptake, affecting corals and other marine life.

Vulnerability and Adaptation

How vulnerable people are to climate change depends on the impacts they face, and on their ability to change their circumstances – 'adapt' – in response to these impacts. In general, poorer countries and regions are the most vulnerable. They tend to have less capacity to deal with disasters, to provide adequate infrastructure and to plan for future change. The adverse impacts from climate change are likely to be greater in tropical regions, which are also home to the majority of the world's poor.

Within each country as well, the poor are the most vulnerable to climate change. They often live in areas that are already prone to natural disasters. They have less access to remedies such as improved housing or health care, and they are less able to reduce their exposure by moving away or changing jobs. Where agriculture is affected by climate change, large numbers of poor farmers will be hurt. The poor are also more immediately affected by measures to reduce greenhouse gases, such as rises in the price of energy or restrictions on the conversion of forests.

Adapting to climate change is important for continued development and economic prosperity. Adaptation can take a wide range of forms, depending on the particular impacts and risks, the existing economic structures and policy frameworks, and people's opportunities and preferences. It could entail, for example, the provision of improved water storage and irrigation systems, strengthened flood defences and diversified transport and energy systems. It could mean developing new crops, altering agricultural growing patterns or introducing new disease monitoring and control systems. All such measures would need to be supported by improvements in public health, emergency management, agricultural extension, urban planning and so forth.

But spending scarce public resources to safeguard against long-term future risks is problematic. It is difficult for developing countries to justify spending big money on structural improvements that will not pay off for many years when they face many more pressing and immediate concerns in areas like health and education.

2   THE EFFECTS OF A CHANGING CLIMATE: IMPACTS ON INDONESIA

Like other countries, Indonesia stands to experience significant impacts from climate change. These include sea-level rise and saltwater inundation, droughts, increased frequency of extreme weather events, heavier rainfall events and flooding, and the spread of diseases. In turn, these may harm the country's agricultural, fishery and forestry industries, threatening both food security and livelihoods. Indonesia's rich biodiversity is also at risk.

Sea-level Rise

One of the best known effects of climate change is sea-level rise, which threatens people in low-lying islands and coastal regions in many countries. As an archipelago with extensive coastal areas relative to its total land mass, Indonesia is particularly vulnerable. Susandi, Firdaus and Herlianti (2008) estimate that a sea-level rise of 0.56 metres would result in the loss of 30,000 square kilometres of land in Indonesia, causing many islands to disappear. Sea-level rise of this magnitude could occur during this century through thermal expansion of the oceans alone, with the risk of much greater sea-level rise if the polar ice shelves disintegrate.

Sea-level rise also causes inundation of coastal freshwater bodies by saltwater, with implications for agriculture, aquaculture and water supplies. Many sections of the coast are rendered even more vulnerable by erosion — often exacerbated by human activity such as the building of jetties and sea walls, the damming of rivers, the mining of sand and coral and the destruction of mangrove forests. Large numbers of Indonesians are at risk: currently around 42 million people inhabit areas that are less than 10 metres above the average sea level (Djajadiningrat 2008: 5–6).

Climate change also has major implications for millions of coastal fishermen. They rely on highly sensitive ecosystems in which even small changes have large effects. Changing water temperatures that damage coral reefs, for example, are likely to exacerbate other human-induced stresses such as pollution and overfishing, thereby causing a reduction in fish stocks. Fishermen will have to cope with more erratic weather. And rising sea levels could inundate many of the shrimp and fish ponds in Java, Aceh and Sulawesi.

Seasonal Cycles and Droughts

Climate change may be a factor contributing to the increased frequency and intensity of droughts observed in recent times. The droughts in Indonesia in 1994 and 1997 were considered the worst of the twentieth century and led to a significant fall in national rice production. In 1994, it is estimated that productivity declined on almost 500 million hectares of agricultural land, and harvests failed on 150 million hectares (Sutardi 2006, cited in PEACE 2007: 47). The 1997–98 El Niño is instructive as an example of how a hotter climate and disrupted hydrological cycle may affect the agricultural sector. During that period, southern Sumatra, Kalimantan, Java and some parts of eastern Indonesia suffered unseasonably dry conditions for several months. The monsoon rains that normally begin in September arrived much later, in November. Large areas of rice-growing land were affected and production of important income-generating non-food crops such as coffee, cocoa and rubber fell sharply.

Drought affects not only crop production but also employment opportunities in rural areas. During times of hardship, unemployed farm workers flock to nearby cities in search of work, increasing the social burden on municipalities. Because of the lack of affordable housing, these itinerant workers tend to squat in public facilities or erect makeshift housing along the river banks.

There are also trade and macroeconomic effects, with rice imports rising sharply during and after droughts. In times of import restrictions on rice, as has been the case since 2004, reductions in domestic rice production have led to sharp spikes in the price of rice (McCulloch and Timmer 2008).

In an analysis of changes in rainfall patterns in Indonesia from 1900 to 2000, Ratag (2007) found that rainfall from September to November had increased in intensity but with fewer rainy days. He also observed shifts in the starting date of the wet season. Compared with the average starting date for 1961–2003, he found that the wet season had shifted forward one to two months in West Papua and some other parts of Indonesia in 1990–2003, but backward in parts of Java and East Nusa Tenggara. These trends are predicted to continue, with dire consequences for agriculture. Farmers will have to adapt to the changes in rainfall patterns and seasons by altering their crop planting and harvesting times, potentially leading to a reduction in productivity (Las 2007).

Although climate anomalies can be predicted with great accuracy three to four months in advance, governments in developing countries lack the resources to collect such information and make it available to farmers. Small farmers find it particularly difficult to adjust to such changes in weather patterns, not just because they lack information, but also because of the difficulty of obtaining agricultural supplies and workers when and where needed (Wiriadiwangsa 2005). To prepare for a shorter growing season, for example, rice farmers would need to obtain adequate amounts of the seed of early crop cultivars (Naylor et al. 2007). But this may take a full cropping season to collect, with further delays likely during distribution (Amien and Runtunuwu 2008: 4).

Extreme Climate Events and Floods

Climate change is set to increase the frequency and intensity not just of droughts but also of floods. Tropical cyclones have become more frequent, triggering unusually high rainfall in many parts of Indonesia. It is believed that the increase in tropical cyclones is linked to rising ocean temperatures.

In Asia, floods are the most frequent and devastating type of disaster (Dutta and Herath 2004). The average of 10 flood events recorded annually in the 1970s became 30 in the 1990s and about 50 events per year in the early 2000s. During 1980–2007, about one-third of all 'registered' natural disasters in Indonesia were floods (CRED 2007).

High rainfall in areas with inadequate drainage systems causes landslides and flooding. More frequent floods will further decrease crop productivity by reducing the area under crops and the quantities harvested. Floods also cause great damage to agricultural and other infrastructure.

Water Resources and Agriculture

One of the most serious potential consequences of climate change is the disruption of regional hydrological cycles, with implications for the quantity and quality of regional water resources (Irianto, Sugianto and Amien 2004). Changes in the hydrological cycle are expected to affect levels of sedimentation and run-off, as well as groundwater and other water resources. Municipal water supplies, reservoirs and irrigation are all under threat.

To adapt to these changes, governments will need to put integrated water resource management plans in place, backed by enhanced collection and dissemination of information on hydrological resources. Water conservation and more efficient and rational use of water in the agricultural sector are likely to be among the measures adopted to protect the nation's freshwater resources (Irianto, Sugianto and Amien 2004).

The additional rainfall expected in some regions under climate change may augment water supplies for irrigation. But conversely, more rapid siltation is likely to reduce the lifetime of reservoirs and irrigation canals, and increased precipitation may accelerate soil erosion. Consequently, soil fertility and land productivity may decline, particularly in upland regions. The anticipated nationwide effect of soil degradation alone is that yields of upland crops such as soy bean and maize could decline by as much as 20–40 per cent; rice yields would generally be less affected, as rice is planted primarily in lowland regions. In addition to deteriorating soil quality, farmers in upland areas will experience abrupt changes in water supply due to soil erosion and new precipitation patterns.

Changing rainfall patterns are already reducing the availability of irrigation and drinking water. On the islands of Lombok and Sumbawa, for example, the number of water sources for irrigation and drinking fell from 580 in 1985 to 180 in 2006. These islands are also suffering from season 'breaks' — droughts during wet seasons. These have become much more common, leading to crop failures. In coastal areas, the loss of groundwater combined with rising sea levels will allow more seawater to intrude, contaminating water resources for both drinking and irrigation (Djajadiningrat 2008: 8).

Health Impacts

Climate change poses serious risks to human health. Importantly, it may increase the spread of infectious and vector-borne diseases (McMichael, Woodruff and Hales 2006). Changes in the hydrological cycle will increase the risk of expansion of water-borne diseases such as diarrhoea and expand the water-based habitats of vector-borne diseases such as malaria and dengue. As the world warms, malaria- and dengue-transmitting mosquitoes will be able to survive at higher altitudes as well as having more watery areas in which to breed. The incubation periods of the vector-transmittable diseases are becoming shorter with higher temperatures, and mutation of the viruses may occur.

Once again, the 1997–98 El Niño event is a good proxy of the impacts of a warming world on public health. By 1997 malaria had spread to high elevations, and for the first time was detected at altitudes above 2,000 metres in the highlands of Irian Jaya (Epstein et al. 1998). In 2004 it appeared that a more virulent strain of the potentially deadly dengue virus had emerged. Dengue fever is now spreading faster and killing more people than in the past.

The impacts on health will be greatest among poor communities that have the least protection. Heavy rainfall and flooding will quickly overwhelm the rudimentary systems of sanitation that prevail in the slum areas of towns and cities, exposing people to water-borne diseases such as diarrhoea and cholera. Those living in flood-prone areas are also the least likely to be able to pay for health care or the reconstruction of their homes. Prolonged, intense heatwaves coupled with high humidity leads to heat exhaustion, particularly among the urban poor and elderly. Poor families are also more likely to be living in environments vulnerable to mosquitoes. Climate change will heighten the risk for young and old alike by allowing mosquitoes to spread to new areas.

Coral Reefs and Fisheries

Increases in ocean temperature pose long-term risks to Indonesia's marine ecosystems. The consequences of ocean warming include coral bleaching, shifting of habitats and, in extreme cases, the disappearance of marine species. Coral bleaching provides the most visible measure of disruption to marine ecosystems. It is marked by a condition in which coral reefs turn white when exposed to stressors such as calcification, pollution, destructive fishing practices, freshwater exposure and increased temperatures. Bleached corals lose their source of energy if their symbiotic algae are exposed to stressors and are killed.

Indonesia has over 50,000 square kilometres of coral reefs, or about 18 per cent of all the world's coral reefs. Data from 414 reef monitoring stations throughout Indonesia found that in 2000 only 6 per cent of the coral reefs were in excellent condition, 24 per cent in good condition and the remaining 70 per cent in either fair or poor condition (Johns Hopkins University and Terangi 2003, cited in PEACE 2007: 52). Pollution and destructive fishing practices are believed to be the main causes of coral bleaching in Indonesia, but further warming of the oceans would probably worsen the situation and prevent the recovery of the reefs.

The 1997–98 El Niño event caused extensive coral bleaching (Setiasih 2006, cited in PEACE 2007: 53). Research carried out in Bali Barat National Park found that the majority of monitored coral segments in the marine park were in poor condition as a result of an outbreak of Acanthaster (a starfish that kills coral), storms and bleaching. During the 1997–98 bleaching event, more than 50 per cent of the hard coral in the national park bleached, leading to up to 100 per cent mortality. The marine park was subsequently classified as a catastrophically affected site.

The sustainability of Indonesia's fisheries is threatened by many factors, including the destruction of coral reefs, the loss of fish nursery areas due to the removal of mangroves, coastal zone reclamation, destructive fishing methods and overfishing, the pollution of water bodies, and excessive aquaculture such as shrimp farming (see also Chapter 8). Climate change could exacerbate this situation in several ways. The warming of ocean waters interferes with the upwelling of cold, nutrient-rich waters, inhibits the development of plankton and thus limits the supply of nutrition in the food chain. This means fewer fish to catch. The geographic distribution of fish species, however, would be determined more by changes in ocean currents than by warming as such, making impacts on fisheries difficult to predict (Merle 1998).

Even a slight rise in water temperature could gravely affect the growth and reproductive rates of tropical marine organisms, which typically live in habitats where temperatures are close to the upper limit of their tolerance. Coral reef destruction will lead to the extinction of marine organisms and affect a variety of fish species. These and other changes in marine habitats have very significant implications for Indonesia's millions of coastal fishermen.

Aquaculture will certainly be affected. If sea levels rise, saltwater may inundate the brackish shrimp and fish ponds increasingly found along the coasts of West, Central and East Java, Aceh and South Sulawesi.

Additionally, increased temperatures will cause higher evaporation rates and thus raise salinity levels (State Ministry of Environment 2003).

Biodiversity

Indonesia is arguably the most important nation for global conservation and is second only to Brazil in terms of terrestrial biodiversity. It has the world's third largest area of tropical forests, and is extremely rich in species. Covering 1.3 per cent of the world's land area, Indonesia has 10 per cent of the world's known species of flora, 12 per cent of the known species of mammals, 7 per cent of the known species of reptiles and 17 per cent of the known species of birds (Bappenas 2003). The island of Kalimantan alone, which covers 0.2 per cent of the earth's land area, provides habitat for 4 per cent of all known plants and 5 per cent of all identified birds and mammals (MacKinnon et al. 1996: 632; see also Chapter 6).

Within Indonesia, eastern Indonesian ecosystems tend to be the most diverse, because of the dynamic and diverse geological and climatic conditions that shaped their evolution. Because of their remoteness, they also tend to be less well studied. Supriatna (1999) estimates that the number of plant species in West Papua may triple from the current known base to 20,000–25,000 once detailed studies have been completed. His prediction is borne out in reports of a recent survey of the Foja mountains in West Papua in which a new bird species (the first in 60 years), 20 new frog species, four new butterflies and a new mammal were recorded (Shatwell 2005).

The significance of Indonesia to global conservation is even more pronounced when marine biodiversity is considered. Indonesia contains 38 per cent of all marine fish species and some 78 per cent of the world's corals. Allen and Adrim (2003) reported 1,111 fish species from a single bay in Flores alone — more than from the entire tropical Atlantic Ocean. Similar diversity has been reported for corals (Connolly, Bellwood and Hughes 2003).

Biodiversity is already under pressure from overexploitation and overharvesting, destructive practices such as blast fishing or the inappropriate use of fire, and the destruction of habitat. Climate change exacerbates these pressures, and adds its own. On land, warming shifts the boundaries of the viable habitat for species upward in altitude. In many instances species will not be able to migrate fast enough, or not be able to migrate at all. The issue at stake is not just the loss of iconic species themselves, but the change in structure of entire ecosystems, with food chains vulnerable to serious disruption if individual animal or plant species decline.

An estimated 12 million eastern Indonesians depend directly on bio-diversity and ecosystem services for their livelihoods and well-being. Those resources are under increasing pressure as global demand rises, as comparable resources in western and central Indonesia are depleted and as regional populations expand due to immigration and local economic and population growth (see Chapter 6).

3   ADAPTATION: DEALING WITH THE INEVITABLE

Some extent of climate change will inevitably occur over the decades to come, with the risk of abrupt and extreme changes. To safeguard living conditions and the underpinnings of economic growth and development, nations need to prepare to deal with the impacts of climate change. This is referred to as 'adaptation' to climate change.

The dominant view in the climate and development community is that climate change adaptation is indispensable for successful development. But although climate change should be considered in development planning, too often it is neglected in development programs and donor-financed projects, even when they are climate change sensitive (Agrawala 2005).

The various climate change impacts for Indonesia, discussed above, show that adaptation is vital across a whole range of development activities. It is particularly important for agriculture, coastal zones, water supplies, the health sector and urban areas, with water playing a cross-sectoral role in all these areas.

Successful adaptation in many instances simply means 'doing things better'. For instance, farmers are best able to adapt to changed agricultural conditions if they are given the best possible information and technical support, and the freedom to choose their own crops. Unencumbered markets for agricultural products are needed to provide the right price signals for supply to respond to market imbalances, and flexibility in land use is needed to allow the switch to the production systems best suited to changed climatic conditions. At the same time it is important to provide a social safety net to cushion people against the hardship caused by events such as droughts and floods. All these factors would generally benefit development even in the absence of climate change.

In other instances, climate proofing requires defensive investments that impose additional costs without appearing to offer much or any short-term gain. Examples would include strengthening physical infrastructure such as coastal installations, dams, roads and so forth. In such cases, developing countries may need to seek increased aid funding from donors.

Above all, adaptation to climate change is an exercise in improved risk management, as climate change adds a dimension of risk to many investments and economic activities. Provision of the best available information about the likely impacts of climate change is therefore critical.

Given the pervasive nature of climate impacts, it is imperative that climate change is 'mainstreamed' into decision making across sectors and across the range of governments. Issues as diverse as poverty alleviation, community development, spatial planning, food security, infrastructure maintenance, disease control, urban planning and disaster management must all be readdressed from the perspective of climate change. The challenge is to 'climate proof' development planning. The impact of climate change on the economy and on human development needs to be properly assessed and mapped out. Adaptation strategies then need to be integrated into plans and budgets, at both the national and local levels. Poverty reduction efforts need to be scaled up in areas especially affected by climate change, and additional investment is needed to reduce the risk of disasters in those areas.

These efforts need to be closely integrated with the efforts of communities and households. They, after all, have had long experience of adaptation — often with measures that have been practised for many centuries. People in flood-prone areas have long built their houses on stilts and many continue to do so, even if they use more modern materials such as concrete pillars and corrugated iron roofs. In areas vulnerable to landslides, people have always built strong retaining walls. Farmers exposed to drought have learned to diversify their sources of income, cultivate drought-resistant crops and optimize the use of scarce water — or even migrate temporarily in search of work elsewhere.

4   GROWING IN THE GREENHOUSE: REDUCING EMISSIONS WHILE ADVANCING DEVELOPMENT

Indonesia is a major emitter of greenhouse gases. The main source of emissions is land-use change and forestry, in particular deforestation and the related emissions from peat lands, which decay or are burned after being drained. According to one set of estimates for the late 1990s, Indonesia's land-related emissions are so great that the country is estimated to be the third largest emitter of greenhouse gases globally behind the United States and China, accounting for over 7 per cent of global emissions (Baumert, Herzog and Pershing 2005). But there is considerable uncertainty around emissions from deforestation and especially peat lands. It appears that deforestation rates are falling and there is debate over estimates of peat soil emissions, so future updates of these numbers may show significantly lower emissions levels.

Although Indonesia is ranked third in total emissions from all sources, its ranking falls to fourteenth when land-use change is excluded, and twentieth when carbon dioxide from fossil fuel burning alone is considered. In terms of emissions per person, Indonesia is well below the global average when emissions from land-use change are excluded.

Curtailing the growth in land-use change and fossil fuel emissions while maintaining high levels of growth is a long-term challenge for Indonesia. The international community now expects all major emitters to make efforts to cut emissions. This presents opportunities for Indonesia to attract international financing and support for investment in cleaner technologies and more efficient equipment.

Fossil Fuel Emissions

The largest component in greenhouse gas emissions globally is carbon dioxide from the burning of coal, oil and gas. Indonesia's fossil fuel emissions account for only a little over 1 per cent of the world total (Baumert, Herzog and Pershing 2005) but they are rising rapidly. In 2005 they were two and a half times greater than in 1990 and have grown slightly faster than those of China over that period. For the world as a whole, the rise since 1990 is about one-third.

Emissions from the burning of fossil fuels will drive Indonesia's future emissions growth. Energy consumption is rising roughly in line with overall economic activity, and a rising share of that energy is from coal, the cheapest source of energy for power generation and industrial use. More plants of average efficiency are planned, using low-grade, high-carbon coal (Narjoko and Jotzo 2007). The reasons are economic. Indonesia has plentiful, easily accessible coal reserves, and coal is the cheapest fuel for electric power generation and some heavy industries. It is more profitable for Indonesia to export its gas to the markets of East Asia than to sell it domestically. Investment in renewables suffers from high up-front costs and long payback periods. The latter is a particular problem when investors feel uncertainty about future laws and regulations in Indonesia.

Yet there are opportunities for Indonesia to follow a lower carbon path. The options include the use of more efficient, energy-saving equipment; greater use of gas rather than oil or coal; an expansion of renewable energy sources such as geothermal and hydropower; and, more controversially, the resurrection of plans to produce biofuels on a large scale (Basri and Patunru 2006). Nuclear power also remains under discussion, although safety and security concerns as well as its prohibitive costs would seem to rule this option out in practice.

The common feature of most low emissions options is that they are more expensive than the high emissions alternatives. In order for them to be taken in preference to the cheaper but more highly emitting alternatives, the international community would need to support Indonesia and other developing countries in these cleaner investment choices. The beginnings of an international 'carbon finance' scheme to support cleaner investment in developing countries were made under the Kyoto Protocol's Clean Development Mechanism, but this would need to be scaled up substantially to have a significant impact.

Deforestation

In line with its development status, eastern Indonesia as defined in this book has relatively low levels of energy use and, consequently, emissions. But the region also has vast forest resources at risk of being converted to other uses, potentially releasing very large quantities of carbon in the process.

Deforestation is thought to account for almost 20 per cent of total global greenhouse gas emissions, with Indonesia and Brazil the largest sources. When land is cleared, carbon stored in trees and in biomass below the ground is released into the atmosphere as carbon dioxide. This occurs through accidental or deliberately lit fires, through the decomposition of debris on site or through the more delayed decomposition of wood and wood products. Tropical forests are often converted for minimal economic gain relative to the amount of carbon dioxide released, if emissions are valued at the prices paid in emerging carbon markets in developed countries (Chomitz 2006).

The drainage of peat lands and subsequent fires and decomposition is an important factor in overall emissions. Many of Indonesia's forests grow in peat lands or other areas where the soil contains high levels of carbon-rich organic matter. When left undisturbed in their anaerobic form, peat lands are sinks and reservoirs of carbon dioxide but a source of methane (CH_4). Drainage of peat lands stops methane emissions but significantly increases carbon emissions through decomposition of the peat when exposed to air. Fires in drained swampland can burn for months and release extremely large quantities of carbon dioxide. Fires in peat lands in Kalimantan and Sumatra have been a major source of carbon dioxide emissions (Page et al. 2002) ; they have also been a big factor in the infamous 'Asian haze' affecting Indonesia's northern neighbours.

The fires of 1997–98 are estimated to have affected nearly 12 million hectares of land, including close to 4 million hectares of lowland and montane forest and over 2 million hectares of peat and swamp forest; the rest was agricultural land (3.5 million hectares), plantations and estates, and grasslands (Tacconi, Moore and Kaimowitz 2007). Kalimantan was the worst affected island, followed by Sumatra and Papua. Fires in Papua are estimated to have affected 1 million hectares of land, including 0.4 million hectares each of lowland/upland forest and peat/swamp forest. The causes of the fires were varied. Recent research suggests that the initial widespread perception that smallholders' agricultural practices were to blame is wrong; instead, it appears that large-scale land clearing following deforestation for land development was mainly to blame (Murdiyarso and Adiningsih 2007). Fires are often used to clear land, and in this case the dry El Niño conditions helped spread the fires.

Forest management is a problematic area in Indonesia. According to the latest estimate, based on Landsat imagery, of the 124 million hectares declared part of the Indonesian forest estate (*kawasan hutan*), only 94 million hectares remained forested in 2005 (Ministry of Forestry 2005). Indonesia has one of the highest rates of deforestation in the world. Almost all of the lowland forests of Sulawesi have been cleared. Lowland forests are becoming scarce in Sumatra and may largely disappear in Kalimantan within the next decade. Papua's forests are possibly the only ones that remain largely intact — but possibly not for long as pressures mount.

Papua is the largest Indonesian province but has the smallest population of all provinces. Around 2 million people inhabit an area of 42 million hectares. It is thought that around 30 million hectares is forested. Of this, more than half has been designated production forest, making it available for commercial use (Anggraeni 2006). Over 60 per cent of Papua is classified as lowland rainforest (Cannon 2006). Around half of this is zoned as production forest and 37 per cent as conservation forest. Because of the altitude and slope of the lands on which they lie, over 90 per cent of the mountain forests of Papua are classified as watershed protection forest. Around 56 per cent of mangroves but only 19 per cent of the southern swamp forests are zoned for conservation. The challenge is to enforce conservation in the areas so declared and, if possible, expand the area of conservation forests.

Policies to Reduce Deforestation

Contemporary forestry policy in Indonesia embraces the concept of resource sustainability. However, what looks good on paper is far less encouraging in reality — unsustainable forestry practices have been the norm rather than the exception. Timber production far exceeds the nationally imposed logging quota because of rampant illegal logging. Moreover, the reforestation effort is far from adequate even though timber concession holders are supposedly responsible for financing reforestation and forest rehabilitation within their concession areas. Forest and land rehabilitation efforts under the current decentralized regime are also discouraging (Resosudarmo 2007).

But there may be some light at the end of the tunnel. On 26 April 2007, the governors of Aceh, Papua and West Papua declared that they were 'committed to a joint policy of environmentally friendly, sustainable economic development, and reduction of greenhouse gas emissions from deforestation (RED) targeted at reducing poverty, protecting community rights over natural resources, stimulating employment, and attracting investment'. This was in recognition of 'the important role that Indonesia plays in global carbon emissions and the overwhelming contribution made by deforestation and land degradation' (Governors of Aceh and Papua 2007).

In the declaration, Governor Barnabas Suebu of Papua and Governor Ataturi of West Papua state their commitment to: (1) recognize, respect and develop the forest ownership rights of the local community, especially customary (*adat*) communities, as stipulated by the Special Autonomy Law for Papua; (2) tackle land conflict by securing community access to forests; (3) prohibit log exports that do not benefit the people of both provinces; (4) accelerate home industry development and community forestry; (5) revoke the licences of some forest concession holders; (6) enforce the law by employing more forest rangers and police and by improving community awareness; and (7) explicitly acknowledge the role of Papua's forests in a low-carbon future — including by developing 'green' industries.

The reality remains, however, that without significant incentives for forest conservation and good forest management to counterbalance the economic incentives to convert land to other uses, many of Papua's forests are unlikely to survive. Such mechanisms are being devised as part of the ongoing UN climate negotiations, with many developed countries showing preparedness to invest in incentives to reduce deforestation in tropical countries. This might entail a global fund to pay for measures to avoid deforestation and degradation, or a mechanism to create tradable offsets for avoided deforestation.

Policies to reduce deforestation must take local conditions into account. For example, Indonesian government legislation calls for zero burning, but this may not be appropriate in all cases. A study of local fire management practices on the islands of Flores and Sumba shows that the local people depend on fire for their livelihoods (Tacconi and Ruchiat 2006). The fires are often lit intentionally to maintain the grasslands that local people use to sustain a variety of livelihood activities, such as cattle rearing, hunting and farming. Possible damage from such fires then needs to be balanced against the need to maintain local livelihoods.

Indonesian provinces that have not yet begun to exploit their natural forest resources on a large scale may be interested in carbon payments as an alternative to large-scale land conversion. The main difficulties will be working out how to channel financial resources from international sources to the local level so that those who actually make land-use decisions face the right incentives, and how to ensure that local communities benefit from protecting forests rather than losing out from diminished employment opportunities.

5 CONCLUSIONS

Climate change is perhaps the largest and most complex environmental challenge for development. This chapter has shown that the impacts of climate change could negate the progress of developmental efforts in many areas of Indonesia and eastern Indonesia. A combination of sea-level rise and changing hydrological cycle may affect already stretched supplies of water and food. Public health could suffer, and biological resources could be diminished.

Adapting to climate change—ideally, 'climate proofing' development—is necessary, and will require careful attention across the arms of government and across the range of donor activities. Adaptation will in some instances impose an additional burden, but in many others it will strengthen the general development effort.

Finally, Indonesia is a major greenhouse gas emitter, in particular because of deforestation. As a developing country, Indonesia needs to grow its economy. On the other hand, it faces increasing pressure from the international community to rein in its greenhouse gas emissions from such economic growth. The regions of eastern Indonesia are generally among the country's least developed. In the pursuit of economic growth and a better quality of life, eastern Indonesia needs to prepare for climate change. It may take a low or high emissions trajectory, depending in large part on the choices made today. In making the choice for a low greenhouse future, eastern Indonesia should call on the international community for financial and technical support. It is, after all, the international community that will reap the benefits of lower levels of climatic change.

REFERENCES

Agrawala (2005), *Bridge over Troubled Waters: Linking Climate Change and Development*, OECD, Paris.

Allen, G.R. and M. Adrim (2003), 'Coral Reef Fishes of Indonesia', *Zoological Studies*, 42: 1–72.

Amien, I. and E. Runtunuwu (2008), 'Impact of and Adaptation to Climate Change: Status and Application in Agriculture', paper presented at the

EEPSEA Climate Change and Southeast Asian Conference, Bali, 13–18 February.

Anggraeni, D. (2006), 'Patterns of Commercial and Industrial Resource Use in Papua', in A.J. Marshall and B.M. Beehler (eds), *The Ecology of Papua*, Periplus Editions, Singapore, 1,149–66.

Bappenas (Badan Perencanaan Pembangunan Nasional) (2003), *Indonesian Biodiversity Strategy and Action Plan*, Jakarta.

Basri, C. and A.A. Pantunru (2006), 'Survey of Recent Developments', *Bulletin of Indonesian Economic Studies*, 42(3): 295–319.

Baumert, K., T. Herzog and J. Pershing (2005), *Navigating the Numbers: Greenhouse Gas Data and International Climate Policy*, World Resources Institute, Washington DC.

Cannon, J.B. (2006), 'Natural Resource Economics of Papua', in A.J. Marshall and B.M. Beehler (eds), *The Ecology of Papua*, Periplus Editions, Singapore, pp. 1,167–98.

Chomitz, K.M. (2006), *At Loggerheads? Agricultural Expansion, Poverty Reduction, and Environment in the Tropical Forests*, World Bank, Washington DC.

Connolly, S.R., D.R. Bellwood and T.P. Hughes (2003), 'Indo-Pacific Biodiversity of Coral Reefs: Deviations from a Mid-domain Model', *Ecology*, 84(2): 178–90.

CRED (Centre for Research on the Epidemiology of Disasters) (2007), *International Disaster Database*, Brussels.

Djajadiningrat, S.T. (2008), 'Climate Change Mitigation and Adaptation in Indonesia: The Role of Environmental Economic Research', paper presented at the EEPSEA Climate Change and Southeast Asian Conference, Bali, 13–18 February.

Dutta, D. and S. Herath (2004), 'Trend of Floods in Asia and a Proposal for Flood Risk Management with Integrated River Basin Approach', in *Proceedings of the 2nd International Conference of Asia–Pacific Hydrology and Water Resources Association*, Volume I, Singapore, pp. 55–63.

Epstein, P.R., H.F. Diaz, S. Elias et al. (1998), 'Biological and Physical Signs of Climate Change: Focus on Mosquito-borne Disease', *Bulletin of the American Meteorological Society*, 78: 409–17.

Garnaut, R. (2008), *The Garnaut Climate Change Review*, Cambridge University Press, Melbourne, available at <http://www.garnautreview.org.au>.

Governors of Aceh and Papua (2007), *Deklarasi Gubernur Provinsi Nanggroe Aceh Darussalam, Papua dan Papua Barat mengenai Perubahan Iklim* [Declaration of the Governors of Aceh, Papua and West Papua on Climate Change], Nusa Dua Bali, 26 April.

IPCC (Intergovernmental Panel on Climate Change) (2007), *IPCC Fourth Assessment Report*, IPCC and Cambridge University Press, Geneva and Cambridge.

Irianto, G., Y. Sugianto and I. Amien (2004), *Dampak dan Adaptasi Perubahan Iklim, Status dan Aplikasinya di Sektor Pertanian* [Climate Change Impacts and Adaptation, Its State and Application in the Agricultural Sector], Departemen Pertanian, Jakarta.

Johns Hopkins University and Terangi (2003), *Coral Reef Education Database*, <http://www.terangi.or.id>.

Las, I. (2007), 'Kebijakan Litbang Pertanian Menghadapi Perubahan Iklim' [Policy on Climate Change, Research and Development Agency, Department of Agriculture], paper presented to the Working Group on Climate Anomalies at the Agricultural Impact of Climate Change: Anticipation Strategy and Adaptation Technology Meeting, 20 August, Bogor.

MacKinnon, K., G. Hatta, H. Halim and A. Mangalik (1996), *The Ecology of Kalimantan*, Periplus Editions, Singapore.

McCulloch, N. and P.T. Timmer (2008), 'Rice Policy in Indonesia: A Special Issue', *Bulletin of Indonesian Economic Studies*, 44(1): 33–44.

McMichael, A.J., R.E. Woodruff and S. Hales (2006), 'Climate Change and Human Health: Present and Future Risks', *Lancet*, 367(9,513): 859–69.

Merle Orstom, J. (1998), *South Pacific Climate Variability and its Impact on Low-lying Islands*, UNESCO, Paris.

Ministry of Forestry (2005), *Forestry Statistics of Indonesia*, Jakarta, available at <http://www.dephut.go.id>, accessed 20 January 2007.

Murdiyarso, D. and E. Adiningsih (2007), 'Climate Anomalies, Indonesian Vegetation Fires and Terrestrial Carbon Emissions', *Mitigation and Adaptation Strategies for Global Change*, 12(1): 101–12.

Narjoko, D.A. and F. Jotzo (2007), 'Survey of Recent Developments', *Bulletin of Indonesian Economic Studies*, 43(2): 143–69.

Naylor R.L., D.S. Battisti, D.J. Vimont, W.P. Falcon and M.B. Burke (2007), 'Assessing Risks of Climate Variability and Climate Change for Indonesian Rice Agriculture', *Proceedings of the National Academy of Sciences of the United States of America*, 104(19): 7,752–7.

Page, S.E., F. Siegert, J.O. Rieley, H.-D.V. Boehm, A. Jaya and S. Limin (2002), 'The Amount of Carbon Released from Peat and Forest Fires in Indonesia during 1997', *Nature*, 420: 61–5.

PEACE (PT Pelangi Energi Abadi Citra Enviro) (2007), *Indonesia and Climate Change: Current Status and Policies*, PT Pelangi Energi Abadi Citra Enviro for World Bank and DFID, Jakarta.

Ratag, M. (2007), 'Perubahan Iklim Indonesia Periode 1900–2000' [Climate Change in Indonesia: 1900–2000], unpublished report, Bureau of Meteorology and Geophysics, Jakarta.

Resosudarmo, I.A.P. (2007), 'Has Indonesia's Decentralization Led to Improved Forestry Governance? A Case Study of Bulungan and Kutai Barat Districts, East Kalimantan', PhD thesis, Australian National University, Canberra.

Setiasih, N. (2006), 'Bali Barat National Park (BBNP) Coral Monitoring Report', Friends of the Reef Project, WWF Indonesia.

Shatwell, J. (2005), 'Mysterious Bird of Paradise: Lost and Found', available at <http://wwww.conservation.org/xp/frontlines/species>, accessed 20 March 2006.

State Ministry of Environment (2003), *National Strategy Study on CDM in the Forestry Sector*, Jakarta.

Stern, N. (2006), *Stern Review on the Economics of Climate Change*, UK Treasury and Cabinet Office, London.

Supriatna, J. (1999), 'The Irian Jaya Biodiversity Conservation Priority-setting Workshop, Final Report', Conservation International, Washington DC.

Susandi, A., Y. Firdaus and I. Herlianti (2008), 'Impact of Climate Change on Indonesian Sea Level Rise with Reference to Its Socioeconomic Impact', paper presented at the EEPSEA Climate Change and Southeast Asian Conference, Bali, 13–18 February.

Sutardi (2006), *Penyelenggaraan Penanggulangan Bencana dan Partisipasi Masyarakat* [Disaster Mitigation Implementation and Public Participation], Department of Public Works, Jakarta.

Tacconi, L. and Y. Ruchiat (2006), 'Livelihoods, Fire and Policy in Eastern Indonesia', *Singapore Journal of Tropical Geography*, 27(1): 67–81.

Tacconi, L., P.F. Moore and D. Kaimowitz (2007), 'Fires in Tropical Forests—What Is Really the Problem? Lessons from Indonesia', *Mitigation and Adaptation Strategies for Global Change*, 12(1): 55–66.

Wiriadiwangsa, D. (2005), 'Pranata Mangsa, Masih Penting untuk Pertanian' [Traditional Calendar, Still Essential to Agriculture], *Tabloid Sinar Tani*, 9–15 March.

PART III

Conflict, Local Development and Health

12 MALUKU: THE LONG ROAD TO RECOVERY

Craig Thorburn

1 INTRODUCTION: AFTER THE STORM

On 27 February 2002, two weeks after the signing of the Malino Peace Accord II (Perjanjian Malino II),[1] a few hundred young Muslim and Christian men from the island of Haruku — one of the tiny Lease islands east of Ambon — rode together into Ambon and began marching through the town, disregarding the barricades that divided the war-torn city into 'red' and 'white' zones. They sang nationalistic songs, hugged spectators and urged them to join the procession. Police and military personnel joined in as the crowd circled its way towards the governor's office. Later that day, Governor Saleh Latuconsina told the cheering crowd, 'From now on, Ambon is free from conflict' (Böhm 2005; *Jakarta Post* 2002a).[2]

Ambon remained partitioned for a few more months, and there continued to be occasional bomb explosions and sniper attacks. The most serious threat to peace came in April–May 2004, when rallies in celebration of the anniversary of the Republic of South Maluku sparked several days of fighting and arson in Ambon. But the people and government of Maluku had clearly had enough, and peace continued to deepen and solidify.

---

1 The first accord was an attempt to end the conflict in Poso, Central Sulawesi.

2 The governor later moderated his remarks, urging the crowd to take heed of any malevolent persons and calling for all parties to begin surrendering their weapons. The conflict continued to sputter and flare for several more months, but this day is widely considered to be a turning point — the day that peace began.

This chapter examines aspects of the conflict in Maluku, analyses factors contributing to the spread and perpetuation of the conflict, and looks at how it finally ended. This is followed by an examination of socio-political trends and developments in the province since the cessation of hostilities. The problems of recently returned or not yet returned refugee families merit special attention, along with the lingering segregation and tensions that still plague communities in many parts of the province. The chapter concludes with a discussion of attempts – by regional government agencies and various civil society actors – to revive and reform customary village (*negeri*) forms of government in an effort to build a more stable and resilient society.

Maluku was split into two provinces, Maluku and North Maluku, in 1999.[3] The fortunes of the two provinces have diverged considerably in the ensuing years (see Chapter 4). This chapter focuses solely on the new province of Maluku, which comprised the Residentie der Zuid Molukken during colonial times and the districts (*kabupaten*) of Central and Southeast Maluku during the post-independence and New Order eras.

2   THE HISTORICAL, ECONOMIC AND CULTURAL ROOTS OF CONFLICT IN MALUKU

Nutmeg and cloves have brought trade to Maluku since at least 300 BC. The 'Spice Islands' were known to Chinese, Javanese, Indian and Arab traders long before the Portuguese 'discovered' Maluku in 1498. From the fourteenth century, the Malukan spice trade was dominated by powerful Islamic sultanates on Ternate, Tidore and Djailolo (Halmahera). It was Maluku that Columbus was searching for when he stumbled on the Americas in 1492. Waves of European merchants and missionaries – first the Portuguese, then the Spaniards and finally the Dutch – attempted to assert monopoly control over the East Indies spice trade. They converted many of the natives to the Catholic and Protestant faiths. This missionary activity was supported by both the Dutch East Indies Company (VOC) and, later, the colonial government of the Netherlands East Indies as a means of countering the political power of the sultans. The attitude of the Dutch colonists towards Islam was that it bred fanaticism and rebellion, and thus constituted a threat to their commercial and state-building

3   Undang-Undang No. 46 Tahun 1999 tentang Pembentukan Provinsi Maluku Utara, Kabupaten Buru, dan Kabupaten Maluku Tenggara Barat (Basic Law No. 46 of 1999 on the Formation of the Province of North Maluku and the Districts of Buru and West Southeast Maluku.)

interests.[4] Historians have noted, however, that Islam tended to spread more rapidly in areas where the Dutch were attempting to increase their influence (Ricklefs 1981; Andaya 1993). Today the province is nearly evenly divided between Muslims and Christians.

The spice trade declined in importance, and the VOC monopoly collapsed into bankruptcy in 1799. By this time, Dutch attention had shifted from Maluku and spices to a plantation-based economy in Java and Sumatra. During the Dutch colonial period (1799–1942), Maluku became a supplier of military manpower to fight for the Dutch against popular uprisings in Java and Sumatra, and of civil servants to manage colonial affairs in Maluku and Papua (both of these drawn almost entirely from the Christian population).

During World War II, Maluku was taken by the Japanese in the first two months of 1942, and recaptured by the Allies in 1945. When Indonesia declared its independence in 1945, many Malukan officers and soldiers of the Royal Dutch Indies Army (KNIL) sided with the Dutch-sponsored Federation of East Indonesian States (NIT) and fought against the republican forces. After Indonesia finally gained its independence in 1949, a group of civilian politicians and KNIL members declared an independent Republic of South Maluku (RMS). The republic was quickly quashed, and in 1950 more than 40,000 soldiers, supporters and their families were evacuated to the Netherlands. The Jakarta government has never forgotten this disloyalty, which continues to colour the politics of the province to the present day.

Colonial officials and missionaries placed great importance on education, and even today Maluku has the highest literacy rate in Indonesia — over 97 per cent. This has not, however, translated into opportunities for economic advancement. The province is rich in natural resources, including forests, minerals and natural gas. Most importantly for both its people and Indonesia as a whole, it also has some of the most productive fishing grounds in the world. Since colonial times, Maluku's economy has been bifurcated into two distinct spheres. Subsistence agriculture and fishing with small-scale trade characterize the livelihoods of most of its people, existing alongside large-scale exploitation of the province's abundant forest and marine resources. The mixed subsistence lifestyle practised by most Malukans combines gardening, hunting and harvesting of forest products, fishing and cash crop farming. Sago and cassava are the main staples, with coconut, cloves and nutmeg grown for market.

---

4 A quote from van Hoëvell (1890: 121), in which he describes Malukan Muslims as 'sly, full of tricks, disloyal, sneaky, quiet and retiring, but cunning and deceitful, mischievous and prideful, and too lazy to do work', typifies the attitudes of colonial civil servants.

Primary exports from the province include plywood, frozen prawns and tuna. Less than 5 per cent of the province's population is employed in the industrial sector (BPS Provinsi Maluku 2005). Local communities derive few benefits from these export industries, and increasingly find that their subsistence livelihoods and commodity production practices are being negatively impacted by overfishing, forest mismanagement and reduced access to hunting, fishing and gathering grounds (Topatimasang 2005; Novaczek and Palyama 1999). As well, trade in the province is largely dominated by non-native groups: Sino-Indonesians control most of the larger enterprises, while local markets are dominated by Buginese, Butonese and Makassarese migrants (commonly referred to collectively as BBM) from the island of Sulawesi.

Maluku is known among scholars and the general public for its array of customary social institutions and structures, particularly *pela* (alliances of friendship and mutual assistance between two or more villages) and *sasi* (spatial and temporal prohibitions on harvesting crops, cutting wood or gathering products from the forest, tidal zone or village-controlled sea, and on untoward behaviour such as cursing, slander, harassing women, and playing loud music).[5] Many of these customary institutions, which have imbued Malukan social structures and regulated relations between people, communities and the human and non-human worlds, have weakened during recent decades due to a variety of factors.

3   OVERVIEW OF THE MALUKU CONFLICT

Fighting broke out in Ambon on 19 January 1999, the Muslim holy day of Idul Fitri. An argument between a Christian public transport driver and at least one Muslim passenger deteriorated into a wide-ranging brawl that escalated into days of mob violence. Within hours of the original encounter, Christian and Muslim groups were attacking neighbourhoods throughout the city, inflicting heavy loss of life and property. In the first few weeks of rioting, much of the city centre of Ambon was reduced to smoking rubble. The fighting spread almost immediately to the nearby islands of Haruku, Seram, Saparua and Manipa, as natives of those islands fled the Ambon fighting, taking with them rumours about the plans of one side (Christian or Muslim) to evict the other group from the province (ICG 2000).

---

5   On *pela*, see Bartels (1977, 2003). On *sasi*, see von Benda-Beckmann, von Benda-Beckmann and Brouwer (1995), Thorburn (2000) and Novaczek et al. (2001).

Ethnic origin was a factor in the first days of fighting, with anger directed at the Muslim BBM migrants.[6] But as most of these migrants fled to their areas of origin in South and Southeast Sulawesi, the fighting quickly spread to local Christian and Muslim communities. Security forces stationed in Ambon were ill-prepared to deal with the violence, despite the rumours that had been swirling for months that various groups were planning to use the religious holidays to launch an offensive. A few months before, hundreds of ethnic Ambonese gang members (*preman*) had been 'deported' to Ambon after a gang fight over control of the entertainment districts in West Jakarta had escalated into mob violence. This, in effect, had exported the turf war between rival Ambonese gangs and their respective backers to Ambon, where it was transformed into religious violence (Human Rights Watch 1999).

Local politicians seemed unable to grasp the seriousness of the situation and did little to defuse it. With no 'official' version of events forthcoming, inflammatory rumour and innuendo ruled (ICG 2000). The military was ineffective in stopping violence during the first 18 months and, indeed, contributed to it: their weapons and tactics under 'shoot-to-kill' orders surely increased the death toll, while some units condoned or actively supported the actions of their coreligionists (Goss 2004).

A cyclical pattern of fighting took hold, increasing in intensity over time. Lulls were followed by new attacks and reprisals. The government of newly elected president Abdurrahman Wahid, preoccupied with an economic crisis and the problems of political transition and fearful of a Muslim backlash, failed to intervene decisively. Wahid did not visit Ambon until he had been president for nearly two months and he was widely criticized for remarking that the Ambonese should sort out their problems themselves (*Asiaweek* 2000). Throughout 1999 violence continued to spread to other parts of the province, first to Buru in Central Maluku, then to Kei and other parts of Southeast Maluku, then finally to North Maluku.[7] Mediation and the segregation of Christian and Muslim communities still managed to create periods of uneasy peace, punctuated by flare-ups and surprise attacks. Over time, both sides became pro-

---

6 The migrants had been arriving in Maluku for decades but their numbers grew rapidly in the 1970s and 1980s. They were estimated to make up about one-third of the Ambon municipality in the 1990s.

7 The province of North Maluku was established in September 1999. Although the violence there was certainly influenced by events in the south, it had its own roots in the resettlement 25 years earlier of a Muslim community in a Christian district, and also an age-old rivalry between the two (Islamic) sultanates of Ternate and Tidore, as the two groups vied for influence in the government of the newly formed province. Fighting there took on its own character and dynamic, and later required a separate peace negotiation.

gressively better armed and organized in the practices of terror. By early 2000, many parts of the province approached a state of civil war (ICG 2000).

The situation took a dramatic turn in mid-2000 when a Java-based fundamentalist Islamic militia, Laskar Jihad, sent several thousand fighters to Ambon to protect its Muslim brethren. With its superior arms and training, and logistical support from elements within the military, Laskar Jihad's arrival escalated the conflict and began to reverse the relative fortunes of the protagonists, particularly in Ambon where Christian forces had made some territorial gains.

In June 2000, President Wahid declared a state of civil emergency, and by July there were 14,000 troops in Maluku. The military established a Joint Battalion (Batalyon Gabungan, or Yon Gab), a centralized mobile reserve drawn from elite forces of the three services. In a context where Muslim militias and Laskar Jihad were gaining ground, the battalion usually found itself confronting Muslim forces and soon gained a pro-Christian reputation (ICG 2002). It effectively crippled Laskar Jihad in several confrontations in 2001, and probably contributed to a decline in the fighting in the province. However, credible allegations about the brutality of some of its members tarnished its reputation and provoked Muslim antagonism (ICG 2002). In November 2001 the battalion was disbanded and replaced by army Special Forces (Kopassus).

Fighting continued for more than three years, claiming over 5,000 lives and displacing more than 700,000 people — roughly one-third of the original province's total population of 2.1 million (Böhm 2005).

The Indonesian government, led by Coordinating Minister for People's Prosperity Jusuf Kalla, mediated a peace agreement in the South Sulawesi town of Malino. The Malino Peace Accord was signed by 35 Muslim and 35 Christian leaders on 12 February 2002. The accord was initially rejected by certain parties. Sporadic bomb blasts, stonings and sniper attacks threatened to disrupt the Malino peace process. These included a vicious attack by black-masked assailants armed with guns and grenades on the Christian village of Soya and a bomb explosion outside a popular restaurant in the Christian section of Ambon, both in April 2002. Other bombs went off in Ambon's Mardika market (in July) and the Lapangan Merdeka soccer stadium (in September). The provincial government stepped up its efforts to 'socialize' the accord, and numerous public organizations spoke out and demonstrated for an end to hostilities.

The civil emergency was finally rescinded at the ceremony to swear in the newly elected governor, Karel Alberth Ralahalu, on 15 September 2003. The next serious threat to peace came in April 2004, prompted by (illegal) ceremonies marking the 54th anniversary of the RMS independence movement. Police hauled down 51 RMS flags. Marches were met by crowds throwing stones, and police began firing on crowds. A curfew was imposed and 200 crack mobile police forces (Brimob) were dispatched from Jakarta. Over the next two weeks, gunfire and explosions killed at least 38 people and wounded hundreds more. Another 536 houses were destroyed during the rioting, along with one church, one mosque and several government, NGO and UN offices. Many of the 38 victims of this outbreak were killed by sniper fire, supporting the widely held view that the latest round of violence—like so many before it—had been 'provoked' (ICG 2004a). The violence was confined to the city of Ambon, and by mid-May had completely subsided. There have been no major outbreaks of violence since those frightening two weeks in April–May 2004.

How and Why Did the Conflict Spread?

The preceding narrative raises some vexing questions, about how a conflict of this nature could spread and escalate, and what contributed to finally bringing about an end to the hostilities.

Although the conflict was portrayed by politicians and the media as a religious war and was largely fought along sectarian lines, Indonesian scholar activists point out that the true basis of the violence was simmering resentment over the impoverishment of the province and its people amid the wholesale pillage of its abundant natural resources (Aditjondro 2001a; Marut 2004; Topatimasang 2005). Clearly control of resources and benefit streams played a central role in the conflict. On the islands of Seram, Ambon and Buru, attacks by mysterious bands of marauders in rural areas often coincided with the clove harvest. Longstanding rivalries between neighbouring villages over boundaries and resources led to violent conflict, prompting Bartels (2003: 141) to claim that 'much of the fighting ... may only be fought under the pretext of religious differences but is in actuality a struggle for the increasing scarce resources of villages—land'. He underscores this point by noting that Christian villages in Saparua frequently clashed over boundaries during the post-independence period, and that one violent battle on the island of Ambon in January 2000 in which three people were killed pitted the residents of Wakal against those of Hitu—both Muslim villages. The latter incident took place at the height of the Christian–Muslim violence in the area, but here boundary disputes superseded any sense of religious solidarity. Other Muslim-on-Muslim violence was reported in Seram in 2001 (Böhm 2005).

Meanwhile, most of the large industries in Maluku—predominantly fisheries and timber—continued to operate despite the chaos. Many of these businesses have military officers as silent partners, or pay protection fees. Giant logging companies such as Barito Pacific and Djayanti Group took advantage of the uncertain political and security situation in the province to secure small to medium-scale timber harvesting permits (IPK) through chicanery and intimidation (Tebiari 2006).

Maluku's economy essentially became a war economy, with members of the security forces playing the dominant role. Everywhere, illegal taxes and fees were levied, and people needing to travel from one district to the other could do so only under the protection of the security forces (ICG 2000; Tapol 2002). In 'secure' villages, soldiers often forced villagers to sell their commodities (such as cloves and resin (*damar*)) through appointed traders (Tebiari 2006). Aditjondro (2001a) traces the links between elements within the Indonesian armed forces (TNI), Christian and Muslim militia leaders, and conglomerates and corporations with close links to the Soeharto family and the state political party, Golkar.

Various theories have been put forward to explain the military's role in inciting and prolonging the conflict. These range from mundane pecuniary interests — opportunities to levy taxes and fees on businesses, sell or lease weapons, provide protection and engage in lucrative illegal businesses (ICG 2002)[8] — to more sinister conspiracy theories about 'rogue elements' and 'entrenched interests' intent on both derailing the reform process and discrediting civilian rule and democracy (Human Rights Watch 1999; Tapol 2002; Aditjondro 2000, 2001b). Evidence put forward for these theories includes the simultaneous and coordinated nature of many of the attacks, which often coincided with increased calls in Jakarta for investigation into Soeharto-related corruption, or international pressure to prosecute human rights violations in East Timor (HPCR 2001). President Wahid frequently complained that disgruntled generals and Jakarta politicians were using the Maluku conflict as a vehicle to undermine his reform agenda (Balowski 2000).

It is unlikely, however, that outside instigation could have provoked and sustained the bellicosity between Malukan Christian and Muslim communities without there being fertile ground for it to flourish. Maluku, with its renowned *pela* tradition,[9] had long been held up by Indonesian politicians and the media as an example of religious tolerance and har-

---

8　About 75 per cent of the Indonesian military's budget is met by informal means and the TNI could not operate if it did not take such payments (IGC 2000). In conflict areas, this proportion increases to as much as 90 per cent (Tapol 2002).

9　*Pela* is a feature of the Ambonese cultural area — that is, Ambon–Lease and West Seram. It is a specific arrangement between particular villages, not a generalized peace pact across the whole of Malukan society, as often characterized in the popular media (Bartels 2003).

mony. How could Indonesia's Shangri-La descend so quickly into paroxysms of bloodletting and retribution?

Several reasons have been put forward, including the effects of demographic change and socio-economic competition, the politicization of ethnicity and religion, the manipulation of religious identity to advance particular political agendas and the 'Indonesianization' of the Ambonese social system. Surely any explanation must include elements of each of these factors.

Discussion of ethnicity, religion, race and class was systematically suppressed during the New Order years, together with political representation on the basis of ethnic or religious identity. This is not to say, of course, that these factors did not play an important role in national or local politics throughout the Soeharto presidency; it simply means that it was forbidden to discuss them. During his first decades in power, Soeharto strategically isolated Islamists by promoting Christian and *abangan* (nominal and syncretist Muslim Javanese) military officers and technocrats (Kingsbury 2005). Later, faced with a rising tide of criticism and calls for reform, he changed course and began to embrace more 'green' (that is, Islamic) politicians and generals. Throughout the 1990s, Indonesia witnessed an upsurge in the social and political profile of Islam (Ramage 1995; Hefner 2000).

The politics and economy of Maluku have been dominated by Christians since colonial times. In the city of Ambon, over one-quarter of the Christian population depends on employment in the civil service or government contracts (Klinken 1999). Family, clan and religious affiliations all figure prominently in gaining employment and contracts. Ambon (and Maluku) is widely perceived as being a Christian society, and many local elites certainly define themselves in that way. But in fact, Muslims now represent a slim majority in the province. This is due in large part to migration, both outward migration of upwardly mobile Christian Malukans and in-migration of Muslims — primarily the spontaneous migration of large numbers of poor landless people from the provinces of South and Southeast Sulawesi, but also of smaller numbers of government-sponsored transmigrants from Java.

From 1992 through to the end of the conflict, the governor of Maluku was a local Muslim. An anonymous pamphlet circulated during the early months of the conflict accused then governor Saleh Latuconsina of replacing 'all 38' of the province's top civil servants with Muslims. He vehemently denied this, but the charge was later repeated by President Wahid, who frequently criticized the governor for his alleged 'Islamic nepotism' (Goss 2004).

Certainly the political and economic fortunes of some of the province's Muslims did advance during the last two decades of the twentieth century, with a concomitant eclipse of the power and wealth of some Christians. In Ambon and other parts of Central Maluku, Christians were displaced from many sectors of the economy by more competitive immigrants. For example, BBM migrants came to dominate the transport and small trade sectors in Ambon and most other towns. Ambonese tend to prefer salaried jobs, and did not compete successfully in the more informal sectors of the economy. There was, as well, a clear 'affirmative action' policy to increase the number of Muslims in the public service (though not to the extent described in the anonymous pamphlet mentioned above).

The successive colonisers — Portuguese, Dutch, Japanese — all manipulated Malukan Muslims and Christians and set them against each other. These machinations involved the local elite, and there is little evidence that they ever instilled deep religious hatred in the general Malukan population (Bartels 2003). Indeed, Muslims and Christians in Maluku often closed ranks to ally themselves against the foreign intruders who were attempting to impose monopoly control on the spice trade. The roots of many intervillage *pela* alliances have their roots in this struggle (Bartels 1977, 2003).

During World War II, the occupying Japanese forces frequently favoured local Muslim leaders and communities, treating Christian Malukans as supporters of degenerate Western values (Chauvel 1990). After the war, many Christians accused the Muslims of collaboration. During the NIT and RMS periods, opposition to Indonesian independence was not entirely confined to Maluku's Christians. Although members of the Dutch-educated Christian elite certainly comprised the majority of the Ambonese nationalist 'Black Dutch' who longed for a return of their erstwhile colonial masters, supporters of the RMS also included a number of traditional (*adat*) Muslim leaders. It was only much later, after this generation of traditional, somewhat colonialist, *adat* leaders died out, that young Malukan Muslims began to perceive the political and economic advantages of aligning themselves with Soeharto's New Order system. It was during this period that the RMS came to be viewed as a Christian endeavour, sometimes sarcastically referred to as the 'Republic of Christian Maluku' (Republik Maluku Serani) (Bartels 2003).

Many authors have asserted that *adat* institutions have for centuries ensured the peaceful coexistence of Maluku's Christian and Muslim communities (Cooley 1962; Bartels 1977, 2003; Turner 2003). Many *pela* pacts link Christian and Muslim villages, representing an enduring and inviolable brotherhood between all peoples of the partner villages. Bartels (2003) points out that although *pela* alliances between Christian and Muslim villages are commonplace, there are no purely Muslim *pela*. These probably existed long ago but have fallen into disuse as Islamic concepts of brotherhood of the broader Islamic community (*ummat*) supplanted the need to maintain special ties between villages. Christian villages, on the other hand, tend to use *adat* rather than a common religion to establish formal ties with other villages.

Two factors have contributed to the weakening of these *adat* institutions: religious purification, and the 'Indonesianization' of Malukan social structures. Throughout Indonesia syncretism has slowly been giving up ground to more fundamentalist interpretations of Islamic and Christian dogma, with Maluku no exception to this trend. On the Christian side, when the Protestant Church of Maluku became independent of the Dutch Reformed Church in 1935, indigenous church leaders continued the attacks made by their European predecessors on *adat*, and there were constant tensions between Christian and *adat* leaders in the villages. These intensified after World War II when groups of young Christian ministers went abroad to study at theological schools in Europe and the United States. These young men returned determined to purify Malukan Christianity by ridding it of customs contrary to Christian beliefs (Bartels 2003). Some church leaders attempted to differentiate between good *adat* (that is, *pela*) and bad *adat*, particularly ancestor worship and idolatry. They slowly succeeded in baptizing many *adat* rituals so that these were conducted in the church and dominated by Christian prayers.

Concurrently, the Islamic leadership emphasized pure Islam at the expense of traditional *adat* beliefs. During the colonial era, Malukan Muslim communities were quite isolated, and Islamic beliefs were deeply intertwined with *adat* beliefs and practices. After independence, the *ummat* concept of universal Islamic brotherhood was extended to all Muslims, making Malukan Muslims more receptive to Islamic ideas and less accepting of other religions than the pre-independence indigenous Ambonese Muslims. Today, young Malukan Muslims embrace Islamic universalism over ethnic parochialism and see advantages in identifying as Indonesians and Muslims in an overwhelmingly Islamic Indonesian nation (Bartels 2003).

In addition to the religious efflorescence described above, the New Order era brought other profound changes to Malukan society. Foremost among these was the radical restructuring of village government, mandated by Law No. 5/1979 on Village Government. In an ingenious attempt to raze local customs and to standardize and rationalize local government, the 1979 law abolished the traditional system of village government based on *adat*, replacing it with a new, pan-Indonesian structure patterned on a Javanese system of village government.

The law incorporated village (*desa*) governments as the lowest tier in the country's territorial government structure. The village head (*kepala desa*) became a salaried employee of the national government, assisted in his job by a small staff that included a village secretary and a few section chiefs (*kepala urusan*). The law also mandated the establishment of village consultative councils (LMD) and village community resilience councils (LKMD) in each *desa*, respectively charged with 'conveying the aspirations of the *desa* community' and 'activating community participation to carry out development in a coordinated way'. The village territorial unit was standardized as well, with all *desa* adhering to minimum and maximum size and population criteria. This led in many cases to the consolidation of several settlements into a single *desa* unit, and in other cases to the subdivision of existing units into smaller *desa*.

Critics of the Village Government Law claimed that it diminished Indonesia's cultural diversity by peripheralizing or negating the autochthonous structures and customs that had developed over generations of intimate interaction between local peoples and their surrounding environment and neighbouring communities, replacing them with standardized forms based on an (idealized) model of Javanese village government (Moniaga 1993; Safa'at 1996). They stressed as well that under this structure village governments drew their authority and power from, and became accountable to, the central government rather than the local community. Traditional office holders were the guardians of *adat*, responsible for passing it on to future generations. The new village bureaucrats, on the other hand, had little interest in transmitting a tradition that was of little benefit to them, and that might even question their own legitimacy.

Some provinces, such as West Sumatra and Bali, attempted to retain aspects of customary local governance when they prepared implementing regulations for the 1979 law. This was not the case in Maluku. Provincial regulations on village government parroted the language of the national law, making no concessions for the rich array of institutions and practices that still prevailed in the province.[10] District and provincial officials did try to take existing leadership structures into account when appointing village government officials. *Raja* became *kepala desa*. Other *adat* functionaries, such as clan heads, village scribes and storytellers, war captains, guardians of the land and sea, and spirit mediums, took most of the other positions (secretary and section chiefs) within the new *desa* government, and staffed the new LMD and LKMD institutions. However, there was not a particularly good fit between the number and

---

10 Instruksi Guburnur Kepala Daerah Tingkat I Maluku Nomor Inst. 08/Gmal/1980 tentang Pelaksanaan Undang-Undang Nomor 5 Tahun 1979 dan Peraturan Pelaksanaannya di Provinsi Daerah Tingkat I Maluku, and Peraturan Daerah Provinsi Daerah Tingkat I Maluku Nomor 414.13-71/07/1981 tentang Pembentukan, Pemecahan, Penyatuan dan Penghapusan Desa, along with many others.

nature of village government positions available and pre-existing polit-ico-religious designations and roles.

In Maluku as in many other parts of Indonesia, the vacuum left by the disempowering of *adat* leaders and structures was filled partly by the Indonesian national ideology (Pancasila) and partly by the accelera-tion of Christianization and Islamization (Bartels 2003). The *adat* fabric of Malukan society was stretched and frayed.

With the fall of Soeharto in May 1998, it became unclear whether the Pancasila ideology that had formed the foundation of the quasi-secular New Order state would continue to define the principles of the Indone-sian nation. Malukan Muslims and Christians alike feared losing their positions and access to resources. Muslims were afraid that Christians would attempt to reassert their political dominance in the province, while the Christians feared further erosion of their status in a state inclined to favour its Muslim majority (Bertrand 2002).

Indeed, many protagonists portrayed the conflict along the same lines: Laskar Jihad, for example, was able to portray itself as an 'Islamic nation-alist' organization, formed to defend both its Malukan coreligionists and the unity and integrity of the Indonesian state. The largely Christian Maluku Sovereignty Forum (FKM), although founded as a 'neutral, non-partisan' organization by a group of intellectuals who were frustrated with the role of the security forces and militia groups in fanning the conflict while the central government watched from the sidelines, later made a political switch and adopted the same position as the RMS, call-ing for an independent Maluku. This gave both radical Muslims groups like Laskar Jihad and the Indonesian government and security forces a pretext to accuse Malukan Christians of wanting to establish a separate republic (Tapol 2002).[11]

Public statements by Malukan Christian leaders generally preached tolerance and conciliation, but many Christian churches and lay activ-ists distributed exaggerated images of their victimization through a sophisticated web presence, using such sites as Ambon Berdarah Online, Suara Ambon Online and the Masariku Network. Several national and international Muslim leaders were quite bold in their calls for religious war in Maluku. Retired brigadier-general Rustam Kastor (2000), a native Malukan and ex-commander of the Pattimura Army Resort Command in

---

11   It is important to note that neither Laskar Jihad nor FKM existed at the time the conflict began in February 1999. Laskar Jihad was founded in Yogyakarta in January 2000, after news reached the outside world of the slaughter of hun-dreds of Muslim villagers near Tobelo in North Maluku in December 1999. FKM was established in December 2000 in response to the activities of Laskar Jihad. Later these two organizations would be blamed for provoking and per-petuating the conflict (*Jakarta Post* 2002d).

Ambon, identified a conspiracy involving remnants of the RMS, the Protestant Church of Maluku and the local chapter of the 'Christian–nationalist' Indonesian Democratic Party of Struggle (PDI-P), which he claimed was part of a global Jewish–Christian conspiracy against the *ummat*. Clerics in Saudi Arabia and Yemen issued *fatwa* that identified Christians in Maluku as 'belligerent infidels' (*kafir harbi*) who could be killed with religious blessing (Goss 2004).

Eriyanto (2003) writes of a second, 'information war', contested on the streets of Jakarta through rallies and marches, and in the public media through books, audiocassettes, videos, and internet sites and mailing lists. The Christians, with their Ambon Berdarah and Suara Ambon Online, were not alone in cyberspace. Militant Muslim sites included the very popular 'Come and Save Muslim', Gema Khadidjah (about the suffering of Muslim women in Ambon) and Laskar Jihad's official site (all now shut down). As the internet war became more sophisticated, sites with spurious names like 'Jahad in Ambon' and 'Laskar Jahar' appeared. At first glimpse the latter appeared to be pro-Laskar Jihad, but actually depicted the group's alleged brutality and duplicity.

Everywhere youth played an important role in the violence. Very often it took the form of gang warfare, even to the extent that participants were identified by their 'colours': white for Muslims and red for Christians. Gang loyalties and motivations were deeply intertwined with religious identity. Religious feeling often plays an important role in communal violence:

> ... because its confessional loyalty translates into clearly defined and durable community and its model of faith counters rational calculation and enlightened self-interest, cultivates a righteous sense of persecution, and provokes a passion against evil that fuels the excesses of group hatred (Goss 2004: 25).

Each of these factors contributed to the explosive violence that beset the province between 1999 and 2004. They still exist today. How and why, then, did the fighting finally stop? The following subsection examines some of the factors that contributed to an end to the violence.

Factors Contributing to the Peace Process

When the fighting finally stopped, most explanations centred on 'war weariness' and the alienation caused by 'extremist' organizations like Laskar Jihad and FKM, which finally caused belligerents on both sides to become receptive to gestures of reconciliation (Goss 2004). Thus, by the time the national government finally secured 70 signatures on the Malino Peace Accord, everyone was ready for peace. These narratives disregard the years of intensive grassroots organizing and lobbying carried out by a wide array of civil society organizations, beginning almost immediately after violence first broke out in 1999. Perhaps the best known of these is Baku Bae,[12] a movement formed by Malukan scholars, NGO activists, lawyers, journalists, and religious and informal leaders, who brokered meetings (usually outside Maluku) between representatives of the opposing sides to try to identify common ground and avenues for accommodation. This was followed by workshops and information gathering in the respective communities, leading to an exchange of views through a sort of 'shuttle diplomacy'. The meetings became larger; over 100 *adat* leaders, youth representatives, NGO activists and 'war leaders' met in Yogyakarta in December 2000. The meetings led to the establishment of neutral zones in Ambon, including a temporary one on the campus of Pattimura University. The university hosted an important meeting of over a hundred *raja* in January 2001. This resulted in an agreement to better integrate educational opportunities in Maluku, a commitment that was later incorporated in the Malino Peace Accord (Goss 2004). Baku Bae also successfully brokered meetings between the military and local communities, leading to vital improvements in relations and cooperation on security.

In March 2001, Jakarta's Go-East Institute, in conjunction with the Crisis Centre of the Diocese of Amboina and local government, held a symposium in Kei entitled 'National Dialogue on Revitalizing Local Culture for Rehabilitation and Development in Maluku towards a New Indonesia'. Attended by almost 1,500 regional leaders, it issued a call for traditional leaders to take a leading role in leading Maluku out of conflict and noted that, although there would continue to be religious and ethnic differences in the province, '*adat* ... and especially *adat* houses, should be permanent meeting points for all' (Böhm 2005: 150).

International organizations also played an important role in the reconciliation process. Throughout the conflict years and during the early phases of recovery, a range of UN, bilateral, non-governmental, religious and professional organizations played a key role in assisting displaced families and victims of the violence, and in creating the conditions for peace. These groups often proved more effective at delivering relief supplies and basic services than their Indonesian government counterparts, being less hampered by bureaucratic structures and procedures and chronic funding delays. In addition to providing emergency relief, they worked to strengthen intercommunity relations through cooperative self-sufficiency projects and capacity-building activities.

Five UN agencies established special offices in Ambon in 2000: the United Nations Development Programme (UNDP), the United Nations

---

12 *Baku bae* is slang in Ambonese Malay for *saling (bersikap) baik*, or being 'good to one another'.

Children's Fund (UNICEF), the World Food Program, the United Nations Population Fund (UNFPA) and the Office for the Coordination of Humanitarian Affairs (OCHA). Other major international relief agencies to establish a presence in the province included the International Medical Corps (IMC), the Red Cross and Red Crescent, Médecins Sans Frontières, Mercy Corps, Action Contre la Faim, the International Catholic Migration Commission (ICMC), Save the Children, Oxfam, World Vision, Project Concern International, the Consortium for Assistance and Recovery toward Development in Indonesia (CARDI)[13] and the Jesuit Refugee Service. These organizations' activities were funded from a range of UN, bilateral, religious and private sources and included health care, emergency assistance (shelter, water and sanitation, distribution of non-food items), education, and economic empowerment projects (micro-credit, fisheries, agricultural activities) for internally displaced persons (IDPs) as well as local communities that had not been displaced but whose livelihoods had been disrupted by the conflict.[14]

Many of these organizations worked closely with local NGOs and community groups, providing grants, training, technical assistance, logistical support and office facilities, and facilitating cooperation and communication among the groups. Most attempted to employ a mixed Christian and Muslim staff and tried to work with communities on both sides of the conflict. By early 2005 all but three of these international agencies had closed their offices in Ambon.

Before the conflict, Maluku had a small but lively NGO community, led by such well-established organizations and networks as Baileo Maluku and Yayasan Hualopu, and regional branches of major national organizations such as the National Family Planning Coordination Agency (BKKBN), the Nahdlahtul Ulama Institute for Human Resource Studies

---

13 CARDI is a coalition of the International Rescue Committee, the Danish Refugee Council, the Norwegian Refugee Council and Stichting Vluchteling.

14 Overall figures for the amount of humanitarian aid that flowed into Maluku during and after the conflict are not available, but the United Nations' Consolidated Inter-Agency Appeal for the Maluku Crisis (OCHA 2000) provides an indication of the level of international support. For 2001, 10 organizations (seven UN agencies plus ICMC, IMC and Mercy Corps) requested a total of US$10,796,977 to cover security; coordination and management; food; health; nutrition; water and sanitation; education; temporary shelter and non-food relief; reconciliation and conflict resolution; community assistance and income generation; and capacity-building activities. This figure does not include direct bilateral assistance from, for example, USAID's Office of Transitional Initiatives, or the large amount of private donations flowing in through church and Islamic channels. Consolidated appeals for subsequent years were similar or slightly lower—for example, US$7,454,651 for 2004 (OCHA 2004).

and Development (Lakpesdam NU) and the Community Recovery Program (PKM/ACE). As occurred in most other parts of the country, the number of local NGOs in Maluku grew dramatically during the financial crisis and in the wake of the downfall of President Soeharto. The motivations, capabilities and sincerity of the new groups were uneven, but many grew to provide valuable support to communities during and after the conflict. Mercy Corps established a community centre in a neutral zone in central Ambon where local NGOs could make use of its office and communications facilities, participate in various training programs, forums and discussions, and build networks (Young 2001). Along with most of the UN and international NGO offices, it was destroyed by arson during the April 2004 flare-up.

The activities of many of these local NGOs were important in assisting families to recover from trauma and maintain livelihoods throughout the conflict period. While the celebrated Baku Bae movement captured donor and press attention (Bäk 2003), it was the unobtrusive, behind-the-scenes activities of many of these local groups that truly helped build and maintain bridges between communities on different sides of the conflict. Baku Bae lost much of its momentum when the organization split due to a leadership struggle between its Ambon and Jakarta contingents in 2003 (Goss 2004), but local NGO activists continued their peace-building activities.

The role of the press was of critical importance in the conduct — and cessation — of the conflict. Sensationalist accounts of gangs of 'religious fanatics' spontaneously 'running amok' tended to reify this interpretation of events, and perhaps helped feed the fury. Different publications demonstrated different biases in their reporting, assigning blame alternately to Christian nationalist/separatist groups, radical Muslims or, most frequently, mysterious *agents provocateur* (Eriyanto 2003).

Before the conflict Ambon had only one newspaper and three private radio stations. Most people in Maluku obtained their external news and commentary from radio or television. The government radio and television stations, RRI and TVRI, reached most of the islands, and people with satellite dishes could watch other national networks such as TPI, SCTV, Indosiar and Metro TV.

Suara Maluku is the oldest newspaper in the province, dating back to 1956. Its offices were located in a Christian section of Ambon and the editorial staff were predominantly Christian. In the months after conflict broke out in 1999, many of the reports submitted by Muslim journalists were not published. Soon, the names of the Muslim journalists disappeared from the masthead. Not long thereafter, the Jawa Pos Group, which owned a majority share in the newspaper, decided to split it into two papers: *Suara Maluku* representing the interests of Christians and

Ambon Expres representing the interests of the Muslim community (ISAI 2004). Not long afterwards, several new radio stations were established. Of the three private stations in existence before the conflict, all were Christian owned, though only one featured religious programming. After 1999, five new stations began broadcasting. Two were explicitly Islamic: Naviri, which broadcast mostly preaching, songs and readings from the Qur'an, and Suara Perjuangan Muslim Maluku (SPMM) — reportedly controlled by Laskar Jihad — which broadcast preaching and chanting of Qur'anic verses (*tablik akba*), ostensibly to encourage Muslim listeners to fight for their beliefs and survival. Christian leaders called on the governor to ban the station (ICG 2002). Eventually, as the partitioning of the city increased, even the government media split into RRI Islam and RRI Kristen, and TVRI Islam and TVRI Kristen.

In 2001, as the conflict continued to gather momentum, several international, national and local organizations — UNDP, UNESCO, the Asia Foundation, International Media Support, the British Council, the BBC, the Institute for the Study of Free Flow of Information (ISAI), the Alliance of Independent Journalists (AJI), Radio 68H and elements of the Baku Bae movement — began working with local journalists, publishers and editors to promote 'peace journalism'. This increasingly popular format stresses a few simple principles to position the press as a tool for peace. These include communicating and supporting peace initiatives; covering both sides of a story; providing background information; avoiding 'spin doctors' who try to manipulate stories and reporting, and not relying solely on 'elites' as sources; publishing accounts of ordinary people; striving to depict the real horrors of war; and avoiding glorifying warfare technology and 'sensationalism' (*Jakarta Post* 2002b).

In early 2002, while the city of Ambon was still partitioned, AJI helped establish the Maluku Media Centre in a neutral zone between Christian and Muslim neighbourhoods in Kampung Mardika as a safe meeting place for journalists from both communities (*Jakarta Post* 2005a). Here they could use the centre's computer, fax, telephone, internet, library and meeting room facilities, attend regular briefings and discussion meetings, arrange to jointly cover news stories in Muslim or Christian areas, and attend training courses on peace journalism and conflict reporting. More than 40 local journalists have participated in training programs at the centre and many more have attended similar courses in other parts of the country.

Informants in the Kei Islands recount how the 'fight went out of them' when they listened to local RRI broadcasts that alternated traditional Kei music with dispassionate accounts of recent incidents of arson and killing (Thorburn 2001). The reporter who prepared those programs later went on to broadcast live accounts of ceremonies held around the islands at the reopening of churches, mosques and schools, and clan meetings where old men chanted legends and songs (*tub*) and recounted family and village histories.

The Cessation of Hostilities

The February 2002 Malino Peace Accord marked an important turning point in the Maluku conflict. However, the rather innocuous language of the 11-point accord hardly captured the behind-the-scenes negotiations that surely took place at the highest levels of Indonesian political and security circles, or the patient work that had been undertaken over the previous two years by local religious, *adat* and NGO leaders on the ground.[15] Nor did it bring an immediate end to the fighting or address all of the belligerents' grievances. Despite its rather uncontroversial content and language, the accord was initially resisted by numerous parties, most notably Forum Komunikasi Ahlus Sunnah wal Jamaah in Yogyakarta (which hosted the Laskar Jihad Online website), the SPMM radio station in Ambon, the Maluku Muslim Defenders Front (FPI Maluku) and FKM (ICG 2002). Polls showed that 20 per cent of the population of Ambon opposed the accord (*Jakarta Post* 2002c). Dissident voices raised questions about whether the delegates were truly representative of the people of Maluku, and whether the commission appointed by the government to investigate the conflict could possibly be impartial given its closeness to government authorities. As well, Muslim groups demanded a formal acknowledgment that Christians were to blame for the violence, while some Christian groups bridled at the term 'separatist' in the accord (Goss 2004). Many were offended by the so-called 'fire engine' approach, in which distant authorities represented themselves as saviours in local conflicts, imposing top-down solutions that frustrated local initiatives (*Jakarta Post* 2003).

The provincial government strove to 'socialize' the accord and most major religious organizations urged their flocks to comply. Local church and Islamic groups continued to channel humanitarian aid, assist IDP groups, gather and disseminate information and organize counselling

---

15 The 11 points were: (1) an immediate cessation of hostilities; (2) upholding law and justice; (3) repudiation of any separatist movements; (4) protecting the unitary state of Indonesia; (5) surrendering of weapons by all belligerent parties; (6) creation of an independent team to investigate the conflict's origins; (7) the return of IDPs to their homes without compulsion; (8) government assistance in rehabilitation and reconstruction; (9) stability and firmness on the part of the national police and military; (10) religious harmony with respect for local diversity and culture; and (11) rehabilitation of an integrated Pattimura University in order to foster common welfare.

and education programs. Often, the synod of the Protestant Church of Maluku, the Amboina Catholic Diocese and the Maluku branch of the Council of Indonesian Ulama (MUI) worked together to provide trauma counselling and joint training programs for communities and social workers, and to organize dialogues between communities, and between communities and the government.

There was an efflorescence of local media in the wake of the Malino accord. In 2003, 13 new local papers were launched – 10 Christian, two Muslim and one neutral – plus at least 10 new private radio stations (Eriyanto 2003). Nearly all situated themselves as champions of peace and reconciliation and they have generally upheld the principles of 'peace journalism'. Many of these operations started out very small, with just an office, a computer or two, and a staff of three or four people. Some lasted for only a few months; others have grown. At present there are seven daily or weekly newspapers publishing in Ambon, and more than a dozen private radio stations operating in the province (ISAI 2004).

Following the Bali bombings in October 2002 (and nearly nine months after the signing of the Malino Peace Accord), Laskar Jihad founder Ja'far Umar Thalib announced that the organization would be disbanded, and it slipped out of Maluku as speedily as it had arrived two years earlier (*Jakarta Post* 2002e). Although the organization was disbanded for 'internal' and 'moral' reasons,[16] there was speculation about secret agreements made at the highest levels of Indonesian politics – as there had been two years earlier when Laskar Jihad was allowed to pass unhindered through the Surabaya and Ambon ports and travel to Ambon on government-owned Pelni ships (Tapol 2002).

As described above, the period following the signing of the accord was punctuated by occasional bombing, arson and sniper attacks. Each of the attacks was calculated to spread fear and rekindle community violence, and at least two of them were successful. After the April 2002 bomb blast in central Ambon on 3 April 2002 killed seven people and injured scores more, angry mobs set fire to the governor's office, claiming that the government was biased towards Muslims and did too little to protect Christian communities. The brazen flag-raising ceremony on the 54th anniversary of the RMS Independence Movement in April 2004

16 The decision to dissolve Laskar Jihad was taken after consultation with Salafi leaders in the Middle East in September 2002. They were concerned that Laskar Jihad and Salafism more generally were being accused of links to al-Qaeda, that Laskar Jihad was taking on the characteristics of a political, as opposed to purely religious, organization, and that its leaders were becoming high-profile media personalities, in opposition to Salafi strictures against the representation, in art or photographs, of living creatures (ICG 2004b).

was met by well-organized Muslim demonstrators, setting off a mêlée that lasted two weeks.

Rivalry between the Indonesian police and the military has also threatened to derail the peace process on several occasions. Though this only occasionally manifests in open battles, the very public argument between provincial police chief Brigadier-General Bambang Sutrisno (a one-star general) and regional military commander Major-General Syari-fuddin Sumah (two stars) after the April 2004 outbreak exposed the level of enmity between the two forces. General Sumah publicly announced that if the police (who had been in charge of security in the province since the civil emergency was rescinded in September 2003) could not handle the situation, his troops were ready to step in (ICG 2004a).

Despite major advances, the peace in Maluku is still quite fragile. The remainder of this chapter examines the steps being taken to strengthen and deepen the peace process, and help the people of Maluku recover from three years of warfare and resume normal productive lives.

4 'NORMALIZATION'

The signing of the Malino Peace Accord marked the beginning of the long process of reconciliation and reconstruction in Maluku. Since then, great strides have been made in rebuilding shattered productive, educational and service delivery infrastructure, returning or resettling displaced peoples and reuniting torn communities, and creating the conditions for peace. This section reviews some of the significant milestones on that journey, and the roles played by different parties.

Governor Karel Alberth Ralahalu and Vice-Governor Mohammad Abdullah Latuconsina were elected by a narrow margin in a plenary session of the regional assembly (DPRD) held on 16 August 2003, after 10 hours of deliberation and two rounds of voting. The entire debate and election were broadcast on local television, closely watched by the people of Ambon. Rahalalu, a Christian, was a retired brigadier-general of the army. He had served briefly as chief military commander in Ambon after the conflict broke out in 1999, but was transferred to Jayapura (Papua) when the civil emergency was declared, and replaced by a commander of higher rank. Vice-Governor Latuconsina was an economist who had been head of the Provincial Revenue Service from 1999 to 2001. These two candidates were nominated by PDI-P, even though Latuconsina, a Muslim, was not a member of the party. PDI-P was identified as a Christian party in Maluku and wanted a Muslim candidate to attract Muslim votes. For Latuconsina, accepting the nomination could be viewed as an astute manoeuvre to protect the interests of the *ummat*. That the single-party Ralahalu–Latuconsina ticket prevailed over coalition candidates representing Golkar and the (Muslim) United Development Party (PPP) demonstrated the esteem in which these two politicians were held by their peers (Ensiklopedia Tokoh Indonesia 2006). The election results were well received by members of the public as well.

The day after the election, on 17 August 2003 (Indonesian Independence Day), acting governor Sinyo Harry Sarundayang ordered all government and private offices that had split to form separate Muslim and Christian entities back to their original offices insofar as these had escaped destruction. This was seen as a major step towards normalizing life in the capital (Böhm 2005).

With the lifting of the civil emergency, responsibility for internal security in the province was officially shifted from the army to the national police. The civil emergency administration was disbanded and numerous emergency decrees and restrictions – including the curfew in Ambon and travel restrictions to and within the province – were rescinded. Troops were pulled off the streets and out of the city centre of Ambon, and the long process of transferring units out of the province began. National and regional business and travel associations predicted that businesses that had fled the province would begin to return, and new investment to flow in, as confidence grew in the provincial and local authorities' capacity to guarantee peace, security and the rule of law (*Kompas* 2003).

Presidential Instruction (Inpres) No. 6/2003 on Accelerating Post-conflict Recovery and Development in Maluku and North Maluku, issued in September 2003, instructs 24 ministers, the commanders of the TNI and police, the heads of the National Boards for Investment, Land Affairs, and Science and Knowledge, and the governors and district heads of Maluku and North Maluku to give special priority to post-conflict recovery and development in the two provinces. It further states that 'all budgetary resources necessary for the recovery and development program will be provided from the national, provincial and district budgets', without further elaboration. The provincial government submitted a request for Rp 4.4 trillion (US$473 million) of post-conflict recovery funding in the form of a Specific Purpose Fund (DAK) grant. After negotiation with the National Development Planning Agency (Bappenas), this amount was reduced to Rp 1.002 trillion. In late 2004, the province received a first instalment of Rp 300 million of the DAK recovery funds (Detik.com 2004). According to the head of the Maluku Regional Development Planning Agency (Bappeda), over 80 per cent of that amount had already been allocated for emergency relief, leaving only Rp 51 million for development support (Detik.com 2004).

Despite these constraints, the province has made significant progress towards reconstruction. By November 2005, Pattimura University had reopened and 55 of the 141 school structures destroyed during the conflict had been rebuilt, with construction under way on many more.[17] Two hospitals and 16 of the 17 damaged community health centres (*puskesmas*) had reopened; reconstruction of two of Ambon city's three markets had been completed; and 25 of 251 houses of worship[18] had been rebuilt or rehabilitated. However, only six of the 106 burned-out government offices had been rebuilt.

Among the many problems still confronting the government and people of Maluku, the return or resettlement of the thousands of families displaced during the conflict is one of the most pressing and, it seems, perplexing. Great strides have been made in returning or resettling most of the 33,000 refugee families, although thousands of cases remain unsettled.

5   THE PLIGHT OF MALUKU'S IDPs

Between 1999 and 2004, nearly one in every three people living in Maluku experienced displacement for some period. Some people who fled their villages when fighting broke out in 1999 are still languishing in camps in and around Ambon. Many others have returned or been resettled. The lingering problem of IDPs remains one of the greatest obstacles to achieving stability and prosperity in the region.

It is virtually impossible to obtain accurate figures on the number of IDPs in the province. Initially this was caused by the volatile nature of the conflict, with the numbers changing from day to day. More recent confusion stems from the lack of coordination among different agencies and between different levels of government, with some agencies inflating figures to augment budget allocations, and district and provincial governments mistrusting one another and jealously guarding 'their' IDP (and budget) figures. There is also ambiguity as to who actually qualifies to be counted as an IDP — and therefore eligible for a government assistance package.

During the first year of fighting, it is generally agreed that 100,000 people were displaced within the province while another 100,000 sought refuge in Southeast Sulawesi (UNDP 2000). These numbers continued to swell, and by September 2000 stood at 215,061 displaced people within the province, 138,481 in Southeast Sulawesi and another 30,000 scattered throughout North Sulawesi, West Papua and East Java (NRC 2001). By

---

17 Five kindergartens, 100 elementary schools, 23 middle schools, 11 high schools and two university campuses had been destroyed.

18 That is, 114 mosques, 134 churches and three Buddhist shrines.

292   Working with Nature against Poverty

this time large amounts of aid had begun flowing through a variety of channels to house, feed and, where possible, return refugees. The Indonesian government released a plan to end the IDP problem, more or less decreeing that it would soon be over. This policy set out three strategies: (1) to return IDPs to their places of origin (the preferred option), (2) to 'empower' refugees by integrating them into the communities to which they had been displaced, supplemented with cash grants to help them start new lives and livelihoods; and (3) to resettle refugees in a new location. The policy further stated that after 31 December 2002, the needs of displaced people would be met within general national poverty alleviation guidelines (Ministry of Social Affairs 2001, cited in Duncan 2003: 36).

Meanwhile, in Maluku, the IDP situation continued to fluctuate. Estimates of IDP numbers in the province reached as high as 332,000 in 2003, although government assistance was flowing well by that time and more than 130,000 people (about 25,000 families) did manage to return to their homes during that year (Global IDP Database 2005). In August 2004, the Maluku Social Affairs Office released new official figures saying that of 70,051 families (331,979 refugees) who had fled the fighting since 1999, 33,673 families (174,570 people) had returned or been resettled, while the remaining 36,378 families (164,189 people) remained scattered across various sites around the province, with the majority concentrated on the island of Ambon (Global IDP Database 2005).

About half of these cases were successfully resolved in 2004 and early 2005, but progress now seems to have stalled. Since June 2005 estimates have continued to hover around 15,800 families, or roughly 60,000 people. Many camps have been closed, but several remain open and full. In addition to the official encampments, thousands of refugee families are living in burned-out shop houses in the city centre and outskirts of Ambon, in rented accommodation or with relatives. Several deadlines for the resolution of the situation have passed. By September 2005, the provincial government appeared ready to be done with the matter, stating that all funds to return, 'empower' or resettle refugees had been dispersed and that any remaining unresolved cases should be handled by the municipal and district authorities. It announced that the remaining refugees would be recounted, to facilitate efforts to finally settle the problem (Jakarta Post 2005b). It set a deadline of 31 December for refugees to vacate the shop houses, to allow the owners — most of whom had fled the province during the violence — to return and reopen their businesses. This was extended to January 2006, then to February (Jakarta Post 2006b).

The Maluku IDP Coalition (KPM) charges the provincial government with not having upheld its obligations under the Malino Peace Accord, causing 15,788 families to continue to live in uncertainty while tens of billions of rupiah in relief funds have been squandered (*Jakarta Post* 2006a; KPM 2004). The government counters that a large number of the remaining unresolved cases have been caused by the IDPs themselves — through ineptitude, lack of ambition or greed. Many are new households formed since the conflict began, through marriage or pregnancy. These families did not lose a house and so do not qualify for assistance. Others are students living in rented accommodation. They too are not eligible for assistance. Still others have taken their assistance money and spent it on consumer goods, and are now using other family members to apply for additional assistance. Some simply prefer to stay in Ambon but have not taken the initiative to find or purchase land, or register for relocation (Soumena, personal communication, 2005).

Long queues of refugees can be seen daily in government offices, asking officials whether their allotments of building materials are ready. Each refugee family is entitled to assistance of up to Rp 12.5 million (US$1,340), comprised of Rp 8.5 million for building materials, Rp 1.5 million for labour and another Rp 2.5 million for 'homecoming' (transport and amenities). The Provincial IDP Coordinating Body divides IDPs into three types: (1) those wanting to return, (2) those who choose to resettle in a new location, and (3) those who are 'resigned' (*pasrah*). These classifications are used to determine the form of assistance the families receive. Returnees are the simplest group. Once they can demonstrate that their dwelling was destroyed, they are provided with building materials and funds to construct their own houses, or government contractors build houses for them. Those choosing to resettle are responsible for acquiring their own land before receiving assistance. There are many instances on Ambon island and elsewhere of groups of refugees having been 'loaned' land by local communities, for purchase when they become capable of paying. For the third group, the provincial government uses the 'homecoming' portion of their assistance allocation to purchase blocks of land, then hires contractors to build houses for them.

The Assistant II (Development) Office of the Maluku provincial government, which bears primary responsibility for coordinating refugee affairs, points out that an integrated approach is needed for each of these groups. In the case of returnees, local communities who receive them need to be 'rewarded' through the provision of new buildings and infrastructure, both to ameliorate jealousy and to foster a sense of well-being. In this way, the recipient community — which was often complicit in these people's exclusion in the first place — can benefit from new infrastructure and services such as clean drinking water, roads, schools and clinics that they may not have enjoyed before. The government also facilitates religious or *adat* welcoming or reconciliation ceremonies in these communities. The resettlement group is generally more dispersed, though there are cases where groups of families have settled together in new communities, allowing the government to again plan for infrastructure development and services that will benefit and reward the broader community. The *pasrah* group has proven the most problematic. These people are now crowded into rows of tiny wooden houses constructed on the outskirts of Ambon. There are two new settlements in Ambon for *pasrah* refugees: Kate-Kate near Passo at the head of the Ambon bay for Muslims, and Kayu Tiga in the hills above the city for Christians.

Charges of corruption and manipulation are rife. District and municipal authorities accuse provincial officials of withholding funds and information. Refugee groups and NGOs charge the government and contractors with squandering funds and supplies, and building substandard houses. Hundreds of government-built houses stand empty, with families refusing to take occupancy because of their very small size and lack of basic facilities such as electricity and water. Many of the intended recipients choose to stay in barracks or camps in Ambon, where they can enjoy such amenities (Global IDP Database 2005).

Throughout the crisis, many of the problems that typically face IDPs, such as communicable diseases, malnutrition, lack of education and other social services, and intimidation and violence, were kept to a minimum. This was largely due to the excellent work of the local and international relief agencies, as well as the ingenuity and initiative of the IDP communities themselves (Soumena, personal communication, 2005).

Returning and relocating IDPs face many serious problems. Many fear for their safety and lack the means to support themselves and their families. The IDP assistance packages do not include provisions for new fishing or farming equipment to replace that lost during the conflict (although various provincial government agencies and NGOs do have budgets and programs for this type of assistance). During the conflict, neighbouring villagers often took over abandoned fields and gardens, usually planting tree crops as a means of staking a claim to the land. Returnees are generally too intimidated to remove these trees and press for the return of their fields. Land ownership in Maluku tends to be complicated and contested, so it seems possible that property disputes will remain a major source of conflict in the province (Goss 2004; Soumena, personal communication, 2005). There are isolated reports as well of returnees being forced to share their meagre assistance allotments as a 'security fee' for the right to return (Global IDP Database 2005). Local networks of mutual support and assistance that help families to survive periods of want are being rebuilt, but most families are struggling to meet their own needs.

In general, however, there is a growing sense that the conflict is over, and that people are ready to get on with their lives. One disturbing outcome of the dislocation and relocation of so many thousands of families is that the city of Ambon—and most other parts of the province—now evince a much sharper spatial segregation than before the conflict, with clearly demarcated Muslim and Christian zones and far fewer mixed communities. The provincial government is pinning its hopes on increased economic activity as a crucible for greater interaction and cooperation between the divided communities. In addition to increased religious segregation, other regional disparities have been exacerbated as well, with an even larger portion of the province's population now concentrated on tiny Ambon island, where most of the province's economic activity is located.[19]

6 LOCAL GOVERNMENT REFORM

The correlation between government decentralization, conflict and resource management is a particularly complex issue, nowhere more so than in Indonesia. Numerous studies (Dermawan and Resosudarmo 2002; ARD 2004; Patlis 2005) point out that, with the passage of the new decentralization laws in 1999, local politicians were quick to take advantage of rent-seeking (or rent-harvesting) opportunities in the management of natural resources and other sources of revenue, and that in many cases there was a sharp increase in the incidence of local conflict over resources and territory. One controversial aspect of the decentralization process is the phenomenon known as *pemekaran*, or administrative fragmentation, whereby a district (*kabupaten*) or group of districts can form a new province, or subdistrict(s) (*kecamatan*) can upgrade to become a new district. The decentralization regulations state that the objectives of any change in the status of a region should be to enhance the delivery of services, speed up democratization, facilitate the realization of a region's potential, enhance law and order, and improve communications between the centre and the regions (ICG 2003).

The ostensible rationale for this fragmentation is to bring government closer to the people and improve the delivery of government services. But as Jones (2004: 2) points out, 'if better service delivery [is] the official reason, the motivation [is] frequently money, power, or the restoration of old historical kingdoms'.

The splitting of Maluku into two provinces in 1999 was a result of this *pemekaran* process. Since then, five new districts have been formed:

---

19 Ambon has a land area of 757 square kilometres, or about 1.4 per cent of the province's total land area of 54,185 square kilometres. Of the province's 1,313,000 people, 360,000 (27 per cent) reside on the island.

Buru in 1999 (along with the splitting of the province); Aru, West Seram and East Seram in 2003; and West Southeast Maluku (comprising Tanimbar and the Southernmost Islands) when Southeast Maluku was split in 2004. There is a move afoot to split West Southeast Maluku yet again, with the Southernmost Islands (Babar, Sermata, Damar, Romang, Leti, Moa, Lakor, Kisar and Wetar) forming their own district. The impact of most of these splits has been positive, as the old districts were among the most geographically vast in all of Indonesia, and government services and programs tended to cluster around the administrative centres. At the very least, the *pemekaran* process has resulted in a slightly more even distribution of government infrastructure development and routine expenditure funds (that is, salaries and amenities for government employees and elected representatives).

There has been an upsurge in local power struggles as various local clans vie for political control of the new districts. Fortunately these tussles have not led to any new violence. Maluku *adat* expert Dr Dieter Bartels (2003: 146) enthuses that dividing Maluku into smaller units will help communities 'to regain a measure of control over their island groups' and 're-emphasize cultural homogeneity'.

As local elites vie for supremacy in the new district governments, a more fundamental reform is taking place at the village level. Maluku's 2003–08 Provincial Strategic Plan emphasizes 'community empowerment' as an underlying principle. The text devotes considerable attention to the issue of building social capital, particularly the consolidation and revitalization of *adat* traditions, norms and practices as key ingredients in promoting social and political harmony. Provincial and district governments are encouraged to conduct detailed studies of the state of *adat* in their respective regions and prepare regulations to facilitate an increased role for *adat* institutions and practices in the social and political life of the province, most particularly at the village level (Provincial Government of Maluku 2004).

When it was introduced over 25 years ago, Law No. 5/1979 on Village Government posed difficult problems for Maluku's *adat* communities. Hereditary clan-based organizations such as *saniri* councils found their ability to control access to and the use of village resources and territories (*petuanan*) slipping away, because their authority was not recognized under Indonesian law. As large-scale natural resource exploitation came to dominate the province's economy, investors and enterprising migrants made deals with village officials and customary leaders alike to obtain access to villages' forest and marine territories, often pitting them against one another and further weakening local control. The central government's village development allocations under the Inpres scheme became another source of conflict, as those local elites who had successfully aligned themselves with the state power structure channelled government projects and contracts to their own clans and neighbourhoods.

The collapse of the New Order government and the promulgation of the new regional government laws of 1999 and 2004[20] changed all of that. Villages are no longer part of the national government hierarchy, but instead enjoy 'natural autonomy' (*otonomi asli*). The new laws supersede Law No. 5/1979 and its hundreds of implementing regulations, and encourage regional governments to devise regulations that support customary forms of village government, while empowering villages to exercise their customary rights and obligations. The 2004 law makes special concessions for new villages established during the past few decades that might not have a customary claim to *adat* lands or seas, or are populated by mixed or non-native people.

The provincial government of Maluku has yet to issue implementing regulations for the 2004 law. Deliberations in the DPRD have been stalled by the Prosperity and Justice Party (PKS) faction, which fears that the new regulations will not protect the rights of the province's large migrant population. Nonetheless, efforts are under way to guide the various district governments through the process of preparing regulations — which can only be issued officially once the provincial regulation is passed — to serve as the framework for the establishment of 'new' village governments throughout the province.

The governor's legal team estimates that at least 10 district regulations will be needed to provide the legal platform necessary to allow villages to exercise their 'natural autonomy'. The term used in many parts of Maluku for a village is *negeri*. The proposed regulations differentiate between *negeri adat* and *negeri administratif*, the former being *negeri* that have existed for many decades and still retain characteristics from the pre-1979 era, and the latter being those that were formed by subdividing larger *negeri* or by establishing new settlements (such as transmigration settlements). *Negeri administratif* do not have a hereditary claim to territories (*petuanan*), and special measures will be necessary for them to be able to exercise territorial control and management authority under an *adat*-based system. According to Malukan *adat*, this latter group of villages is located within the pre-existing *petuanan* of older *negeri*.

The draft regulations identify seven basic characteristics of a *negeri adat*:

1 an *adat* community;
2 a clearly defined area (*petuanan*) still controlled by *adat* law;

---

20 Undang-Undang Nomor 22 Tahun 1999 tentang Pemerintahan Daerah, and Undang-Undang Nomor 32 Tahun 2004 tentang Pemerintahan Daerah.

298 *Working with Nature against Poverty*

3 *adat* institutions (*latupati, raja, saniri negeri, soa, matarumah, kewang* and so on);
4 a connection between the community and the region/area, with *adat* regulations on management, control and use of land and sea *petuanan* that are still in force;
5 customary social institutions (such as *sasi*);
6 *adat* symbols and structures (*baileo, batu pamale, adat* costumes and so on); and
7 other *adat* characteristics (the belief that a *raja* or *kepala soa* is a descendent of a particular lineage, *adat* marriage ceremonies, dress, language and so on).

The first three are 'essential characteristics' and the remaining four are 'complementary characteristics'. *Negeri adat* must possess all seven, while those *negeri* that do not have their own *petuanan*, customary social institutions, symbols and structures will be classified as *negeri administratif*. According to the provincial legal team, *negeri administratif* can be guided and developed to one day become *negeri adat*.

Both types of *negeri* government will be empowered to regulate village affairs, including routine government matters, community social and economic development, revenues and disbursements, infrastructure, and cooperation with other villages and government institutions. The primary difference between *negeri adat* and *negeri administratif* is that the former are entitled to exercise 'customary' or 'original' rights (*hak asal-usul*). A vague but powerful legal concept, this basically translates to customary control of territory and resources. Perhaps most significantly for the communities of Maluku, this customary control can extend over marine territories up to four and a half nautical miles from the coastline (half a mile beyond district or municipal seas, which comprise one-third of the province's 12-mile coastal sea zone). This authority will only be accorded to *negeri* that can demonstrate that they have active *adat* institutions and practices in place to manage access to and exploitation of coastal waters, and that members of the *negeri* community still utilize those seas and resources themselves (that is, the rights have not been contracted to migrant fishers or outside commercial interests). Otherwise, management control (and revenues) revert to the district government. This important right will probably be available only to *negeri adat*, while other communities and enterprises will be required negotiate with *adat* communities for rights within marine *petuanan* where these are still in force, or with district officials for those seas that are no longer under *adat* control. As most Malukan communities depend on the sea for their subsistence needs and livelihoods, the proposal to afford legal recognition of territorial seas to village communities has profound implications.

While the provincial DPRD deliberates and the governor's legal team provides guidance to district officials, many local communities in the province have decided not to wait for new regulations before restoring *adat* governance. Local and regional NGOs such as Baileo Maluku and its many network partners are actively engaging with village communities and leaders in Seram, Ambon, Kei, Aru and Tanimbar to investigate and record oral histories and customary beliefs and practices, and to revitalize old structures and institutions. These NGOs provide training in legal drafting, and assist village communities to prepare *negeri* charters and regulations. Many communities have been galvanized by the commercial exploitation of *petuanan* resources, particularly small-scale IPK timber concessions issued by district governments during the early days of decentralization. Groups such as the *adat* community of Honitetu, in West Seram, assert that the IPK permits were issued without consultation with local *adat* leaders, and that they comprise a violation of the *negeri* community's customary rights (*hak asal-usul*). Other communities, such as Haruku in the Lease islands and Debut in Kei Kecil, believe that the restoration of robust *adat* structures and traditions is the only way to address conflicts with neighbouring villages over access to marine territories and resources. So far the neighbourhood of Batumerah in Ambon is the only urban community to attempt to reactivate a *saniri negeri* government structure. After sustaining heavy damage during the conflict years, Batumerah is now recovering more rapidly than other parts of the city (Papilaja, personal communication, 2005). A strong grassroots movement is emerging province-wide as village groups and NGOs meet and exchange views and experiences, and attempt to duplicate the successful models pioneered by these and other village communities in different parts of the province.

Far from being merely a 'salvage' or 'restoration' operation, this movement is seeking ways to craft new institutional forms and practices that combine the advantages of customary governance with democracy, equity and environmental sustainability concerns. Nearly all *adat* governance throughout Maluku is based on heredity, with particular clans and families exercising near-absolute power over decision-making processes, resource management and benefit streams. Issues of precedence and ancestral heritage permeate all aspects of local governance in the province. As discussed earlier, the potency and authority of *adat* have diminished in most Malukan societies, and continual change is placing new strains on local leadership and community cohesion. The challenge is to retain some of the power and efficacy of *adat* forms, while assuring that all sectors and factions within village society are fully represented in deliberative processes and the allocation of benefits. Fortunately, nearly everyone involved in the process is cognisant of the need to go beyond simplistic Hobbesian narratives advocating a 'return to the old ways' as a panacea for all the province's woes. *Adat* norms, practices and institutions have evolved over centuries (and, indeed, continue to evolve), constantly responding to changes in the social, political, economic and natural world in which they inhere. After 25 years of being sidelined and overridden, Malukan *adat* is now back at the centre of the changes swirling through the region today.

Of all the changes that have taken place since the cessation of hostilities in 2003–04, the reform of local government holds the greatest promise for effecting a lasting recovery. The problems that beset the province before the outbreak of hostilities in 1999 are still present—indeed, in many cases are now worse. Poverty levels province-wide have only just recovered to pre-conflict levels, while the economy continues to be dominated by large-scale fisheries and forestry, with few benefits flowing to local communities. Local subsistence livelihood patterns continue to be disrupted. Many populations lack access to basic services, markets and information. Furthermore, as a consequence of the displacement and resettlement processes, Malukan communities are more segregated than they were before the conflict began. Fear and suspicion still impede full resumption of local production and intercommunity relations. In 1999, President Wahid was roundly criticized for his remark that it was up to the Malukans to sort out their problems themselves. In retrospect, this comment may merely have been premature. It is indeed up to the people of Maluku to solve their own problems, and the best place to start is in the villages where they live.

REFERENCES

Aditjondro, G. (2000), 'The Political Economy of Violence in Maluku', *Green Left Weekly Online*, No. 397, 15 March, available at <http://www.greenleft.org.au/back/2000/397/397p18.htm>, accessed 24 May 2006.

Aditjondro, G. (2001a), 'Di Balik Asap Mesiu, Air Mata dan Anyir Darah di Maluku' [Beneath the Smoke of Explosives, Tears and the Stench of Blood], in Z. Salampessy and T. Husain (eds), *Ketika Semerbak Cenkih Tergusur Asap Mesiu* [When the Perfume of Cloves Is Pushed aside by the Smoke of Explosives], Tapak Ambon, Jakarta, pp. 131–70.

Aditjondro, G. (2001b), 'Gajah Lawan Gajah Berlaga, Orang Maluku Mati di Tengah-Tengah' [Elephants Do Battle, Malukans Die in Between], in Z. Salampessy. and T. Husain (eds), *Ketika Semerbak Cenkih Tergusur Asap Mesiu* [When the Perfume of Cloves Is Pushed aside by the Smoke of Explosives], Tapak Ambon, Jakarta, pp. 42–7.

Andaya, L.Y. (1993), *The World of Maluku: Eastern Indonesia in the Early Modern Period*, University of Hawaii Press, Honolulu.

ARD Inc. (2004), 'Growing Conflict and Unrest in Indonesian Forests: A Summary Paper', paper submitted to USAID/ANE/TS under the Biodiversity and Sustainable Forestry (BIOFOR) IQC, available at <http://pdf.dec.org/pdf_docs/PNADD200.pdf>, accessed 29 May 2006.

Asiaweek (2000), 'Stop the Mayhem', 9 June 2000, available at <http://www.pathfinder.com/asiaweek/magazine/2000/0609/edit2.html>, accessed 30 May 2006.

Bäk, M.L. (2003), 'Slouching towards Democracy: Social Violence and Elite Failure in Indonesia', in T.D. Nguyen and F.J. Richter (eds), *Indonesia Matters: Diversity, Unity and Stability in Fragile Times*, Times Editions, Singapore, pp. 73–89.

Balowski, J. (2000), 'Indonesia: Behind the "Religious" Violence in Maluku', *Green Left Weekly Online*, No. 411, 12 July, available at <http://www.greenleft.org.au/back/2000/411/411p16.htm>, accessed 24 May 2006.

Bartels, D. (1977), 'Guarding the Invisible Mountain: Intervillage Alliances, Religious Syncretism and Ethnic Identity among Ambonese Christians and Moslems in the Moluccas', PhD thesis, Cornell University, Ithaca NY.

Bartels, D. (2003), 'Your God Is No Longer Mine: Moslem–Christian Fratricide in the Central Moluccas (Indonesia) after a Half-Millennium of Tolerant Coexistence and Ethnic Unity', in S. Pannell (ed.), *A State of Emergency: Violence, Society and the State in Eastern Indonesia*, Northern Territory University Press, Darwin, pp. 128–53.

Bertrand, J. (2002), 'Legacies of the Authoritarian Past: Religious Violence in Indonesia's Moluccan Islands', *Pacific Affairs*, 75(1): 57–85.

Böhm, C.J. (2005), 'Brief Chronicle of the Unrest in the Moluccas, 1999–2005', unpublished manuscript, Crisis Centre Diocese of Amboina, Ambon.

BPS (Badan Pusat Statistik) Provinsi Maluku (2005), *Maluku dalam Angka 2004* [Maluku in Figures 2004], Ambon.

Chauvel, R. (1990), *Nationalists, Soldiers and Separatists: The Ambonese Islands from Colonialism to Revolt*, KITLV Press, Leiden.

Cooley, F. (1962), *Ambonese Adat: A General Description*, Yale University Press, New Haven CT.

Dermawan, A. and I.A.P. Resosudarmo (2002), 'Forests and Regional Autonomy', in C.J. Pierce Colfer and I.A.P. Resosudarmo (eds), *Which Way Forward? People, Forests and Policymaking in Indonesia*, RFF Press, Washington DC, pp. 325–57.

Detik.com (2004), 'Dana Pemulihan Pasca Konflik Maluku Rp 300 M' [Rp 300 Million in Post-conflict Aid Funds for Maluku], 23 October, available at <http://www.detiknews.com/index.php/detik.read/tahun/2004/bulan/10/tgl/23/time/233552/idnews/229525/idkanal/10>, accessed 5 March 2006.

Duncan, C. (2003), 'Confusing Deadlines: IDPs in Indonesia', *Forced Migration Review*, 17: 35–6, available at <http://www.fmreview.org/FMRpdfs/FMR17/fmr17.15.pdf>, accessed 6 April 2006.

Ensiklopedia Tokoh Indonesia (2006), 'Karel Alberth Rahalalu, Gubernur Maluku 2003–2008' [Karel Alberth Rahalu, Governor of Maluku 2003–2008], available at <http://www.tokohindonesia.com/ensiklopedi/k/karel-ralahalu/index.shtml>, accessed 26 February 2006.

Eriyanto (2003), *Media dan Konflik Ambon* [The Media and the Ambon Conflict], Kantor Berita 68H, Jakarta.

Global IDP Database (2005), *Profile of Internal Displacement: Indonesia*, Norwegian Refugee Council, Helsinki, available at <http://www.internal-displacement.org/8025708F004BE3B1/(httpInfoFiles)/57A5AC883A7FCA55802570BA00552E12/$file/Indonesia+-May+2005.pdf>, accessed 16 March 2006.

Goss, J. (2004), 'Understanding the "Maluku Wars": An Overview of the Sources of Communal Conflict and Prospects for Peace', *Cakalele*, 11–12: 7–39.

Hefner, R. (2000), *Civil Islam: Muslims and Democratization in Indonesia*, Princeton University Press, Princeton NJ.

HPCR (Program on Humanitarian Policy and Conflict Research) (2001), 'Building Human Security in Indonesia' available at <http://www.preventconflict. org/portal/main/maps_maluku_actors.php>, accessed 24 May 2006.

Human Rights Watch (1999), 'Indonesia: The Violence in Ambon', available at <http://www.hrw.org/reports/1999/ambon/>, accessed 22 May 2006.

ICG (International Crisis Group) (2000), 'Indonesia: Overcoming Murder and Chaos in Maluku', ICG Asia Report No. 10, 19 December 2000, available at <http://www.crisisgroup.org/library/documents/report_archive/ A400320_19121999.pdf>, accessed 11 December 2005.

ICG (International Crisis Group) (2002), 'Indonesia: The Search for Peace in Maluku', ICG Asia Report No. 31, 8 February 2002, available at <http://www. crisisgroup.org/library/documents/report_archive/A400544_08022002. pdf>, accessed 11 December 2005.

ICG (International Crisis Group) (2003), 'Indonesia: Managing Decentralization and Conflict in South Sulawesi', ICG Asia Report No. 60, 18 July 2003, available at <http://www.crisisgroup.org/library/documents/report_archive/ A401055_18072003.pdf>, accessed 29 May 2006.

ICG (International Crisis Group) (2004a) 'Indonesia: Violence Erupts Again in Ambon', ICG Asia Briefing, 17 May 2004, available at <http://www.crisis group.org/library/documents/report_archive/A400544_08022002.pdf>, accessed 29 May 2006.

ICG (International Crisis Group) (2004b) 'Indonesia Backgrounder: Why Salafism and Terrorism Mostly Don't Mix', ICG Asia Report No. 83, 13 September 2004, available at <http://www.crisisgroup.org/library/documents/asia/ indonesia/83_indonesia_backgrounder_why_salafism_and_terrorism_don_ t_mix_web.pdf>, accessed 10 June 2006.

ISAI (Institut Studi Arus Informasi) (2004), 'The Role of Media in Supporting Peace-building and Reconciliation Efforts in Central Sulawesi, Maluku and North Maluku', final draft report, Jakarta.

Jakarta Post (2002a), 'Muslims, Christians Rally Joyfully in Ambon', 1 March 2002, available at <http://www.thejakartapost.com/Archives/ArchivesDet2.asp? FileID=20020301.@01>, accessed 13 January 2006.

Jakarta Post (2002b), 'Peace Journalism a Model for Reporting on Conflicts', 12 October 2002, available at <http://www.thejakartapost.com/Archives/ ArchivesDet2.asp?FileID=20021012.B08>, accessed 12 March 2006.

Jakarta Post (2002c), 'Peace Elusive in Maluku Despite Accord', 3 November 2002, available at <http://www.thejakartapost.com/Archives/ArchivesDet2. asp?FileID=20020311.A05>, accessed 26 May 2006.

Jakarta Post (2002d), 'FKM, Laskar Jihad Not the Root of Conflict', 14 May 2002, available at <http://www.thejakartapost.com/Archives/ArchivesDet2. asp?FileID=20020514.A01>, accessed 29 May 2006.

Jakarta Post (2002e), 'Laskar Jihad Dissolved, Ends Ambon Presence', 16 October 2002, available at <http://www.thejakartapost.com/Archives/Archives Det2.asp?FileID=20021016.@03>, accessed 29 May 2006.

Jakarta Post (2003), 'Deliver Promises to Prevent Further Violence', 28 October 2003, available at <http://www.thejakartapost.com/Archives/Archives Det2.asp?FileID=20031027.B01>, accessed 26 May 2006.

Jakarta Post (2005a), 'Responsible Reporting during Religious Wars', 5 March 2005, available at <http://www.thejakartapost.com/Archives/Archives Det2.asp?FileID=20050305.F04>, accessed 29 May 2006.

Jakarta Post (2005b), 'Displaced People in Ambon City to be Recounted', 28 September 2005, available at <http://www.thejakartapost.com/Archives/ArchivesDet2.asp?FileID=20050928.D08>, accessed 16 March 2006.

Jakarta Post (2006a), 'Ambon Refugees Still Waiting 7 Years On', 3 February 2006, available at <http://www.thejakartapost.com/Archives/ArchivesDet2.asp?FileID=20060203.D11>, accessed 16 March 2006.

Jakarta Post (2006b), 'Refugees in Ambon to Be Relocated' 24 February 2006, available at <http://www.thejakartapost.com/Archives/ArchivesDet2.asp?FileID=20060224.D01>, accessed 29 May 2006.

Jones, S. (2004), 'Comprehending Contemporary Causes of Conflict in Indonesia', address to a public seminar organized by the Centre for Strategic Studies, New Zealand and the Asia 2000 Foundation, available at <http://www.vuw.ac.nz/css/docs/seminars/Sidney_Jones.pdf>, accessed 29 May 2006.

Kastor, R. (2000), *Fakta, Data, dan Analisa Konspirasi RMS dan Kristen untuk Menghancurkan Umat Islam di Ambon-Maluku* [Facts, Data and Analysis of the RMS and Christian Conspiracy to Destroy the Muslim Community of Ambon-Maluku], Wihdah Press, Yogyakarta.

Kingsbury, D. (2005), *The Politics of Indonesia*, third edition, Oxford University Press, Melbourne.

Klinken, G. (1999), 'What Caused the Ambon Violence?', *Inside Indonesia*, 60 (October–December), available at <http://www.insideindonesia.org/edit60/ambon.htm>, accessed 26 May 2006.

Kompas (2003) 'Dunia Usaha Minta Status Darurat Sipil Maluku Dicabut' [Businessmen Request that the Maluku Civil Emergency Be Lifted], 31 August, available at <http://www.kompas.com/kompas-cetak/0308/31/utama/525468.htm>, accessed 26 February 2006.

KPM (Koalisi Pengungsi Maluku) (2004), 'Overcoming IDP Problem', open letter to the chairs of the MPR, DPR and President of Indonesia, available at <http://www.internal-displacement.org/8025708F004CE90B/(httpDocuments)/587AA076DCFB34C6802570B700594455/$file/Maluku+IDP+Coalition.pdf>, accessed 16 March 2006.

Marut, D. (2004), 'Petuanan dan Sasi: Hak Komunal & Management Sumberdaya Alam di Maluku' [*Petuanan* and *Sasi*: Communal Management of Natural Resources in Maluku], in P.M. Laksono and R. Topatimasang (eds), *Ken Sa Faak: Benih-Benih Perdamaian dari Kepulauan Kei* [Ken Sa Faak: Seeds of Peace from the Kei Islands], INSIST Press, Yogyakarta, pp. 243–73.

Ministry of Social Affairs (2001), 'National Policies on the Handling of Internally Displaced Persons/Refugees in Indonesia', Jakarta.

Moniaga, S. (1993), 'Toward Community-based Forestry and Recognition of *Adat* Property Rights in the Outer Islands of Indonesia', in J.J. Fox (ed.), *Legal Frameworks for Forest Management in Asia: Case Studies of Community/State Relations*, East-West Center Program on Environment, Honolulu, pp. 131–50.

Novaczek, I. and R. Palyama (1999), 'Dig It Up and Ship It Out? Resistance to Mining in the Lease Islands', *Cakalele*, 10: 37–47.

Novaczek, I., I. Harkes, J. Sopacua and M. Tatuhey (2001), 'An Institutional Analysis of Sasi Laut in Maluku', Technical Report No. 59, ICLARM, Manila.

NRC (Norwegian Refugee Council) Global IDP Project (2001), 'The Maluku Provinces', available at <http://www.maluku.org/portal/portal.php3?oid=226533&key=3>, accessed 16 March 2006.

OCHA (Office for the Coordination of Humanitarian Affairs) (2000), 'United Nations Consolidated Inter-agency Appeal for the Maluku Crisis 2001', 20 December, available at <http://www.reliefweb.int/rw/rwb.nsf/db900SID/ACOS-64CE4Z?OpenDocument&cc=idn>, accessed 30 May 2006.

OCHA (Office for the Coordination of Humanitarian Affairs) (2004), 'Indonesia 2004: Consolidated Appeals Process (CAP)', April, available at <http://www.reliefweb.int/appeals/2004/files/idn04.pdf>, accessed 30 May 2006.

Papilaja, M.J. (2005), personal communication, Office of the Mayor of Ambon, 12 November.

Patlis, J. (2005), 'New Legal Initiatives for Natural Resource Management in a Changing Indonesia: The Promise, the Fear and the Unknown', in B. Resosudarmo (ed.), *The Politics and Economics of Indonesia's Natural Resources*, Institute for Southeast Asian Studies, Singapore, pp. 217-33.

Provincial Government of Maluku (2004), *Rencana Strategis (RENSTRA) Provinsi Maluku Tahun 2003-2008* [Five-year Strategic Plan for the Province of Maluku, 2003-2008], Bappeda, Ambon.

Ramage, D. (1995), *Politics in Indonesia: Democracy, Islam and the Ideology of Tolerance*, Routledge, New York NY.

Ricklefs, M.C. (1981), *A History of Modern Indonesia*, Macmillan, London.

Safa'at, R. (1996), *Masyarakat Adat Yang Tersingkirkan dan Terpinggirkan: Studi Dampak Undang-Undang Nomor 5 Tahun 1979 tentang Pemerintahan Desa Terhadap Masyarakat Adat* [*Adat* Communities That Have Been Sidelined and Marginalized: Study of the Impact on *Adat* Communities of Law No. 5 on Village Government], Lembaga Studi dan Advokasi Masyarakat (ELSAM), Jakarta.

Soumena, R. (2005), personal communication, Office of the Assistant II (Development) to the Provincial Secretary of Maluku, 16 November.

Tapol (2002), 'Maluku Is Now a Closed Territory', Tapol Bulletin No. 168, available at <http://tapol.gn.apc.org/bulletin/2002/bull168.htm#maluku>, accessed 22 May 2006.

Tebiari, P. (2006), 'Memperjuangkan "Otonomi Asli" di Negeri Honitetu—Nu Dua Siwa, Seram Barat' [Struggling for 'Natural Autonomy' in Negeri Honitetu—Nu Dua Siwa, West Seram], paper presented at the 11th Biennial Conference of the International Association for the Study of Common Property, Ubud, 19-23 June.

Thorburn, C. (2000), 'Changing Customary Marine Resource Management Practice and Institutions: The Case of Sasi Lola in the Kei Islands, Indonesia', *World Development*, 23(8): 1,461-79.

Thorburn, C. (2001), 'Kei Islands Peace Building Programme: Challenges and Opportunities for Programme Development', report prepared for the UNDP Kei Islands Peace Building Programme, INS/00/023, November.

Topatimasang, R. (ed.) (2005), *Orang-Orang Kalah: Kisah Penyingkiran Masyarakat Adat Kepulauan Maluku* [Those Who Lose: Tales of the Marginalization of *Adat* Communities in the Maluku Islands], INSIST Press, Yogyakarta.

Turner, K. (2003), 'Myths and Moral Authority in Maluku: The Case of Ambon', *Asian Ethnicity*, 4(2): 241-63.

UNDP (United Nations Development Programme) (2000), 'Maluku Crisis: Umbrella Support Project for the Relief, Reconciliation and Recovery Strategy of the Government of the Republic of Indonesia', Jakarta.

van Hoëvell, G.W.W.C. (1890), 'De Kei Eilanden' [The Kei Islands], *Tijdschrift voor de Indische Taal-, Land- en Volkendunde*, Volume 33.

von Benda-Beckmann, F., K. von Benda-Beckmann and A. Brouwer (1995), 'Changing Indigenous Environmental Law in the Central Malukus: Communal Regulation and Privatization of *Sasi*', *Ekonesia*, 2: 1-38.

Young, A. (2001), 'Ambitions in Ambon, Indonesia', *Bridge*, third quarter: 6, available at <http://www.mercycorps.org/files/file1136577045.pdf>, accessed 29 May 2006.

13 IMPROVING THE LIVELIHOODS OF THE POOR: CHALLENGES AND LESSONS FROM EAST NUSA TENGGARA

Astia Dendi, Heinz-Josef Heile and Stephanus Makambombu

1 INTRODUCTION

Developing a livelihood development policy that effectively alleviates poverty while protecting the environment has been the focus of much study and debate in developing countries for several decades. This issue is highly relevant for Indonesia, where problems of poverty, unemployment and environmental degradation remain pervasive. In 2003, around 16 million Indonesians, or 7.5 per cent of the population, were living on less than US$1 per day, the poverty line set by the World Bank (Kerstan et al. 2004; *Kompas*, 1 November 2004).[1] But the number of Indonesians vulnerable to poverty, that is, living on less than US$2 per day, was far

1 The full description of this international poverty line is 'US$1 per capita per day, 1993 PPP'; that is, the World Bank uses purchasing power parity (PPP) exchange rates to calculate how much of the local currency is required to purchase the same amount of goods and services that US$1 would buy in the United States (Zeller 2004). When adjusted for inflation and cost-of-living differences between countries, this came out at around Rp 2,476 per person per day for Indonesia in 2003. Indonesia's central statistics agency, BPS, calculated a poverty line of Rp 4,600 per person per day for urban areas and Rp 3,500 for rural areas in 2003, that is, somewhat higher than the international poverty line (see also Appendix A2.1, Chapter 2). It has been estimated that the proportion of the Indonesian population living in poverty in 2003 was 17.4 per cent (BPS NTT and Bappeda NTT 2005).

higher, at more than 110 million people, or around 53 per cent of the population (Kerstan et al. 2004). In the 2004 *Human Development Report*, Indonesia was ranked 111th out of 177 countries on the human development index (HDI), a widely used measure of the health, education and standard of living of a country's population (UNDP 2004: 141).

Since the mid-1990s, a number of livelihood development programs have been implemented in eastern Indonesia to alleviate poverty. They include the government livelihood development program for 'left-behind' villages (IDT), the World Bank-funded Subdistrict Development Project (PPK) and the Poverty Alleviation and Support for Local Governance Program (PROMIS) implemented by the German government-sponsored agency, GTZ. This chapter assesses the performance and effects of PROMIS in East Nusa Tenggara to extract lessons for future livelihood development programs. Particular attention is paid to the impact of this program on poverty and the environment.

The next section of the chapter provides a brief overview of the local context in East Nusa Tenggara, and of the province's development policies. It is followed by a section describing the concept behind PROMIS and examining the strategic instruments applied in East Nusa Tenggara. The fourth section discusses the effects of the program on local livelihoods from the perspective of the local economy, the social setting and the environment. The last section contains the authors' conclusions.

2   THE DYNAMICS OF DEVELOPMENT POLICY IN EAST NUSA TENGGARA

The notion of livelihood is grounded in a dynamic and people-centred concept of development. A definition of livelihood frequently cited by scholars is that introduced by Carney in 1998:

> A livelihood comprises the capabilities, assets and activities required for a means of living. A livelihood is sustainable when it can cope with, and recover from, shocks and maintain or enhance its capabilities and assets, both now and in the future, while not undermining the natural resource base (Carney 1998, cited in Kleih, Greenhalgh and Oudwater 2003: 35–6).

This definition informs our assessment of local vulnerability to poverty in East Nusa Tenggara and the impact of livelihood development programs in the province.

Local Vulnerability to Poverty

East Nusa Tenggara faces huge and entrenched problems of poverty. Its people are heavily reliant on agriculture, in particular food crops, livestock and marine fisheries. Farmers are able to produce only low volumes of generally substandard commodities for sale on local markets. Part of the problem lies in the province's unfavourable climatic and other conditions, including its low and variable rainfall and infertile soils, which increase the vulnerability of crops to pests and disease. These have been a driving factor in seasonal food shortages, unemployment and farmers' increasing indebtedness to traders and money lenders. But it has also been argued that current levels of agricultural output in the province are far below potential levels of productivity (GTZ and MHA 2002). Farmers do not make optimal use of family labour, lack access to technology that has been adapted for local conditions and fail to institute adequate pest and disease controls (GTZ and MHA 2002; Heile and Dendi 2004). In East Sumba, for example, the failure to control grasshoppers has resulted in severe crop losses for nearly a decade. Farmers also lack investment capital and strong supporting organizations. Marketing of major products tends to be controlled by a few pre-eminent traders and moneylenders, with market information largely unavailable at the village level (GTZ and MHA 2002). Poor public infrastructure has also hindered economic development in the province. As a consequence, the region continues to miss out on opportunities for private sector investment.

Livelihood Development Programs

In the 1970s and 1980s, the Indonesian government adopted a centralized, top-down approach to development that relied heavily on intervention in specific sectors to promote strong economic growth. During this period, the government's approach to regional agricultural development and poverty reduction was built around providing farmers with a 'green revolution package' consisting of new, high-yielding seed varieties, credit schemes and input subsidies, backed by rural infrastructure development (roads and irrigation) and public investments in agricultural research and extension. Through widespread and intensive implementation of the green revolution package in lowland areas, rice self-sufficiency was achieved in Indonesia in 1984. In upland areas such as those in East Nusa Tenggara, however, farmers were less able to take advantage of the green revolution package and did not experience the same improvements in livelihood.[2]

In the early 1990s, thinking on livelihood development programs shifted from a top-down and narrow sectoral approach that saw the poor

---

2 See Adiningsih and Fairhurst (1998); Dendi and Shivakoti (2003); Dendi et al. (2005); personal communication, Ambrosius Mifa, head of the Ombay Community Development Institute, Alor, 2006.

as a problem to be solved, to a more holistic approach that viewed them as potential actors in solving local developmental and environmental problems. Several non-government organizations (NGOs) began to take a more participatory approach to poverty reduction and natural resource management in the regions. The government, too, rethought its approach to implementing livelihood development programs. In 1994, it introduced a new program of presidential grants designed to speed up poverty reduction at the village level throughout Indonesia: the well-known IDT program. Under this program, the government agreed to provide grants of about Rp 20 million to each village deemed to have been left behind by the development process. The funds were to be distributed to several self-help groups in each recipient village to support income-generating activities. The groups were expected to repay the funds over time so that the money could be made available to other self-help groups. Although the IDT program had a positive effect on poverty, it was discontinued in 1997 because of the severe impact of the Asian economic crisis (Alatas 2000).

In East Nusa Tenggara, many of the self-help groups that received funding under the IDT program did not perform well, with members either unable or unwilling to repay their loans.[3] A number of factors have been identified as contributing to the poor performance of the self-help groups, in particular:

- group members used IDT funds for consumption rather than productive activities;
- crop failures affected the ability of some farmers to repay their loans;
- group members lacked a common understanding of the collective nature of fund ownership;
- there was a lack of trust and mutual support in some groups, leading to a failure by members to support the group's activities;
- some groups were established too quickly, overlooking the diversity of members' individual interests; and
- groups suffered from inadequate guidance and a lack of monitoring and supervision.

3   PROMIS: A PRO-POOR DEVELOPMENT INITIATIVE

The PROMIS livelihood development program was implemented in 1998–2005 by GTZ on behalf of the German Ministry for Economic Coop-

---

3 Suryani et al. (2005); personal communication, Ambrosius Mifa, head of the Ombay Community Development Institute, Alor, 2006; personal observation of Stephanus Makambombu (one of the authors), East Sumba, 2002.

eration (BMZ), together with the Indonesian Ministry of Home Affairs, provincial and district-level development planning boards, and community empowerment agencies. It had two components, one focusing on poverty alleviation and the other focusing on local governance. The goal of the former component was to accelerate poverty alleviation in a sustainable way, by enabling rural populations and organizations to expand their economic activities and achieve their development potential. The goal of the latter component was to enhance the capacity of public and private service providers at the village and district levels better to meet the needs of the poor.

PROMIS and Poverty Alleviation

The poverty alleviation component of PROMIS took on board the lessons from the IDT program, particularly the need to provide intensive guidance and assistance to self-help groups and to monitor closely their activities and use of funds. The program also took account of the major institutional changes that were occurring in Indonesia in the late 1990s and early 2000s. During this period Indonesia experienced a transition of power from a highly authoritarian regime to a more democratic form of government. For the first time, Indonesians were able to elect directly the country's president and vice-president, provincial governors and district/municipality heads. In 1999 the new democratic government passed laws devolving many central government functions to the regions.[4] The main beneficiaries of this decentralization program, implemented throughout Indonesia in 2001, were district and municipal governments.

The new powers given to local governments under decentralization gave NGOs increased opportunities to develop programs that could respond more effectively to local needs. Thus, the poverty alleviation component of PROMIS sought to tap into and strengthen the capacity of rural villagers, community groups and organizations to help themselves. It focused on developing strategies to enhance local economic potential, strengthen village institutions, build human and institutional capacity, support income-generating activities, and promote secure access to capital, markets and resources. These goals were to be achieved by establishing revolving funds to finance self-help groups, by providing advice on agro-processing and marketing, by facilitating access to material resources and by establishing food-for-work projects. During its period of operation, the PROMIS scheme assisted more than 1,000 self-help groups throughout Nusa Tenggara. While many of these were former partici-

---

4 The functions still under central government control are foreign affairs, defence, security, justice, monetary policy, fiscal policy and religion.

Figure 13.1   The Village Motivator System in East and West Nusa Tenggara

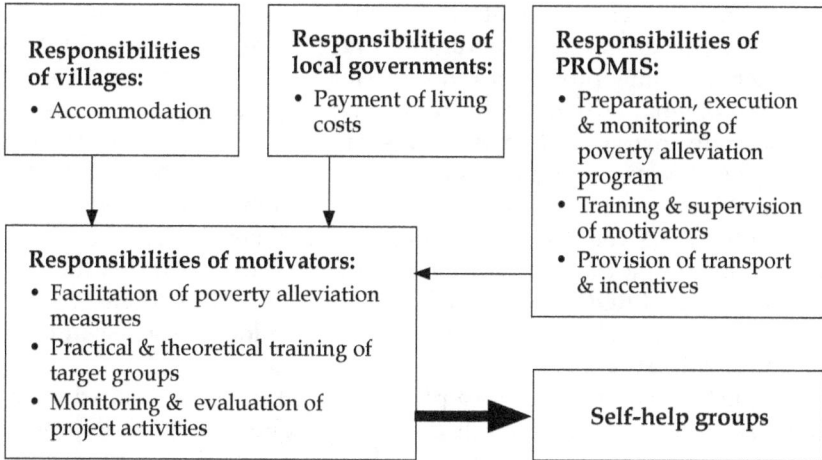

Responsibilities of villages: • Accommodation	Responsibilities of local governments: • Payment of living costs	Responsibilities of PROMIS: • Preparation, execution & monitoring of poverty alleviation program • Training & supervision of motivators • Provision of transport & incentives

Responsibilities of motivators:
• Facilitation of poverty alleviation measures
• Practical & theoretical training of target groups
• Monitoring & evaluation of project activities

Self-help groups

Source: GTZ and MHA (2002: 7).

pants in the IDT program, a considerable number were highly motivated non-IDT groups that had applied to be included in the program.

A crucial element of the program was to recruit and train young, educated people to act as 'motivators' in the villages. Living in the villages themselves, they were paid by local governments to help self-help groups carry out their activities and to provide administrative, financial and technical training. They also acted as an important conduit for conveying information and feedback between the villages and local governments, thus increasing the stake of villagers in public planning and decision making. Figure 13.1 shows how the system worked.

Revolving funds were another strategic tool used by PROMIS to enable self-help groups to accumulate sufficient capital to set up agricultural and other ventures. In East Nusa Teggara, the funds were mainly used to purchase cattle and initiate fishery projects; in West Nusa Tenggara, they also funded the purchase of chickens, ducks and hand tractors. The funds were distributed only after an intensive period of consultation with and training of beneficiary groups. This process began with the identification of eligible groups, followed by a participatory process (through workshops) to formulate and disseminate rules and regulations. Where necessary, the program coordinators helped groups develop workable action plans as well as providing appropriate technical training. Once income was being generated by the venture, each member was required to make monthly payments that could be used, once sufficient capital had accumulated, to fund that person's future economic activities. It was believed that the strong social pressures at work in the villages would ensure that groups met their commitments under the revolving fund system.

In addition to providing funding and support on the ground, PROMIS conducted training programs and workshops to help farmers realize the market potential of their agricultural products, increase their access to market information and raise their awareness of possible marketing strategies. A separate fund was established to provide seed capital for projects directly related to agro-processing activities. Interested groups and individuals could apply for funding after developing a business plan, undergoing training and paying a contribution towards the cost of the project. PROMIS vetted the processing schemes to ensure that they were financially sustainable and could provide a reliable source of income for the rural poor.

While PROMIS was at core a people-centred program, limited material inputs were provided to self-help groups. These included improved seed varieties, irrigation devices, tools and materials for small-scale infrastructure construction, and cleaner, energy-saving cooking stoves.

A food-for-work scheme in which members of self-help groups could work to earn the money to buy basic necessities such as food was another important element of PROMIS. The projects financed through the scheme were mainly small-scale village infrastructure projects (such as the construction of water basins, bridges, access roads and irrigation channels) and projects aimed at ensuring the sustainable use and protection of natural resources (such as land rehabilitation, reforestation and the planting of living fences). Like the revolving funds system, the food-for-work project aimed to give poor people the means not only to pay for the basic necessities of life, but to accumulate capital. This was achieved by requiring workers to pay one-third of their food-for-work earnings into group funds.

PROMIS and Local Governance

The strategic focus of the local governance component of PROMIS was to encourage a more participatory approach to development planning, and to promote the development of effective and efficient budgetary processes at the village and district levels. PROMIS worked to build the capacity of development planners and local policy makers (including both executive and legislative personnel) to formulate policy while making persistent efforts to encourage the construction of a policy framework that would be conducive to development. It concentrated its efforts on the following activities.

- It supported the annual updating of local governments' medium-term development plans based on an evaluation of the results of programs implemented during the previous year.
- It encouraged the development of bottom-up planning processes at the village, subdistrict and district levels, including the development of guidelines on methodology, the training of facilitators and so on.
- At the sectoral level as well, it supported the development of bottom-up planning processes accompanied by guidelines on methodology and training, with a special focus on the health sector.
- It encouraged local government institutions to formulate specific local indicators that could be used to monitor the development process, by conducting field studies, training and workshops.
- It lobbied district and village-level members of parliament and government institutions to develop non-distorting tax policies, providing research to show the benefits of such policies.
- It attempted to increase the transparency of local budgetary processes by arguing for the holding of public hearings, the publication of budget analysis and so forth.
- It argued for the need to develop a process to better link mid-term development planning and mid-term budgeting.
- It provided assistance to district authorities in the drafting of regulations on village budgets.

With the underlying objective of strengthening the local economy, PROMIS concentrated in particular on the need for policy adjustments and institutional development. For example, it commissioned a study on local fees and taxes and local investment policies in selected districts, and advised district, provincial and national-level officials accordingly.

4 ASSESSMENT OF THE PROGRAM'S PERFORMANCE

Our assessment of the performance and impact of PROMIS is based mainly on a study conducted by Dendi et al. (2005) in the districts of Alor, East Sumba and Ende, East Nusa Tenggara, in 2004–05. As well as collecting data from the administrative arm of PROMIS, the authors interviewed households and key persons both within and outside PROMIS program areas. The non-program areas selected by the authors were villages that had been targeted under the national IDT program; they were located close to the villages engaged in PROMIS activities.

The household interviews involved a total of 465 respondents: 310 in program areas and 155 in non-program areas. Of the respondents in the program areas, 100 were from Alor, 120 from East Sumba and 90 from Ende. Of those in the non-program areas, 50 were from Alor, 60 from

East Sumba and 45 from Ende. The key persons interviewed included traditional leaders, self-help group leaders, village heads, NGO personnel, local government representatives and other prominent community leaders.

Some caveats are in order regarding this survey. First, the sample was small. Second, the study did not take into account the problem of selection bias; that is, those who were willing to be involved in the PROMIS program may have had advantages compared with those who were not. Third, in the analysis, many variables were not controlled for; thus, there may have been additional factors at work that were not tested for in the study. Finally, no cost–benefit analysis was conducted. With these limitations in mind, the evaluation nevertheless gives some useful insights.

Revolving Funds

Rather than distributing new revolving funds, in the early period of implementation PROMIS concentrated on helping local governments recover funds held by members of non-performing IDT self-help groups. The funds that were recovered from members were then pooled as group assets, with groups that had performed well in the past eligible to lend the funds to their members. Columns 1 and 2 of Table 13.1 show the total number of groups and the total amount of IDT funds collected in Alor, Ende and East Sumba. As is evident from the table, the amount of funds collected per group varied greatly.

The assets were then redistributed to some of the self-help groups, but this time PROMIS provided intensive guidance and assistance to the beneficiary groups before making the funds available. Overall, the number of self-help groups remained the same. A comparison of columns 3 and 5 in Table 13.1 shows that, in the six years from 1999 to 2005, the funds held by self-help groups increased in all three districts in nominal terms. However, when adjusted for inflation, the real value of the funds increased only in Alor, and actually declined in Ende and East Sumba (column 7). It should also be noted that the 2005 amount may have included mandatory savings from food-for-work activities and bank interest derived from groups' savings.

In 2001, PROMIS started distributing its own revolving funds. In that year, eight self-help groups in Alor and nine in East Sumba received sufficient funding to purchase 8–9 cows per group. In the same year, 14 groups in Alor and seven in East Sumba were able to buy boat engines for their small boats (*sampan*). In 2003, seven groups in Ende each purchased 8–9 cows (Table 13.2).

By 2005, the total number of cows owned by the self-help groups in Alor had almost tripled, the number owned by groups in Ende had dou-

Table 13.1   Growth in Funds Collected from Self-help Groups Formerly in the IDT Program (Rp million)

District	No. of Groups	1999		2005			
		Total[a]	Average per Group[a]	Total[a]	Average per Group[a]	Total[b]	Average per Group[b]
	(1)	(2)	(3)	(4)	(5)	(6)	(7)
Alor	204	1,051	5.15	2,136	10.47	1,118	5.48
(% change since 1999)				(103)		(6)	
Ende	175	721	4.12	925	5.29	484	2.77
(% change since 1999)				(28)		(−33)	
E. Sumba	230	860	3.74	1,192	5.18	624	2.71
(% change since 1999)				(39)		(−27)	

a   Current rupiah.
b   1999 rupiah.
Source: Dendi and PROMIS Monitoring Team (2005).

Table 13.2   Use of PROMIS Revolving Funds

	No. of Groups Involved	No. Purchased Initially	No. Currently Owned
Cows[a]			
Alor	8	75	222
East Sumba	9	80	128
Ende	7	61	135
Total	**24**	**216**	**485**
Boat engines			
Alor	14	15	19
East Sumba	7	16	20
Total	**21**	**31**	**39**

a   Groups in Ende purchased the cows in 2003; other groups purchased them in 2001.
Source: Dendi and PROMIS Monitoring Team (2005).

Table 13.3 Households Engaged in New Income-generating Activities

	Alor		East Sumba		Ende	
	Program Areas	Non-program Areas	Program Areas	Non-program Areas	Program Areas	Non-program Areas
No. of respondents	100	50	120	60	90	45
Households engaged in new activities						
(no.)	82	27	72	36	90	23
(%)	82	54	60	60	100	51

Source: Dendi and PROMIS Monitoring Team (2005).

bled, and the number owned by groups in East Sumba had increased by 60 per cent (Table 13.2). The total number of boat engines also increased in both Alor and East Sumba. However, once again the groups in Alor performed better, not only increasing the number of engines owned but also accumulating enough capital to buy more. At a time when the market price of an engine was around Rp 2.6 million, the Alor groups had accumulated approximately Rp 20 million that they could use to buy more boat engines.

Several factors seem to have contributed to the better performance of self-help groups in Alor than in Ende and East Sumba as measured by their ability to capitalize on the use of revolving funds. First, the self-help groups in Alor were more cohesive and more successful at capacity building than groups elsewhere. Second, they were more successful in creating a common understanding among members of the collective nature of fund ownership. And finally, they benefited from a variety of institutional, performance-based initiatives provided by the district government of Alor, such as the opportunity to enrol in training courses and access to credit from the provincial bank, Bank NTT, without collateral.

New Income-generating Activities

It is important to provide income-generating opportunities for the poor, to give them the means to shift away from a subsistence-level existence. The move to a more market-oriented economy in which a broader spread of income-generating opportunities is available also helps to diversify household and village economies, making them more resilient to shocks such as drought or floods. Table 13.3 shows the number and propor-

Table 13.4 Newly Established Economic Activities by Type of Activity (%)

	East Sumba		Ende		Alor	
	Program Areas	Non-program Areas	Program Areas	Non-program Areas	Program Areas	Non-program Areas
Tree & crop cultivation	53	50	56	71	66	43
Forest products	1	11	2	6	10	3
Fisheries	1	2	3	0	1	0
Trade	16	9	13	15	10	35
Livestock	10	24	17	3	9	0
Home industries/ handicrafts	12	2	10	6	4	8
Other	7	2	0	0	1	11
Total	**100**	**100**	**100**	**100**	**100**	**100**

Source: Dendi and PROMIS Team Monitoring (2005).

tion of respondent households in Alor, East Sumba and Ende engaging in new income-generating activities between 1997 and 2005. In general, it appears that households involved in PROMIS were more willing to engage in new market-oriented activities than households outside the program. Among the households in the program, those in Ende were the most active and households in East Sumba the least active. The majority of new activities involved tree and crop production, followed by trading sector activities (Table 13.4). The main factors enabling respondent households to develop new income-generating activities were access to finance; improved self-confidence; support from other members of the group; collaboration among groups; guidance in developing new ideas and skills; and access to new technology and tools.

Household Living Conditions

The key persons interviewed by Dendi et al. (2005) generally concluded that the approach adopted by PROMIS (namely IDT plus comprehensive assistance) was useful, for the following reasons.

- It increased the incomes of villagers.
- It induced visible diversification of village economies between on-farm and off-farm income-generating activities.
- It promoted economies of scale among existing enterprises.

Table 13.5   Households with Poor Living Conditions (%)[a]

	1997	2000	2004
Alor			
Program areas	84	42	4
Non-program areas	–[b]	–[b]	33
Ende			
Program areas	77	12	0
Non-program areas	54	15	15
East Sumba			
Program areas	80	31	20
Non-program areas	33	63	60

a   Respondents were asked to self-assess changes in their individual living conditions between 1997 and 2004 by applying a three-point scale, namely 'poor', 'medium' and 'good'.

b   No data are available.

Source: Dendi and PROMIS Monitoring Team (2005).

- It ensured secure ownership of assets.
- It focused on building information and marketing networks.
- It strengthened the foundations for sustainable use of the resource base (through the planting of hedgerows and construction of terraces, for example).
- It helped farmers and other small producers (such as people producing handicrafts) to achieve higher prices for their products, primarily through improvements in product quality and better access to market information.

Households were asked to rate their living conditions in 1997, 2000 and 2004 on a three-point scale. The results showed that the majority of households engaged in PROMIS activities felt that their living conditions had improved over the previous five years (Table 13.5). Among the households not involved in the program, the picture was more mixed: households in Ende felt that their situation had improved while those in East Sumba felt that it had worsened (with no data for Alor). The reasons households typically gave for an improvement in living conditions were the existence of common goals among group members; fair rules for each group supported by adequate conflict resolution mechanisms; mutual trust; transparent procedures; access to secure assets; and high-quality training and assistance.

Ecological Impact

Although no systematic assessment of the environmental impact of PROMIS was conducted, the comments of interviewees indicated that the program had made a substantial contribution to reducing the negative effects of poverty on the local environment. In Alor and East Sumba, there was a significant reduction in destructive practices such as the use of explosive devices for fishing. In Alor, the extent and frequency of forest fires declined. Moreover, after intensive discussion with PROMIS's village motivators and technical staff, the Alor district government passed several local government regulations (*perda*) to protect the environment. These included Perda No. 8/1999 on the prevention of forest burning and Perda No. 14/2005 on the management and protection of coastal resources.

5   FINAL REMARKS

The main goal of this chapter has been to extract lessons from the PROMIS program, as implemented in the districts of Alor, East Sumba and Ende, East Nusa Tenggara, for use in future poverty alleviation programs. We do not mean to argue that PROMIS has achieved all its envisaged goals, or that it has performed better than any other poverty alleviation program conducted in eastern Indonesia.

An important feature of PROMIS was that it constituted an integrated approach to poverty alleviation. It gave the poor access to financial resources while encouraging individual participation and creativity in the use of those resources. The program coordinators also worked with village and district governments to promote a participatory approach to developing policies and budgets that would help the poor. In areas where poverty was particularly intransigent or local infrastructure especially poor, PROMIS conducted food-for-work programs.

The data used to assess the program were collected by Dendi et al. (2005). Although their study had a number of limitations, it nevertheless yielded some useful lessons. First, the main factors enabling the poor to accumulate capital were effective formation and capacity building of self-support groups; a common understanding of the collective nature of ownership of group funds; and appropriate rewards for good performance, such as the provision of special loans from local banks without needing to provide collateral. Second, the conditions that enabled the poor to develop new income-generating activities were access to adequate financial resources; improved self-confidence; support from other members of the group; collaboration among groups; guidance in developing new ideas and skills; and access to new technology and tools.

Third, both within self-help groups and in members' interactions with society, people felt that their livelihoods improved when they were working towards common goals; when fair rules were backed up by adequate conflict resolution mechanisms; when they knew they could trust those around them and were trusted in return; when decision-making, administrative and distribution procedures were transparent; when they had access to secure assets; and when they received high-quality training and assistance.

Fourth, people seemed to prefer the integrated approach of PROMIS to the approach of programs like IDT which provided funding but almost no guidance. People believed that the more integrated approach was effective in increasing the incomes of villagers; inducing visible diversification of village economies between on-farm and off-farm income-generating activities; developing economies of scale among existing enterprises; securing ownership of assets; building information and marketing networks; strengthening the foundations for sustainable use of the resource base; and achieving higher prices for products, primarily through improvements in product quality and better access to market information.

Finally, it seems that a properly integrated, bottom-up approach may be good for the environment. During the period in which PROMIS was implemented, Alor produced the best outcomes among the districts studied in terms of meeting the program's immediate objectives, while also achieving an improvement in environmental conditions.

ACKNOWLEDGMENTS

The authors gratefully acknowledge the financial support of the Multi-donor Support Office for Eastern Indonesia and the invaluable assistance with data collection and processing provided by PROMIS, the local governments of Alor, East Sumba and Ende, and NGOs. Among the latter, we would particularly like to thank the Ombay Community Development Institute in Alor, KSU-Panutan in Ende, Pusat Studi dan Pemberdayaan Masyarakat in East Sumba and the Center for Development Studies in Bima. We are indebted to Mr K.D. Peters (former GTZ team leader of Poverty Alleviation in Nusa Tenggara) and Dr Birgit M. Kerstan (former team leader of PROMIS) for help in conceptualizing our approach to the research; to the people of Alor, East Sumba and Ende for their genuine willingness to share their experiences with us; to Mr G. Sippel, a principal adviser with GTZ, for organizing a very fruitful discussion session; and to Dr Manfred Poppe for editing our English as well as for constructive discussions.

REFERENCES

Adiningsih, S. and T.H. Fairhurst (1998), 'The Use of Reactive Phosphate Rock for the Rehabilitation of Anthropic Savannah in Indonesia', in A.E. Johnston and J.K. Syers (eds), *Nutrient Management for Sustainable Crop Production in Asia*, World Phosphate Institute and CAB International, New York NY, pp. 159–74.

Alatas, V. (2000), 'Evaluating the Left Behind Villages Program in Indonesia: Exploiting Program Rules to Identify Effects on Employment and Expenditures', Princeton University, Princeton NJ (mimeo).

BPS NTT and Bappeda NTT (Badan Pusat Statistik Provinsi Nusa Tenggara Timur and Badan Perencanaan Pembangunan Daerah Provinsi Nusa Tenggara Timur) (2005), *Nusa Tenggara Timur dalam Angka 2004/2005* [East Nusa Tenggara in Figures, 2004/2005], Kupang.

Carney, D. (ed.) (1998), *Sustainable Rural Livelihoods: What Contribution Can We Make?* Department for International Development, London.

Dendi, A. and PROMIS Monitoring Team (2005), 'Laporan Lokakarya Serah Terima Hasil-hasil dan Aset-aset PROMIS-NT' [Workshop Report on Handing over Results and Assets of PROMIS-NT], unpublished paper, PROMIS-NT, Mataram.

Dendi, A. and G.P. Shivakoti (2003), 'Assessment of Participatory Extension Approaches for Sustainable Agriculture Development in Uplands of West Sumatra, Indonesia', *Asia–Pacific Journal of Rural Development*, 13(2): 19–43.

Dendi, A., G.P. Shivakoti, R. Dale and S.L. Ranamukhaarachchi (2005), 'Evolution of the Minangkabau's Shifting Cultivation in the West Sumatra Highland of Indonesia and Its Strategic Implications for Dynamic Farming Systems', *Land Degradation and Development*, 16: 13–26.

GTZ and MHA (Deutsche Gessellschaft für Technische Zusammenarbeit and Ministry of Home Affairs) (2002), *Raising Capacities of the Poor: Experiences of Nusa Tenggara Project*, Jakarta.

Heile, H.-J. and A. Dendi (2004), *Agro-processing and Marketing: Approach and Strategy for Alleviating Poverty*, GTZ and Ministry of Home Affairs, Jakarta.

Kerstan, B., A. Dendi, H.-J. Heile, Mahman, R. Hilaliah and R. Saleh Haryono (2004), *Alleviating Poverty through Local Economic Development: Lessons from Nusa Tenggara*, GTZ and Ministry of Home Affairs, Jakarta.

Kleih, U., P. Greenhalgh and N. Oudwater (2003), *A Guide to the Analysis of Fish Marketing Systems Using a Combination of Sub-sector Analysis and the Sustainable Livelihoods Approach*, Natural Resources Institute, Chatham.

Suryani, S., U.H. Ara, K.A. Rewa, A.K. Hudang and E.K. Kiha (2005), 'Laporan Hasil Penelitian: Keberlanjutan Investasi Program Padat Karya Pada Level Pokmas' [Research Report: Continuation of Investment in the Food-for-Work Program at the Community Group Level], unpublished paper, Pusat Kajian Pembangunan dan Pemberdayaan Masyarakat, Sekolah Tinggi Ilmu Ekonomi Kristen Wira Wacana Sumba.

UNDP (United Nations Development Programme) (2004), *Human Development Report 2004: Cultural Liberty in Today's Diverse World*, New York NY.

Zeller, M. (2004), 'Review of Poverty Assessment Tools', report submitted to IRIS and USAID as part of the Developing Poverty Assessment Tools Project, available at <http://www.povertytools.org/>.

14 HOW FAR IS PAPUA FROM ACHIEVING THE GOALS OF HEALTHY INDONESIA 2010?

Endang R. Sedyaningsih and Suriadi Gunawan

1 INTRODUCTION

The vision for health development in Indonesia was formulated by the Ministry of Health in 2000. Called 'Healthy Indonesia 2010', it aims to create an environment conducive for human beings to achieve their optimal health status, a community with proactive behaviour to promote health and prevent disease, and a heath care system with sufficient capacity to provide quality health services. The principles on which Healthy Indonesia 2010 are based include equitable and even development, with priority to be given to remote areas (Ministry of Health 2000).

Papua, the easternmost province of Indonesia and often regarded as the most culturally distinct, is most in need of priority.[1] Despite the province's abundant natural resources, Papuans are poorer than other Indonesians. Papua has Indonesia's highest poverty rate, with 41.8 per cent of the population living on less than US$1 per day, more than double the national average of 18.2 per cent (BPS, Bappenas and UNDP 2004: 187).

Papua continues to face problems of poor quality and uneven provision of health services, local political instability, the emergence of new diseases and persistence of old ones, and low levels of education. Although vital indicators show that there have been some improvements, the province still lags behind the western part of Indonesia. It ranked 29th out of

---

Indonesia's then 30 provinces on the 2004 human development index (HDI), which measures longevity, educational attainment and standard of living (BPS, Bappenas and UNDP 2004: 109). Malaria continues to be the most frequent cause of mortality and morbidity,[2] and a serious AIDS epidemic is emerging.

This chapter discusses the current health problems facing Papua and reviews the capacity of the province to improve the health status of Papuans. Will Papua achieve the aims set out for it in Healthy Indonesia 2010?

2 STRUGGLING FOR HEALTH

Under the Dutch administration, health care services in Papua were managed by the Public Health Service (Dienst van Gezondheidszorg), a very active government department providing health care services down to the village level. The first government post in the highlands was established in 1938, in Enarotali in the centre of Papua, near the Paniai lakes. This post was abandoned during World War II but was reopened in 1946. The eastern region of the Papuan highlands, Baliem valley, was more difficult to reach. It was only in 1955 that a government post was established in Wamena. The intensity of contacts then increased with the gradual addition of government as well as mission posts (Gunawan 1990).

At the conclusion of World War II, the Dutch re-established control over Papua. For the next decade and a half the Public Health Service was again vigorous in conducting government health programs. Between 1 October 1962 and 1 May 1963, Papua was ruled by a transitional government led by the United Nations Temporary Executive Authority. During this period Dutch personnel were gradually replaced by Indonesians, including Papuans (Gunawan 2005). Indonesia then assumed full administration of the area, which it renamed West Irian.

The next five years were very difficult ones for Indonesia. In the face of national political and economical upheaval, the government found it hard to maintain its planned funding arrangement for Papua. Inflation was high and goods were scarce. A shortage of competent technicians and administrators led to a deterioration in most services, including medical services.

Economic conditions began to improve following the change of government from President Soekarno to President Soeharto in 1966. Begin-

---

2 Morbidity is a rough indicator to show the health status of a population; it indicates the percentage of people who are ill at the time a survey is conducted relative to the total population in the area.

ning in 1969, the administration implemented a series of five-year plans (Repelita) aimed at lifting development outcomes. With the assistance of the Fund of the United Nations for the Development of West Irian, the Indonesian government began to undertake some rehabilitation and revitalization of public health programs. However, disparities in the distribution of health services meant that many rural areas were still neglected. Only after a large demonstration in Jakarta in 1974 did the government undertake to introduce corrective measures to address this problem of equity. West Irian, now called Irian Jaya, also gained from these policies. Health care coverage in rural and remote areas started to improve.

The Presidential Instruction (Inpres) program of central government grants extended basic health services to all subdistricts (*kecamatan*, called *distrik* in Papua) in the 1980s, and maternal and child health services to 50 per cent of villages in the 1990s. The World Health Organization (WHO), the United Nations Development Programme (UNDP), the World Bank and the German government-owned development bank, KfW, helped train more health personnel to staff the expanding health facilities. The total number of health workers in Papua increased from 2,500 in the 1970s to around 7,000 in the late 1990s. But the Inpres program was uniform across Indonesia; no modifications for local conditions were possible. This caused problems in acceptance and implementation, especially in a province with a culture as distinct as that of Irian Jaya (Gunawan 2005).

The fall of Soeharto in 1998 ushered in a new era of political reform (*reformasi*). Papuans fought for greater autonomy and some demanded independence. In 2001 the province was given special autonomy, renamed Papua and divided into two provinces, Papua and West Irian Jaya. The number of autonomous districts (*kabupaten*) rose from 12 to 29, each with its own Kabupaten Health Service. The emphasis on the creation of new provinces and districts has taken attention away from social issues such as health care. The political changes have set back the provision of health services; there are not enough qualified staff to operate the newly established Kabupaten Health Services, for example.

3   THE HEAVY BURDEN OF COMMUNICABLE DISEASES

Papua has extensive lowlands in the coastal regions and a huge mountain chain across its centre. The types of health problems experienced in the province are closely related to its topography. Because there are fewer mosquitoes at high altitudes, for example, malaria is less of a problem in the mountains than in the lowlands. On the other hand, cold weather diseases like influenza spread very fast and kill many people in the highlands, where people live in overcrowded conditions in cool mountain valleys.

The main sources of health data for Papua are health service records and reports, as surveys are conducted only infrequently, especially in the highlands. Papua was included in some of the national health and demographic surveys carried out by Statistics Indonesia (BPS), the National Family Planning Coordinating Board (BKKBN) and the Ministry of Health in 1991, 1994 and 1997. But together with the provinces of Aceh and Maluku, Papua was left out of the national Demographic and Health Survey for 2002–03 because of security concerns (BPS 2003).

Infectious diseases are the dominant health issue in Papua. In 2003, 36.5 per cent of morbidity reported for all patients in government health facilities was caused by malaria, followed by diarrhoea (9.7 per cent) and acute respiratory infections (3.5 per cent). Other common diseases were worm infestations (hookworm, roundworm and whipworm), pneumonia, tuberculosis, yaws,[3] meningitis[4] and leprosy[5] (Papua Provincial Health Office 2004).

Malaria: The Greatest Killer

Malaria is responsible for over 20 per cent of outpatient consultations, 16 per cent of hospital admissions and 15 per cent of hospital deaths (mainly of children) in Papua. It is hyper-endemic to meso-endemic[6] in the coastal and lowland areas, and unstable[7] and potentially epidemic in the highlands (Gunawan 1985). In 2003, a total of 187,383 cases of malaria were reported to the provincial health services. The estimated annual malaria incidence was 74 per 1,000 people, the second highest rate in Indonesia after the province of East Nusa Tenggara. These data are not very reliable, since they are based on reported cases in hospitals and health centres, usually clinically diagnosed without laboratory con-

---

3 Yaws is a skin and bone disease caused by bacteria *Treponema pallidum pertenue*. Its characteristic manifestation is large skin papilloma. Bone involvement may cause deformities.

4 Meningitis is an infection of the nerve coating (meninges) caused by bacteria or viruses; viral meningitis is generally less severe, while bacterial meningitis can be devastating. Its characteristic manifestations are fever, stiff neck and seizures.

5 Leprosy is a skin and nerve disease caused by bacteria *Mycobacterium leprae*. Its characteristic manifestations are anaesthetic skin patches and nodules, and *leonine facies* (lion face). The nerve damage is irreversible and may cause deformities.

6 Hyper-endemic: spleen rate or parasitic rate in children aged 2–9 years constantly over 50 per cent; meso-endemic: spleen rate or parasitic rate in children aged 2–9 years of 11–50 per cent.

7 Unstable malaria: malaria transmission not occurring at the same rate over the year.

firmation. Many of these cases may not have been malaria; on the other hand, many affected people would not go to health facilities but simply treat the symptoms themselves.

Malaria causes loss of productive days, poor quality of life due to severe anaemia and profound weakness, disability and death. In pregnant women, it increases perinatal deaths. Malaria is a major cause of death in young children in particular.

The main malaria vectors in Papua are mosquitoes of the *punctulatus* group. They breed indiscriminately in all types of water collections, their only need being some sunshine. Such water collections are often man-made — ditches, footprints, wheel ruts, vegetable beds, canoes, empty drums and cans — or animal-made (pools produced by the digging and bathing activities of pigs). Indonesia has over 24 mosquito groups of malaria vectors but they mostly breed in more selective environments. This makes them less widely distributed than the *punctulatus* group.

The specific behaviour of *punctulatus* mosquitoes poses a serious obstacle to the control of malaria by house spraying: they bite both inside and outside the house, and they leave the house after biting. The semi-nomadic way of life of some people in the villages also favours transmission and interferes with the effectiveness of insecticide house spraying. This wandering habit appears to inhibit the effectiveness of impregnated mosquito nets in the rural areas of Papua.

A significant setback in malaria treatment and control is the emergence of chloroquine resistance among two of the four species of malaria parasites (Taylor, Richie and Tjitra 1995). As chloroquine, the traditional anti-malarial drug, becomes ineffective, second-line malaria drugs will be needed. However, these are more expensive and not yet widely available. For example, combinations of artemisinine with other malaria drugs cost US$3 per treatment course, compared with 50 cents for chloroquine.

Malaria is a serious impediment to socio-economic development in Papua. Clearly, better anti-malaria programs are essential to the sound economic development of the province. These programs could consist of such simple activities as providing and distributing mosquito nets, conducting some vector control, providing rapid testing for early diagnosis and implementing a clinical algorithm for presumptive diagnosis, in addition to the use of effective drugs, at least in and around areas under development.

The Persistence of Tuberculosis

Tuberculosis is still being reported with increasing frequency. In 1999, a total of 2,545 cases of active tuberculosis were detected; in 2003, 4,519 cases of clinical and laboratory-confirmed tuberculosis were reported.

Tuberculosis is the sixth leading cause of death in the province, causing 6.7 per cent of all mortality (Papua Provincial Health Office 2004). Following the national tuberculosis control program, the Directly Observed Treatment Short Course (DOTS) strategy was introduced in Papua.[8] However, it has not been a complete success: the cure rate is only around 50 per cent and the drop-out rate is about 10 per cent (Gunawan 2005).

The highlands were free of tuberculosis until the mid-1980s. A tuberculin survey in the Baliem valley in the 1960s did not reveal any positivity among the local population; that is, at that time nobody had ever been infected by the tuberculosis bacterium. But in 1986 a total of 33 cases were reported in Jayawijaya (Gunawan 1990), and in 1999 over 50 cases were reported in Wamena (Gunawan 2005).

The current policy of passive case finding will inevitably have a low case-detection rate in a geographically difficult area like Papua where health services are not easily accessed. In this situation, the infection will still be rampant even if the cure rate increases and the drop rate decreases — especially with the emergence of HIV/AIDS, which can perpetuate the manifestations of tuberculosis (Harries and Maher 1996).

HIV/AIDS: A Rising Health and Social Problem

According to an evaluation conducted in 2005 by the Papua Province AIDS Commission, the number of people living with HIV in Papua is around 12,000, or 1 per cent of the adult population (KPAP 2005). This number is predicted to increase to 30,000 in 2010 and 60,000 in 2015 if no effective interventions can be implemented (Kaldor et al. 2006). This will place a heavy burden on Papuan health services and have a measurable impact on the economy.

HIV infection was first detected in 1992 among Thai fishermen and female sex workers in Merauke. Each year since then, the number of AIDS cases reported in Papua has increased (Figure 14.1). By June 2006 Papua had reported a total of 2,703 HIV/AIDS cases with a male to female ratio of 55:45. Of these, 364 were in Merauke, 56 in Jayapura, 121 in Biak, 104 in Nabire and six in Manokwari (Papua Provincial Health Office 2006). These reported cases represent just the tip of the iceberg.

The reported case rate in 2002 was 20.4 cases per 100,000 people, a striking contrast to the rest of Indonesia, which had only 0.42 cases per 100,000 people (Ministry of Health 2003a). In 2006, the rate had risen to

---

8 DOTS is a WHO strategy consisting of: (1) government commitment to a national tuberculosis program; (2) passive case finding; (3) short-course chemotherapy under direct observation; (4) supply of essential anti-tuberculosis drugs; and (5) monitoring and evaluation.

Figure 14.1   Number of HIV/AIDS Cases Reported in Papua, 1992–2006 (cumulative)

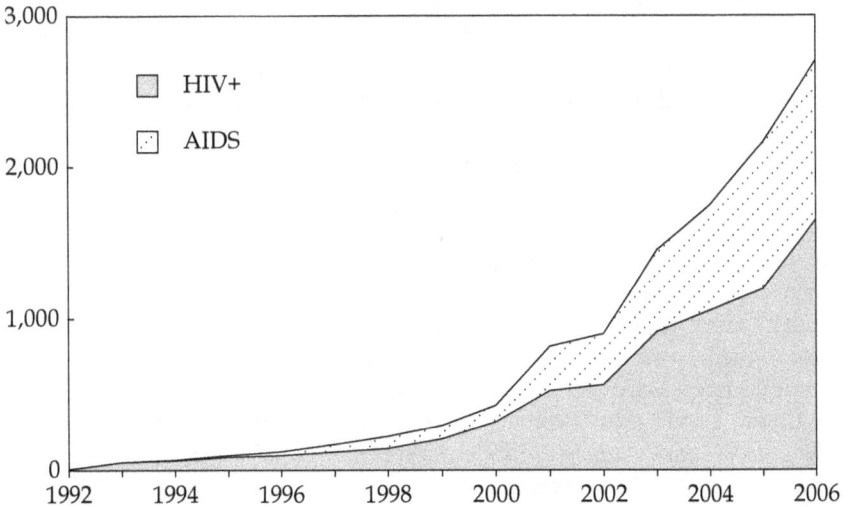

Source: Papua Provincial Health Office (2006).

50 cases per 100,000 people, 15.8 times the national average of 3.2 per 100,000 (Ministry of Health 2006). Table 14.1 shows the provinces with the eight highest rates in Indonesia.

Some districts where studies of pregnant women have been done (such as Merauke and Timika) show an HIV prevalence rate of over 1 per cent.[9] This means that these areas are already experiencing a generalized HIV/AIDS epidemic (WHO and UNAIDS 2000; KPAP 2005).[10] The

---

9   The HIV prevalence rate in pregnant women is based on active HIV sero-surveillance among this population, while the AIDS reported case rate is based on reported cases divided by the number of the whole population. Since sero-surveillance is based on voluntary participation, participation is skewed towards those who are aware that they may be at risk because of their husbands' behaviour.

10 According to WHO and UNAIDS (2000), there are three different epidemic states: low-level, concentrated and generalized. A low-level epidemic is one in which HIV infection may have existed for many years but has not spread to a significant extent in any subpopulation. The numerical proxy for this situation is HIV prevalence that has not consistently exceeded 5 per cent in any defined subpopulation. A concentrated epidemic is one in which HIV has spread rapidly in a defined subpopulation but is not well established in the general population. The numerical proxy for this situation is HIV prevalence that is consistently over 5 per cent in at least one defined subpopulation, but still consistently below 1 per cent in pregnant women in urban areas. A gen-

Table 14.1   *Reported AIDS Case Rate in Provinces with the Eight Highest Rates in Indonesia, 2005 (no. cases per 100,000 people)*

Province	Reported AIDS Case Rate
Papua	50.0
Jakarta	26.5
Bali	9.0
Maluku	8.5
West Kalimantan	6.0
Riau & Riau Islands	5.7
North Sulawesi	5.0
Bangka-Belitung	4.8

Source: Ministry of Health (2006).

prevalence of HIV infection among female sex workers in 2005 was 16 per cent in Sorong, 13 per cent in Nabire, 9 per cent in Timika/Mimika and 5 per cent in Jayapura (KPAP 2005).

Factors that promote HIV transmission in Papua are the high rates of sexually transmitted diseases (STDs) — other than AIDS — among sex workers and the general population, and the high proportion of the population having unprotected sex outside of marriage. Figure 14.2 shows the prevalence of STDs among sex workers in Jayapura in 2003 and 2005. The rates are not substantially different to those among sex workers in other Indonesian cities (Silfanus et al. 2006a, 2006b).

Behaviour surveillance surveys conducted in 2003 found that 30 per cent of adult males in Merauke, Jayapura and Sorong had purchased sex and 40 per cent of these had had sex with more than one partner in the previous year (Ministry of Health and BPS 2003). Premarital sex among young women aged 15–19 years was also high: 64 per cent in Merauke, 20 per cent in Jayapura and 30 per cent in Biak. Other behaviour that may facilitate the spread of HIV infection is high alcohol use among men, especially in the towns.

Condom use is very low. Despite the targeted condom promotion program executed by the government and non-government organizations (NGOs) among sex workers, the proportion of female sex workers in Jayapura who always used condoms was only 39 per cent in 2003 and 40 per cent in 2005 (Jazan et al. 2004; Silfanus et al. 2006a).

---

eralized epidemic is one in which HIV is firmly established in the general population. The numerical proxy for this situation is HIV prevalence that is consistently found in over 1 per cent of pregnant women.

Figure 14.2   Prevalence of Sexually Transmitted Diseases among Sex Workers in Jayapura, 2003 and 2005

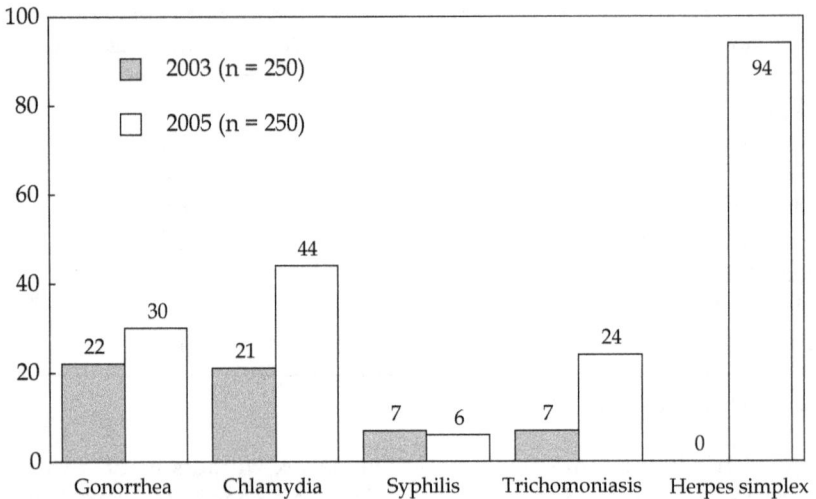

Source: Jazan et al. (2004); Silfanus et al. (2006a).

From a program point of view, HIV prevention activities are sporadic and the general AIDS awareness campaigns inadequate. Moreover, there is still a reluctance to promote condom use. The situation is exacerbated by inadequate service delivery, especially to treat STDs (Butt, Numbery and Morin 2002).

As well as being a serious health problem, HIV/AIDS has significant political overtones because of its association with moral and cultural values. Attempts to raise HIV/AIDS awareness often fail because they stigmatize Papuans (Butt, Numbery and Morin 2002). Intervention programs proven to be effective elsewhere cannot just be imported and implemented without change in Papua. They need to be introduced in a culturally sensitive fashion and tailored to the local situation. For example, planners need to understand and accept the existence of culturally valued practices such as polygyny and wife swapping in order to be able to create a program that is appreciative of the local culture while also promoting safe sex.

It is encouraging that international donors like AusAID, USAID, the Global Fund and UNICEF (with Dutch and New Zealand funding) have implemented projects to prevent the spread of HIV/AIDS in Papua. Appropriate programs are certainly needed to prevent the epidemic from escalating to rates commonly reported in Sub-Saharan Africa, where some countries experience HIV prevalence as high as 10–24 per cent in the general population (UNAIDS 2006). These programs should include increasing awareness of HIV, AIDS and other STDs, promoting safe sex, providing voluntary counselling and HIV testing, increasing the availability and accessibility of STD and AIDS treatment, and providing home care and shelter for AIDS patients and orphans.

4 OTHER HEALTH PROBLEMS

Other Communicable Diseases

In addition to the three major diseases discussed above, Papuans are at risk of several other communicable diseases.

STDs are a growing health problem in Papua. Increased prostitution in urban areas and in logging, fishing and mining regions is an important factor in the spread of STDs including HIV. A high incidence of syphilis, gonorrhoea, chlamydia and trichomoniasis is found among female sex workers, especially those who work on the streets (Figure 14.2). Improvements in road access have aided the spread of STDs from coastal areas into the highlands. Providing better services for the treatment of STDs is an important strategy to prevent these diseases from spreading further.

Between 1999 and 2004, leprosy had a steady prevalence of four cases per 10,000 people. During this period nearly 1,000 cases were treated each year, most of them in the Sorong area and about one-fifth of them children under 15 years of age (Papua Provincial Health Office 2005). The highlands remain free of leprosy, but this may change as access improves and more people move into the highland areas. The present program initially aimed to eliminate leprosy (no new cases) by 2005, but this goal is unlikely to have been achieved.

Yaws can still be found in the more isolated areas of the highlands. The current health program aimed to eliminate yaws by 2005, but a total of 2,618 cases were reported in 2004 (Papua Provincial Health Office 2004), more than the 1,793 cases reported in 2000 (Gunawan 2005). Nearly half of the cases were among 5–14 year olds. Just treating people with yaws and their contacts does not provide good results, since housing and environmental conditions, as well as personal hygiene, influence the spread of the disease. The government is now considering conducting a mass campaign to treat everybody in villages where yaws is still found.

Dengue hemorrhagic fever[11] first became a problem in the 1980s and the number of cases has continued to increase since then. The disease has

---

11 Dengue fever is a viral infection spread by mosquitoes (*Aedes aegypti*). Infection produces a spectrum of clinical illnesses ranging from a non-specific viral syndrome to severe and fatal hemorrhagic disease.

a seasonal pattern, peaking around the months of February and March (Papua Provincial Health Office 2005). It is important to attack the source of the disease though larval control of *Aedes aegypti* mosquitoes, especially in urban areas.

Taeniasis and cysticercosis[12] were first detected in Enarotali in 1972 (Gunawan, Subianto and Tumada 1976). This coincided with an increase in the number of burns patients admitted to Enarotali hospital, some of them grand mal epileptic patients with cerebral cysticercosis who had fallen into fire in their own homes. Attempts to control the disease through health education, the introduction of latrines and treatment with the drug praziquantel have been only partially successful. The prevalence of taeniasis/cysticercosis in the Paniai area has decreased but it has spread to other areas of the highlands and is now a major problem in the Baliem valley. Mass treatment with praziquantel or abendazole combined with a culturally appropriate health education campaign will be needed to control the disease.

Fumacosis has been described by Vriend (2003), a doctor who worked in the highlands for many years (1962–92). It is a chronic obstructive pulmonary (lung) disease caused by air pollution from the smoke of fires inside the home. Traditional houses in the highlands, designed to protect against the cold, are filled with smoke from fires that burn constantly to provide warmth. A large proportion of adults suffer from the disease, whose symptoms include cough, sputum and breathlessness. The solution to this problem would lie in modification of houses to produce smoke-free cooking and sleeping facilities, while still ensuring warmth. This means the construction of chimneys, closed fireplaces and stoves, and the introduction of blankets.

Whooping cough and measles epidemics occasionally sweep through the Papuan highlands, causing significant morbidity and mortality. In addition, cholera epidemics have been reported in coastal towns (Gunawan 2005). Seasonal influenza is often accompanied by a remarkably high fatality rate due to severe complications such as pneumonia, especially in the highlands (Gunawan 1990).

Infectious disease epidemics occur frequently in Papua. More often than not they take an immense death toll, especially when they occur among the isolated populations in the highlands. Some of these diseases

---

12 Taeniasis is caused by tapeworms (*Taenia spp.*). It is the most common cause of acquired seizure disorder in the developing world, causing neurological disease. Humans acquire taeniasis by ingesting undercooked meat (mostly pork) containing tapeworm larvae. Cysticercosis is caused by the larva of *Taenia spp.* It is acquired, not by eating infected meat, but by ingesting food contaminated with human faeces containing eggs or larvae. The clinical manifestations include seizures and other neurological symptoms.

could be prevented by immunization, if the difficulties of transportation and geographical terrain, insufficient human resources and inadequate cold storage facilities could be overcome.

The Emergence of Non-communicable Diseases

Non-communicable diseases mainly affect urban populations and are not considered a top public health issue. Cases of diabetes, obesity, hypertension, stroke, coronary heart disease, cancer, accidents and mental health problems are reported with increasing frequency. Scattered surveys and research in the 1970s showed very low rates of hypertension among highland populations, but increasing rates among urban populations where people had adopted a more modern lifestyle (Gunawan 2005). Given the vast extent of Papua's mining industry, significant occupational health problems, especially accidents and injuries, are likely to occur.

To anticipate the non-communicable disease burden in Papua, anti-smoking campaigns and other measures to promote a healthy lifestyle, as well as occupational health programs, must be initiated. Some indications of future conditions can be seen in a snapshot health survey conducted in the Tembagapura supermarket on National Health Day (12 November) in 1995. Of the 267 people examined (mainly PT Freeport Indonesia employees and dependants, including Papuans), 54 (20 per cent) had raised blood pressure and 16 (6 per cent) had diabetes (Gunawan 1997).

The incidence of mental health illnesses is also predicted to rise, due to the pressures caused by increasing urbanization, rising population densities, migration/transmigration and cultural/intergroup conflict, changing value systems (including ways of dealing with conflict), unemployment, and intergenerational and marital conflict.

5   NUTRITIONAL STATUS

A shortage of dietary protein is one of the most important nutritional problems in Papua, especially in the highlands. Sago is the staple food in the coastal areas, and sweet potato, taro and yam are the primary foods in the highlands. Rice is becoming the staple food in towns, but it has to be imported. The prevalence of malnutrition in Papua fell from 24.8 per cent in 1999 to 18 per cent in 2003 (Papua Provincial Health Office 2004), compared with a national figure of 28 per cent (Ministry of Health 2005a).

Another health issue associated with chronic malnutrition is anaemia (Ministry of Health 2003b). The estimated prevalence of malnutrition-related anaemia among young girls ranges from 17.6 per cent in Sorong to 73.6 per cent in Jayawijaya. Those at highest risk are children aged less than five (where the prevalence is greater than 40 per cent) and pregnant women (where the prevalence is greater than 50 per cent) (Gunawan et al. 1978).

Vitamin deficiencies are rare among Papuans living in their natural surroundings. However, beri-beri and other vitamin deficiencies may be observed in closed artificial communities such as the barracks of logging operations, prisons or boarding schools.

In the 1970s, a significant incidence of iodine deficiency was observed among many segments of the Papuan population in the highlands. In response to this issue, the government implemented a program to provide iodized oil injections to high-risk populations in many highland regions (Sumule 2003). This program was quite successful as measured by the continuing low prevalence of goitre in those regions. However, three coastal districts, Manokwari, Sorong and Jayapura, continue to experience high levels of iodine deficiency, with an average goitre prevalence of 13 per cent (Papua Provincial Health Office 2004).

6 HEALTH RESOURCES

The ratio of health care personnel per head of population in Papua is one of the highest in Indonesia, but the ratio of health care facilities per square kilometre is quite low. In 2003, the various health services employed a total of 9,245 health care personnel, approximately 83 per cent of them in health centres and hospitals and the remaining 17 per cent in administrative and support positions (health offices, laboratories, training institutions). These health care personnel included 72 specialist doctors, 224 other doctors, 4,980 paramedics (mainly nurses and midwives), 50 dentists and 19 pharmacists. The province had 217 community health centres (*puskesmas*), 903 sub-*puskesmas*, 388 mobile health care centres and 2,714 integrated community health care posts (*posyandus*). It had 25 hospitals: 13 district hospitals (1,560 beds), six military hospitals (238 beds) and six private hospitals (444 beds) (Papua Provincial Health Office 2004).

A report on health facilities in 2005 showed that the number of facilities had increased slightly. However, only 48 per cent of health care centres had a qualified doctor on staff and only 15 per cent of the *posyandus* were active. This was worse than in previous years, before decentralization and the granting of special autonomy status (Papua Provincial Health Office 2005).

Spending on health accounts for about 15 per cent of the Papua government budget, a proportion that is considered ideal by the Indonesian

Ministry of Health. In 2003, the health budget was Rp 171 billion (US$17.1 million), consisting of a special autonomy budget of Rp 85 billion, a routine budget of Rp 21 billion and a deconcentration budget of Rp 65 billion (Papua Provincial Health Office 2004). Per capita spending was Rp 68,000. This was higher than the national figure of around Rp 50,000, but lower than the estimate of Rp 300,000 put forward by the working group that had prepared the draft special autonomy law (Sumule 2003). An insight into the health spending of one of Papua's districts, Yapen Waropen, is given in Box 14.1.

BOX 14.1   VIEW FROM THE LOCAL LEVEL: YAPEN

The district of Yapen Waropen (not to be confused with the district of Waropen) was established in 2002. Yapen comprises several islands south of the Biak archipelago, northeast of Jayapura and north of Cendrawasih Bay. In 2003 the district had a population of 70,000, growing at a rate of 2.5 per cent annually. The population density is around 35 people per square kilometre, relatively high for Papua; the most densely populated area is Serui, the capital. The majority of the population are fishers (30 per cent) and farmers (30 per cent). The percentage of poor people was 43 per cent in 2004, compared with 38 per cent for Papua as a whole.

In 2002, around 20 per cent of the Yapen population died before reaching the age of 40 (compared with a national average of 15 per cent), 90 per cent had no access to clean water (national average: 45 per cent) and 36 per cent had no access to medical facilities (national average: 23 per cent). Only 33 per cent of houses had proper sanitation facilities in 2000, compared with 75 per cent nationally (BPS, Bappenas and UNDP 2004).

In 2003, 43.6 per cent of births were assisted by health personnel. The infant mortality rate was about 58 deaths per 1,000 live births. In addition, 18.5 per cent of under-five-year-olds were malnourished (Papua Provincial Health Office 2004).

The reported morbidity rate, on the other hand, was relatively low, at 8 per cent in 2002 (compared with a national average of 15 per cent). The percentage of the population perceiving themselves to be ill was also low at 12 per cent (national average: 25 per cent). However, the majority of the population does not have access to medical facilities and staff, so these figures should be regarded as gross underestimates. Additionally, most people (77 per cent) prefer to self-treat all but the most serious health problems.

With one government official for every 24 people, Yapen has a relatively high ratio of government officials to population by Indonesian standards. But around 80 per cent of these officials are located in urban areas, effectively leaving rural areas without public services.

In 2003, total government spending in Yapen by all levels of government was around Rp 408 billion, or Rp 5.8 million per capita. About 76 per cent of these funds (Rp 310 billion) came from the district government, 16.7 per cent from the provincial government and 6.6 per cent from the central government. The district's own-source revenues amounted to only 0.6 per cent of total spending. Total spending on health (including salaries) was around Rp 34.7 billion (8.5 per cent of total district government expenditure), or Rp 500,000 per capita.

The Special Autonomy Law for Papua explicitly states that health and education expenditure should comprise 30 per cent of total district expenditures. The local government of Yapen spent around 20 per cent of its budget on education in 2003 (Rp 81.6 billion). Therefore, its total spending on health and education reached 28.5 per cent of total government spending—relatively close to the target set by the law (Table 14.2).

Table 14.2   Government Spending in Yapen, 2003

Source	Total Expenditure		Health (Rp billion)	Education (Rp billion)
	(Rp billion)	(%)		
Central government	27.4	6.7		
Provincial government	68.2	16.7		
District government	310.0	76.0		
District revenue	2.4	0.6		
Total expenditure	**408.0**		**34.7**	**81.6**
Total health & education expenditure			Rp 116.3 billion (28.5% of total expenditure)	

Source: Tim UNIPA (2005).

Government spending per capita in Yapen is relatively high compared with the national figure of around Rp 150,000 per capita. Even so, it is not enough to provide adequate infrastructure and health services in remote regions. To expand health services in rural areas without sacrificing spending on education, Yapen needs to increase its revenues and spend existing funds more effectively. Its ability to generate its own revenue is limited. Therefore, it will need more support from the central and provincial governments.

Elina Situmorang
Faculty of Economics, University of Papua

7   ACHIEVEMENTS IN HEALTH STATUS

The vision for health development in Papua is set out in Healthy Papua 2005, a milestone on the way to Healthy Papua 2010, itself part of the Healthy Indonesia 2010 program. The goal was to achieve a strong base for the development of health-related human resources by 2005. This would be marked by an improvement in the health status of Papuans, that is, an improvement in nutritional status, a decrease in infant, maternal and productive-age mortality, a decrease in the incidence and prevalence of major diseases, and an increase in people's satisfaction with health care services. It would be achieved through: (1) health-oriented provincial development; (2) empowering people to lead healthy lives; (3) maintaining and improving the quality, accessibility and distribution of health care services; (4) maintaining and improving individual, family, community and environmental health; and (6) improving the quality of health-related human resources (Papua Provincial Health Office 2004).

The health development programs conducted in Papua have slowly been improving the health status of Papuans. Life expectancy, for example, increased from 57.9 years in 1986 to 66.2 years in 2004. In 1998 the crude birth rate for Papua was higher than the average for Indonesia (29 births per 1,000 people compared with 22.8 for Indonesia), while the crude death rate was lower (6.0 deaths per 1,000 people compared with 7.7 for Indonesia) (Table 14.3).

Some other health indicators, however, paint a bleaker picture. A Rapid Survey conducted in 2000–01 found an infant mortality rate of 122.2 deaths per 1,000 live births and an extremely high maternal mortality rate of 1,161 deaths per 100,000 live births (Hidayat 2001). These figures differ substantially from projections based on the national Demographic and Health Survey conducted in 1997 (BPS 1997). It predicted a 2001 infant mortality rate for Papua of 50 deaths per 1,000 live births (compared with a national figure of 46 deaths) and a maternal mortality rate of 396 deaths per 100,000 live births (compared with a national figure of 334 deaths) (Table 14.3). The two surveys used different sampling methods. The Demographic and Health Survey probably better reflected the situation in urban areas, while the Rapid Survey better reflected the situation in rural areas.

According to the Rapid Survey, in 2001 Papua had infant and maternal death rates that were nearly three times those for the whole of Indonesia. The maternal mortality rate refers to deaths among women related to pregnancy, childbirth and the puerperal period. More than half of these fatalities were due to the three classical causes of maternal death: bleeding, infections and eclampsia (Ministry of Health 2003b); malaria caused nearly one-quarter of them.

Table 14.3   Comparison of Papuan and National Health Indicators

Indicator	Papua	Indonesia
Crude birth rate, 1998 (births per 1,000 people)	29.0	22.8
Crude death rate, 1998 (deaths per 1,000 people)	6.0	7.7
Infant mortality rate, 2001 (deaths per 1,000 live births)		
Rapid Survey	122.2	46.0
Demographic and Health Survey	50.0[a]	
Maternal mortality rate, 2001 (deaths per 100,000 live births)		
Rapid Survey	1,161	334
Demographic and Health Survey	396[a]	

a   Projection.

Source: Crude birth and death rates: Papua Provincial Health Office (2005); Rapid Survey: Hidayat (2001); Demographic and Health Survey: BPS (1997).

The latest data reveal that the coverage of antenatal care is insufficient: only 65.7 per cent of women received one antenatal visit in 2001, falling to 54.4 per cent in 2003, and even fewer received four antenatal visits (40.7 per cent in 2001 increasing to 44 per cent in 2003). Furthermore, only 55 per cent of births were attended by a health professional (the national average was 65 per cent). Nevertheless this was better than in some other provinces in Indonesia (see Figure 14.3). Within Papua, the proportion varied widely across districts, with the worst situation found in the district of Jayawijaya and the best in the city of Sorong (Papua Provincial Health Office 2005). These inadequacies were caused not only by the reluctance of pregnant women to attend maternal clinics or hospitals, but also by the difficulty of access to health providers such as doctors and village midwives.

Immunization coverage is also poor; it ranges from 45 to 75 per cent for polio, DPT (diphtheria, pertussis and tetanus), measles and tuberculosis. The global commitment to reach a 90 per cent universal child immunization rate is clearly far away for Papua. As one would expect, the less accessible districts had the lowest immunization rates (about 23 per cent for Paniai in 2003, for example). Among females, the average vaccination rate against tetanus—a relatively new program—was 6.4 per cent for the whole province in 2003, ranging from zero in the district of Jayawijaya to 41.2 per cent in Puncak Jaya (Papua Provincial Health Office 2005). Overall, immunization coverage has decreased significantly

Figure 14.3   Births Attended by Trained Personnel by Province, 2004

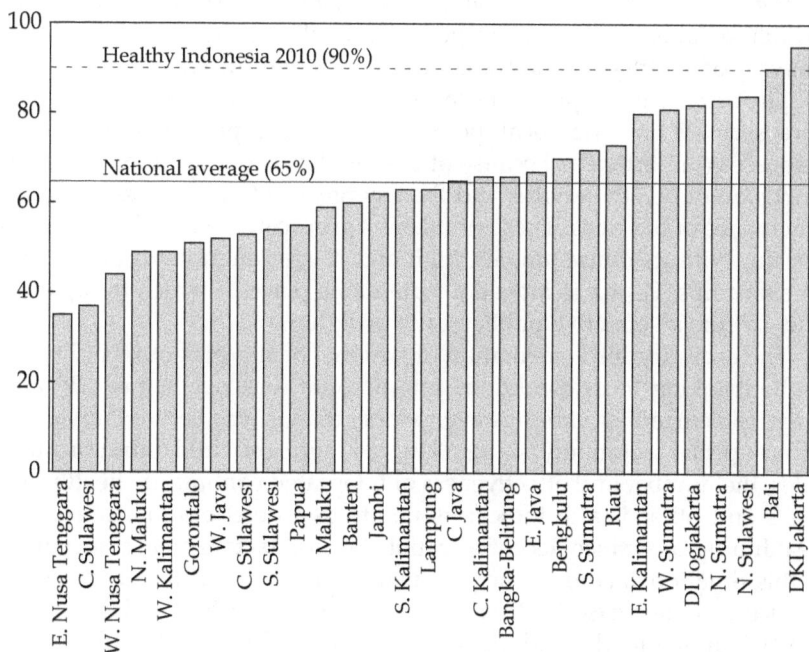

Source: Ministry of Health (2005b).

in recent years, with 20 per cent of villages receiving no coverage at all because of the difficulty of access (Papua Provincial Health Office 2005).

8   DISCUSSION

The first problem that emerged when planners were trying to assess the health situation in Papua was the scarcity of reliable data. Data on some basic health indicators had been collected regularly as part of the national health surveys, but there were periods in which the surveys did not cover Papua for security reasons. Moreover, what were called 'Papuan' data were actually only measurements taken in a few districts, and therefore unrepresentative of the true situation in more remote areas. That is, there were contradictions between the records and the actual situation in the field.

Since the end of World War II, efforts to improve health care in Papua have been directed at increasing the number and capability of health care providers (nurses, doctors and midwives) and increasing government expenditures on health. Since decentralization and special autonomy in

2001, the provision of health care services has been the responsibility of local governments, especially at the district level. The central Ministry of Health remains responsible for policy and still sets the standards for the delivery of health care and the control of epidemic diseases.

The difficulties Papua faces in its struggle to deliver adequate health care services include local political instability, poor-quality human resources (in particular because of the low levels of education), uneven provision of health services and the emergence of new diseases and re-emergence of old ones. These problems are exacerbated by the country's terrain. With its dense jungles, high and rugged mountains and extensive swamps, Papua is indeed a formidable place in which to organize and execute an effective public health program.

The arbitrary implementation of national health programs in Papua, without taking local conditions into account, has not helped. By and large, the current situation is even worse than it was before Papua was given special autonomy status. The evidence on child immunization rates, the number and effectiveness of integrated community health care posts and other health indicators points to a deterioration in existing health programs since decentralization. Several factors have contributed to this situation, including the poor management of health and education services; the decrease in disease surveillance, recording and reporting; the lack of qualified health personnel to staff Kabupaten Health Service offices and reach the vast inland regions; and poor transportation.

Papua also has several strengths: health expenditure comprises 15 per cent of the total local government budget and the province has a higher ratio of health personnel to population than the national average. Papua's health and educational programs are also supported by significant amounts of international donor aid. But if the available funds and personnel are to be translated into effective programs to achieve the goals of Healthy Papua 2010, they will need to be distributed more evenly and more efficiently across the province.

9 CONCLUSION

Papua faces great challenges in improving the health of its people. The main health problem remains communicable diseases, with malaria continuing to be the most frequent cause of mortality and morbidity. Diarrhoea, acute respiratory infections and tuberculosis are still present, and in recent years a very serious HIV/AIDS epidemic has emerged.

Although indicators show some improvements, the province still lags behind many Indonesian provinces, especially Java and Bali. Papua ranked 29th out of 30 provinces on the 2004 human development index

(BPS, Bappenas and UNDP 2004: 109). Evidently, the vision expressed in Healthy Indonesia 2010 remains a far-off destination for Papua.

Papua needs to develop a health service model based on primary health care and community self-help. There will need to be more emphasis on capacity building and the strengthening of health services. Both the national government and foreign donors are able to assist Papua in this respect. The province's special autonomy status should be seen as an opportunity to develop the region in line with the cultural, spiritual and intellectual aspirations of Papuans within the unitary state of Indonesia. Good governance and reconciliation are part of the solution. Above all, the people of Papua themselves must make their own voluntary contribution to improve the health and promote the development of their own communities.

ACKNOWLEDGMENTS

The authors would like to thank Dr Gunawan Ingkokusumo in Jayapura for his assistance in collecting documents, and Dr Shannon D. Putnam for editing the initial draft of the manuscript.

REFERENCES

BPS (Badan Pusat Statistik) (1997), *Indonesia Demographic and Health Survey 1997*, BPS in collaboration with BKKBN and the Ministry of Health, Jakarta.
BPS (Badan Pusat Statistik) (2003), *Indonesia Demographic and Health Survey 2002–2003*, BPS in collaboration with BKKBN and the Ministry of Health, Jakarta.
BPS, Bappenas and UNDP (Badan Pusat Statistik, Badan Perencanaan Pembangunan Nasional and United Nations Development Programme) (2004), *Indonesia Human Development Report 2004. The Economics of Democracy: Financing Human Development in Indonesia*, Jakarta.
Butt, L., G. Numbery and J. Morin (2002), 'The Smokescreen of Culture: AIDS and the Indigenous Papuan, Indonesia', *Pacific Health Dialog*, 2(2): 283–9.
Gunawan, S. (1985), 'A Review of the Malaria Situation in Irian Jaya', *Bulletin of Health Studies*, 13(3–4): 1–13.
Gunawan, S. (1990), 'Health Conditions and Disease Patterns in the Central Highlands of Irian Jaya', paper presented to the Conference on the Mek and Their Neighbours, Seewiesen, 17–22 October.
Gunawan, S. (1997), 'Environmental Impact Assessment Study of PT Freeport Indonesia Mine Operations in Irian Jaya (Public Health)', unpublished report, PT Freeport Indonesia, Jakarta.
Gunawan, S. (2005), 'Health Services in Papua 1963–2000', in J.P. Verhave and H.W.A. Voorhoeve (eds), *De Dienst van Gezondheidszorg in Papoea 1950–2000* [Health Services in Papua 1950–2000], Netherlands Society of Tropical Medicine and International Health, Wageningen, pp. 144–62.

Gunawan S., D.B. Subianto and L.R. Tumada (1976), 'Taeniasis and Cysticercosis in the Paniai Lakes Area of Irian Jaya', *Bulletin of Health Studies*, 4(1–2): 9–17.

Gunawan S., E. Utomo, B. Subianto and Kartono (1978), 'Gondok dan Kretinisme Endemik di Irian Jaya [Goitre and Endemic Cretinism in Irian Jaya], in R. Djokomoeljanto et al. (eds), *Naskah Lengkap Seminar Nasional I Gondok dan Kretin Endemik* [Proceedings of the National Seminar on Goitre and Endemic Cretinism], Faculty of Medicine, University of Diponegoro, Semarang, pp. 29–35.

Harries A.D. and D. Maher (1996), 'TB/HIV: A Clinical Manual', WHO/TB/96.200, Geneva, World Health Organization.

Hidayat, Melania (2001), *Survey Cepat Angka Kematian Ibu Propinsi Papua Tahun 2000–2001* [Rapid Survey on the Maternal Mortality Rate in Papua Province in 2000–2001], Papua Provincial Health Office, Jayapura.

Jazan S. et al. (2004), *Prevalensi Infeksi Saluran Reproduksi pada Wanita Penjaja Seks di Jayapura, Indonesia, 2003* [The Prevalence of Reproductive Tract Infections among Female Sex Workers in Jayapura, Indonesia, 2003], Ministry of Health, ASA-FHI-USAID Jakarta, Jakarta, October.

Kaldor, John et al. (2006), *Impacts of HIV/AIDS 2005–2025 in Papua New Guinea, Indonesia and East Timor: Synopsis Report of the HIV Epidemiological Modelling and Impact (HEMI) Study*, AusAID, Canberra, available at <http://www.ausaid.gov.au/publications/pdf/hivaids_synopsis.pdf>.

KPAP (Komisi Penanggulangan AIDS Provinsi Papua) (2005), 'Rangkuman Hasil Pemetaan Respon Tanah Papua' [Summary of Response Mapping in Papua], Jayapura, 17–21 October.

Ministry of Health (2000), *Indonesia Sehat 2010: Visi Baru, Misi, Kebijakan dan Strategi Pembangunan Kesehatan* [Healthy Indonesia 2010: A New Vision, Mission and Policy for Health Development], Jakarta.

Ministry of Health (2003a), 'HIV Surveillance Report, December 2002', Directorate General of Communicable Disease Control and Environmental Health, Jakarta, January.

Ministry of Health (2003b), *Data/Informasi Kependudukan menurut Sensus Penduduk Tahun 1971, 1980, 1990, 2000 dan SUPAS 1995 serta Proyeksinya* [Population Data/Information according to the Censuses of 1971, 1980, 1990, 2000, and SUPAS 1995], Centre of Data and Information, Jakarta.

Ministry of Health (2005a), *Survei Sosial Ekonomi Nasional* [National Socio-economic Survey], Jakarta.

Ministry of Health (2005b), *Indonesia: Sub-national Health System Performance Assessment*, National Institute of Health Research and Development, Jakarta.

Ministry of Health (2006), 'HIV Surveillance Quarterly Report, June 2006', Directorate General of Disease Control and Environmental Health, Jakarta, June.

Ministry of Health and BPS (Badan Pusat Statistik) (2003), 'Report on Behavioural Surveillance Survey 2003 in Jayapura, Sorong, Merauke, Ambon, Bitung, Surabaya, Semarang, Bandung, Jakarta, Palembang, Tanjung Pinang and Medan', Jakarta.

Papua Provincial Health Office (2004), *Health Profile of Papua Province 2003*, Jayapura, November.

Papua Provincial Health Office (2005), 'Beban Ganda Permasalahan Kesehatan di Papua' [The Double Disease Burden in Papua], paper presented to Seminar Beban Ganda dalam Permasalahan Kesehatan di Indonesia [Seminar on the Double Disease Burden in Indonesia], Jakarta, 15 November.

Papua Provincial Health Office (2006), *Informasi HIV/AIDS Provinsi Papua Triwulan II* [HIV/AIDS Information for the Province of Papua, Second Quarter], Jayapura.

Silfanus F. et al. (2006a), *Prevalensi Infeksi Saluran Reproduksi pada Wanita Penjaja Seks di Jayapura, 2005* [The Prevalence of Reproductive Tract Infections among Female Sex Workers in Jayapura, 2005], Ministry of Health, Family Health International, Jakarta.

Silfanus F. et al. (2006b), *Prevalensi Infeksi Saluran Reproduksi pada Wanita Penjaja Seks di 10 Kota di Indonesia, 2005* [The Prevalence of Reproductive Tract Infections among Female Sex Workers in 10 Cities in Indonesia, 2005], Ministry of Health, Family Health International, Jakarta.

Sumule, Agus (ed.) (2003), *Mencari Jalan Tengah, Otonomi Khusus Provinsi Papua* [Seeking the Middle Way, Special Autonomy for Papua Province], PT Gramedia Pustaka Utama, Jakarta.

Taylor W.J.R., T.L. Richie and E. Tjitra (1995), 'Antimalaria Drug Evaluations: NAMRU-2 and Indonesian Partnership', *Bulletin of Health Studies*, 23(3): 49–58.

Tim UNIPA (2005), *Laporan Akhir Kajian Kapasitas Pemerintah Daerah Delapan Kabupaten Terpilih di Papua* [Final Report on Capacity Assessment of Eight Selected Districts in Papua], Kerjasama Universitas Negeri Papua dengan UNDP, Jayapura.

UNAIDS (Joint United Nations Programme on HIV/AIDS) (2006), *2006 Report on the Global AIDS Epidemic*, Geneva, available at <http://www.unaids.org/en/HIV_data/2006GlobalReport/default.asp>, accessed 4 October 2006.

Vriend, W.H. (2003), 'Smoky Fires: The Merits of Development Cooperation for Inculturation of Health Improvements', PhD thesis, Free University, Amsterdam.

WHO and UNAIDS (World Health Organization and Joint United Nations Programme on HIV/AIDS) (2000), 'Guidelines for Second Generation HIV Surveillance for HIV: The Next Decade', WHO/CDC/EDC/2000.05, Geneva.

INDEX

GDP by sector, 41
geographic conditions, 48, 339
Gini ratio, 43
government income and
   expenditure, 61
health, 3, 14, 34, 61, 64, 65, 321–40
health indicators, 337
Healthy Papua 2010, 336–8
housing, 101
human development index
   (HDI), 31–2, 47, 227, 322, 339
imports, 36, 37, 39
indigenous Papuans, 47
infrastructure, 60, 64, 69–70, 92
in-migration, 6, 11, 27, 31
institutions, 60, 67, 72
investment, 70–71
map, 22
manufacturing, 41
migrants, 29–31
mining, 39, 40, 41, 42, 61, 68,
   147–73
natural resources, v–vi, 6, 7–9,
   23, 24
personal consumption
   expenditure (PCE), 42–3, 47
politics, 24–7, 67, 154
population, 6, 28–9, 34, 45, 165–6,
   261
poverty, 6, 7, 21, 37, 40–47, 56, 233
poverty rate, 321
religion, 29–30
social indicators, 3, 31–4
socio-economic indicators, 38
Special Autonomy Law, 11, 15,
   23–7, 33, 60–65, 157–8, 227, 335
statistics, quality of, 50–53
Tangguh gas operation, 39, 70,
   129, 169
topography, 48, 339
trade, 37–9, 61, 193, 204, 209, 215,
   219–20
trade, hotels and restaurants, 33,
   39–40, 41
transport and communications,
   40, 41, 51, 61, 70
Yapen, 334–5
see also Rendani Protection Forest
Papua Conservation Fund, 141

Papua New Guinea, 36–7, 153
   comparison of socio-economic
   indicators with Papua, 38
Papuan People's Assembly (MRP),
   24–6
Papuan Tribal Council, 23
PDAM, *see* Municipal Drinking Water
   Enterprise
PDI-P, *see* Indonesian Democratic
   Party of Struggle
peat lands, 258, 260, 261
Pepela port, 211–12, 212–14, 215, 221,
   222
   bodi voyages and catch rates, 220
personal consumption expenditure
   (PCE), 42–3, 47
Philippines, 7, 137
PHKA, *see* Forest Protection and
   Nature Conservation agency
physicians, 38
PKS, *see* Prosperity and Justice Party
plantations, 16, 40, 71, 86, 104, 228,
   243
plywood, 37, 81, 272
police, 67, 68, 167, 168, 172, 241, 242.
   244, 269, 289, 290
politics, 11, 23–7, 67, 110–11, 160, 163,
   271, 277, 288
population, 2, 4, 6, 12, 28–9, 34, 38,
   45, 77, 78, 87, 88, 96, 104–5, 125,
   165–6, 261
   densities, 4, 7, 9, 104
   migrant proportion of urban/
   rural, 29, 30, 31
   Rendani Protection Forest, 228,
   230
   urban/rural proportion, 30, 77
poverty, 2, 6, 7, 11, 14, 21, 37, 40–47,
   74, 86–7, 88, 94, 104, 119, 120, 130,
   233, 275, 300, 305–19
   alleviation, 10, 14, 15, 47, 102, 107,
   113–15, 117, 306, 309–11
   data trends, 3
   educational attainment and
   employment status of poor
   people, 46, 86–8
   expenditure required for basic
   needs, 55
   human poverty index (HPI), 37,
   38, 43–4